Gregg Dictation and Introductory Transcription

Shorthand written
by Charles Rader

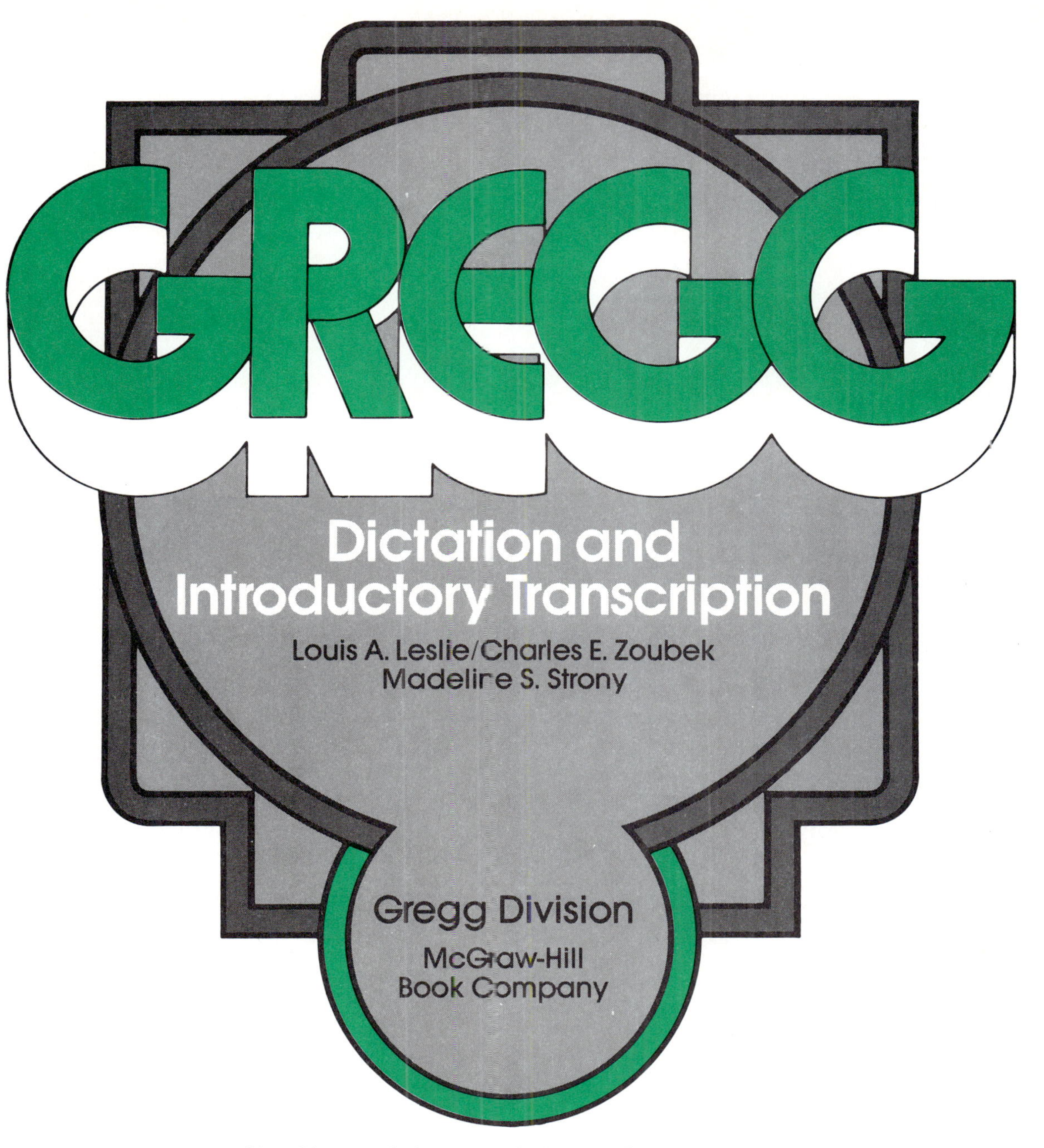

GREGG

Dictation and Introductory Transcription

Louis A. Leslie/Charles E. Zoubek
Madeline S. Strony

Gregg Division
McGraw-Hill
Book Company

New York / St. Louis / Dallas / San Francisco
Auckland / Bogotá / Düsseldorf / Johannesburg / London
Madrid / Mexico / Montreal / New Delhi / Panama / Paris
São Paulo / Singapore / Sydney / Tokyo / Toronto

Library of Congress Cataloging in Publication Data

Main entry under title:

Gregg dictation and introductory transcription, series 90.

Includes index.

1. Shorthand—Gregg—Exercises for dictation.

I. Leslie, Louis A., date.

Z56.G8368 653'.427042'4 77-4166

ISBN 0-07-037735-9

Gregg Dictation and Introductory Transcription, Series 90

6 7 8 9 0 DODO 8 6 5 4

Preface

Gregg Dictation and Introductory Transcription is the second volume in Series 90 of Gregg Shorthand. It is designed to follow *Gregg Shorthand, Series 90,* or *Gregg Shorthand, Functional Method, Series 90,* and serves as a link between shorthand theory and advanced dictation and transcription. For some students *Gregg Dictation and Introductory Transcription* may also serve as a terminal course in shorthand.

Objectives

Gregg Dictation and Introductory Transcription, Series 90, has the following major objectives:

1 To review and strengthen the students' knowledge of Gregg Shorthand.

2 To develop their ability to construct outlines for unfamiliar words under the stress of dictation.

3 To increase their dictation speed to the highest point possible.

4 To increase their knowledge of the basic nonshorthand elements of transcription.

5 To lay a solid foundation for rapid and accurate transcription—the students' ultimate goal.

6 To give students the ability to transcribe mailable correspondence.

7 To make the students aware of the desirable traits and characteristics of a good secretary.

Organization

Gregg Dictation and Introductory Transcription, Series 90, is divided into 16 chapters, each containing 5 lessons, or a total of 80 lessons. Each lesson consists of three parts:

1 Developing Phrasing or Word-Building Power

2 Building Transcription Skills

3 Reading and Writing Practice

Developing Phrasing or Word-Building Power

The five lessons in each chapter contain a carefully planned cycle of phrasing and word-building drills that provide a quick, intensive recall in list form of the important elements of Gregg Shorthand. Selected words and phrases in these drills are used in the Reading and Writing Practice exercises. In addition, other words using these principles are often also included in the Reading and Writing Practice.

Lesson 1 in each chapter is devoted to building phrasing skill. It opens with a number of lists of commonly used phrases selected from a study made by one of the authors of the phrase content of more than 3,000 business letters. These lists are followed by a specially prepared phrase letter, which serves as a source for warm-up practice throughout the chapter.

Lesson 2 in each chapter is devoted to a brief-form review. It opens with a chart of brief forms and derivatives. There is also a brief-form letter that contains a high concentration of brief forms and derivatives. Lesson 2 provides, in addition, a drill on cities, states, and other geographical expressions.

Lesson 3 in each chapter is devoted to a study of shorthand word families. These shorthand word families enable the students to take advantage of a very effective aid in word building—analogy. The students' practice on these word families helps them to develop their ability to construct outlines for unfamiliar words.

Lesson 4 in each chapter deals with the word beginnings and word endings of Gregg Shorthand. Through these lists the students review intensively all the word beginnings and word endings at least once.

Lesson 5 in each chapter contains a shorthand vocabulary builder that concentrates on the major principles of Gregg Shorthand—blends, vowel omissions, abbreviations, and so on.

Building Transcription Skills

It is a well-known fact that the weakest link in the transcription chain is the students' inability to handle the mechanics of the English language. The cry of the business executive has long been that the stenographer cannot spell, cannot punctuate, and cannot use correct grammar. One of the major objectives of *Gregg Shorthand, Series 90,* is to strengthen this link.

In *Gregg Shorthand, Series 90,* a number of features designed to develop the students' mastery of the mechanics of the English language were introduced. In *Gregg Dictation and Introductory Transcription, Series 90,* the emphasis on this phase of transcription is extended and intensified. From the very first lesson of this text, mastery of the mechanics of the English language and the development of shorthand speed proceed side by side.

SPELLING

Two types of spelling exercises are provided in *Gregg Dictation and Introductory Transcription, Series 90*:

1 **Marginal Reminders** As in *Gregg Shorthand, Series 90,* words selected from the Reading and Writing Practice have been singled out for special spelling atten-

tion. These words are printed in a second color in the shorthand and appear in type, correctly syllabicated, in the margins next to the shorthand.

2 **Spelling Families** These spelling families group words that have a common spelling problem—words that are spelled *-ant, -ent; -ious, -eous;* and so on.

PUNCTUATION

In *Gregg Shorthand, Series 90,* the students studied nine of the most frequent uses of the comma. They will continue to drill on those uses of the comma in *Gregg Dictation and Introductory Transcription, Series 90.* In addition, they will study more advanced problems of punctuation, such as the use of the semicolon, the hyphen, and the apostrophe.

To test the students' grasp of the punctuation rules they have studied, a Transcription Quiz is provided in each lesson, with the exception of the fifth lesson of each chapter. This quiz consists of a letter in which the students must supply all internal punctuation. In the later lessons the Transcription Quizzes provide an additional challenge—the students must supply from context words that have been omitted in the shorthand.

VOCABULARY DEVELOPMENT

Three types of exercises are provided to help the students expand their vocabulary and develop their understanding of words.

1 **Business Vocabulary Builder** In each lesson the students study words and expressions, selected from the Reading and Writing Practice, with which they may not be familiar. The definition provided for each word or expression is the one that applies to its use in the Reading and Writing Practice.

2 **Similar-Words Drill** One of the common reasons for transcription errors is the students' inability to choose the correct word from pairs of similar-sounding words—*accept-except,* for example. In *Gregg Shorthand* the students studied several common pairs of similar words; in *Gregg Dictation and Introductory Transcription,* they study 12 more.

3 **Common Prefixes** As the students learned in *Gregg Shorthand,* the study of common prefixes is an effective device for increasing their command of words. In *Gregg Dictation and Introductory Transcription,* they study seven prefixes.

GRAMMAR CHECKUP

There are seven lessons that contain drills dealing with common rules of grammar that are often misapplied or misunderstood by stenographers. Correct applications of these rules are included in the Reading and Writing Practice exercises.

TYPING STYLE STUDIES

In the Typing Style Studies the students learn the correct way to transcribe dates, street addresses, amounts of money, times of day, and so on.

In Lessons 41 and 52 the students are taught how to place short letters and average-length letters attractively on a letterhead. This feature will be especially valuable to those students whose shorthand training will end with *Gregg Dictation and Introductory Transcription.*

INTRODUCTORY TRANSCRIPTION

Beginning with Lesson 41 the students are introduced step by step to elementary transcription. The *Instructor's Handbook for Gregg Dictation and Introductory Transcription, Series 90,* includes letters for the students to transcribe in letter form.

OFFICE-STYLE DICTATION

In Chapters 13 through 16 a number of problems of office-style dictation are introduced. Each problem is explained and then illustrated in shorthand. This feature will also be valuable to those students who are taking their last term of shorthand.

Reading and Writing Practice

An essential part of the students' practice program is the reading and copying of quantities of well-written shorthand. This reading and copying provides a constant, automatic review of the principles of the system. In addition, it stocks the students' minds with the correct joinings of shorthand characters and with the shapes of the individual characters so that they can quickly construct an outline for any word that is dictated. *Gregg Dictation and Introductory Transcription, Series 90,* provides the student with 67,476 running words of practice material in the form of business letters and interesting, informative articles.

Nearly all of the material in this edition is new; that which has been retained from the former edition has been revised and brought up to date.

The connected material in each of the 16 chapters relates to a specific business or department of business in order to give the students the dictation "flavor" of many kinds of businesses. Each chapter opens with a brief description of the business or business function that is the subject of the chapter.

An extremely helpful and interesting feature of the Reading and Writing Practice for the fifth lesson of each chapter is an actual secretarial case study entitled "The Secretary on the Job." Each case emphasizes the importance of some desirable traits or characteristics of a good secretary, effective secretarial procedures, and so on.

The publishers are confident that this text will enable teachers to do an even more effective job of training accurate and rapid stenographers.

The Publishers

Contents

PART

Your Speed-Building Program

Before you begin your work on the second phase of your shorthand development—speed building—let us take an inventory of what you have already accomplished. You may not realize it, but you have taken a long step toward your goal of becoming a stenographer and secretary.

You have learned the alphabet of Gregg Shorthand and thus have the means with which to form an outline for any word in the language—whether the word is familiar or unfamiliar.

You have learned many useful abbreviating devices, such as brief forms, word beginnings and endings, and phrases that will help you to write more easily.

You have improved your ability to spell and to punctuate; you have increased your vocabulary of business terms; and you have brushed up on a number of rules of grammar.

If you have faithfully practiced the lessons in *Gregg Shorthand*, you now have a firm foundation for the task ahead—developing your ability to take dictation on new material easily and rapidly and to transcribe on the typewriter. With this foundation, you will experience the thrill of watching your shorthand speed grow and your ability to handle the mechanics of the English language improve almost from day to day!

YOUR PRACTICE PROGRAM AT HOME

Here is what you should do at home as you practice the lessons in *Gregg Dictation and Introductory Transcription*:

Read the word and phrase drills. For some of them, a time goal is provided. Try to reach or, better still, exceed that goal.

Study the Transcription Skill Builder.

Read and copy the Reading and Writing Practice in this way:

■ **1** Always read all shorthand before you copy it. This is important! Read aloud, if possible.

■ **2** If as you read you come across an outline you cannot decipher, spell the shorthand characters in it. If this spelling does not give the meaning of the outline to you, refer to the *Student's Transcript of Gregg Dictation and Introductory Transcription* if it is available. If it is not available, write the outline on a slip of paper and find out its meaning from your teacher the next day. Do not spend more than a few seconds trying to decipher an outline. Fortunately, at this stage there will not be many outlines that will give you trouble.

■ **3** After you have read the material, make a shorthand copy of it. Read a convenient group of words—aloud, if possible—and then write that group in your notebook. Write as rapidly as you can, but be sure what you write is legible.

■ **4** If time permits, read what you have written. You will be glad you did if you are called upon to read back from your homework in class the next day!

■ **5** Complete the corresponding lesson in the *Workbook for Gregg Dictation and Introductory Transcription* if you have been provided with one.

YOUR PRACTICE PROGRAM IN CLASS

During the first part of the term, most of your class time will be devoted to taking dictation at constantly increasing speeds. Your teacher will see to it that you get the right kind of dictation at the proper speeds so that your dictation skill will increase steadily and rapidly. During the latter part of the term, part of your time will be devoted to transcribing shorthand on the typewriter.

CHAPTER

Goodwill

Goodwill is important in business, just as it is in your private life. An asset, but not a commodity, goodwill can't be measured in dollars and cents; its value is impossible to estimate. Perhaps that is why goodwill is consciously projected—and consciously sought—by everyone who participates in a successful business relationship.

Does that sound like a riddle? Actually, goodwill is so essential to our lives that we all experience it, whether or not we define or discuss it in exactly the same terms. For goodwill is many things, most of them having to do with attitudes of interest, concern, and regard—and the ways in which people express these feelings. Although a business or an institution benefits from expressions of goodwill, it is the people involved who create those feelings.

One way goodwill is created is through service. For example, a department store that is well known for quality goods at fair prices, that is staffed by people who seem to enjoy their work, and that is generally considered a pleasant place to shop earns the goodwill of the consumer.

Another way to create goodwill is to provide the unasked for *extra*—extra service, extra thoughtfulness, extra responsiveness to people's needs. One large chain of clothing stores wins countless friends and customers by inviting readers of their ads to bring to the stores' tailors any clothing that needs to have a button replaced. The service is free; it is also graciously and expertly provided. The feelings of goodwill between the store and the public as a result of this gesture cannot be measured in terms of tailoring costs; both the store and the public are the beneficiaries.

Goodwill is also evident in the small courtesies, familiar in your daily life, that are transferred to a business relationship. Among business associates, courtesy may mean taking the time to write a thank-you note, to send a congratulatory telegram, or to write a thoughtful letter of condolence. These are small gestures, perhaps, but they are meaningful in terms of confirming good relations—another term for goodwill.

The expressions of goodwill just discussed are not costly in time or money. Yet they can pay large dividends. Some businesses consider establishing goodwill essential, and executives are encouraged to include it as an important item in their advertising or public relations budgets. As a business expense, goodwill may take the form of a contribution to a worthwhile community project, a scholarship designated for training a talented young person in a particular field, or a fund set up to promote certain professional achievements. Again, both the public and the business organization are the beneficiaries in these expressions of goodwill.

Whether goodwill is manifested by a receptionist's welcoming smile or by a company's underwriting the cost of a needed park or playground, it remains the basic ingredient of successful business—and personal—relationships.

Comma Brushup

As you learned in *Gregg Shorthand,* secretaries must be able to punctuate correctly if they are to turn out letters that their employers will have no hesitation in signing. In *Gregg Shorthand* you studied nine of the simpler uses of the comma as they occurred in the Reading and Writing Practice.

In *Gregg Dictation and Introductory Transcription* you will take up new and more advanced points of punctuation. Before you are introduced to these new points, however, you will "brush up" on the uses of the comma that you studied in *Gregg Shorthand.* In Chapter 1 of *Gregg Dictation and Introductory Transcription* you will review five of those uses; in Chapter 2, the remaining four.

Practice Procedures

To be sure that you derive the greatest benefit from your study of punctuation and spelling in each Reading and Writing Practice, follow these practice suggestions:

■ **1** Read carefully each punctuation rule and the illustrative examples.

■ **2** Continue to read each Reading and Writing Practice as you have always done.

■ **3** Each time you see a circled comma, note the reason for its use, which is indicated directly above it.

■ **4** As you copy the Reading and Writing Practice, insert the commas in your shorthand notes, encircling them.

, parenthetical

In order to make the meaning clearer, a writer sometimes inserts a comment or an explanation that could be omitted without changing the meaning of the sentence. These added comments and explanations are called *parenthetical* and are separated from the rest of the sentence by commas.

If the parenthetical word or expression occurs at the end of a sentence, only one comma is needed.

His main job, of course, *is to repair cars.*

I am sure, Mrs. Jones, *that you will like our representative.*

We will send you a copy of the new book, of course.

Each time a parenthetical expression occurs in the Reading and Writing Practice, it will be indicated as shown in the margin:

par

, apposition

Sometimes a writer mentions a person or thing and then, in order to make the meaning perfectly clear to the reader, says the same thing again in different words. This added explanation is known as an expression in *apposition.*

An expression in apposition is set off by two commas, except at the end of a sentence, when only one comma is necessary.

Our representative, Miss Jane Jones, *will come to see you soon.*

The meeting will be held on Monday, October 23, *at the Hotel Baker.*

Meet my assistant, Carlos Lear.

Each time an expression in apposition occurs in the Reading and Writing Practice, it will be indicated as shown in the margin:

, series

When the last member of a series of three or more items is preceded by *and, or,* or *nor,* place a comma before the conjunction as well as between the other items.

She is a person of integrity, dependability, and initiative.

The meeting will be held January 3, 4, and 5.

My duties consisted of receiving callers, answering the telephone, and opening the mail.

Each time a series occurs in the Reading and Writing Practice, it will be indicated as shown in the margin:

ser

(,)

, conjunction

A comma is used to separate two independent clauses that are joined by a conjunction.

I placed my order over three months ago, but *I have not heard from you.*

The last supplies were delivered before the holidays, and *I will soon need more.*

Each time this use of the comma occurs in the Reading and Writing Practice, it will be indicated as shown in the margin:

conj

(,)

, and omitted

When two or more adjectives modify the same noun, they are separated by commas.

She was a quiet, efficient *person.*

However, the comma is not used if the first adjective modifies the combined idea of the second adjective plus the noun.

Lee wore a beautiful blue *coat.*

Each time this use of the comma occurs in the Reading and Writing Practice, it will be indicated as shown in the margin:

and o

(,)

Building Phrasing Skill

1 Phrase Builder

In the following list there are 48 phrases that are frequently used in business letters. Can you read the entire list in 48 seconds or less?

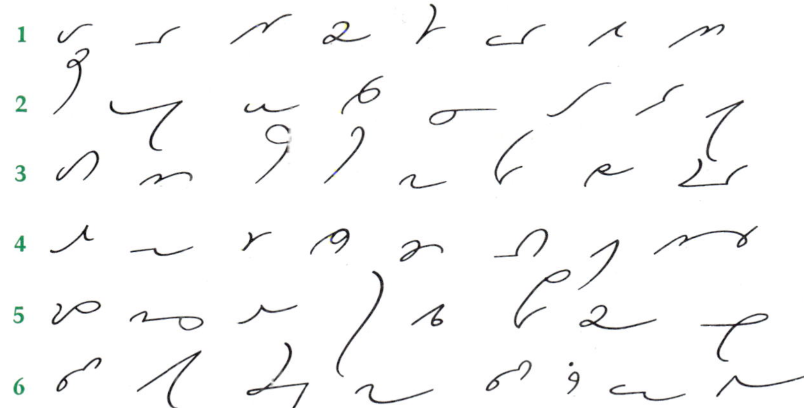

1. *Of the, in the, to the, we are, for the, on the, it is, to you.*
2. *We have, will be, of our, that the, I am, and the, at the, to be.*
3. *Of this, you can, I have, you have, you are, by the, they are, from the.*
4. *There is, in our, is the, that is, we can, in this, to have, to get.*
5. *So that, you may, there are, have been, to see, about the, we will, may be.*
6. *With you, would be, very much, you will, with us, he is, on our, it will.*

2 Warmup Phrase Letter

The following 134-word letter, which is your warmup letter for Chapter 1, contains 32 useful phrases. Can you read it in 1 minute? Can you copy it from the shorthand in 2 minutes or less?

[134]

Building Transcription Skills

3 BUSINESS VOCABULARY BUILDER The Business Vocabulary Builders in *Gregg Dictation and Introductory Transcription* will help you improve your command of business terminology. In each Business Vocabulary Builder, business words and expressions selected from the Reading and Writing Practice of the lesson are briefly defined.

Study the definitions carefully, notice them in the Reading and Writing Practice, and later use them in new sentences.

Business Vocabulary Builder

complimentary Flattering.

processing Moving along.

imminent About to occur.

Reading and Writing Practice

4

com·pli·men·ta·ry

ap

pro·cess·ing

im·mi·nent par

[100]

5

friend ap

rec·om·men·da·tion

de·light·ed

ma·te·ri·als ser

par

conj

[128]

6

re·ceived

ap

plan·ning

conj

sub·stan·tial

par

and o

com·plete

[101]

7

ap·point·ment

conj

and o

[90]

conj

10

afraid

fa·mil·iar

conj

[120]

8

and o

gen·u·ine

9

buf·fet

[87]

10 Transcription Quiz From your work with *Gregg Shorthand,* you are already familiar with the Transcription Quiz, which gives you an opportunity to see how well you can apply the punctuation rules you have studied. There will be a Transcription Quiz at the end of the first four lessons in each chapter of *Gregg Dictation and Introductory Transcription.* In Chapters 1 and 2 the Transcription Quiz will contain the same type of exercises as those in *Gregg Shorthand.* In later lessons, as new and advanced points of punctuation are introduced, these quizzes will become more challenging.

As you read the Transcription Quiz letter, decide what punctuation should be used. Then make a shorthand copy of the letter and insert the correct punctuation marks in the proper places in your notes.

For you to supply: 7 commas—2 commas conjunction, 3 commas parenthetical, 2 commas series.

[106]

Warmup A "warmup" is a profitable way to make use of the few minutes between the time you enter the shorthand classroom and the time your teacher starts the day's lesson. Unless your teacher instructs you otherwise, turn to the phrase letter on page 17 and see how fast you can copy it.

Developing Word-Building Power

11 Brief-Form Chart

The following chart contains 30 frequently used brief forms. You have practiced them many times while you were studying from *Gregg Shorthand,* so you should be able to read them rapidly. First, read the brief forms on each line from left to right. Your reading goal on your first reading is 35 seconds. Then read the brief forms down each column. You will, of course, be able to read them faster the second time.

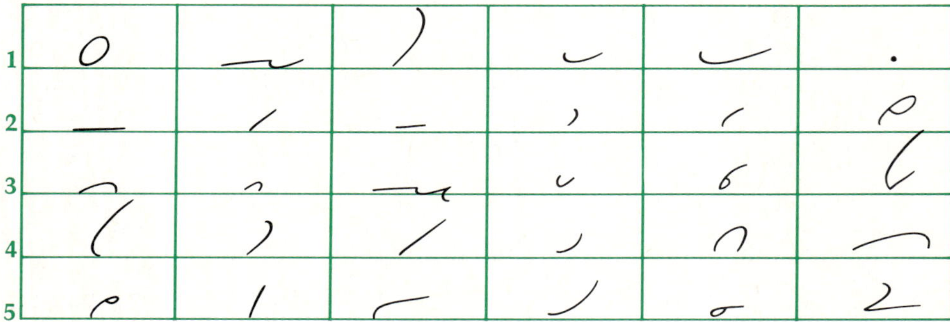

1. *I, Mr., have, are-our-hour, will-well, a-an.*
2. *Am, it-at, in-not, is-his, the, that.*
3. *Can, you-your, Mrs., of, with, but.*
4. *Be-by, for, would, there (their), this, good.*
5. *They, which, them, and, when, from.*

12 Geographical Expressions

1. San Francisco, New York, Newark, Hartford, Seattle, Chicago, Los Angeles.
2. California, Oregon, New Jersey, Connecticut, Kentucky, Illinois, Tennessee, Washington.

Building Transcription Skills

13 SIMILAR-WORDS DRILL *In Gregg Dictation and Introductory Transcription* you will continue your study of similar words—words that sound alike and words that sound or look *almost* alike. Such words are responsible for many of the errors that shorthand writers make when they transcribe.

Study each definition carefully. As you read and copy the Reading and Writing Practice of the lesson, watch for these similar words.

SIMILAR-WORDS DRILL accept, except

accept *(verb)* To take.

He has convinced me to accept the position.

except *(preposition)* Omitted; left out.

She will take over the entire territory except *California.*

---

14 Business Vocabulary Builder

lucrative Profitable.

designated Chosen.

associates *(noun)* Co-workers.

Reading and Writing Practice

15 Brief-Form Letter

The following letter of 124 words contains 67 brief forms or brief-form derivatives.

Can you read the entire letter in 75 seconds or less? Can you make a shorthand copy of it in 2 minutes or less?

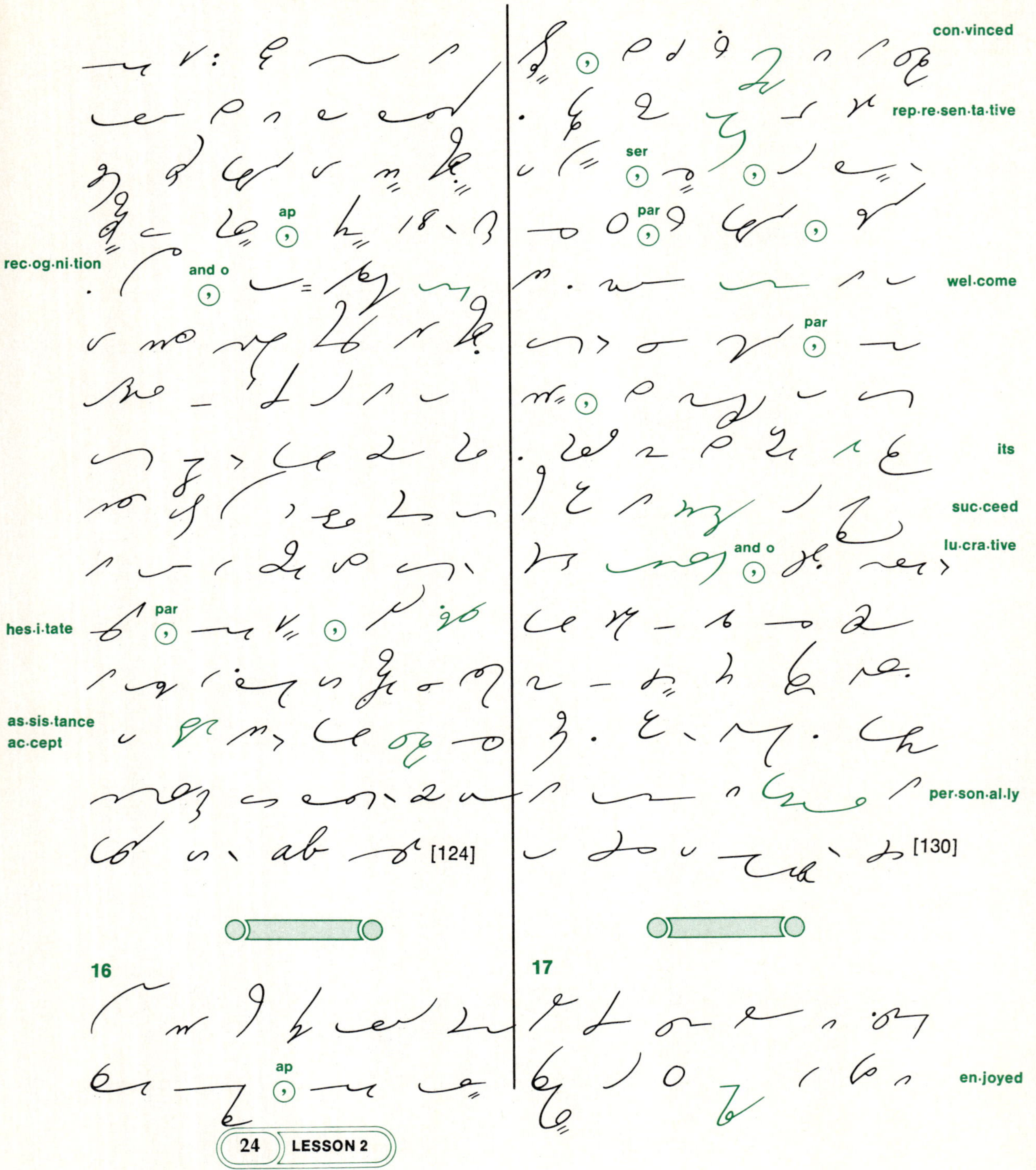

25

touched

as·so·ci·ates

par

too

scroll

par

[160]

18

ap

ser

ac·cept

des·ig·nat·ed

ex·cept

par

conj

help·ful

and o

ap

Feb·ru·ary

[134]

19

im·pressed

ser

par

stud·ied

conj

ex·cept

[109]

20 Transcription Quiz For you to supply: 9 commas—2 commas apposition, 4 commas parenthetical, 2 commas conjunction, 1 comma *and* omitted.

[119]

Warmup A few minutes of warmup will help you get off to a good start on your day's dictation. Turn again to page 17 and write the warmup phrase letter as rapidly as you can, being sure, however, to write readable shorthand.

Developing Word-Building Power

21 Word Families

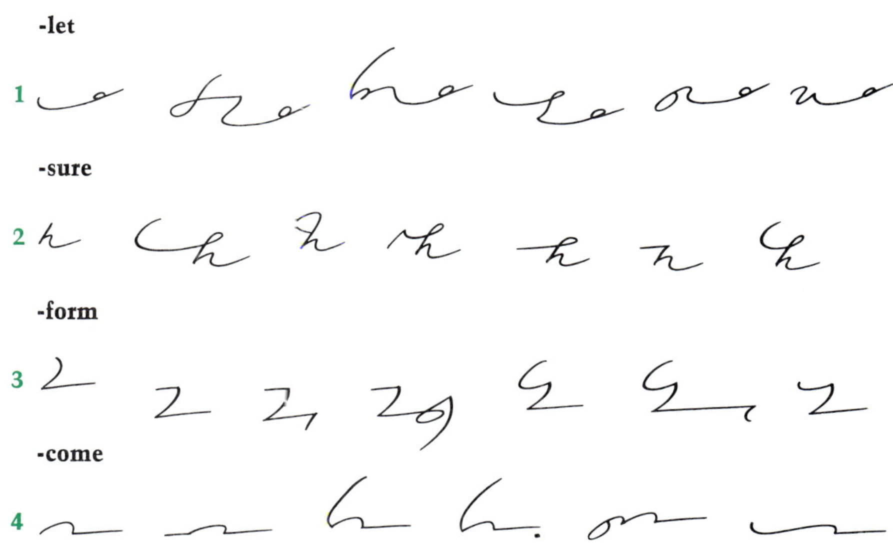

1. *Let, pamphlet, booklet, leaflet, outlet, wallet.*
2. *Sure, pleasure, assure, treasure, measure, insure, pressure.*
3. *Form, inform, information, informative, perform, performance, reform.*
4. *Come, income, become, becoming, outcome, welcome.*

Building Transcription Skills

22 SPELLING FAMILIES ie, ei In this text you will continue to study spelling families. Study the spelling words carefully and watch for examples of the families in the Reading and Writing Practice. In the lists a dot is placed in the words where they may be divided on the typewriter.

One of the most troublesome spelling families in the English language is the *ie, ei* group. Grammarians tell us that:

1 i comes before e:

achieve	**chief**	**piece**
be·lief	**friend**	**re·lief**
brief	**niece**	**yield**

2 except (a) after c:

re·ceipt	**re·ceive**	**de·ceit**

and (b) when the combination has the sound of a:

eight	**their**	**heir**

This rule, like any other, has its exceptions. A few words used frequently in business that are exceptions to the rule are given below.

ef·fi·cient	**for·eign**	**nei·ther**
ei·ther	**lei·sure**	**suf·fi·cient**

---

23 Business Vocabulary Builder

with our compliments Free.

stationery Letter paper.

fascinating Extremely interesting.

Reading and Writing Practice

24

friend

neigh·bor

ap

15

ser

re·ceive

par

de·li·cious

[96]

25

par

de·pos·i·tor

de·scribes

par

with·draw·als

ex·cept

conj

con·ve·nient

[157]

26

ap

pam·phlet

par

plea·sure

com·pli·ments

re·ceipt

practical

and o

efficiency

[111]

27

expressing

ap

stationery

ap

believe

fascinating

par

[84]

28

thoughtfulness

cooperation

[98]

29

conj

at·mo·sphere

guests

conj

par

col·or·ful

[144]

30 Transcription Quiz For you to supply: 6 commas—2 commas apposition, 2 commas parenthetical, 2 commas series.

[111]

Warmup Don't you find that a brief warmup before the shorthand class starts really gets you ready for the day's dictation? Turn once again to the warmup phrase letter on page 17 and write it as rapidly as you can.

Developing Word-Building Power

31 Word Beginnings and Endings

Un-

-tion (-sion)

Re-

Con-

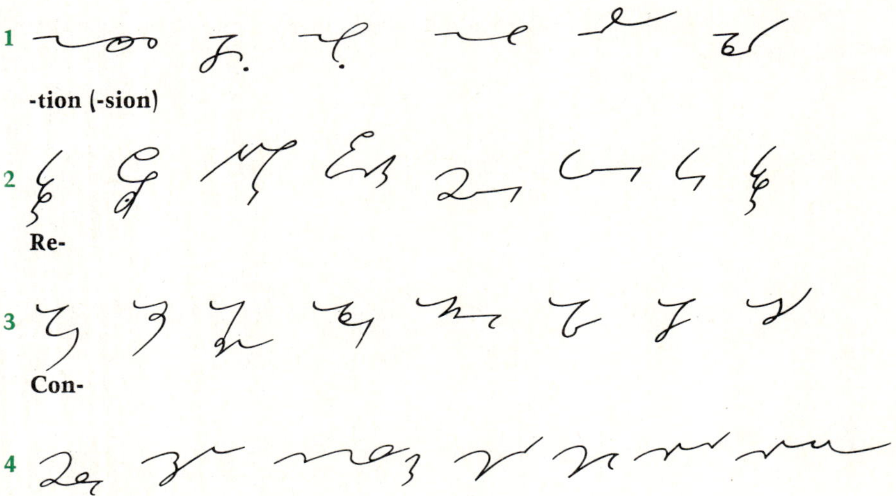

1. *Unlikely, unpacking, unwrapping, unless, until, uncertain.*
2. *Positions, appreciation, distribution, expectations, confirmation, permission, pension, possessions.*
3. *Representative, receive, register, research, resumes, report, repeat, recent.*
4. *Conference, consider, congratulations, confident, confidence, contract, control.*

Building Transcription Skills

32 GRAMMAR CHECKUP pronouns

A pronoun must agree with its antecedent in person, number, and gender.

These books *are worth* their *cost.*

After reviewing your plan, *I have decided to use* it.

Each *of the girls must carry* her *(not* their) *own luggage.*

---

33 Business Vocabulary Builder

relish To enjoy or delight in something.

attendees Those who are present at an event.

reciprocate To repay.

Reading and Writing Practice

34

ap

pen·sion

and o

de·vel·op·ments

conj

ap

fair

par

conj

man·ag·ing

[124]

35

ap

hearty

ser

pos·ses·sions

conj

chore

de·scrip·tion

par

555-1187

[163]

36

ap

and o

beau·ti·ful·ly

par

conj

par

ex·ceed

[102]

37

ap·pre·ci·ate

sights

wound·ed

par

re·cip·ro·cate

[94]

38

Chem·i·cal

15

di·rec·tor

ap

de·vel·op·ments

30

at·tend·ees

conj

sense

par

[137]

39

re·tail·ers

conj

car·pet·ing

20

[109]

oc·cu·pant

40

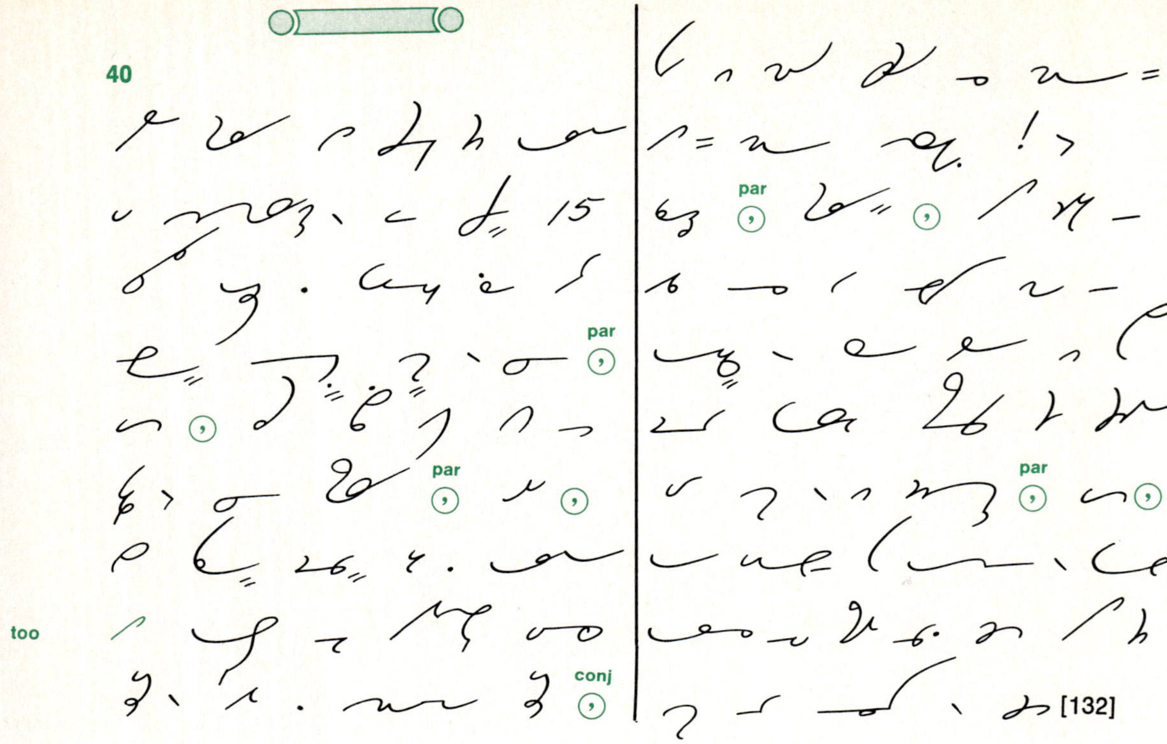

par par par conj too par par

[132]

41 Transcription Quiz For you to supply: 7 commas—4 commas apposition, 1 comma conjunction, 2 commas series.

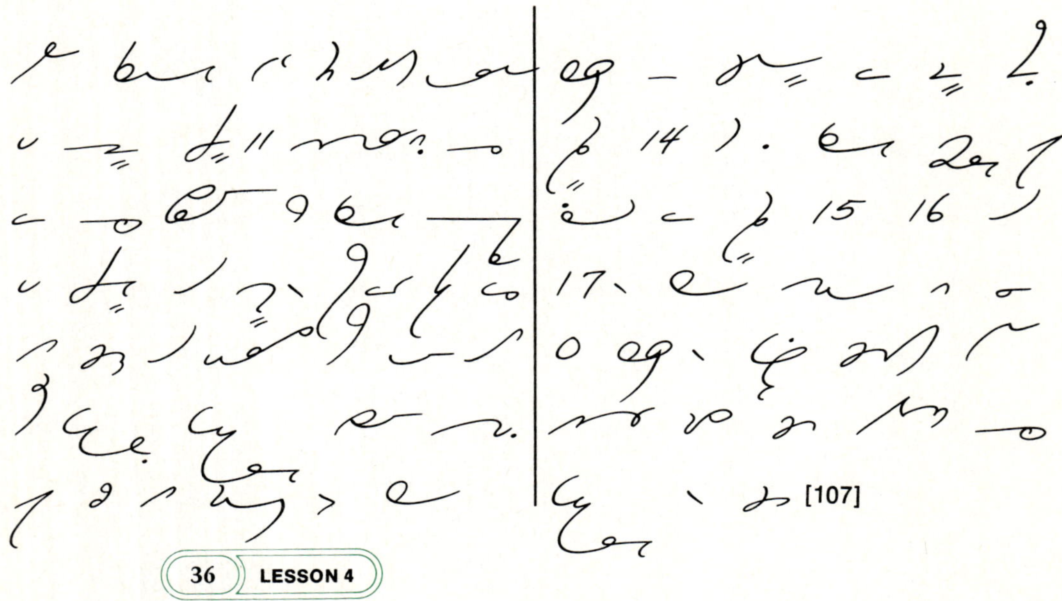

Warmup Turn once again—for the last time—to the warmup phrase letter on page 17. The phrases in that letter should now be so familiar to you that you should be able to write the entire letter in about one minute. Can you do it?

Developing Word-Building Power

42 Shorthand Vocabulary Builder

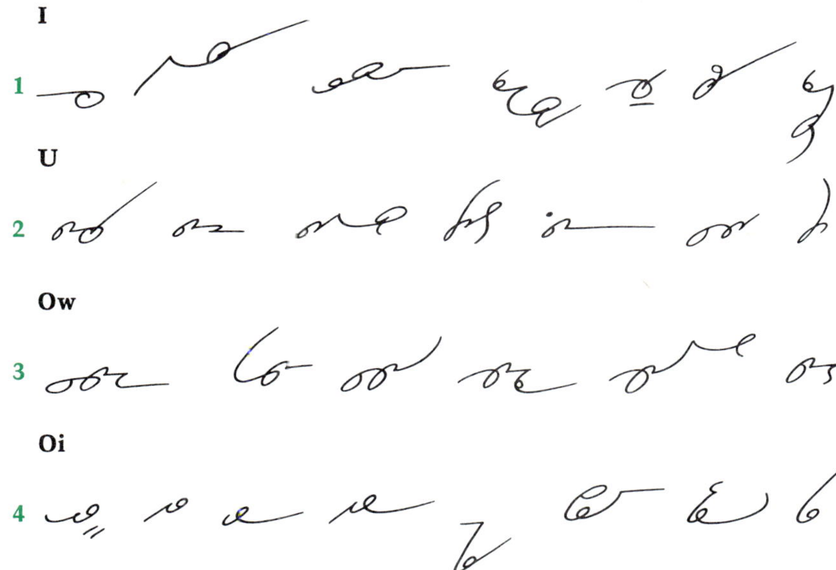

1. *My, delighted, retirement, surprised, quite, excited, survive.*
2. *United, union, utilize, beautiful, human, acute, view.*
3. *Announcement, brown, account, counsel, countless, ounces.*
4. *Roy, toy, oil, toil, enjoyed, appointment, spoiled, boy.*

Building Transcription Skills

43 Business Vocabulary Builder

suite A group of rooms occupied as a unit.

indispensable Essential.

anxious Uneasy; distressed.

Reading and Writing Practice

44

fi·nan·cial

ap

suite

as·sis·tants

conj

[114]

45

sore·ly

ex·pan·sion

par

viv·id·ly

anx·ious

conj

com·pe·tent

par

en·cour·age·ment

ad·vice

[140]

46

edi·tion

ap

16

in·dis·pens·able

par

rec·og·ni·tion

conj

15

[127]

47

25

conj

sat·is·fied

grat·i·tude

par

al·ways

coun·sel

[104]

The Secretary on the Job

48 BUSINESS BEHAVIOR

The habit

Any list

Consideration for Others.

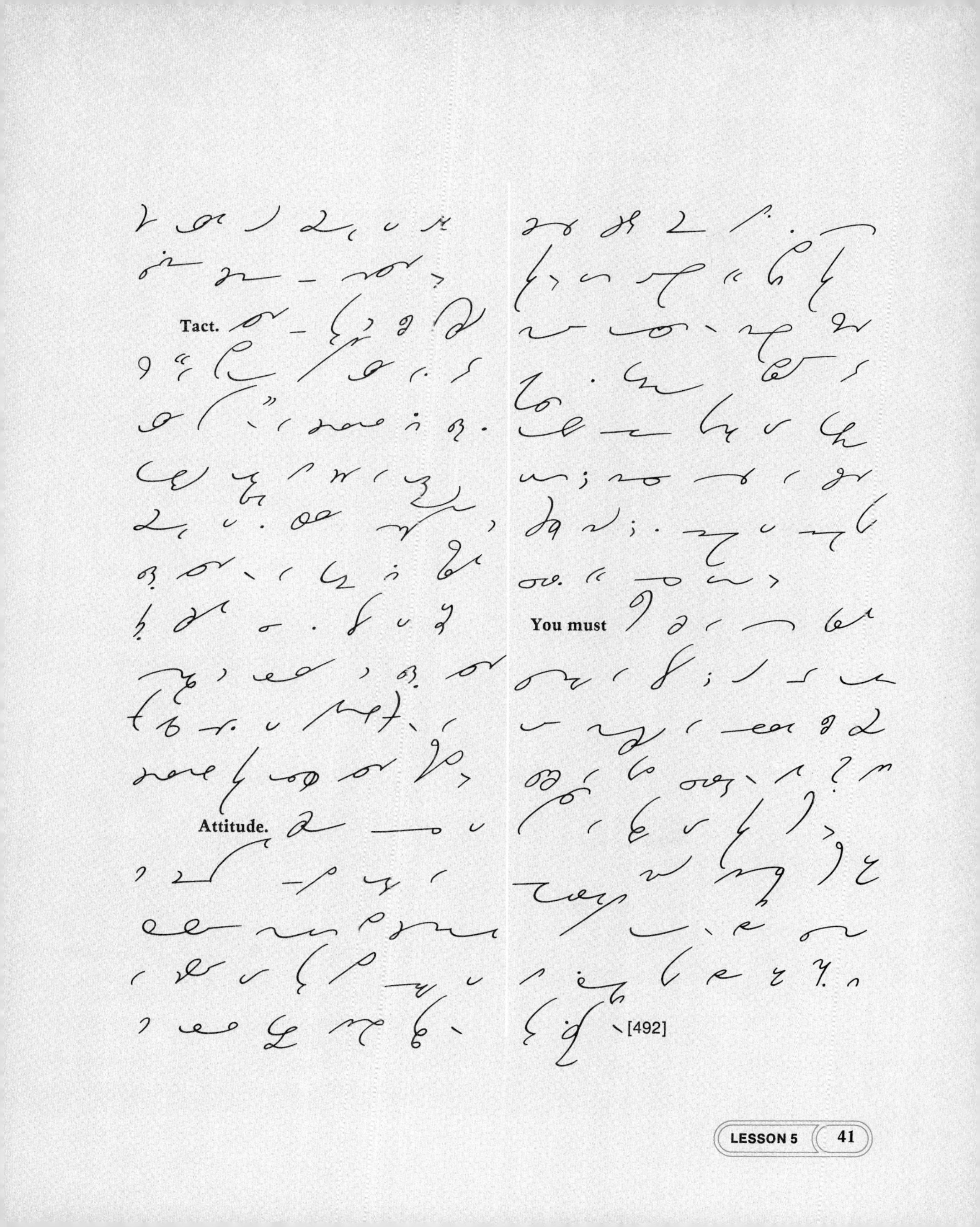

Tact.

Attitude.

You must

[492]

CHAPTER

2 Employment

The task of looking for a job is big business, both for the people who are hunting and for those who are involved in helping them. As the number and types of jobs as well as places to work increased in this country, the need to help job-seekers find positions and to help companies find suitable employees became apparent. Out of these needs, a large new business area sprung up—the employment field.

Almost everyone who is looking for a job uses the services of an employment agency at one time or another. Private employment agencies keep a current list of available jobs and help companies find the right people to fill them. They charge a fee for their services, which in some cases is paid by the employer and in other cases is paid by the job applicant.

People who work in employment agencies must be in constant contact with businesses in their area in order to keep a current listing of all job openings and the requirements of applicants to fill those jobs. They must also make the jobs they have available known to job seekers by placing advertisements in local newspapers on a regular basis. Interviewers at the agency screen all applicants, decide what jobs they would be suitable for, contact the proper person at the company that is hiring, and set up an interview. If a job cannot be found right away, the agency keeps the applicant's name, résumé, application form, and contract on file for future reference.

Some agencies specialize in placing temporary workers. They often train the workers themselves and then place them on jobs which may last from one day to as much as several months. The worker actually is employed by the agency—not the business in which he or she is working. The business pays the agency a set amount, and the agency pays the worker's salary from this amount. Of course, not all the money paid by the business goes to the employee. Some of it goes to pay the administrative costs of the agency and some of it goes to the agency in the form of profit.

Businesses find this type of service extremely valuable, especially for seasonal work when there is a heavy volume of work for only a short period of time. Employees often like to work for temporary agencies because this type of work lets the employee work the days and hours that he or she selects. The temporary employment field is a large field and one that continues to gain popularity.

Many companies have employment divisions of their own. These divisions keep track of job openings within the company and are responsible for interviewing applicants from within the company itself, from employment agencies, and from direct inquiries by job seekers. The people who work in an employment division not only interview job applicants but also keep records of an employee's job history, and they perform all other functions related to taking or leaving a job.

The employment business is a people-oriented business. It involves matching the right person with the right job. The letters in this chapter deal with employment.

Comma Brushup (concluded)

In Chapter 1 you reviewed five of the uses of the comma that you studied in *Gregg Shorthand.* In Chapter 2 you will review the remaining four uses of the comma that were presented in that book—commas with introductory expressions. As in *Gregg Shorthand,* introductory commas will be treated under the four headings listed below. Next to each of these headings is the indication that will appear in the shorthand for that use of the comma.

At the beginning of a sentence all dependent clauses beginning with words other than *if, as,* and *when* will be classified as "introductory."

If you need the supplies now, please telephone us.

As you know, we are closed on Saturdays.

When the work is finished, we will return home.

Unless we receive your check, we will have to close your account.

When the main clause comes first, however, no comma is used between the main clause and the dependent clause.

Please telephone us *if you need the supplies now.*

We are closed on Saturdays *as you know.*

We will return home *when the work is finished.*

We will have to close your account *unless we receive your check.*

A comma is also required after introductory words and explanatory expressions such as *frankly, consequently, on the contrary, for instance.*

Frankly, I do not want to go.

On the contrary, he is the one who made the error.

Building Phrasing Skill

49 Phrase Builder

The following four groups contain 41 phrases. Can you read all the phrases in these groups in 50 seconds or less?

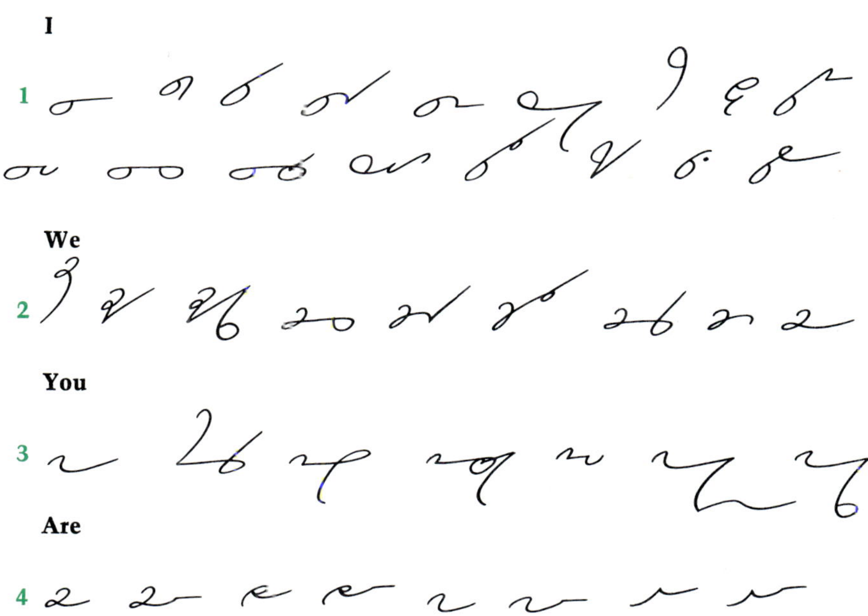

1. *I am, I wish, I would, I could, I cannot, I will be, I have, I was, I do not, I know, I may, I might, I wrote you, I did, I should, I think, I tell.*
2. *We have, we should, we should be able, we may, we could, we did, we made, we can, we will.*
3. *You will, you have made, you may be, you might be, you know, you will be glad, you will be able.*
4. *We are, we are not, they are, they are not, you are, you are not, there are, there are not.*

50 Warmup Phrase Letter

The following letter, consisting of 103 words, contains 21 phrases that are frequently used in business letters. Can you read the entire letter in 45 seconds or less? Can you make a shorthand copy in 1½ minutes or less?

This will be your warmup letter for Lessons 6-10.

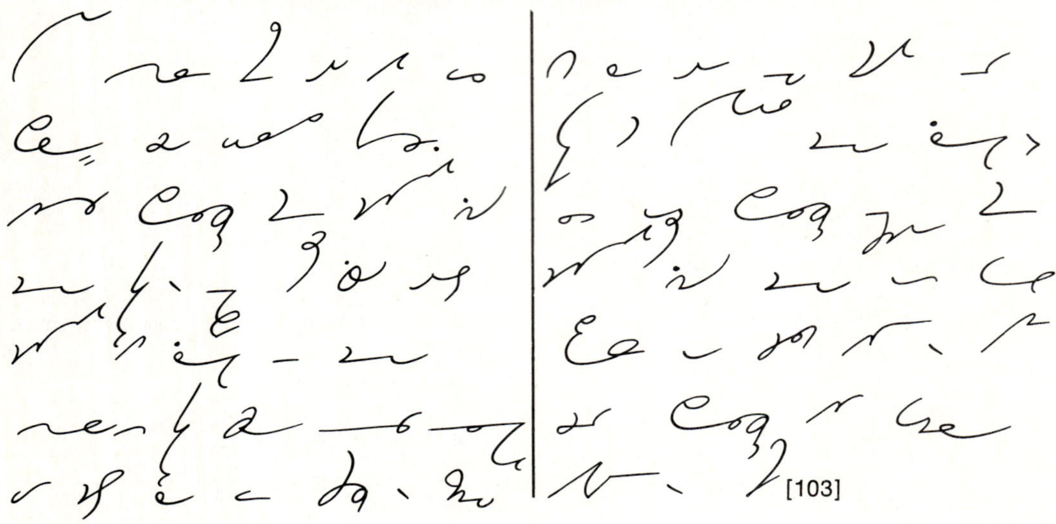

Building Transcription Skills

51 Business Vocabulary Builder

credentials Written evidence of status or qualifications.

prominence The state of being widely known.

colleagues Friends; co-workers.

● Reading and Writing Practice

52

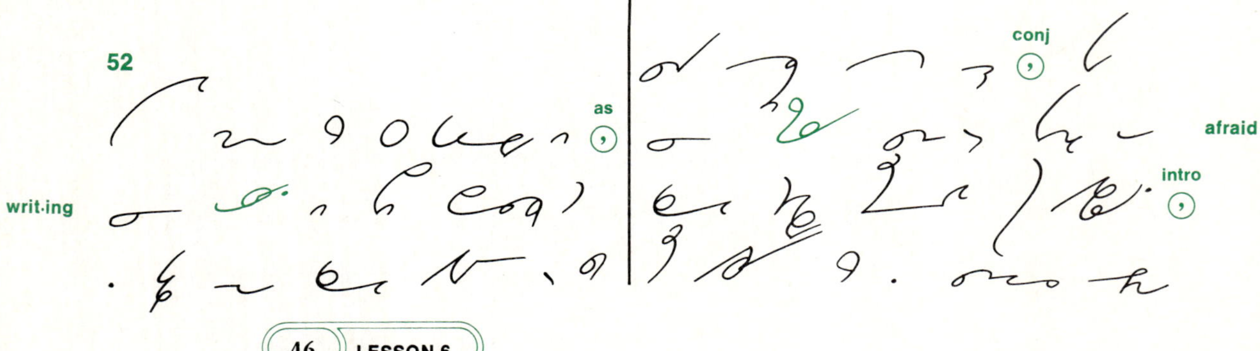

if

par

sub·mit·ting

[111]

53

re·ferred

fa·vor·ably

conj

tem·po·rary

ser

[83]

54

ap

col·leagues

as

and o

par

[97]

con·ve·nient

55

intro

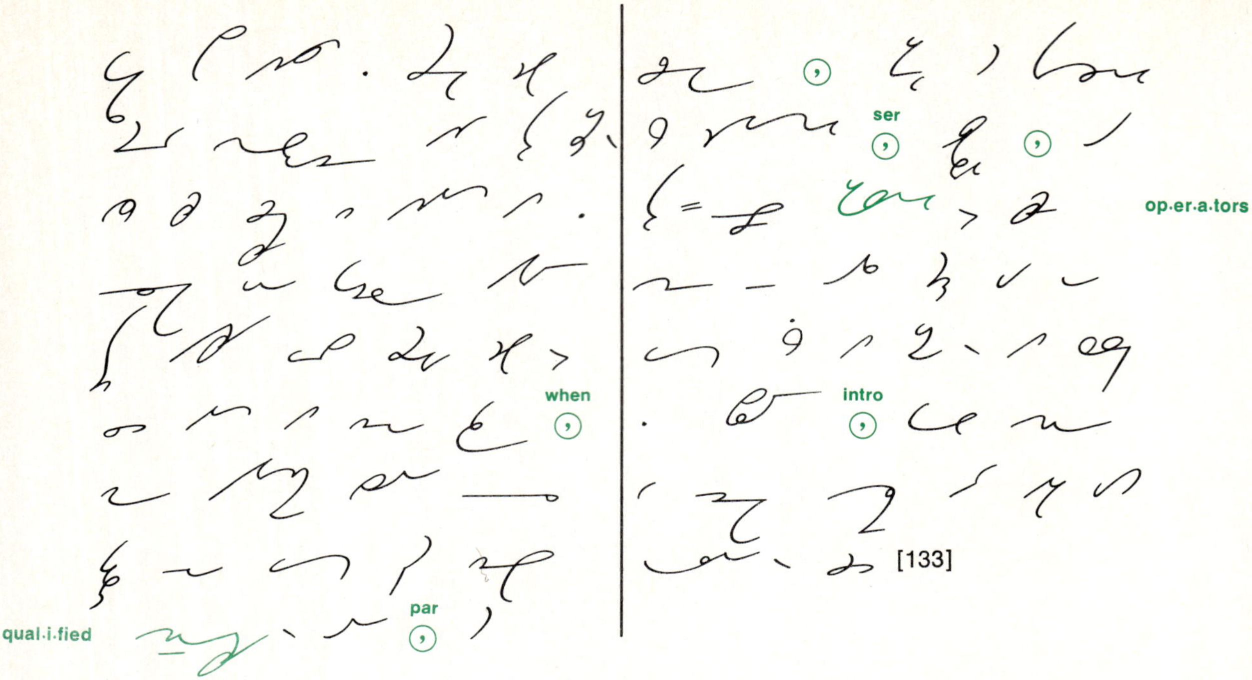

ser

op·er·a·tors

when

intro

[133]

qual·i·fied

par

56 Transcription Quiz For you to supply: 6 commas—1 comma *when* clause, 2 commas parenthetical, 1 comma conjunction, 1 comma *as* clause, 1 comma *if* clause.

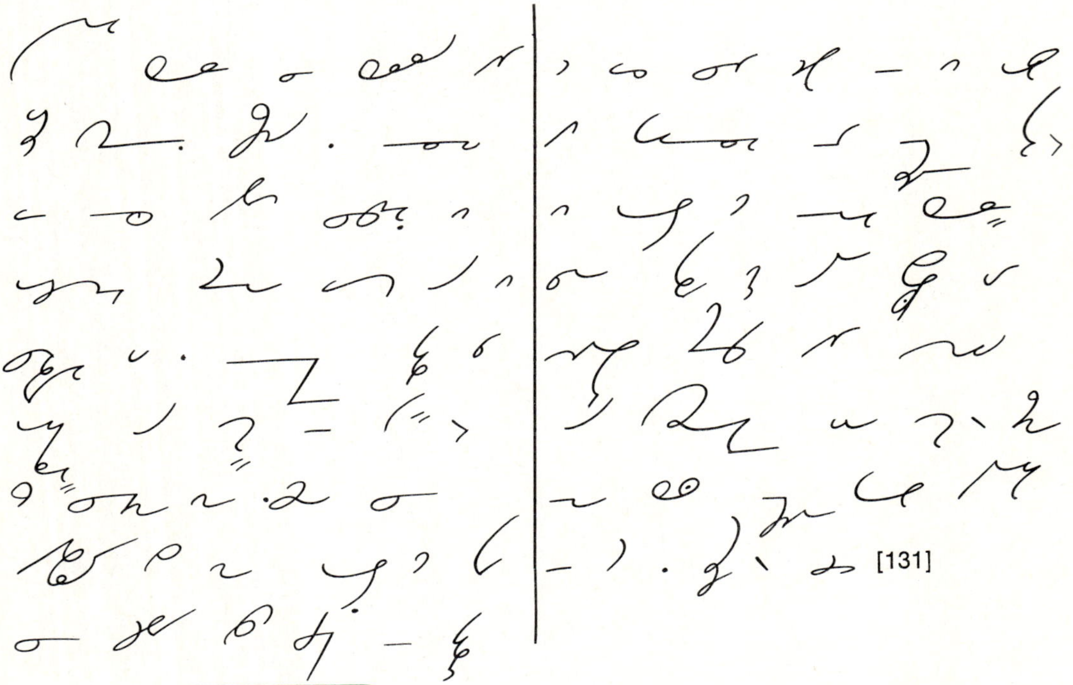

[131]

Warmup For your warmup during the first few minutes of the period, copy the phrase letter on page 46. Write as rapidly as you can, but be sure that your shorthand notes are readable.

Developing Word-Building Power

57 Brief-Form Chart

The following chart contains 30 brief forms. Can you read it in 35 seconds or less?

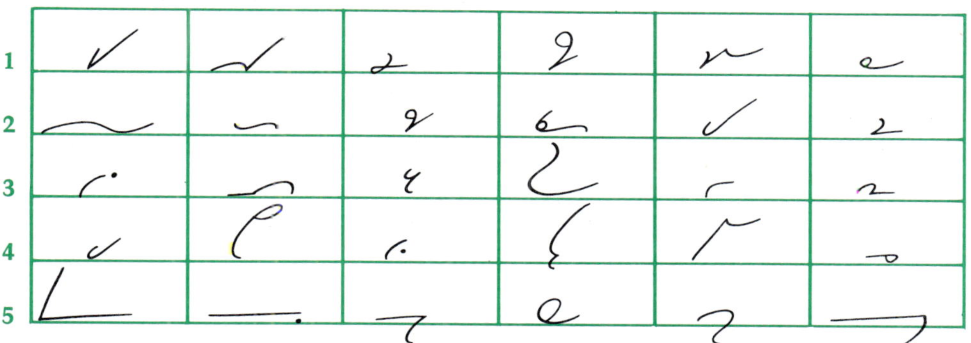

1. *Should, could, send, after, street, were.*
2. *Glad, work, yesterday, circular, order, soon.*
3. *Thank, enclose, was, value, than, one (won).*
4. *What, about, thing-think, business, Dr., any.*
5. *Gentlemen, morning, important-importance, where, company, manufacture.*

58 Geographical Expressions

1

2

1. *Boston, Des Moines, Miami, Indianapolis, Minneapolis, St. Paul, Philadelphia.*
2. *Massachusetts, Iowa, Florida, Indiana, Minnesota, Ohio, Pennsylvania.*

Building Transcription Skills

59 SIMILAR-WORDS DRILL affect, effect

affect To change.

This won't affect *you.*

effect Influence.

Absences can have a great effect *on your business.*

---

60 Business Vocabulary Builder

legitimate Authentic; genuine.
urban Pertaining to a city or town.
extraordinary Unusual.

Reading and Writing Practice

61 Brief-Form Letter

The following letter of 149 words contains 62 brief forms or brief-form derivatives. Can you read the entire letter in 75 seconds or less? Can you make a shorthand copy of it in 2 minutes or less?

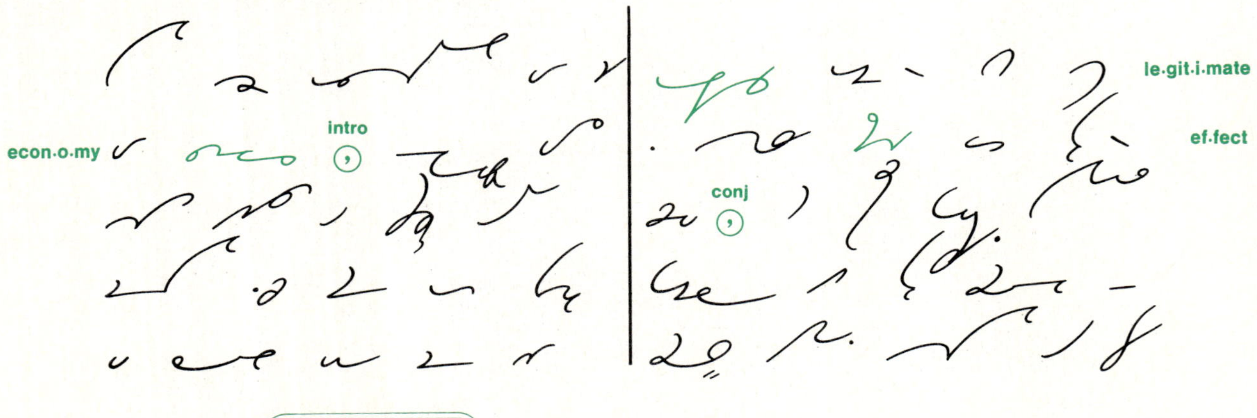

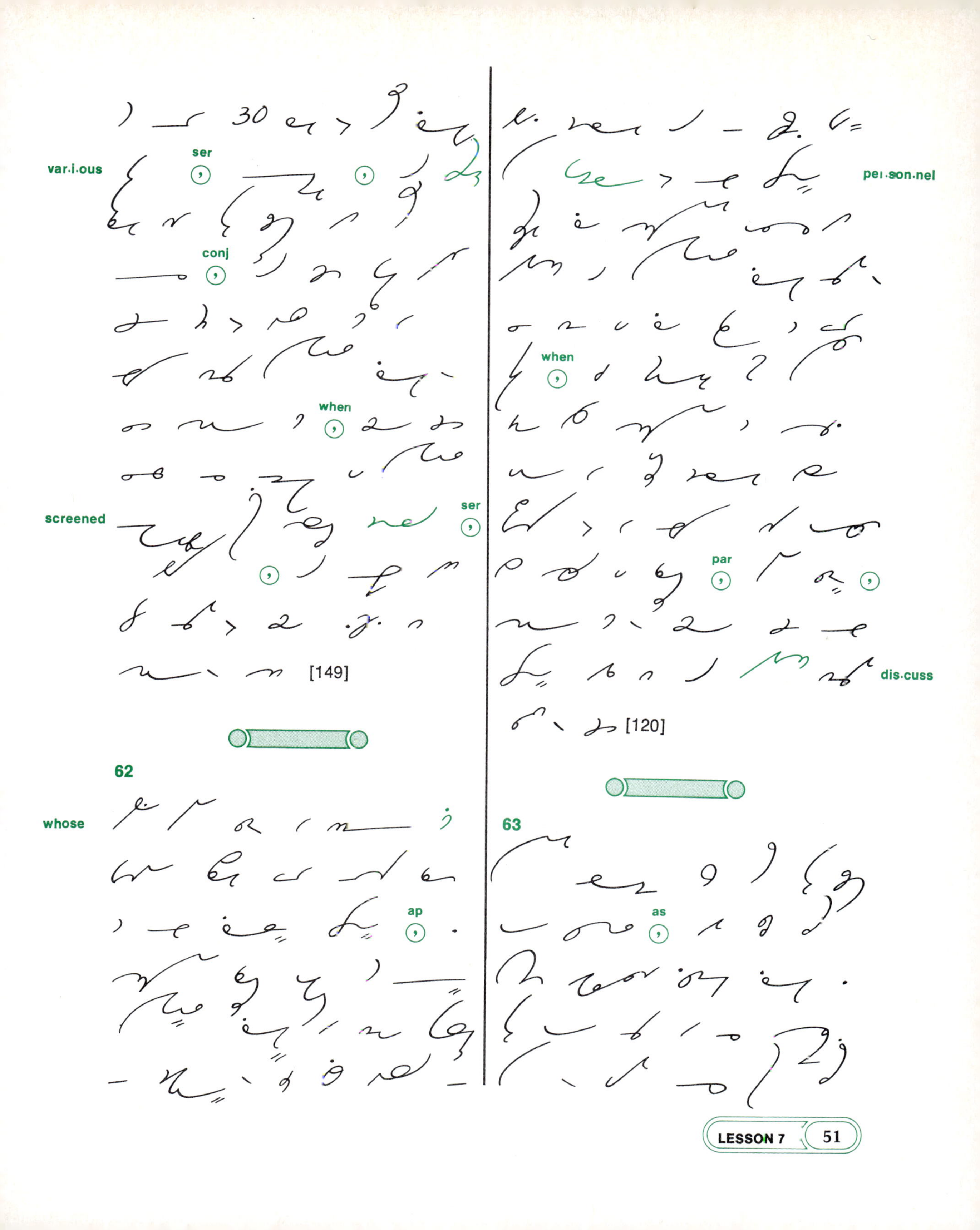

30

various

ser

conj

when

screened

ser

[149]

62

whose

ap

personnel

when

par

discuss

[120]

63

as

conj

af·fect

if

when

pro·duc·tiv·i·ty

555-1166 [134]

ser

ex·traor·di·nary

intro

em·pha·sis

10

and o

chal·leng·ing

[147]

64

su·per·vi·sor

65

per·son·al

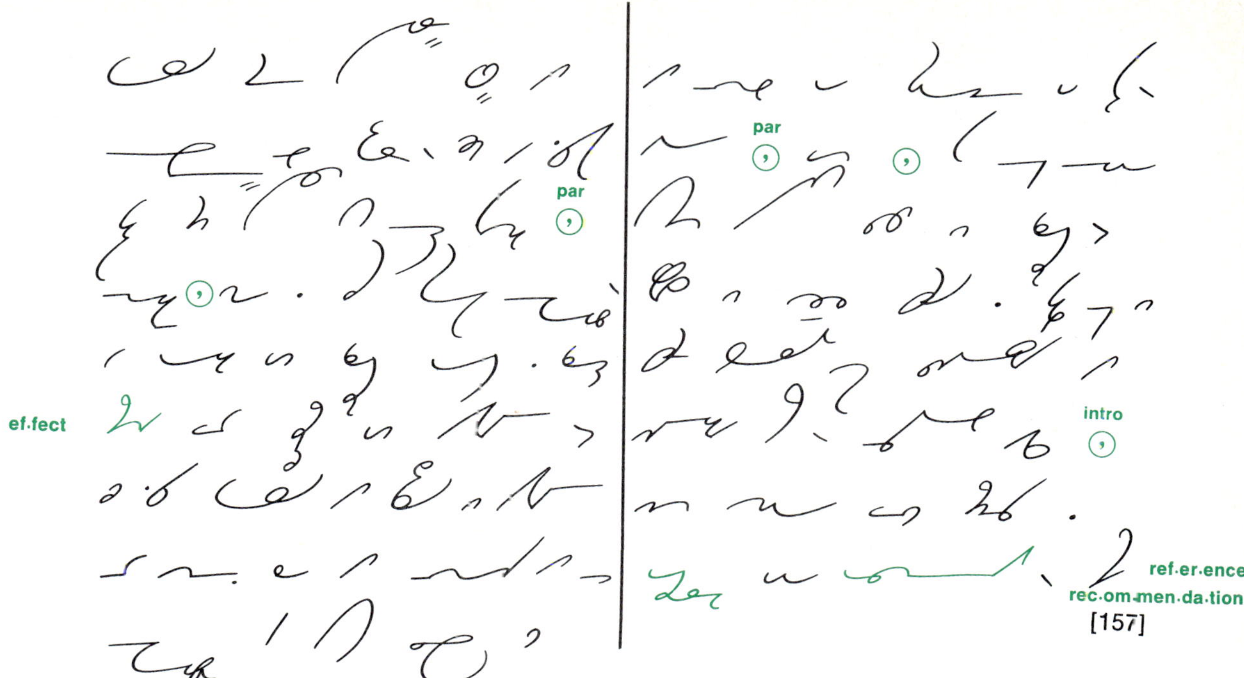

66
Transcription Quiz
For you to supply: 6 commas—2 commas apposition, 2 commas parenthetical, 1 comma conjunction, 1 comma *if* clause.

[131]

Warmup Your warmup letter is on page 46. Can you copy it faster than you did in Lesson 7?

Developing Word-Building Power

67 Word Families

1. *Student, confident, president, resident, accident, incident, evident.*
2. *Point, appoint, appointment, appointed, disappoint, disappointment, reappoint.*
3. *Illness, sickness, friendliness, fairness, kindness, witness, usefulness.*
4. *Side, sides, aside, decide, outside, inside, reside, resided.*

Building Transcription Skills

68 SPELLING FAMILIES -ance, -ence Always be careful when you transcribe a word ending in the sound of *-nce*—sometimes the ending will be spelled *-ance,* sometimes *-ence.*

Words Ending in -ance

ac·cep·tance	bal·ance	in·sur·ance
as·sis·tance	cir·cum·stance	per·for·mance
as·sur·ance	in·stance	re·li·ance

Words Ending in -ence

con·fer·ence	ev·i·dence	in·de·pen·dence
con·fi·dence	ex·cel·lence	oc·cur·rence
con·ve·nience	ex·pe·ri·ence	ref·er·ence

69 Business Vocabulary Builder

managerial Pertaining to a manager or management.

sole Only.

impeccable Without flaw; faultless.

Reading and Writing Practice

70

rise

par

conj

em.ploy.ees

man.a.ge.ri.al

conj

and o

[133]

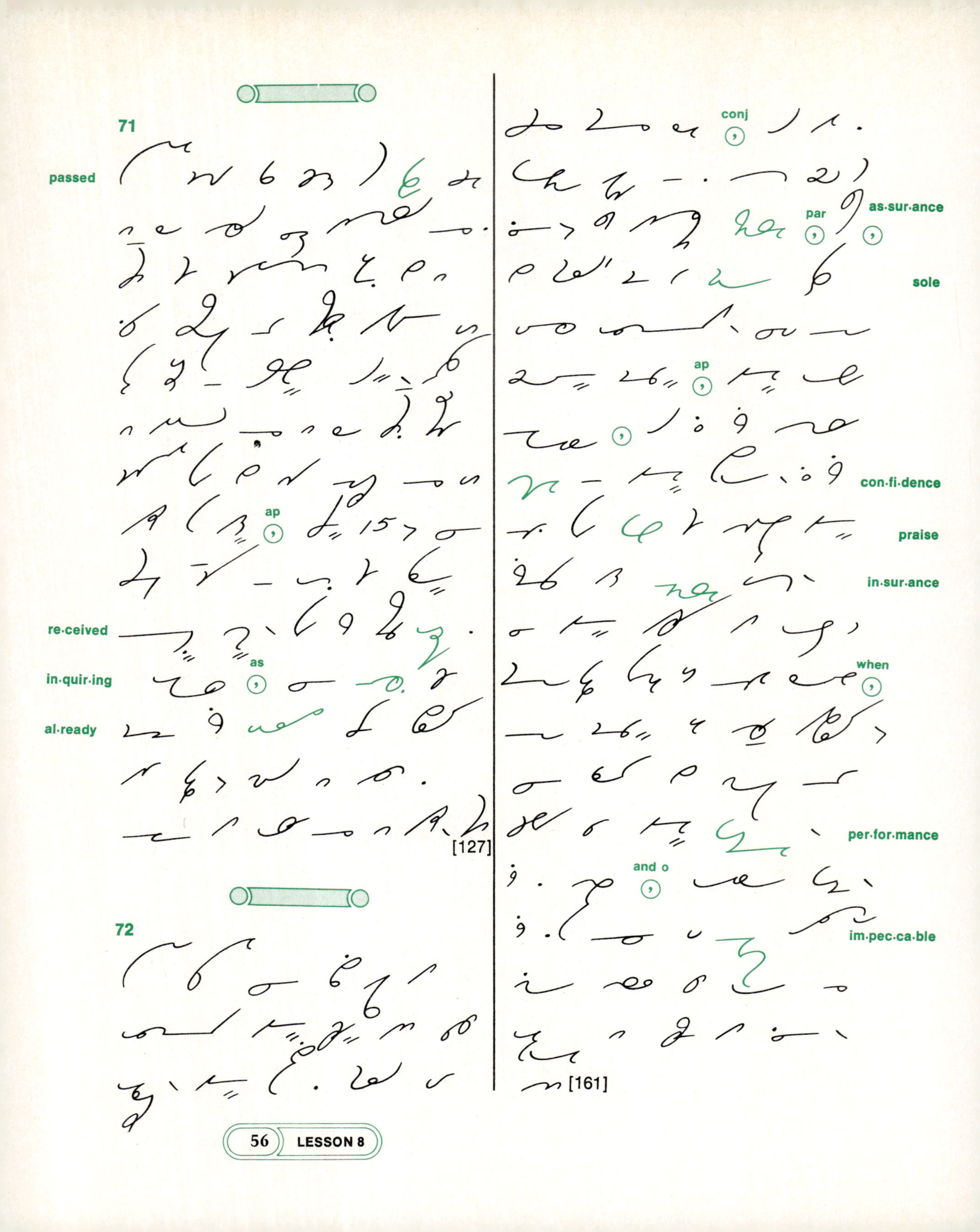

71

passed

re·ceived

in·quir·ing

al·ready

ap

as

[127]

72

conj

par

as·sur·ance

sole

ap

con·fi·dence

praise

in·sur·ance

when

per·for·mance

and o

im·pec·ca·ble

[161]

73

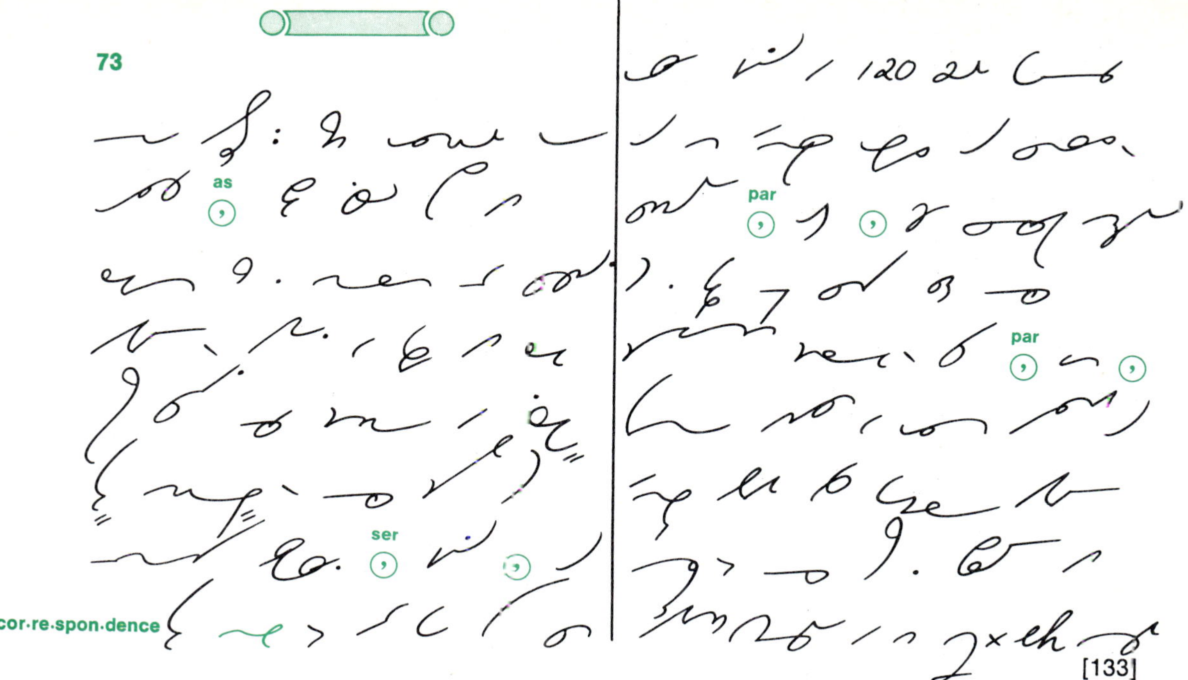

74 Transcription Quiz For you to supply: 7 commas—4 commas parenthetical, 1 comma introductory, 1 comma conjunction, 1 comma *if* clause.

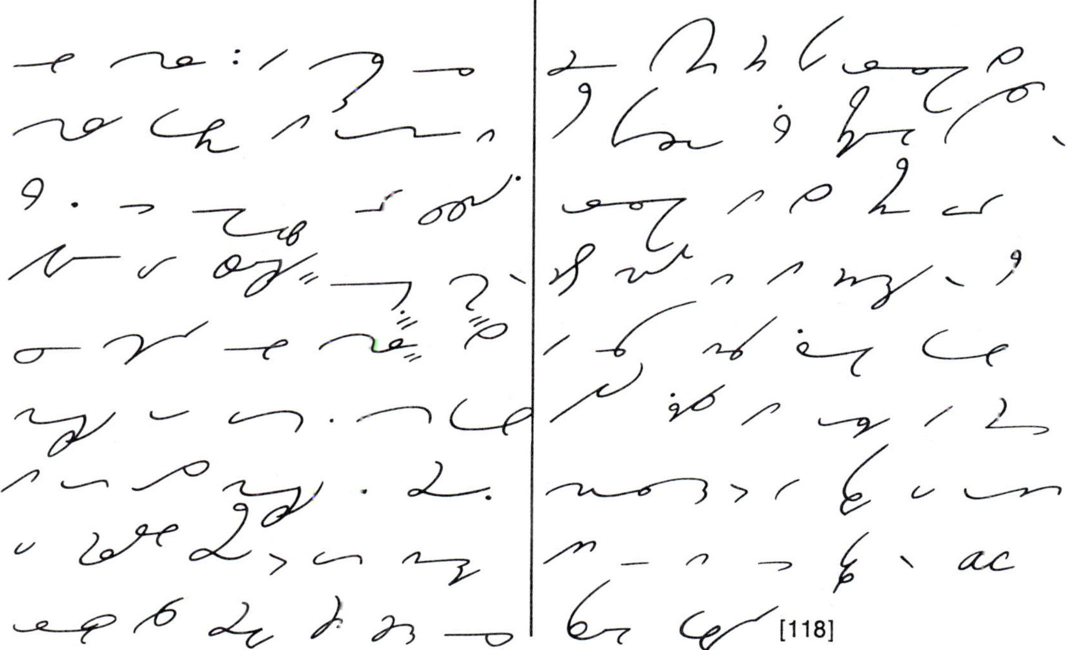

Warmup Your warmup once again is the phrase letter on page 46. How fast can you write it, legibly of course?

Developing Word-Building Power

75 Word Beginnings and Endings

Self-

1

-ward

2

Electric, Electr-

3

Inter-, Intr-

4

1. *Self-reliant, self-satisfied, self-satisfaction, self-confident, selfish, self-made, self-respect.*
2. *Rewarding, unrewarding, forward, inward, outward, afterward, eastward, backward.*
3. *Electric, electric company, electronic, electrical, electrician, electrify, electricity.*
4. *Interest, interested, interview, international, interpret, interfere, internal, intricate, introduce.*

Building Transcription Skills

76 GRAMMAR CHECKUP between, among

Between is used when referring to two things or persons; *among*, to more than two.

> Between *you and me, I do not believe we can finish the job.*
>
> *The work was divided equally* among *the three people—Mr. Smith, Mrs. Moreno, and Ms. Baker.*

Remember that when *between* is used as a preposition, any pronoun that follows it must be in the objective case. Careless writers and speakers often incorrectly say "between you and *I*" instead of "between you and *me*."

---

77 Business Vocabulary Builder

intensive Concentrated and exhaustive.

equivalent Equal in substance, degree, or value.

warrant *(verb)* To justify.

Reading and Writing Practice

78

dis·sat·is·fied

war·rant

ap·peal·ing

ser

if

ser

en·gi·neer·ing

conj

if

at·mo·sphere

[171]

79

cli·ents

in·tri·cate

if

equiv·a·lent

par

ser

if

if

[198]

80

ap·ti·tude

if

if

intro

ser

if

ser

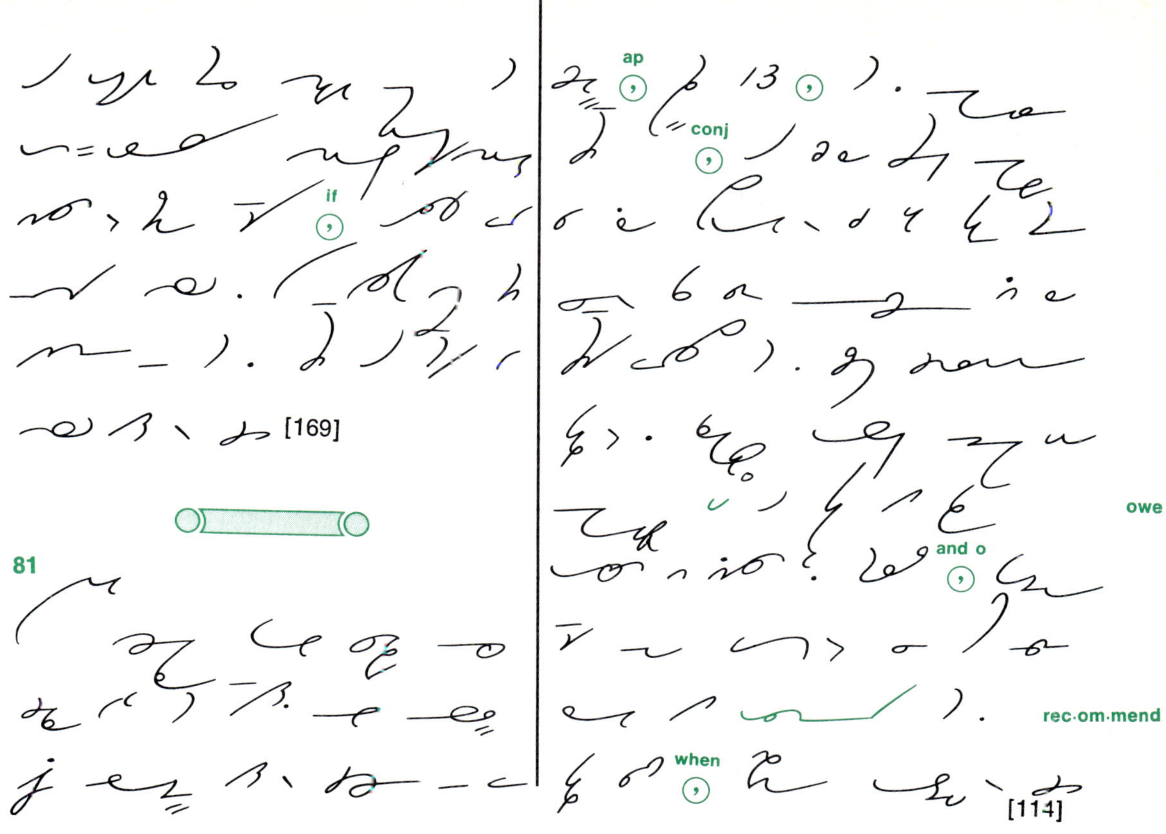

82 Transcription Quiz For you to supply: 6 commas—1 comma apposition, 1 comma introductory, 1 comma *as* clause, 1 comma conjunction, 2 commas parenthetical.

[116]

Warmup Copy the warmup phrase letter on page 46. This will be the last time you will use that letter for your warmup. Can you copy it in 75 seconds?

Developing Word-Building Power

83 Shorthand Vocabulary Builder

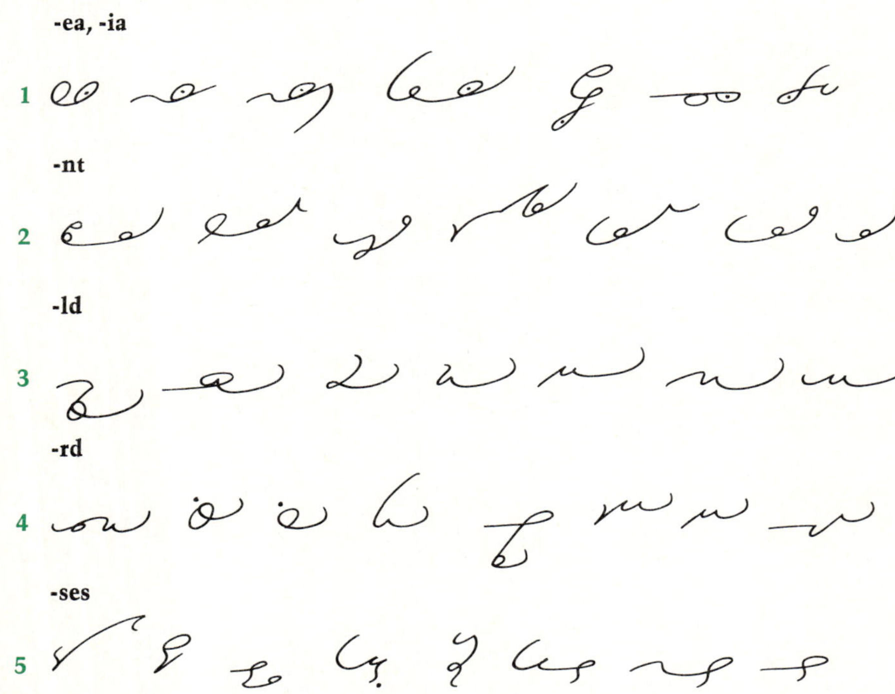

1. *Area, create, creative, brilliant, appreciate, mania, piano.*
2. *Excellent, talents, recently, standpoint, printer, plenty, rent.*
3. *Compiled, mild, field, sold, told, called, rolled.*
4. *Record, hired, hard, board, majored, stored, toward, motored.*
5. *Systems, assist, necessary, processing, offices, promises, classes, masses.*

Building Transcription Skills

84 Business Vocabulary Builder

drastically Extremely.

retrench To cut down.

majored Pursued academic studies in a chosen field.

compiled Brought together; collected.

Reading and Writing Practice

85

bear·er

ap

ex·cel·lent

conj

intro

dras·ti·cal·ly

conj

if

and o

cre·ative

fur·ther

if

[138]

86

intro

conj

re·trench

par

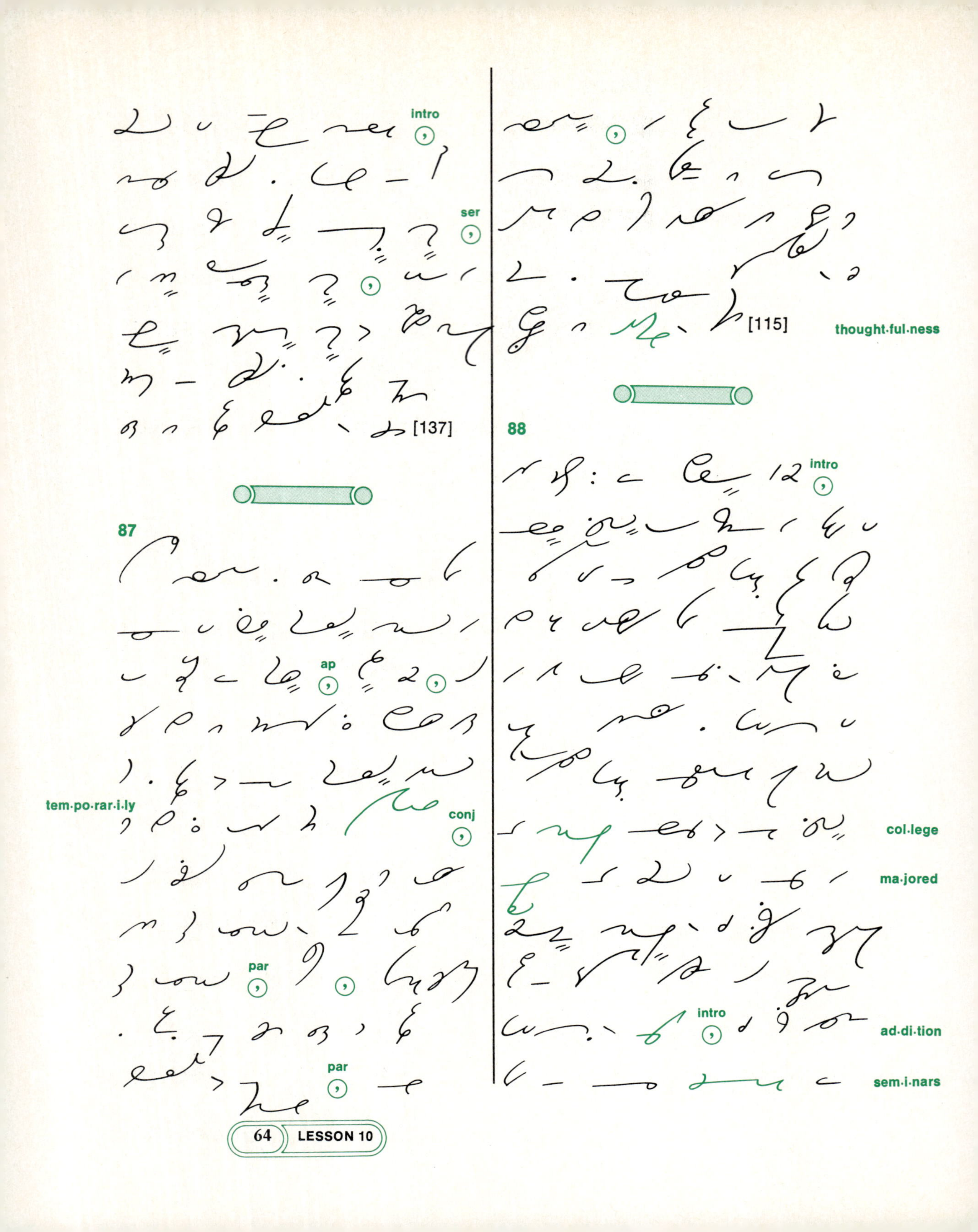

intro

ser

[137]

87

ap

tem·po·rar·i·ly

conj

par

par

intro

[115]

thought·ful·ness

88

intro

col·lege

ma·jored

intro

ad·di·tion

sem·i·nars

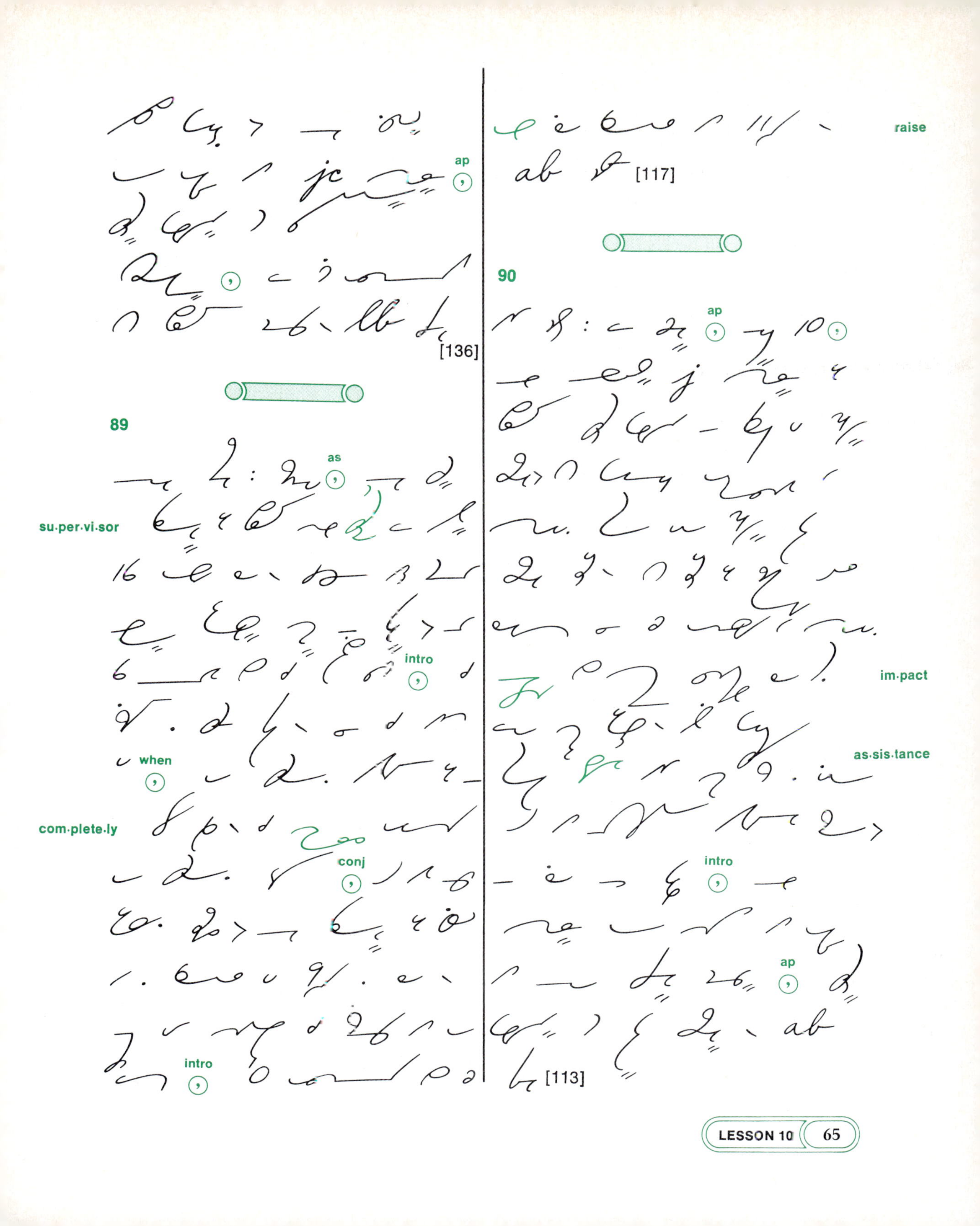

ap

[136]

89

as

su·per·vi·sor

intro

when

com·plete·ly

conj

intro

raise

[117]

90

ap

im·pact

as·sis·tance

intro

ap

[113]

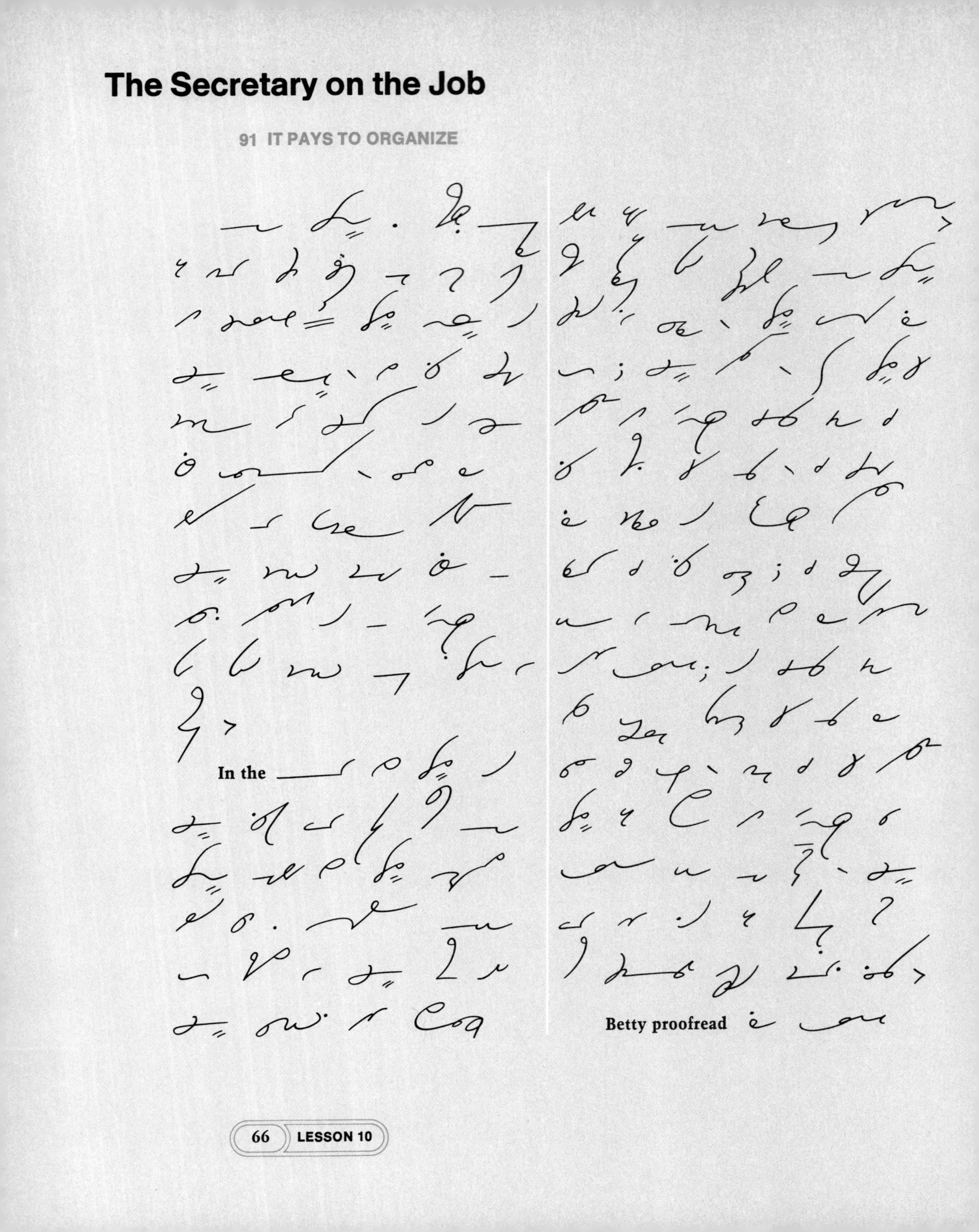

The Secretary on the Job

91 IT PAYS TO ORGANIZE

In the

Betty proofread

[327]

Good human relations skills do not just happen; they must be developed. In the office, the secretary has many opportunities every day to develop human relations skills. Using the telephone, greeting visitors, and working with peers all give the secretary valuable practice in dealing with people.

CHAPTER

Personnel

In most business organizations, the personnel office is the threshold you must cross before obtaining the job you want. The personnel department acts as a kind of clearinghouse, accommodating both those who seek jobs and those who would like to fill positions on their staffs.

Depending on the size of the company or organization, the personnel department takes on many of the responsibilities of recruiting, interviewing, testing, and placing job applicants. For example, it is not unusual for a large company to send members of its personnel department to high schools and colleges to talk to graduating students about the merits of a career in a particular company. For students who are almost ready to seek jobs, the visits by representatives of various companies are stimulating and helpful.

The personnel department of most companies is usually headed by a personnel director who, in turn, supervises a staff of specialists. The size of the personnel staff depends, of course, on the size of the company it must service. But whether the personnel staff is large or small, its chief purpose is to find the most desirable new employees from among the many who routinely apply for positions.

In this important function, the personnel department works in behalf of the company's executives who require additional staff but have little time to interview and screen a succession of job applicants. The personnel department—supplemented usually with questionnaires and tests—can handle this task expertly.

The work of the personnel department benefits the company's employees in other important ways too. It is usually the personnel department that handles the health and life insurance programs, the policies governing retirement benefits, and the guidelines for salary and wage incentives, vacations, and the like.

Each time a company welcomes a new employee, the personnel department steps in to introduce the newcomer to the company, to co-workers, and to the policies of the company. Often the new employee is invited to attend an orientation meeting (usually scheduled for a number of new employees) in order to learn about the company's services, products, history, and aspirations. The new employee also learns about his or her potential with the company.

The personnel department is the repository of all the records concerning every employee in the company—from the application form through progress reports, data on training, and promotions. These statistics are recorded on many different kinds of forms—usually considered confidential—and are kept by the personnel department. Inquiries and replies regarding these records may take the form of letters and memorandums.

The secretary who works in the personnel department has diverse duties and responsibilities—in one of the most interesting departments of any company or organization. As you practice working on letters in this chapter, you will better appreciate the continually interesting work of people in the personnel department.

Building Phrasing Skill

92 Phrase Builder

The following groups contain 41 phrases. Can you read the entire list in 45 seconds or less?

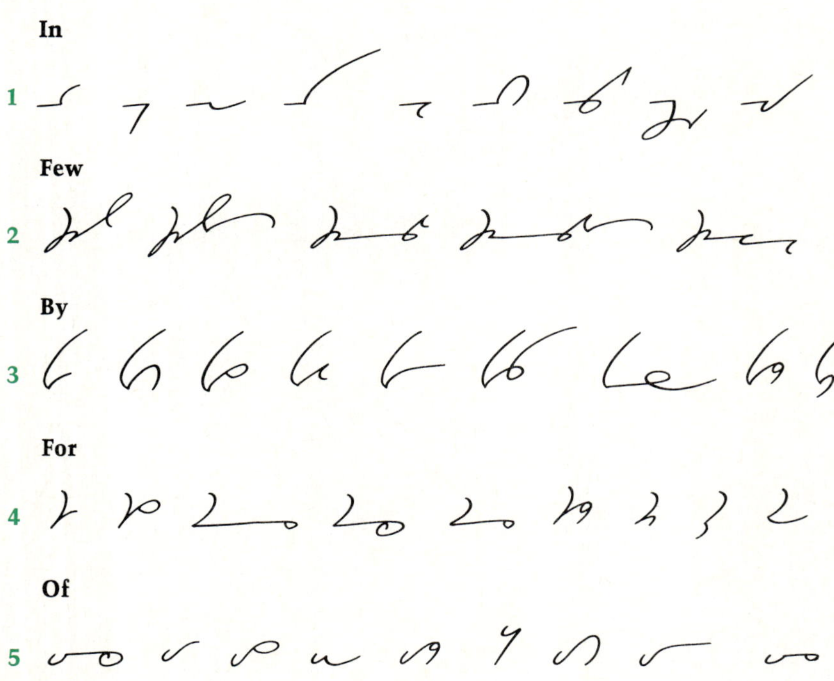

1. *In the, in which, in our, in time, in his, in this, in addition, in fact, in order.*
2. *Few days, few days ago, few minutes, few minutes ago, few moments.*
3. *By the, by this, by that, by its, by them, by that time, by mail, by these, by us.*
4. *For the, for that, for many, for my, for me, for these, for your, for his, for our.*
5. *Of my, of the, of that, of our, of these, of which, of this, of them, of any.*

93 Warmup Phrase Letter

The following letter, consisting of 131 words, contains 28 phrases that are frequently used in business letters. Can you read the entire letter in 1 minute or less? Can you make a shorthand copy in 2 minutes or less?

This will be your warmup letter for Lessons 11-15.

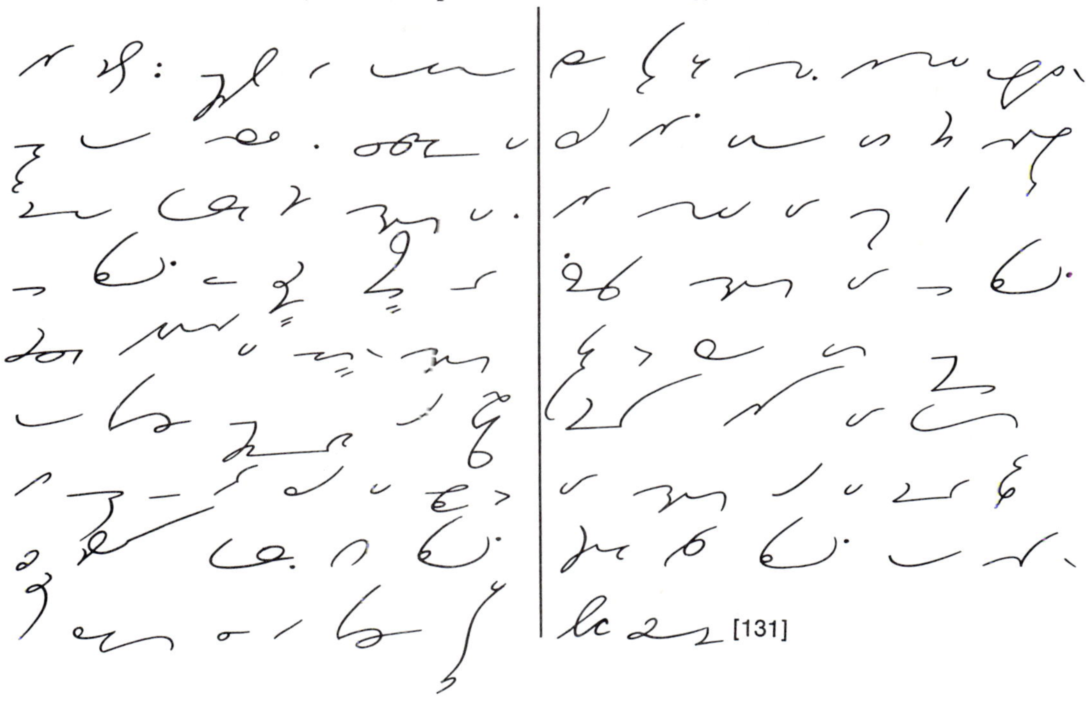

Building Transcription Skills

94 PUNCTUATION PRACTICE Thus far you have been reviewing the uses of the comma you studied in *Gregg Shorthand.* Beginning with this lesson, you will take up new punctuation pointers.

• • •

, nonrestrictive A *nonrestrictive* clause or phrase is one that may be omitted without changing the meaning of the sentence. It is sometimes called *nonessential.* Nonrestrictive clauses and phrases are set off by commas and might be classified as parenthetical. It is important that you grasp the meaning of the sentence in order to identify nonrestrictive clauses and phrases and punctuate them correctly.

Nonrestrictive—commas *Lee Pulaski, who is old enough to vote, should register.*

Restrictive—no commas *All persons* who are old enough to vote *should register.*

In the first sentence, *who is old enough to vote* is a nonrestrictive descriptive or parenthetical clause that must be set off with commas. It is not essential to identify the particular person who should register and could be omitted without changing the meaning of the sentence.

In the second sentence, *who are old enough to vote* is a restrictive clause and *must not* be set off by commas. The expression identifies the persons who should vote. The expression is essential to the meaning of the sentence.

Each time a nonrestrictive use of the comma occurs in the Reading and Writing Practice, it will be indicated in the shorthand thus: nonr (,)

95 Business Vocabulary Builder

entail To involve.

in the red The condition of showing a loss.

tentatively Not definite.

of the essence Of immediate importance.

Reading and Writing Practice

96

con·sid·er·a·bly

nonr

ad·e·quate

re·quire·ments

par

and o

nonr

nonr

ap

[138]

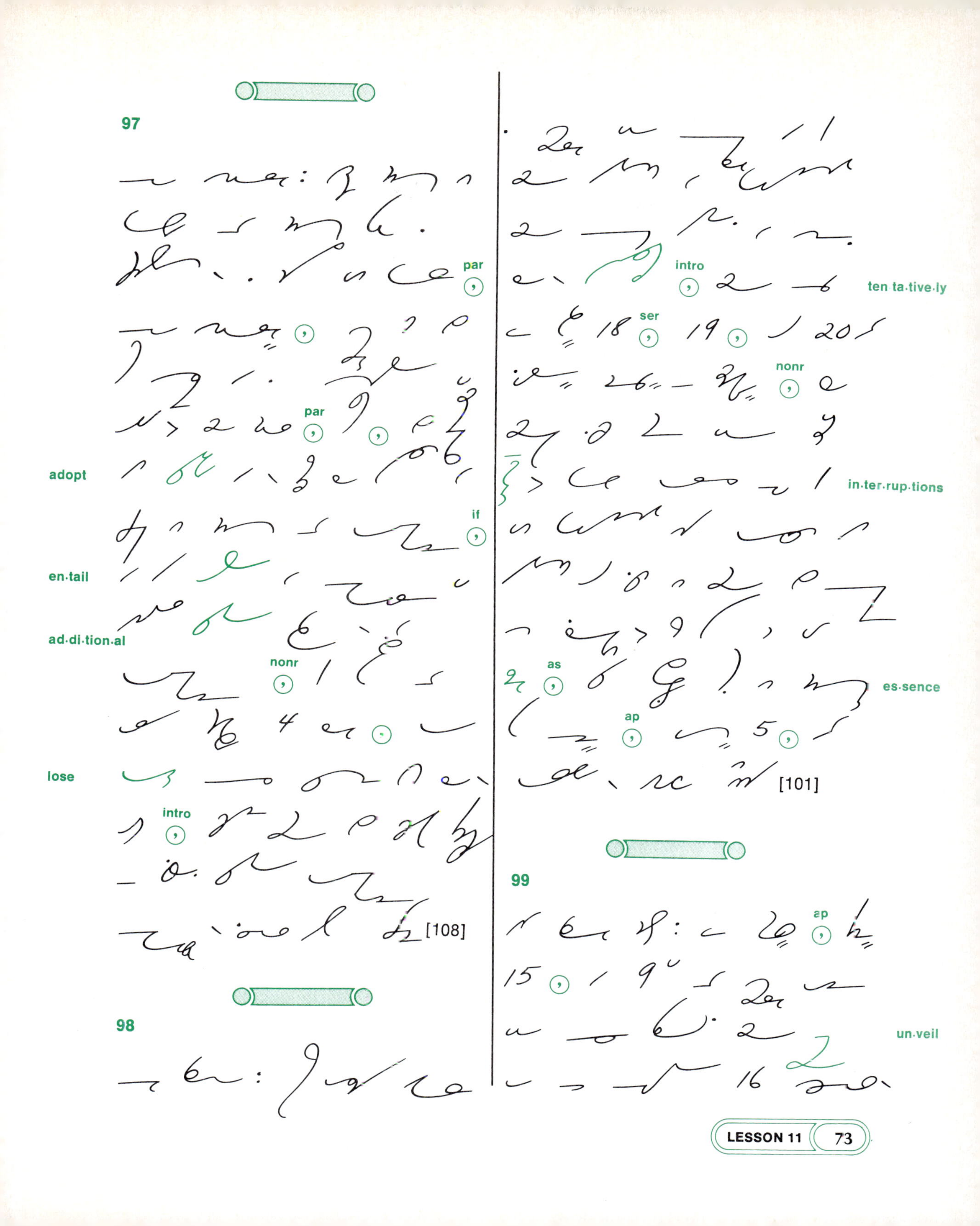

97

adopt

en·tail

ad·di·tion·al

lose

[108]

98

ten·ta·tive·ly

in·ter·rup·tions

es·sence

[101]

99

un·veil

en·gi·neers

if

[87]

100 Transcription Quiz In this and following Transcription Quizzes, a challenging new feature will be added. In addition to supplying the commas necessary to punctuate the letter correctly, you will have to supply a number of words that have been omitted from the printed shorthand.

Occasionally, a shorthand writer will omit a word when taking dictation, either through lack of attention or because of a distraction. Then as the meaning of the sentence becomes clear, the stenographer will supply the missing word when transcribing.

You should have no difficulty supplying the missing words in these Transcription Quizzes since in each case only one possible word makes sense.

For you to supply: 3 commas—1 comma introductory, 1 comma conjunction, 1 comma nonrestrictive; 2 missing words.

[130]

Warmup For your warmup, copy the phrase letter on page 71. Write as rapidly as you can, but be sure that your shorthand is readable.

Developing Word-Building Power

101 Brief-Form Chart

The following chart contains 30 brief forms. Can you read the entire chart in 35 seconds or less?

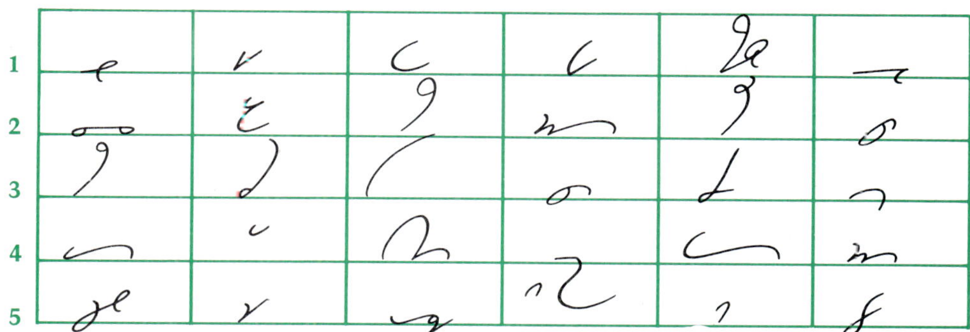

1. *Next, short, present, part, advertise, Ms.*
2. *Immediate, opportunity, advantage, suggest, several, out.*
3. *Every-ever, very, time, acknowledge, general, question.*
4. *Organize, over, difficult, envelope, progress, success.*
5. *Satisfy-satisfactory, state, request, under, wish, particular.*

102 Geographical Expressions

1. *Atlanta, Denver, Fort Worth, Phoenix, Dallas, Salt Lake City.*
2. *Alabama, Colorado, Utah, Idaho, New Mexico, Texas, Georgia, Arizona.*

Building Transcription Skills

103 TYPING STYLE STUDY numbers

■ 1 Spell out numbers 1 through 10.

We rode the bus four *times.*

■ 2 Use figures for numbers above 10.

There were 12 *students.*

■ 3 If several numbers both below and above 10 are used in the same sentence, use figures for all numbers.

The vote was 5 *for Tom,* 15 *for Sally, and* 6 *for Lee.*

■ 4 Spell out a number at the beginning of a sentence.

Twenty *people were there.*

■ 5 Express percentages in figures and spell out the word *percent.*

We will receive a 5 percent *discount.*

■ 6 To express even millions or billions in business correspondence, use the following style:

25 million *100 billion*

The correct form for typing numbers will occasionally be called to your attention in the margins thus: ***Transcribe:*** **25 million**

---

104 Business Vocabulary Builder

candid Without prejudice; impartial; fair.

confidential Private; secret.

receptacles Containers.

interoffice Between two offices.

Reading and Writing Practice

105 Brief-Form Letter

The following letter of 149 words contains 67 brief forms and derivatives. Your reading goal: 75 seconds; your writing goal: 2¼ minutes.

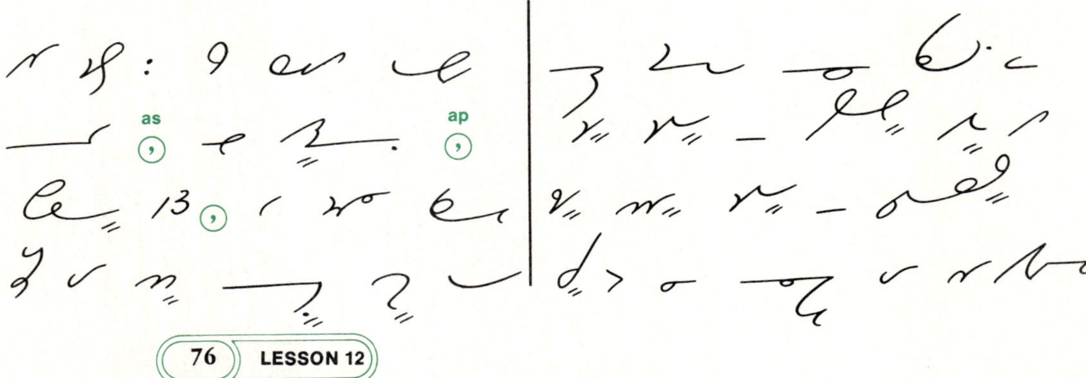

when

in·ter·of·fice

par·cels

Transcribe: three

if

[149]

106

par

en·joyed

and o

un·bi·ased

ques·tion·naire

ap

if

strict·ly

[129]

107

Transcribe: Eight

ser

intro

Transcribe:
10
11
12

ser

intro

intro

nonr

ser

Transcribe:
two

[126]

if

lose

intro

par

de·vel·op·ing

par

par

com·mis·sions

[177]

108

ap

109

ser

dis·tressed

intro

Transcribe: 20 percent

20,

if

if

ser

any·one

[140]

110 Transcription Quiz For you to supply: 6 commas—1 comma introductory, 2 commas series, 2 commas parenthetical, 1 comma *if* clause; 2 missing words.

[148]

Warmup Your warmup phrase letter is again No. 93 on page 71. Copy it as rapidly as you can, being sure to write readable shorthand. Try to cut a few seconds off the time it took you to copy the letter when you were in Lesson 12.

Developing Word-Building Power

111 Word Families

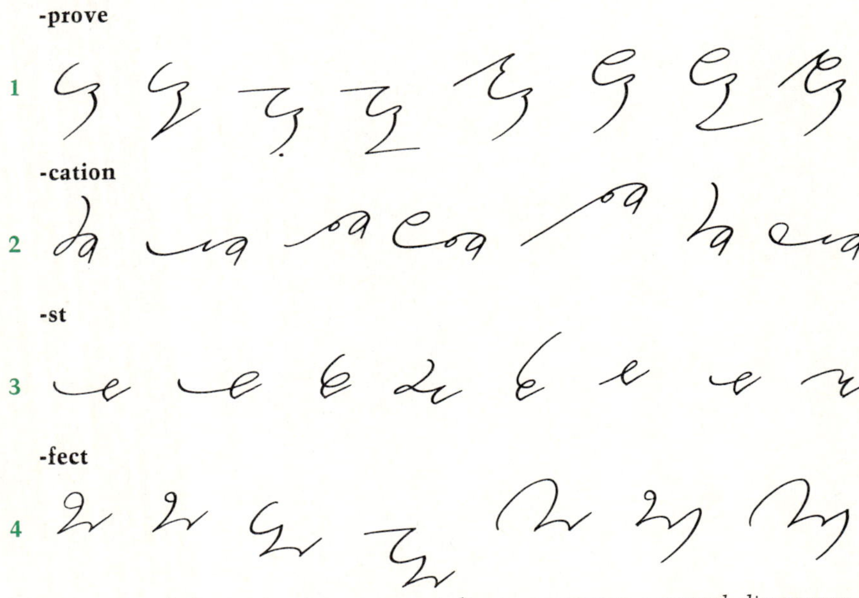

1. *Prove, proved, improving, improvement, disprove, approve, approval, disapprove.*
2. *Vacation, location, indication, application, dedication, vocation, allocation.*
3. *List, last, past, first, best, test, rest, cost.*
4. *Affect, effect, perfect, imperfect, defect, effective, defective.*

Building Transcription Skills

112 PUNCTUATION PRACTICE commas in numbers

■ 1 When a number contains four or more digits, a comma is generally used to separate thousands.

1,000 *167,181* *351,000*

■ 2 Commas are not used in serial numbers, house or store numbers, telephone numbers, page numbers, zip codes, and between the digits of a year.

No. 15181 *3156 Lexington Avenue* *Telephone number 564-1414*

page 1515 *New York, NY 10036* *the year 1776*

The generally recommended usage will be called to your attention in the margin of the Reading and Writing Practice thus: **Transcribe: 5,000** **Transcribe: 3116**

113 Business Vocabulary Builder

stagger To arrange in alternating or overlapping time periods.

participants Those who take part in something.

inducted Formally installed, as in an office or club position.

Reading and Writing Practice

114

Transcribe: 5,000

ser

Transcribe: 5850

ef·fec·tive

if

ab

[109]

115

stag·ger

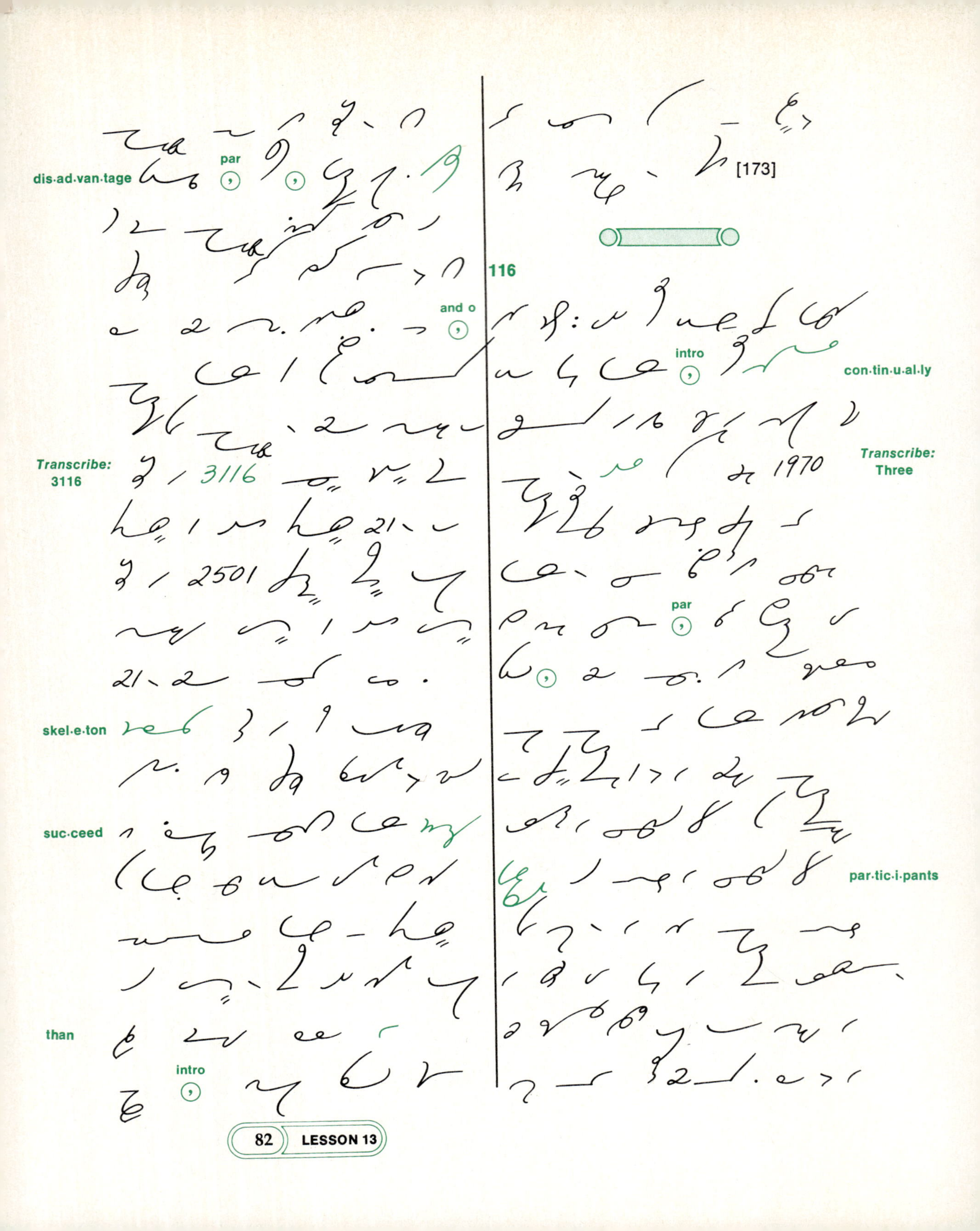

dis·ad·van·tage

par

Transcribe: 3116

skel·e·ton

suc·ceed

than

intro

[173]

116

intro

con·tin·u·al·ly

Transcribe: Three

par

par·tic·i·pants

as

af·fect

if

555-1261

[183]

117

an·nu·al

ap

18

1418

Transcribe:
1418
Twenty

80202

20

and o

[81]

118 Transcription Quiz For you to supply: 8 commas—2 commas apposition, 2 commas nonrestrictive, 2 commas conjunction, 2 commas parenthetical; 2 missing words.

[79]

Warmup Can you copy the phrase letter on page 71 faster than you did last time? If there is time to do so, copy the letter a second time in your best shorthand.

Developing Word-Building Power

119 Word Beginnings

Em-, Im-

1

Dis-

2

En-

3

Ex-

4

1. *Employees, employment, embarrassed, empower, emphasis, empire, implement, implementation, improper, import, importation, imposter.*
2. *Distribute, distributed, discussion, disappear, dismiss, discover, disappoint.*
3. *Enlightening, enjoyable, endeavor, encourage, encouragement, engage, engineer.*
4. *Exception, expect, explaining, export, extension, exterminate, extremely, exist.*

Building Transcription Skills

120 PUNCTUATION PRACTICE ; no conjunction

A semicolon is used to separate two independent but closely related clauses when no conjunction is used between them.

Althea finished the lesson in a few minutes; her sister did not finish the lesson.

The above sentence could be written as two sentences.

Althea finished the lesson in a few minutes. Her sister did not finish the lesson.

Because the two thoughts are closely related, the use of the semicolon is more appropriate than the use of the period.

Each time this use of the semicolon occurs in the Reading and Writing Practice, it will be indicated in the shorthand thus: (;) nc

---

121 Business Vocabulary Builder

implement *(verb)* To put into effect.

endeavor *(verb)* To try.

welfare State of being well.

Reading and Writing Practice

122

sup·pli·ers

nc

intro

ex·cep·tion

led

par

ac·cept

intro

im·ple·ment

conj

if

em·bar·rassed

[137]

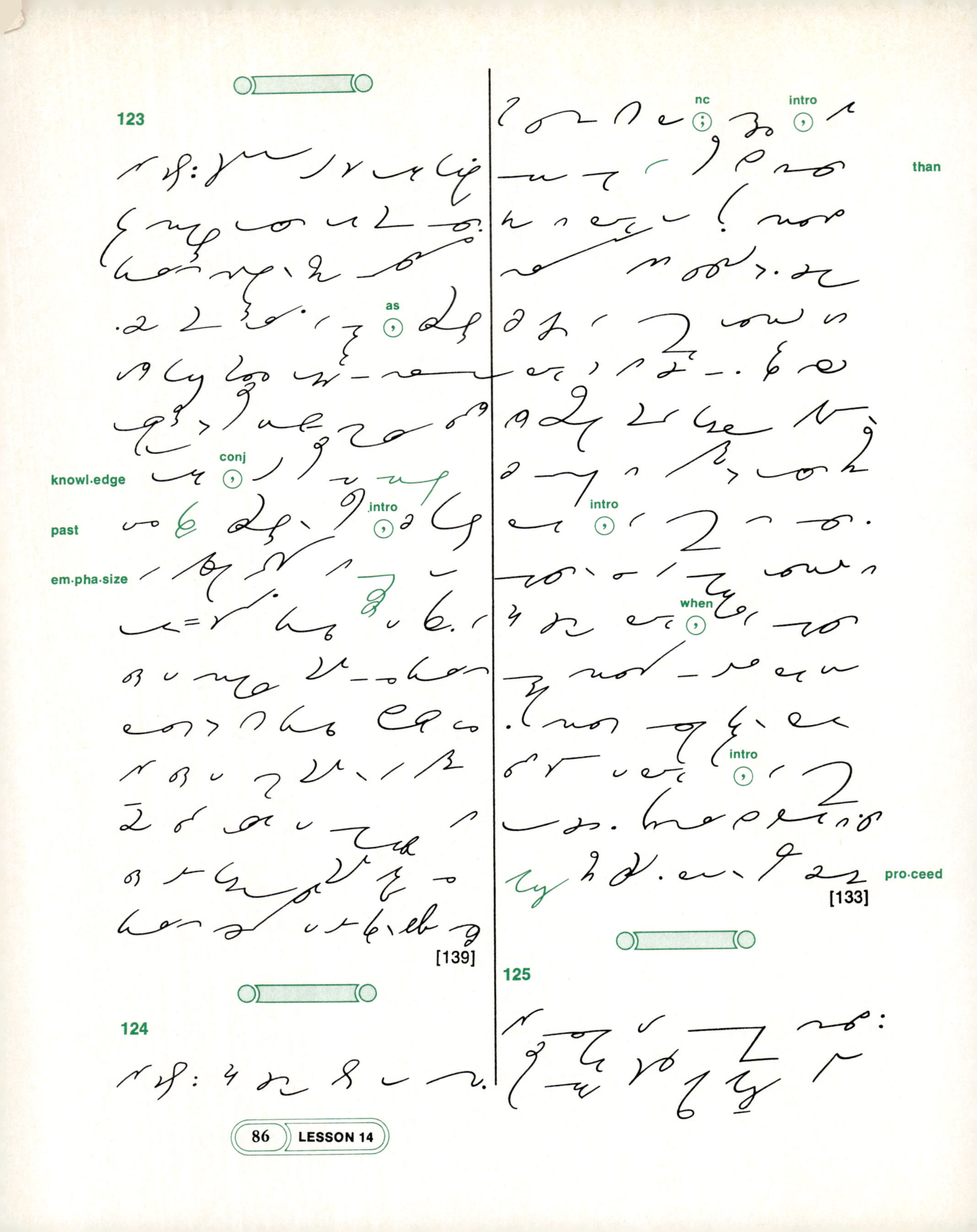

123

as

conj

knowl·edge

past

intro

em·pha·size

[139]

124

nc

intro

than

intro

when

intro

pro·ceed

[133]

125

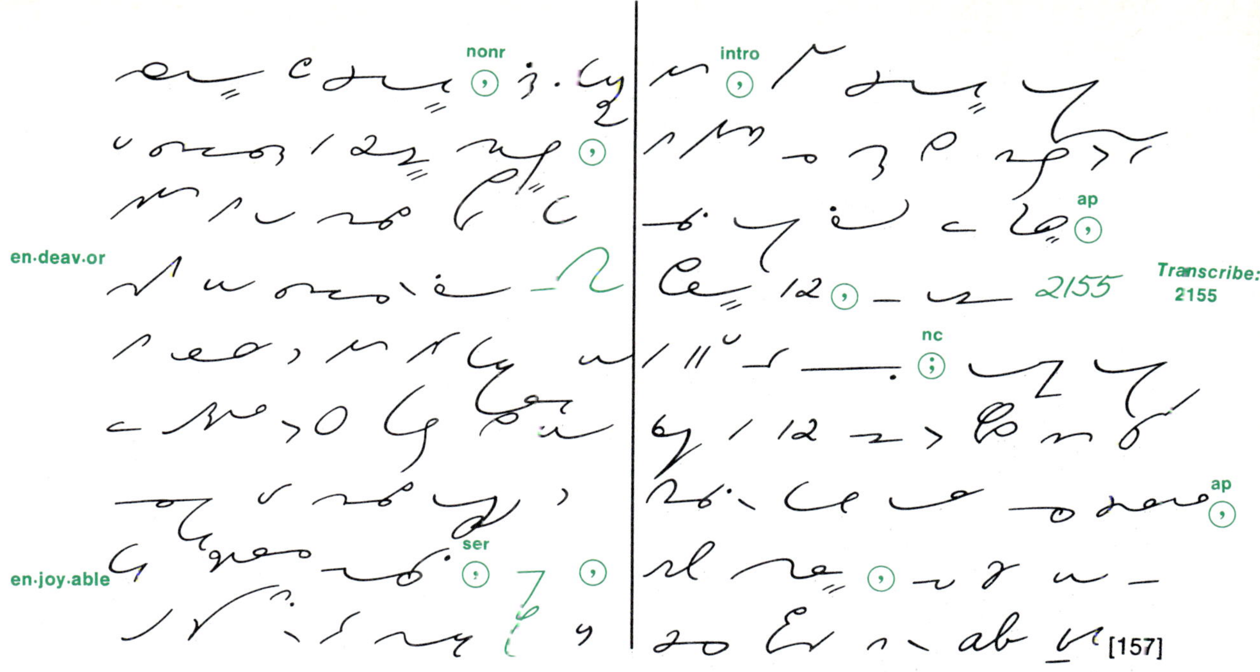

126
Transcription Quiz

For you to supply: 5 commas—1 comma *and* omitted, 1 comma conjunction, 2 commas series, 1 comma parenthetical; 1 semicolon no conjunction; 2 missing words.

[133]

Warmup This will be the last time that you will copy the phrase letter on page 71 as your warmup. If time permits, copy it once as rapidly as you can; then copy it a second time in your best shorthand for control.

Developing Word-Building Power

127 Shorthand Vocabulary Builder

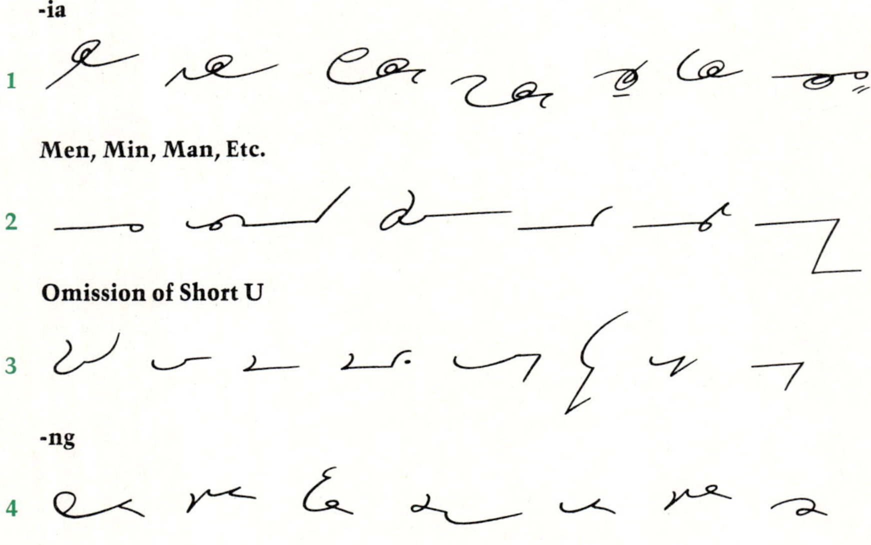

1. *Dial, trial, appliance, compliance, quiet, prior, Miami.*
2. *Many, recommend, firemen, month, minutes, management.*
3. *Front, run, some, something, lunch, budget, rushed, much.*
4. *Along, strong, spring, single, wrong, string, king.*

Building Transcription Skills

128 Business Vocabulary Builder

instituted Established, organized, and set in operation.

query A question; an inquiry.

itinerary Proposed outline of a trip.

humid Containing moisture.

Reading and Writing Practice

129

when

in·sti·tut·ed

que·ry

ser

ser

par

ser

nc

and o

[161]

130

ap

conj

ap·pli·ca·tion

ap·prov·al

if

[101]

131

vi·cin·i·ty

nc

ar·ea

fa·mil·iar·ize

par

re·sponse

and o

en·sure

[146]

132

nonr

hu·mid

Transcribe: Fifteen

15

nc

Transcribe: ten

10

ap

nc

conj

ful·filled

[124]

re·bel·lious

if

[112]

134

133

as

intro

intro

ap

pres·ence

intro

conj

itin·er·ary

[83]

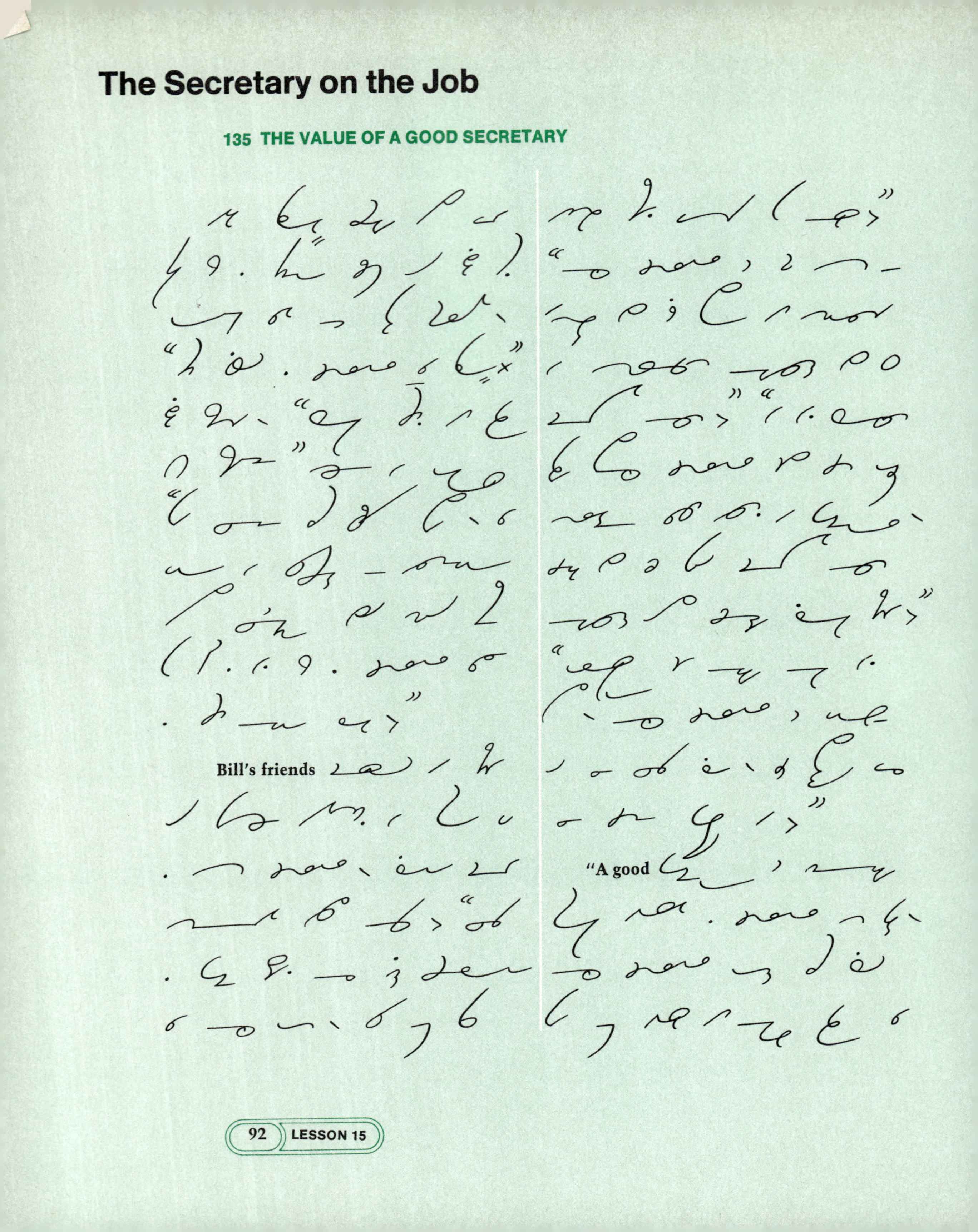

The Secretary on the Job

135 THE VALUE OF A GOOD SECRETARY

Bill's friends

"A good

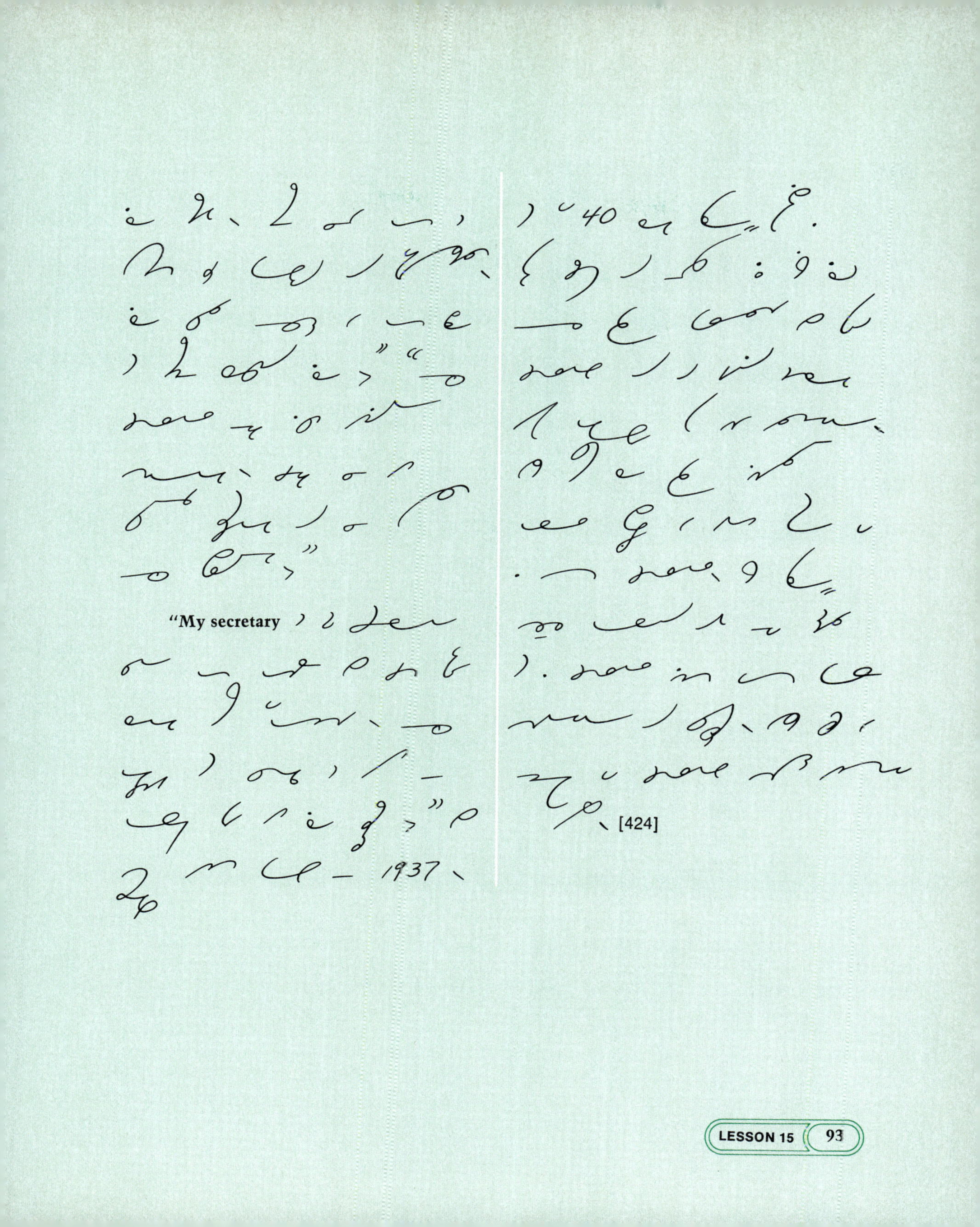

“My secretary

[424]

CHAPTER

Advertising

Which detergent is best? Which margarine? Which toothpaste? Research indicates that although most consumers are concerned primarily with price when choosing a brand, the next most important reason consumers select one brand rather than another is advertising. When faced with a choice between brands, consumers tend to reach for the one that seems most familiar—usually the brand whose advertising has made the greatest impact.

Advertising surrounds us during all our waking hours. We are in constant contact with advertising messages of one sort or another. It may be the sign on a coffee shop that simply says "Eat," the matchbook with its sales message, the advertising letters and pamphlets that arrive in the mail, the billboards on the road or the placards on buses and subways, or the commercials on radio and television.

It has been estimated that a "typical" family is exposed to 1,500 advertising messages a day, and this is a very conservative figure. If you traveled even a short distance to school today, you could have passed 100 shop signs and posters along the way. If you stopped at a drugstore, you could have seen a myriad of counter advertising cards, interior signs, and packages printed with advertising messages. While glancing through a monthly magazine, you would encounter at least 100 ads. And if you read the evening paper or watched television, the total number of advertising messages you were exposed to during the day becomes even more impressive.

Advertising is a sales message directed at a mass audience that seeks through persuasion to sell goods, services, or ideas on behalf of a sponsor. Business executives in every kind of commercial activity use advertising in one form or another as a selling tool.

Developing an advertising program for a company begins with researching information about who buys the product or service and why it is bought. Then the creative people—writers and artists—prepare the ads. Production people make sure the ads are produced according to specifications for the proper media. Specialists analyze the best media package—newspaper, magazine, radio, television, and so on, or a combination of one or more of these—for presenting the client's ads, and they buy the space and time for the client's message.

There is another side to advertising that differs markedly from the process of developing an ad campaign—selling space and time. Magazines, newspapers, television and radio stations, and other media that depend on advertisers for revenue need sales forces to sell advertisers on placing their advertisements in the vehicle they offer.

The purpose of the advertising business is to help sell goods and services. Because it is always challenging and because, to be successful, it requires the application of creativity, advertising can be stimulating, exciting, and rewarding. The letters in this chapter deal with the field of advertising.

Building Phrasing Skill

136 Phrase Builder

The following groups contain 45 phrases. Can you read the entire list in 50 seconds?

For

1

As

2

Of

3

That

4

If

5

1. *For the, for these, for this, for that, for it, for your information, for me, for his, for us, for them.*
2. *As the, as you will, as you, as you can, as you are, as you know, as you may, as you would be.*
3. *Of the, of them, of these, of your, of our, of which, of time, of their, of this.*
4. *That is, that is not, that are, that will, that would, that it will, that it will be, that they.*
5. *If you, if you are, if you will, if you can, if you have, if you would, if you know, if it is, if it will, if they.*

137 Warmup Phrase Letter

The following 118-word letter contains 29 phrases. Your reading goal: 50 seconds; your copying goal: 1¾ minutes.

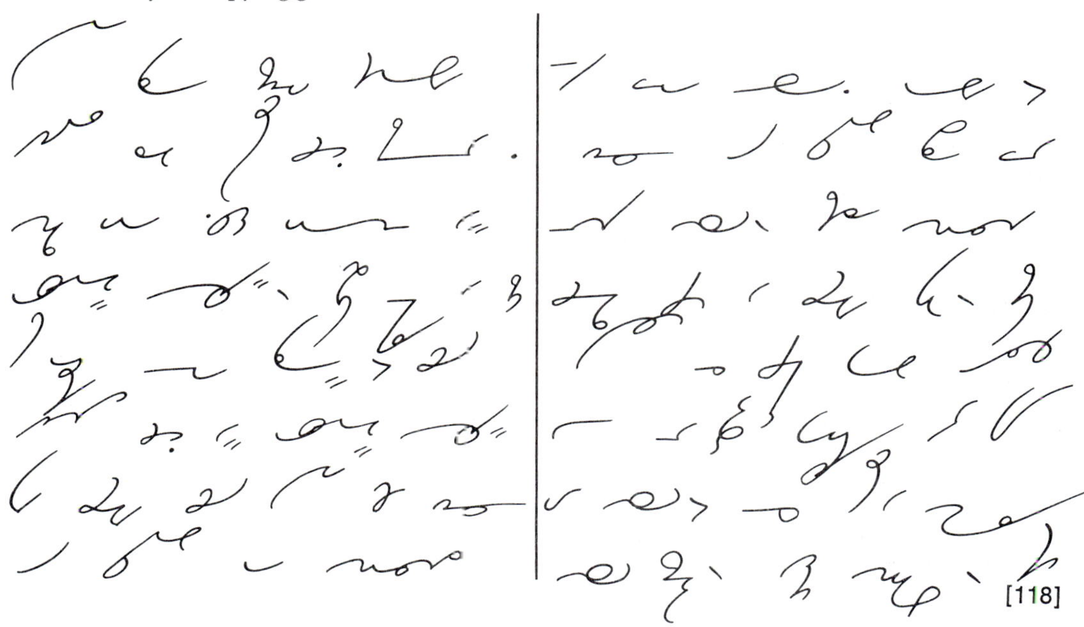

Building Transcription Skills

138 PUNCTUATION PRACTICE . courteous request

Very often one person may wish to persuade another to take some definite action. The request for action could be made in a direct statement such as:

I want your check by return mail.

A direct statement of this type, however, might antagonize the reader. Many people, therefore, prefer to make such a request in the form of a question.

May I have your check by return mail.

Such a request should be followed by a period.

This is how you can decide whether to use a question mark or a period:

■ 1 When a question calls for *definite action*, a *period* is used at the end of the sentence.

■ 2 When a question calls for a *yes-or-no response*, a *question mark* is used at the end of the sentence.

Whenever the period is used in this situation in the Reading and Writing Practice, it will be indicated in the shorthand thus: cr ⊙

139 Business Vocabulary Builder

deletions Eliminations.

buttress To support.

sublet To rent to another.

Reading and Writing Practice

140

conj

as

sim·i·lar

intro

cr

conj

[114]

141

ap

bud·get

and o

conj

de·le·tions

fac·tors

but·tress

par [152]

when

ad

142

555-5115

ad·ver·tis·ers

va·ri·ety

nc

intro

nc

555-5115 [144]

143 Transcription Quiz For you to supply: 6 commas—2 commas series, 1 comma nonrestrictive, 1 comma *as* clause, 1 comma *if* clause, 1 comma introductory; 1 period courteous request; 2 missing words.

4 15

[88]

Warmup Your warmup is Letter 137 on page 97. This time, instead of warming up on the entire letter, use only the first paragraph. Write the paragraph slowly at first, in your best penmanship. Then write it again as rapidly as you can.

Developing Word-Building Power

144 Brief-Form Chart

Can you read the 30 brief forms and derivatives in this chart in 35 seconds or less?

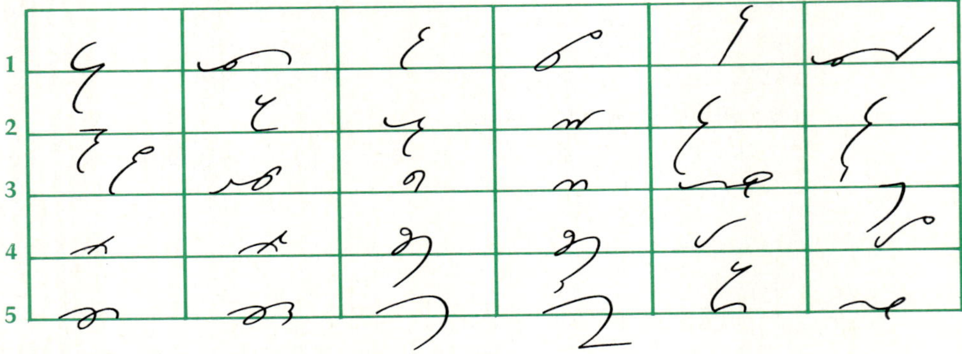

1. *Probable, regular, speak, idea, subject, regard.*
2. *Newspaper, opinion, responsible, worth, public, publish-publication.*
3. *Experience, throughout, usual, world, recognize, never.*
4. *Quantity, quantities, executive, executives, ordinary, ordinarily.*
5. *Character, characters, govern, government, object, correspond-correspondence.*

145 Geographical Expressions

1. *Wilmington, Baltimore, Richmond, Charleston, Columbus.*
2. *Delaware, Maryland, Virginia, West Virginia, South Carolina, North Carolina.*

Building Transcription Skills

146 PUNCTUATION PRACTICE hyphens

Hyphenated Before Noun
No Noun, No Hyphen
No Hyphen After ly

You can quickly decide whether to use a hyphen in compound expressions like *up to date* or *high level* by observing these rules:

■ **1** If a noun follows the expression, use a hyphen.

It is an up-to-date *bank (noun).*

She holds a high-level *job (noun).*

Whenever a hyphenated expression occurs in the Reading and Writing Practice, it will be called to your attention in the margin thus: **up-to-date** ***hyphenated before noun***

■ **2** If *no* noun follows the compound expression, do not use a hyphen.

The book is up to date.

His job is on a high level.

Occasionally, these expressions in which a hyphen is not used will be called to your attention in the Reading and Writing Practice thus: **up to date** ***no noun, no hyphen***

■ **3** No hyphen is used in a compound modifier where the first part of the expression is an adverb that ends in *ly*.

It is a privately owned *business.*

To be sure that you are not tempted to put a hyphen in expressions of this type, your attention will occasionally be called to them in the Reading and Writing Practice thus: **pri·vate·ly owned** ***no hyphen after ly***

---

147 Business Vocabulary Builder

expeditiously Carried out with dispatch; finished quickly.

innovative Creative.

stimulate To cause action.

● Reading and Writing Practice

148 Brief-Form Letter

The following letter contains 151 words, of which many are brief forms or brief-form derivatives. Your reading goal on this letter: 90 seconds; your writing goal: 2½ minutes.

when

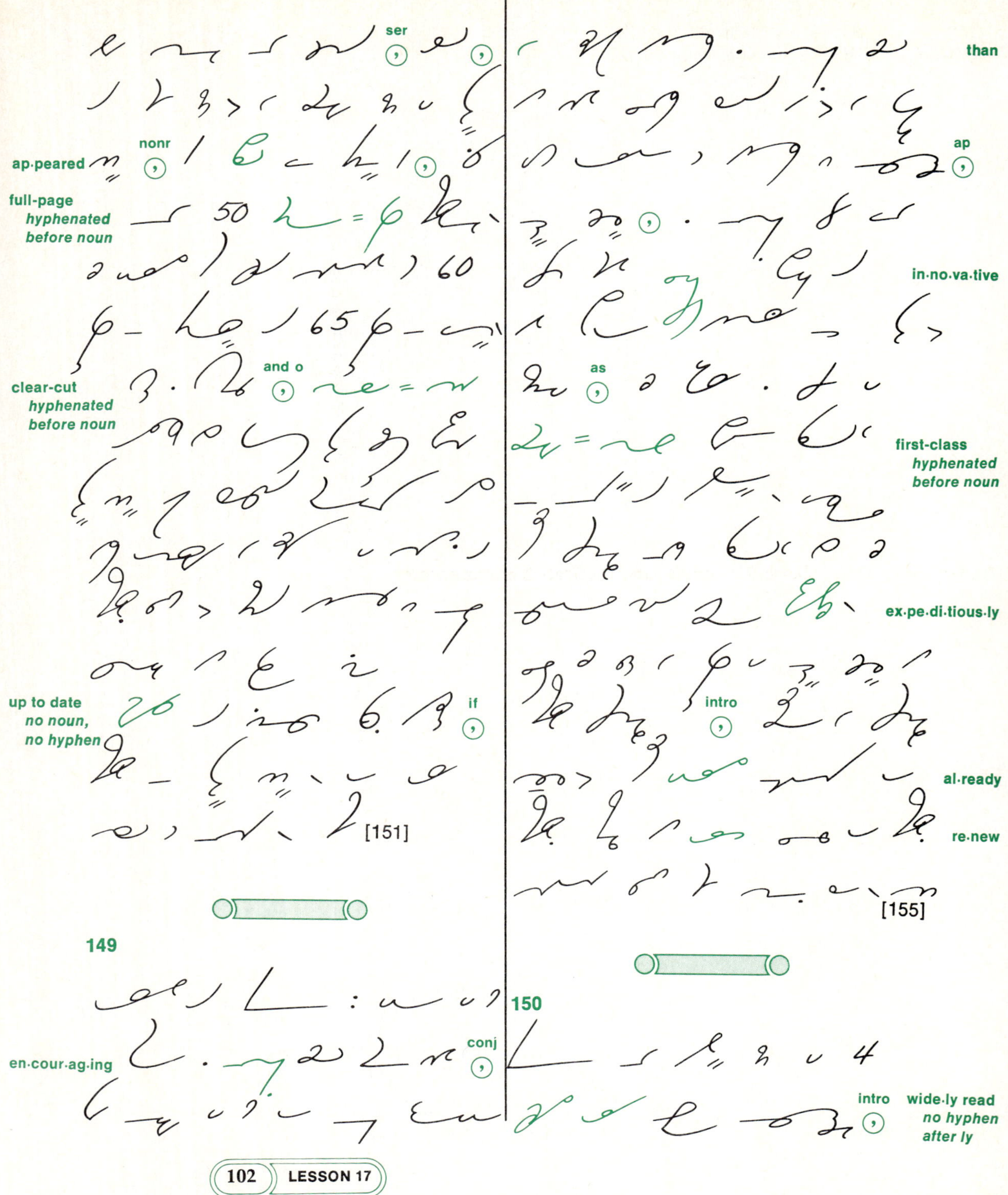
ser
than
nonr
ap·peared
ap
full-page
hyphenated
before noun
50
60
in·no·va·tive
65
and o
as
clear-cut
hyphenated
before noun
first-class
hyphenated
before noun
ex·pe·di·tious·ly
up to date
no noun,
no hyphen
if
intro
al·ready
re·new
[151]
[155]
149
150
en·cour·ag·ing
conj
intro
wide·ly read
no hyphen
after ly

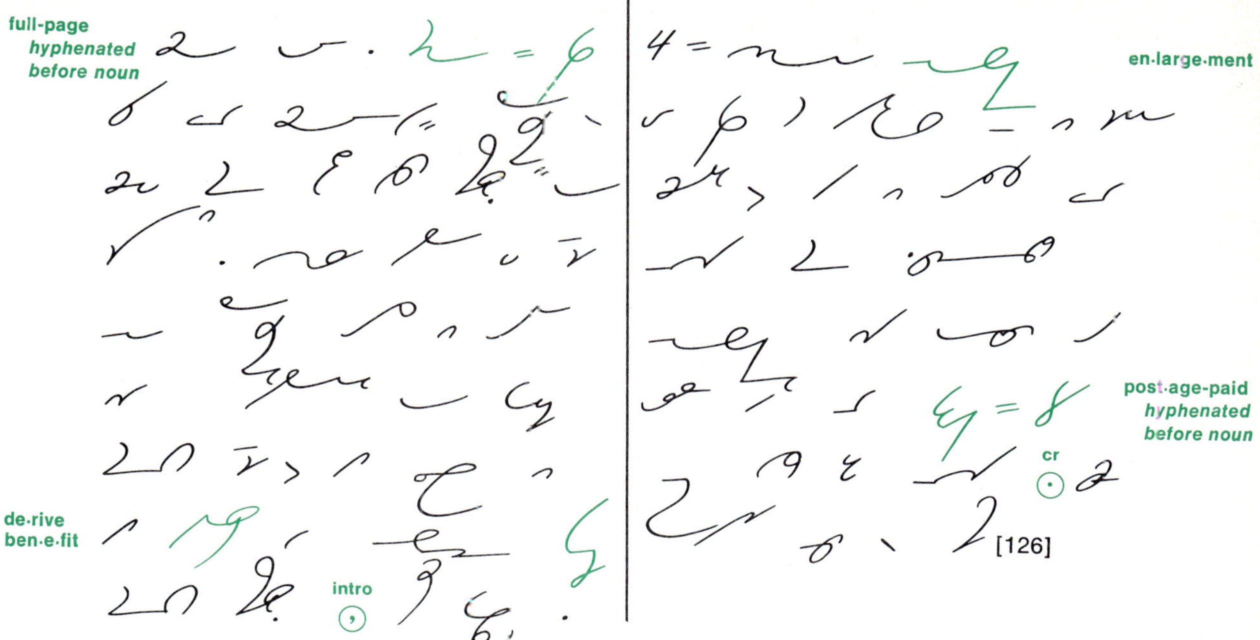

151 Transcription Quiz For you to supply: 6 commas—2 commas series, 1 comma conjunction, 1 comma *as* clause, 2 commas parenthetical; 2 missing words.

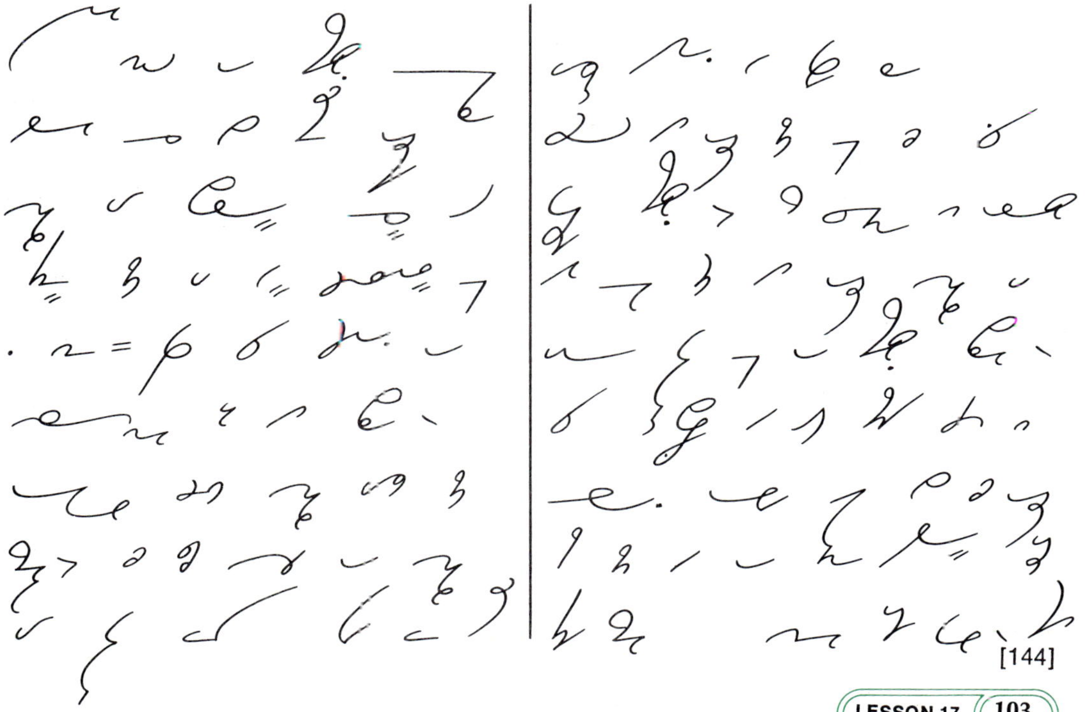

[144]

Warmup Once again, warm up on the phrase letter on page 97. This time warm up on the second paragraph in the same way you warmed up on the first paragraph of the letter.

Developing Word-Building Power

152 Word Families

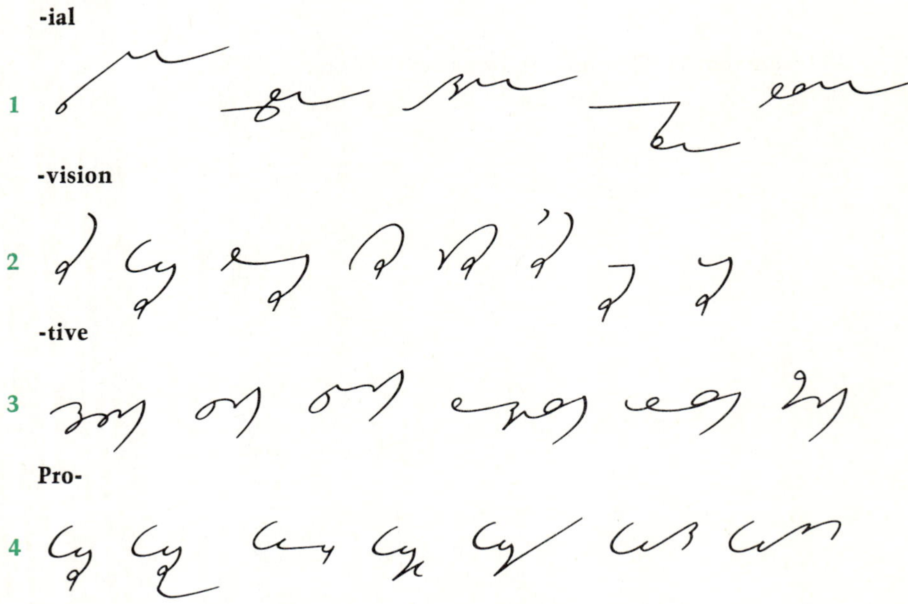

1. *Editorial, material, industrial, managerial, territorial.*
2. *Vision, provision, television, division, subdivision, supervision, envision, revision.*
3. *Consecutive, active, attractive, illustrative, relative, effective.*
4. *Profession, professional, promotion, profits, profited, produce, production.*

Building Transcription Skills

153 PUNCTUATION PRACTICE the apostrophe

■ 1 A noun that ends in *s* and is followed by another noun is usually a possessive, calling for an apostrophe before the *s* when the word is singular.

The company's *new building is under construction.*

Mr. Brown's *work is satisfactory.*

■ 2 A plural noun ending in *s* calls for an apostrophe after the *s* to form the possessive.

Several workers' *salaries were adjusted.*

All contractors' *bids will be studied.*

■ 3 An irregular plural requires an apostrophe before the *s* to form the possessive.

The new store doesn't sell children's *clothes.*

The store does carry women's *suits.*

■ 4 The possessive forms of pronouns do not require an apostrophe.

You will be saving your time as well as ours.

This record is yours, *not* ours.

These books are theirs, *not* ours.

The company submitted its *report on time.*

---

154 Business Vocabulary Builder

consecutive Continuous; one after the other.

graphics Of or relating to drawing or writing.

undisputed Unquestioned.

deplane To get off an airplane.

Reading and Writing Practice

155

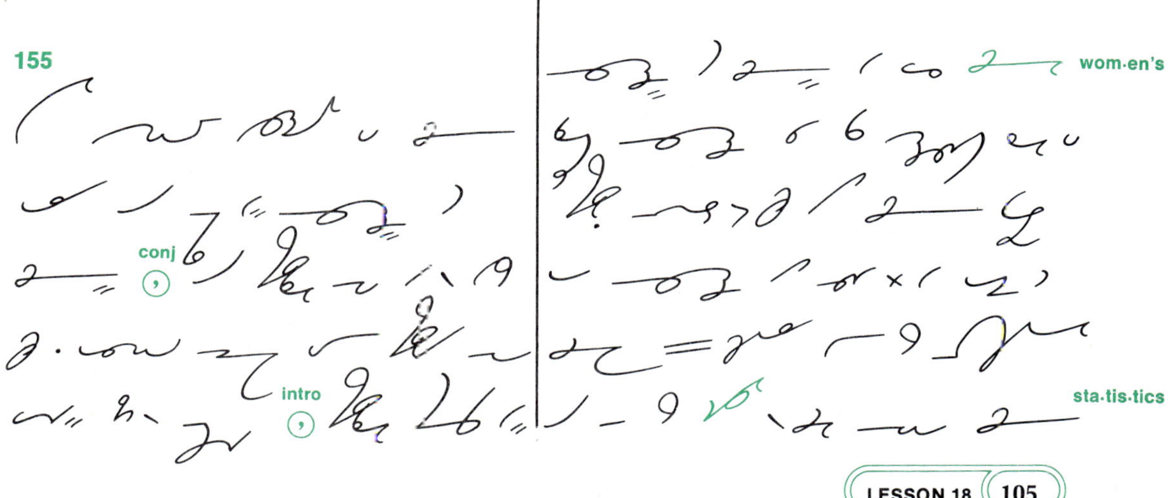

intro

ad·ver·tis·ers'

com·pa·ny's

full-page *hyphenated before noun*

[133]

156

Transcribe: 12

graph·ics

Transcribe: three

when

ours

coun·try's

intro

[125]

157

na·tion's

air·line's

de·plane

its

nonr

intro

ap

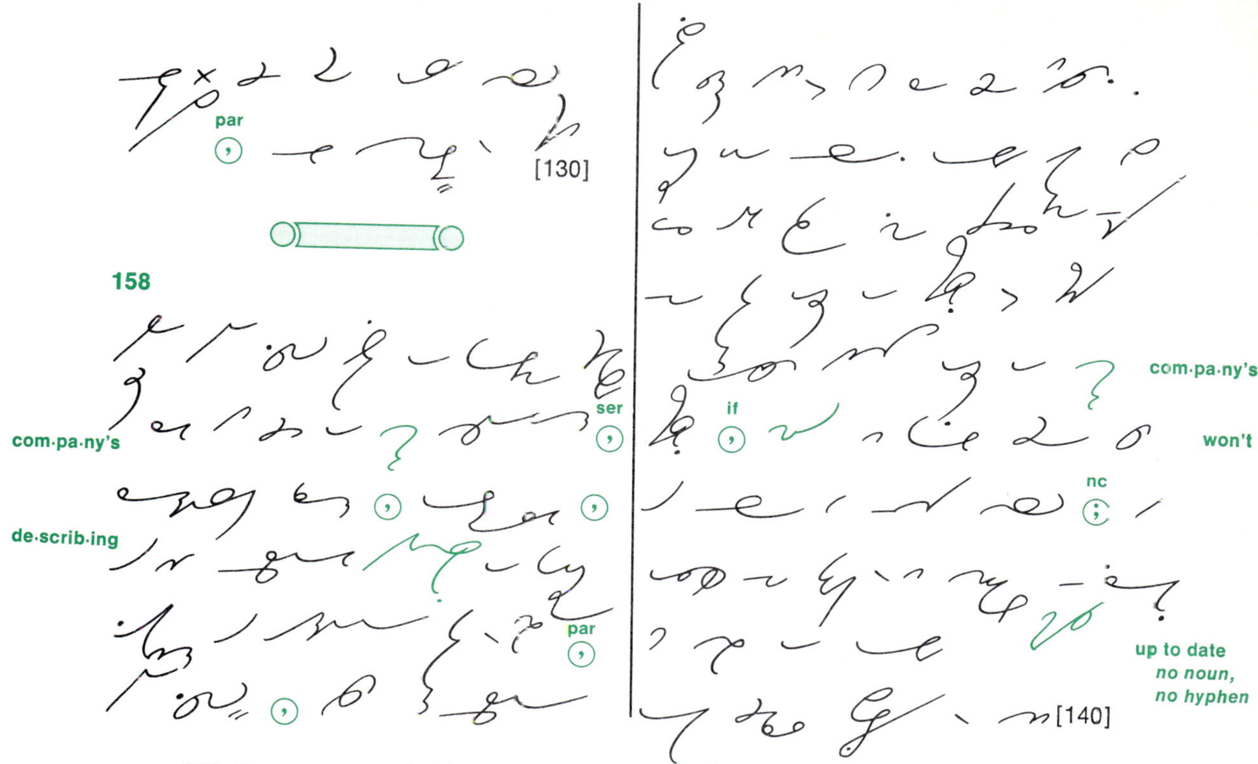

159 Transcription Quiz For you to supply: 5 commas—1 comma *as* clause, 2 commas nonrestrictive, 1 comma conjunction, 1 comma *and* omitted; 2 missing words.

[137]

Warmup Your warmup letter is paragraph 137 on page 97. Practice the third paragraph of this letter as you practiced the first paragraph for your warmup when you were working on Lesson 17. Don't foget the final writing for control.

Developing Word-Building Power

160 Word Endings

-cal, -cle

1

-ful

2

-ble

3

-ment

4

1. *Technical, periodicals, medical, logical, chemicals, articles.*
2. *Helpful, useful, careful, thoughtful, doubtful, mindful, delightful.*
3. *Possible, available, profitable, reliable, applicable, agreeable, terrible.*
4. *Apartment, requirement, advertisement, department, moment, compartment, torment.*

Building Transcription Skills

161 PUNCTUATION PRACTICE commas with geographical expressions

Place a comma between the name of a city and state.

Glenn lived in Richmond, Virginia.

If the name of the state does not end the sentence, place a comma after it also.

Lee visited our Wilmington, Delaware, *office.*

Each time a comma is used with a geographical expression, it will be shown thus: (,) geo

---

162 Business Vocabulary Builder

summarize To restate briefly.

periodicals Publications issued at regular intervals.

ultimately In the end.

Reading and Writing Practice

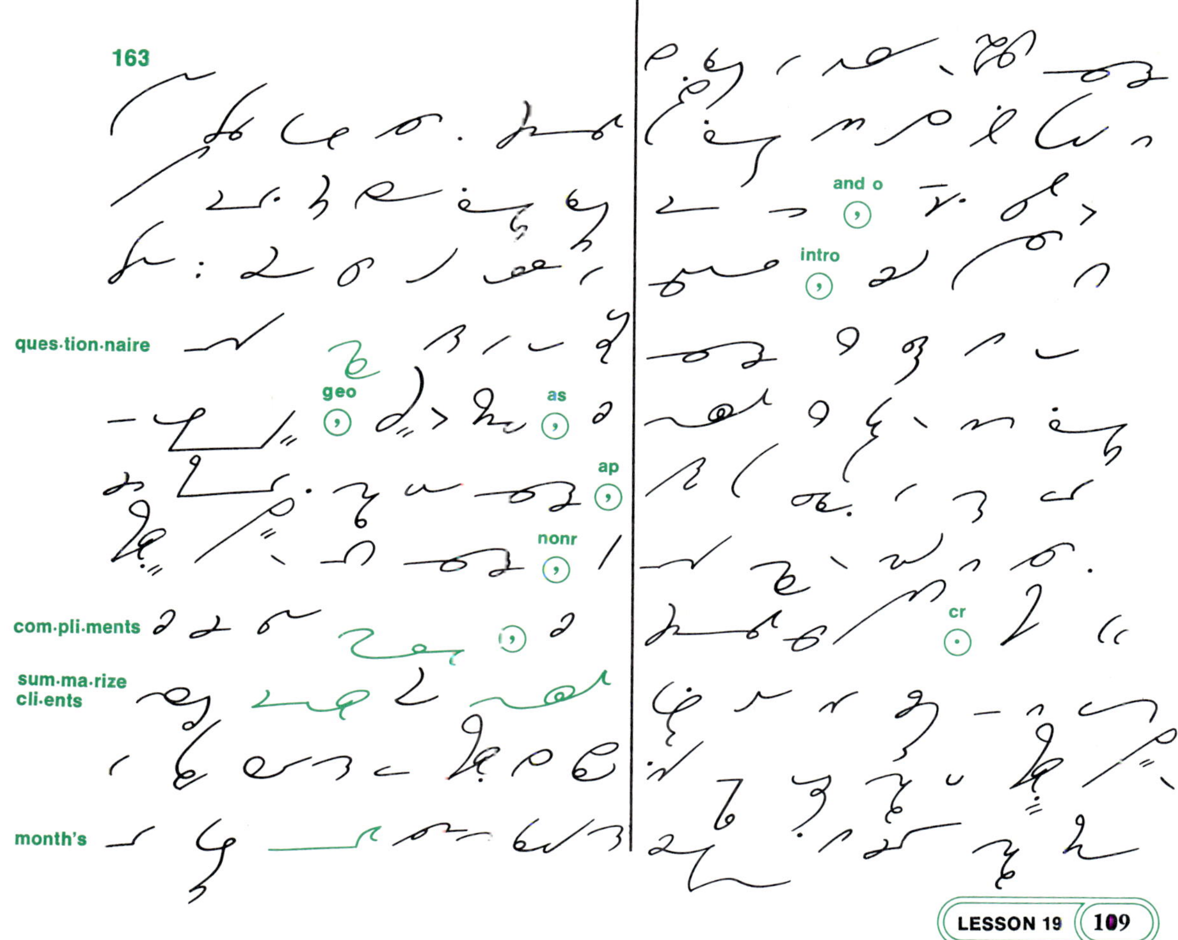

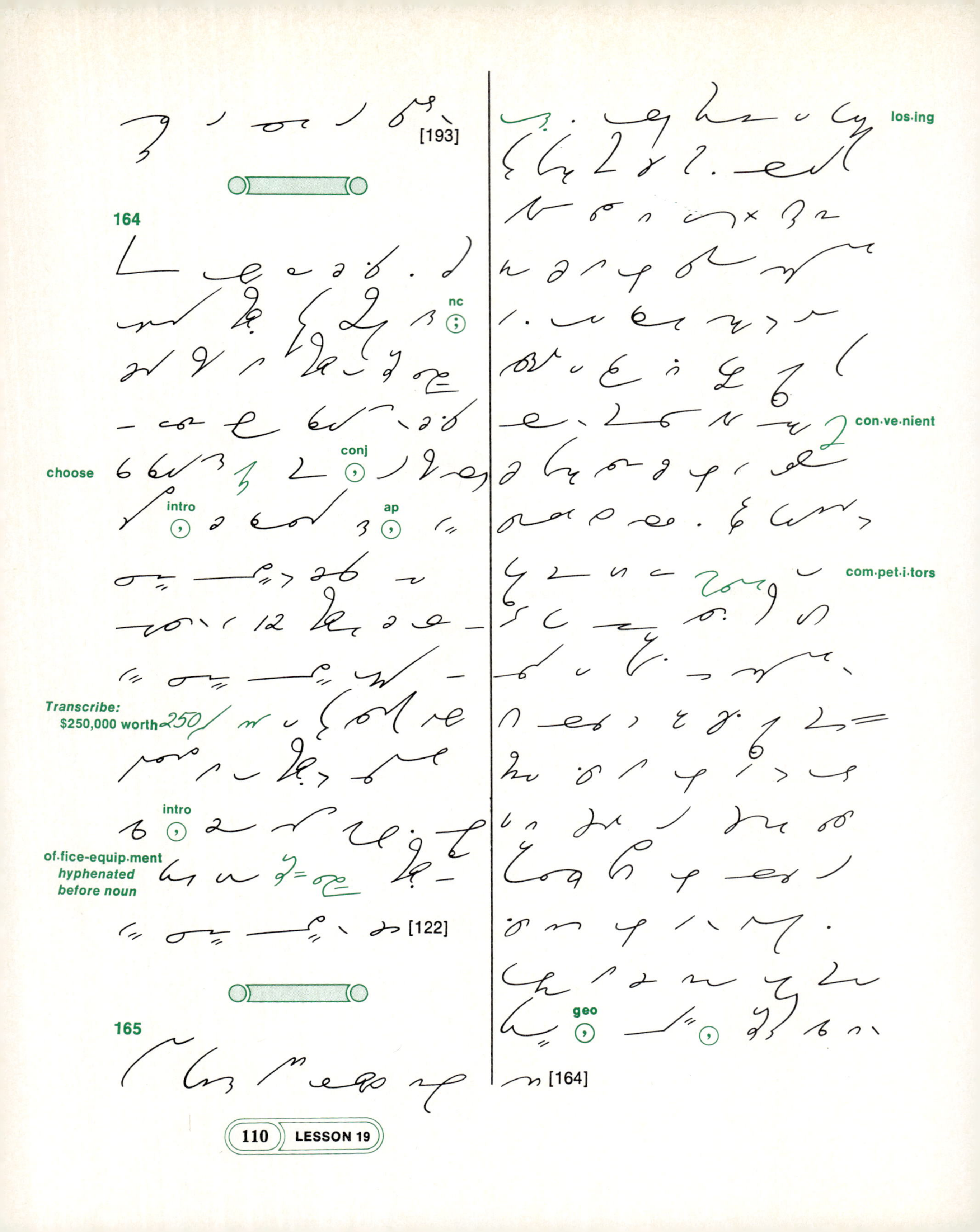

[193]

164

nc

choose

conj

intro

ap

Transcribe: $250,000 worth

intro

of·fice-equip·ment *hyphenated before noun*

[122]

165

los·ing

con·ve·nient

com·pet·i·tors

geo

[164]

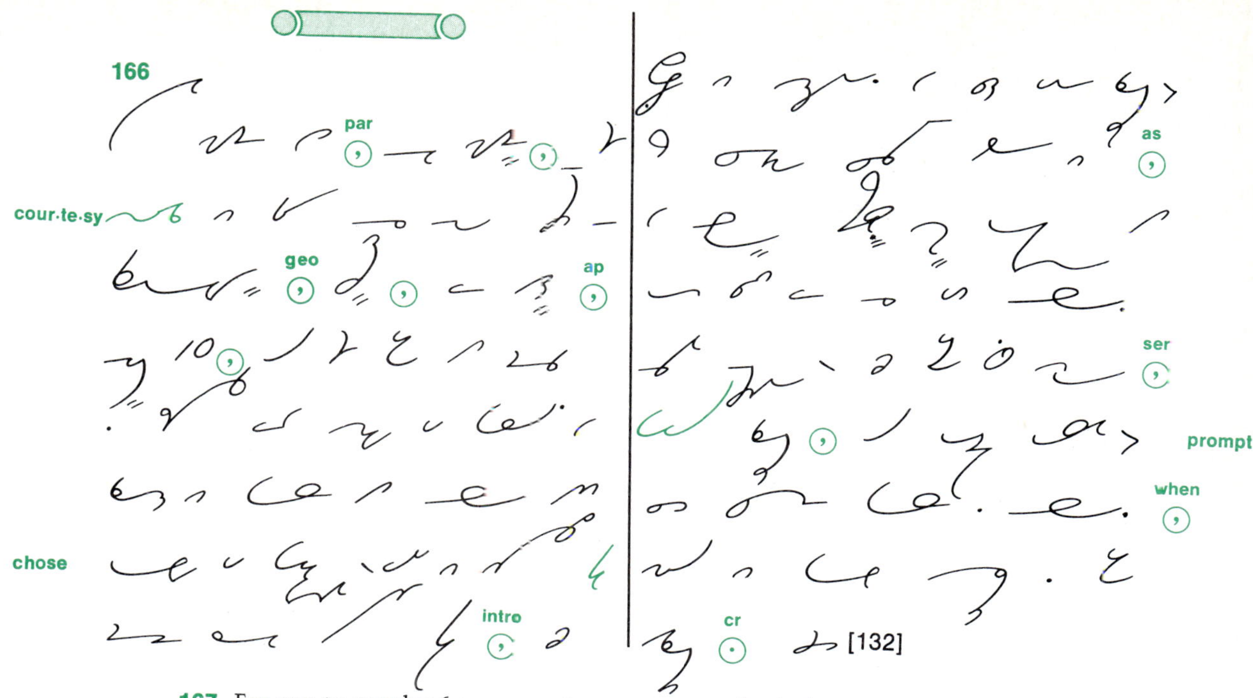

167 Transcription Quiz For you to supply: 6 commas—1 comma parenthetical, 1 comma apposition, 1 comma geographical, 1 comma *if* clause, 1 comma conjunction, 1 comma introductory; two missing words.

555-1181

[124]

Warmup Your warmup letter, which you will use for the last time, appears on page 97. Copy the letter as many times as you can as rapidly as possible.

Developing Word-Building Power

168 Shorthand Vocabulary Builder

Amounts

1

Ten, Etc.

2

Omission of Vowel in -ition, -ation

3

OO Hook on Its Side

4

O Hook on Its Side

5

1. *100,000; $200; $100; 110,000; a dollar; several dollars; few thousand dollars, a hundred, a million.*
2. *Written, stand, substantial, attend, constantly, standard, tonight, sentence.*
3. *Edition, quotation, information, additional, permission, recommendation, condition.*
4. *New, noon, number, Monday, numerous, manuscript, move.*
5. *Stone, grown, promotion, omit, nominate, ownership, honesty.*

Building Transcription Skills

169 Business Vocabulary Builder

incredible Unbelievable.

recur To happen again.

commitment A pledge to do something.

Reading and Writing Practice

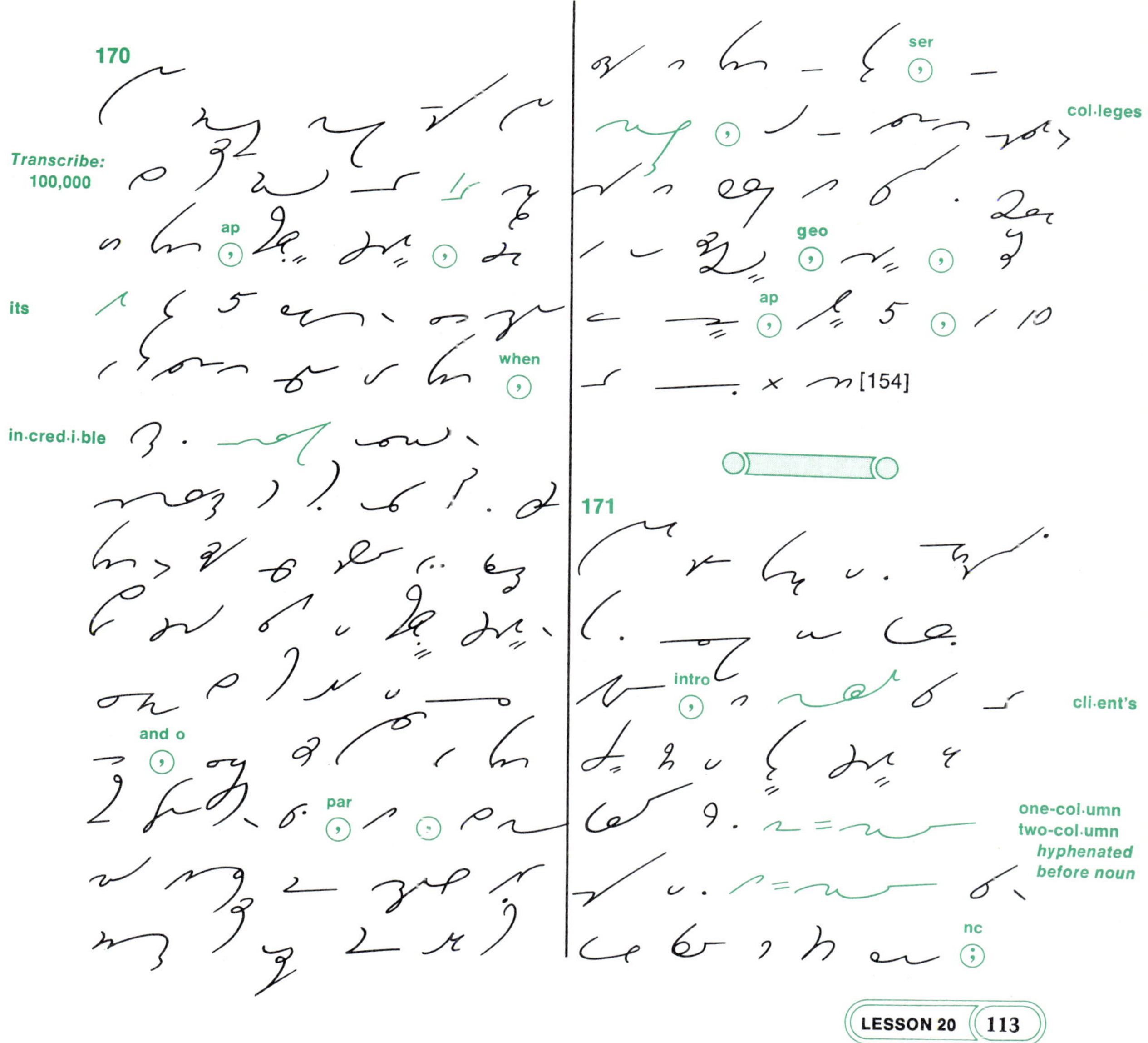

re·cur

Transcribe: $200

nonr

nonr

[107]

172

ap

as

grown

conj

Transcribe: 90,000 110,000

par

nc

intro

intro

if

[159]

173

rel·a·tive·ly

intro

intro

re·ac·tion
typ·i·cal

[124]

174

ap

intro

nc

intro

ser

com·mit·ment

par

and o

[127]

Superior secretaries never make major decisions when they are not feeling well or when they are in a bad mood. Making major decisions should be postponed if a person is under undue stress.

The Secretary on the Job

175 ROBERT BAKER, TIMESAVER

Robert put

1. Urgent.

2. Correspondence to Be Answered.

3. **Correspondence to Be Read.**

4. **Miscellaneous Reading.**

[355]

There is no secret about the best way to obtain shorthand speed. All that is required is the reading of large amounts of printed shorthand and the writing from dictation of even larger amounts of the right kind of dictation given in the right way.
Martin J. Dupraw—World's Champion Shorthand Writer

The Champion's Notes

When Martin J. Dupraw won the world's shorthand championship, he established some remarkable records for accuracy. On a speech dictated at 200 words a minute for five minutes, he made only one error. On court testimony dictated at 280 words a minute for five minutes, he made only two errors. These and many other records that he has established are due, in large measure, to the amazing legibility of his shorthand notes.

When you examine Mr. Dupraw's shorthand notes on the following page, one thing will immediately impress you—the careful attention to proportion.

Notice, for example, how large he makes the *a* circles and how small he makes the *e* circles. There is never any question whether a circle represents *a* or *e*. Notice, too, how much larger his *l's* are than his *r's*. As you read Mr. Dupraw's notes, you will observe many more examples of good proportion.

Another thing that will strike you as you examine Mr. Dupraw's notes is the way he rounds off angles. He does not consciously do this; rounding angles comes naturally to him as a result of his high speed. As your speed increases, you, too, will find that you will naturally round off angles.

In the selection that Mr. Dupraw has written in his beautiful shorthand, he discusses the size of notes. You will notice that he has a fairly large shorthand style, just as he has a large longhand style. Don't try to imitate Mr. Dupraw's style of writing; take the advice he gives in his article, "How Big Should My Shorthand Be?"

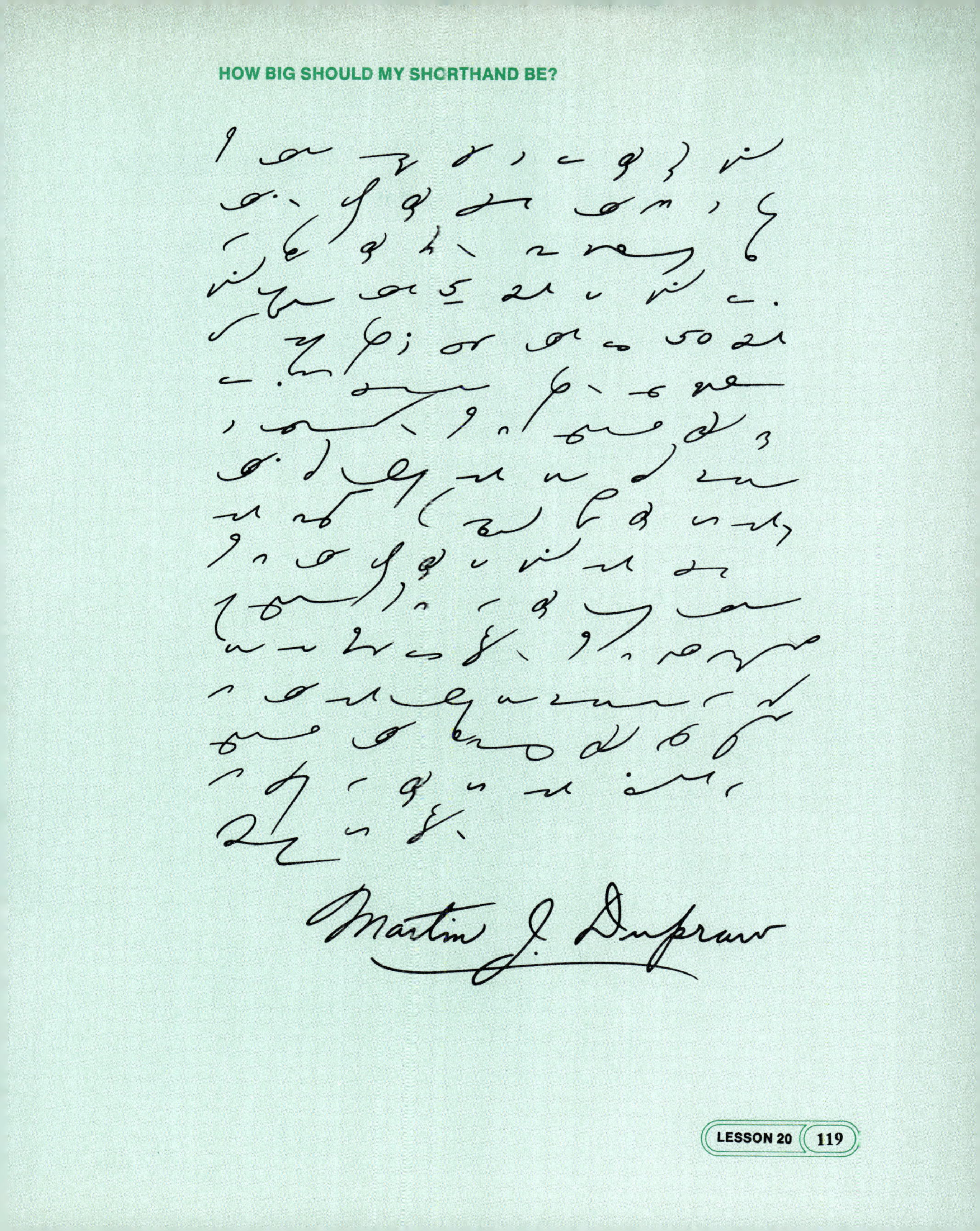

HOW BIG SHOULD MY SHORTHAND BE?

Martin J. Dupraw

PART

Taking New-Matter Dictation

By this time, you are no doubt taking dictation on new material, material that you have not previously practiced. If you have been doing the lessons in this book faithfully—and continue to do so—your ability to write new matter will develop rapidly, and you will experience a real thrill as you find yourself taking dictation at faster and faster rates.

Here are some suggestions that will be helpful to you in taking new-matter dictation:

During dictation, don't stop to improve an outline once you have written it. Every shorthand writer, no matter how skillful, will occasionally write a poor outline during dictation. When you do this, do not make the mistake of scratching out the outline and rewriting it. The dictator will not wait while you are "patching up" your notes, and you may find yourself hopelessly behind as a result. Once you have written an outline, leave it. Even though you may have written it poorly, in most cases you will be able to transcribe it with the aid of the context.

When the dictator uses a word that is unfamiliar to you, write something down—don't stop writing. In your practice work and in your dictation on the job, you will constantly be encountering words that are unfamiliar to you. When one of these words comes along, try to write it in full; write all the sounds you hear. If you cannot do this, try to get down at least the beginning. Often this beginning, along with the context, will be sufficient to enable you to find the correct word in the dictionary.

There will be times when you are unable to write anything for an unfamiliar word. When that happens, leave a space in your notes and continue writing. Don't spend so much time trying to form an outline for the word that the dictation gets too far ahead of you. You will be surprised how often you will be able to fill in the word or supply an equally acceptable one—with the aid of the context.

Never stop writing. There will be times in your speed-development work when the dictation will be too fast for you and you will miss some of it. You must not let this worry you. If you always took dictation at speeds that you could write easily, you would make little progress. In order to build up your speed, you must practice at speeds beyond the rate that you can write easily. When you find yourself getting behind in your notes, hang on as long as you can. Something may happen that will enable you to catch up—the dictator may stop to take a breath or there may be an easy spot in the dictation or a nice phrase may come to your rescue.
If, however, you are so far behind that you feel nothing will help you, drop the words that you have not yet written and pick up the dictation again. But don't decide to drop too soon—and never stop writing!

Don't try to phrase too much. Some writers have the feeling that the key to shorthand speed is phrasing. Phrases will help in gaining shorthand speed only if they can be written without hesitation. Remember, too, that dictators may not always say a phrase as one piece. They may say one word in a phrase and then pause before saying the remaining words. When that occurs, you will probably have the first word written before you hear the rest of the phrase. You should then write the remaining words of the phrase as though no phrase were involved. Under no circumstances should you scratch out the word that you have already written and then write the phrase.

CHAPTER

Credit

Many years ago getting into debt was considered a moral transgression as well as a money matter, and it was commonplace at one time for a debtor to be thrown into prison. But times have changed, and in today's economy debt is no longer considered sinful. As a matter of fact, buying on credit has become an integral part of the life-style in the United States.

Stated simply, credit is trust in a person's ability to pay later. Consumers find buying on credit to be convenient, and business firms find offering credit to be profitable, because it encourages people to buy things even if they do not have the cash available at the moment to pay for them.

Credit enables consumers to buy goods such as automobiles, refrigerators, and television sets that may be too expensive to be paid for out of one paycheck but can be paid for from a number of upcoming paychecks.

In addition, for certain services, credit can be more convenient than cash payment. For example, consumers use gas and electricity in their homes and are billed later for what they use. This is actually a form of credit. Think how inconvenient it would be if utility companies required us to pay every day for the gas and electricity we consumed. Many consumers also find charging purchases at retail stores more convenient than carrying cash to pay for merchandise.

Credit in some form is used by just about every adult consumer in the United States. Goods may be purchased with the agreement that payment must be made within a certain period of time, such as 30 days after the bill is mailed, or a finance charge will be added to the cost of the merchandise. Or a relatively expensive item such as a color television set may be sold under an agreement in which the consumer makes periodic payments until the full price is paid. A finance charge is added to such installment purchases.

The growth in the use of credit has brought with it a number of jobs. Every business that provides credit needs a credit department to handle billing and collection. Bills must be issued on a regular basis to credit customers; letters requesting payment must be sent to people who fall behind in their payments; arrangements for payment must be worked out with customers who have difficulty meeting the regular payments; and sometimes lawsuits must be initiated to force customers to meet their obligations.

The letters in this chapter deal with many types of credit in modern business.

Charter
New York
Banks
Car Loans
Personal Loans...
Now
Apply Today!

Building Phrasing Skill

176 Phrase Builder

The following five groups contain 36 useful phrases. Can you read the entire lesson in 40 seconds or less?

Let Us

1

Very

2

From

3

Thank

4

To

5

1. *Let us, let us know, let us have, let us see, let us make, let us say.*
2. *Very much, very important, very well, very glad, very soon, very low, very little.*
3. *From the, from you, from that, from these, from our, from us.*
4. *Thank you, thank you for, thank you for your, thank you for the, thank you for this, thank you for your order, we thank you, I thank you, to thank you.*
5. *To you, to the, to them, to this, to these, to that, to their, to think.*

177 Warmup Phrase Letter

Your warmup phrase letter for this chapter contains 125 words. In the letter there are 32 useful business letter phrases. How fast can you read the letter? How fast can you copy it?

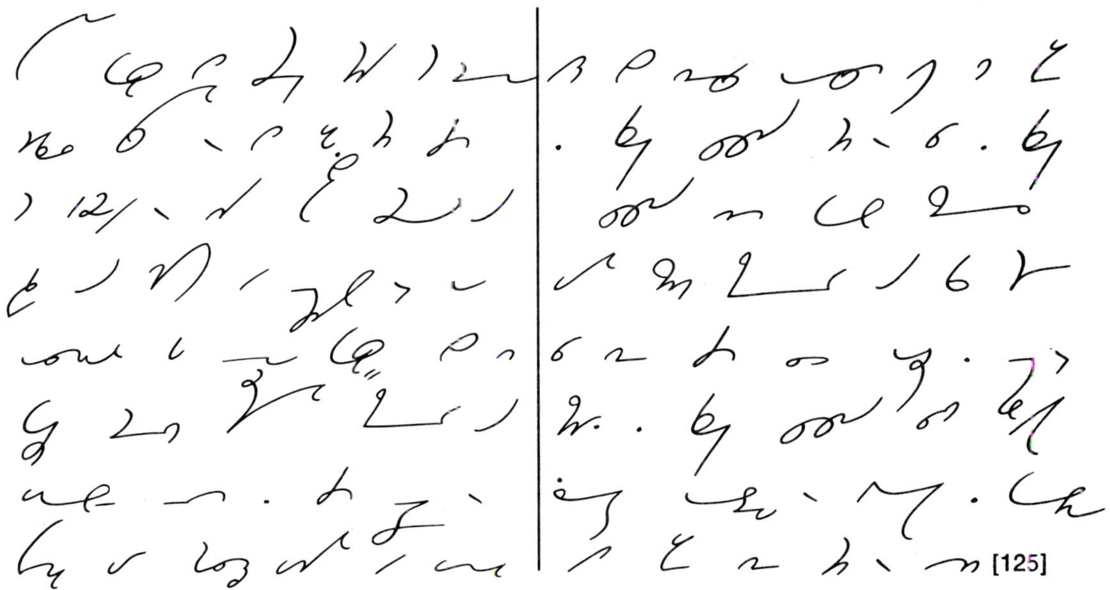

Building Transcription Skills

178 TYPING STYLE STUDY dates

■ 1 If the name of the month precedes the day, do not use *th, st,* or *d* after the number.

On August 21, 1975, *she left the company.*

When a date is expressed in this manner, there is a comma both *before* and *after* the year.

■ 2 If the day precedes the month, *th, st,* or *d* should be included.

On the 21st of December *we will leave on vacation.*

When dates appear in the Reading and Writing Practice, they will be called to your attention in the margin thus: ***Transcribe:*** **January 28**

---

179 Business Vocabulary Builder

merit *(verb)* Deserve.

adapt To make suitable; to adjust.

complicated Complex; hard to understand.

Reading and Writing Practice

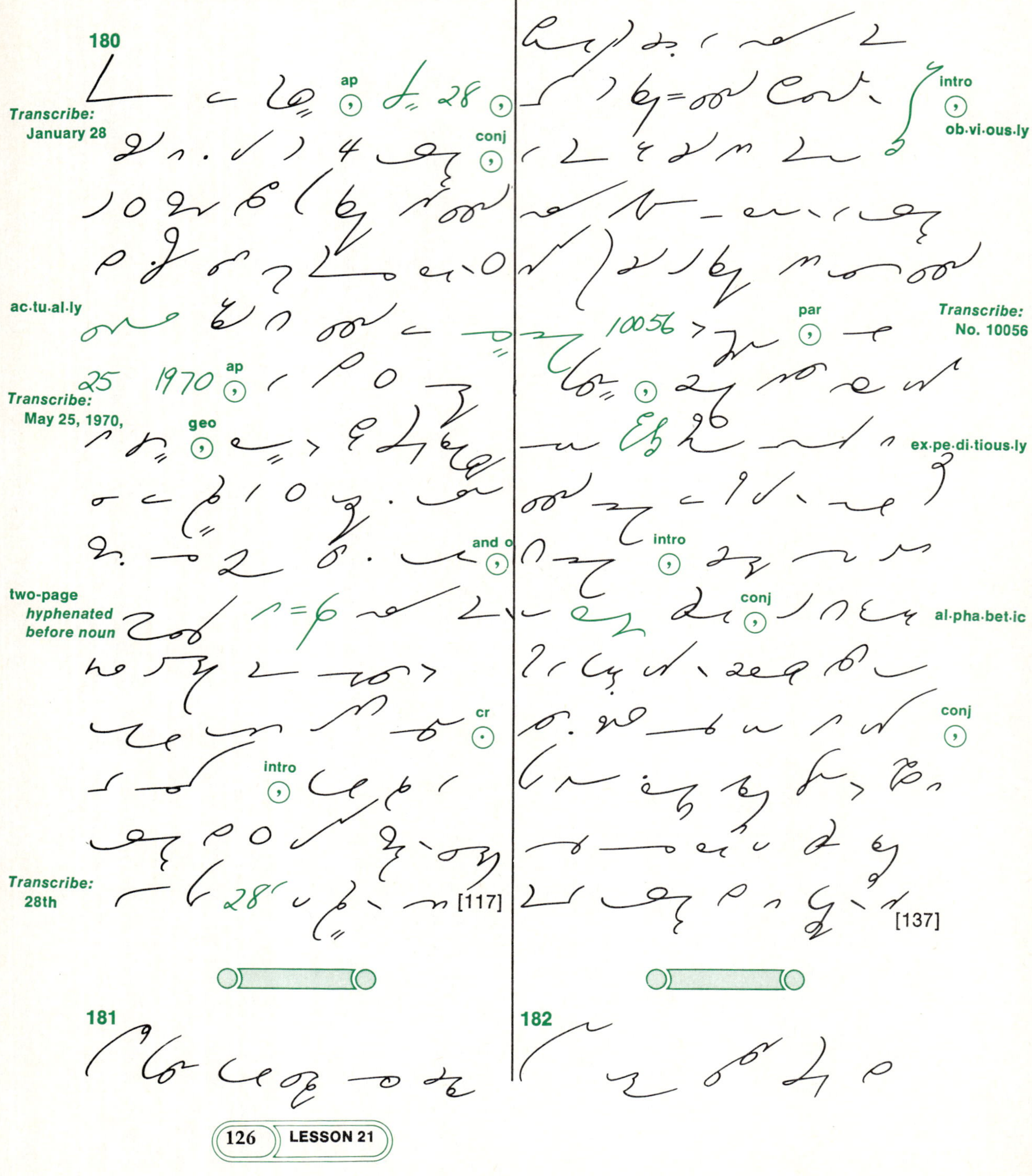

sig·nif·i·cance

Transcribe: March 10, 1976,

par

Wil·son's

fre·quent·ly

par

[107]

183

its

ap

ap

re·mit·tances

adapt

intro

nonr

[175]

184

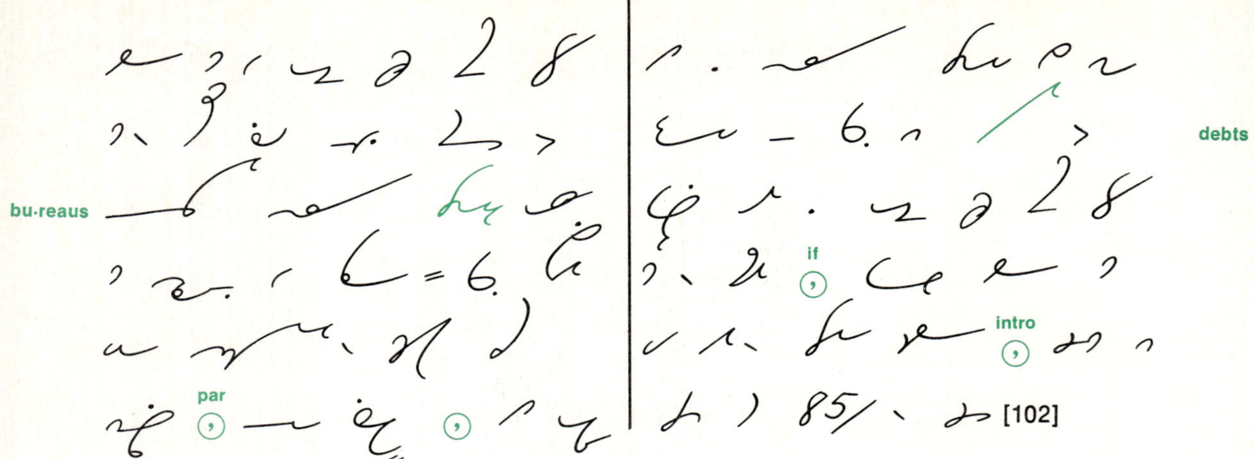

185 Transcription Quiz The transcription quizzes hereafter will be a greater challenge to you. Thus far you have had to supply only commas to punctuate a letter correctly; hereafter, you will also have to supply semicolons.

For you to supply: 7 commas—1 comma *as* clause, 2 commas *if* clause, 1 comma conjunction, 2 commas series, 1 comma *when* clause; 1 semicolon no conjunction; 2 missing words.

[127]

Warmup Your warmup letter is on page 125. Practice it a paragraph at a time. Today write the first paragraph slowly the first time, as rapidly as you can the second time, and in your best shorthand the third time.

Developing Word-Building Power

186 Brief-Form Chart

Your reading goal: 30 seconds or less.

1. *Recognize, should, advertise, advertisement, advertisements, advertised.*
2. *About, morning, soon, and, are-our-hour, correspond-correspondence.*
3. *Any, it-at, be-by, business, that, but.*
4. *Acknowledge, there (their), speak, street, can, subject.*
5. *Advantage, them, success, character, thank, than.*

187 Geographical Expressions

1. *Little Rock, Milwaukee, Providence, New Orleans, Jackson.*
2. *Arkansas, Wisconsin, Rhode Island, Louisiana, Mississippi, Washington, Indiana.*

Building Transcription Skills

188 TYPING STUDY STYLE addresses in sentences

■ 1 Use figures for house numbers. Spell out *Road, Street,* etc.

She lived at 300 River Road.

■ 2 Spell out numbers below 11 in street names.

He works at 215 Third Avenue.

■ 3 Use figures for numbered street names 11 and above. Omit *th, st,* and *d* from numbered street names if a word such as *East* or *West* separates the building number from the street number.

Her address is 21 West 81 Street.

When street addresses occur in the Reading and Writing Practice, they will occasionally be called to your attention in the margin of the shorthand thus: ***Transcribe:*** **14 East 81**

---

189 Business Vocabulary Builder

commendatory Serving to recommend or praise; approving.

in arrears The state of being behind in fulfilling contracted obligations or payments.

hesitant Holding back in doubt.

Reading and Writing Practice

190 Brief-Form Letter

The following letter contains 150 words, many of which are brief forms or brief-form derivatives. How fast can you read this letter? Copy it?

conj ,
conj ,
par ,
,
doesn't
nc ;
ap ,
nonr ,
com·pa·ny's
conj ,

[150]

191

ap

mov·ing

nonr

ap

nonr

geo

Mil·wau·kee

par·ents'

nonr

330

Transcribe:
Fifth Avenue

[136]

192

as

15

com·men·da·to·ry

ap

ser

char·ac·ter

bill-pay·ing
hyphenated before noun

when

Transcribe:
$600

ser conj

ac·knowl·edged

Transcribe: 14 East 81

14 81

geo

02904

if

intro

[157]

ref·er·ences

par

5

and o

[139]

193

nonr

Transcribe: 600

6

194

re·in·stat·ed

sep·a·rate·ly

as

can·cel·la·tion

re·ceipt

par

conj

if

intro

if

re·mit·tance

[74]

[65]

195

al·ready

196

Transcription Quiz

For you to supply: 5 commas—1 comma *as* clause, 2 commas parenthetical, 1 comma *when* clause, 1 comma introductory; 1 semicolon no conjunction; 2 missing words.

[116]

LESSON 23

Warmup Use the second paragraph of the phrase letter on page 125 for your warmup. Remember to write the paragraph slowly on your first writing and then as rapidly as you can, keeping your shorthand readable; finally, write it in your best shorthand.

Developing Word-Building Power

197 Word Families

-rate

1 

-ount

2 

-ol

3 

-ter

4 

1. *Rate, concentrate, cooperate, illustrate, operate, overrate, accurate, considerate.*
2. *Count, account, discount, recount, amount, surmount.*
3. *All, ball, call, fall, small, recall.*
4. *Better, later, letter, matter, adjuster, faster, roster.*

Building Transcription Skills

198 TYPING STYLE STUDY amounts of money

■ **1** When transcribing whole dollar amounts in business letters, do not add a decimal point or zeros.

The check for $175 *(not $175.00) was mailed yesterday.*

■ **2** In business letters use the word *cents* in amounts under $1.

The cost was only 29 cents *(not $.29).*

■ **3** Even millions and billions of dollars may be transcribed in numbers and words for easier reading.

The city budget is $25 million.

When amounts such as the above appear in the Reading and Writing Practice, they will occasionally be called to your attention in the margin of the shorthand thus:

Transcribe: $100

---

199 Business Vocabulary Builder

loath Unwilling; reluctant.

oblige Do a service or favor for; perform a courtesy.

depleted Used up; exhausted.

Reading and Writing Practice

200

as

nc

loathe

intro

nonr

Transcribe: $250

intro

30-day hyphenated before noun

if

Transcribe: $100

[138]

201

Transcribe: 98 cents

as

conj

de·plet·ed

par

conj

intro

ready-cred·it *hyphenated before noun*

[110]

202

ap

apol·o·giz·ing

Transcribe: $1,200

conj

par

par

and o

[123]

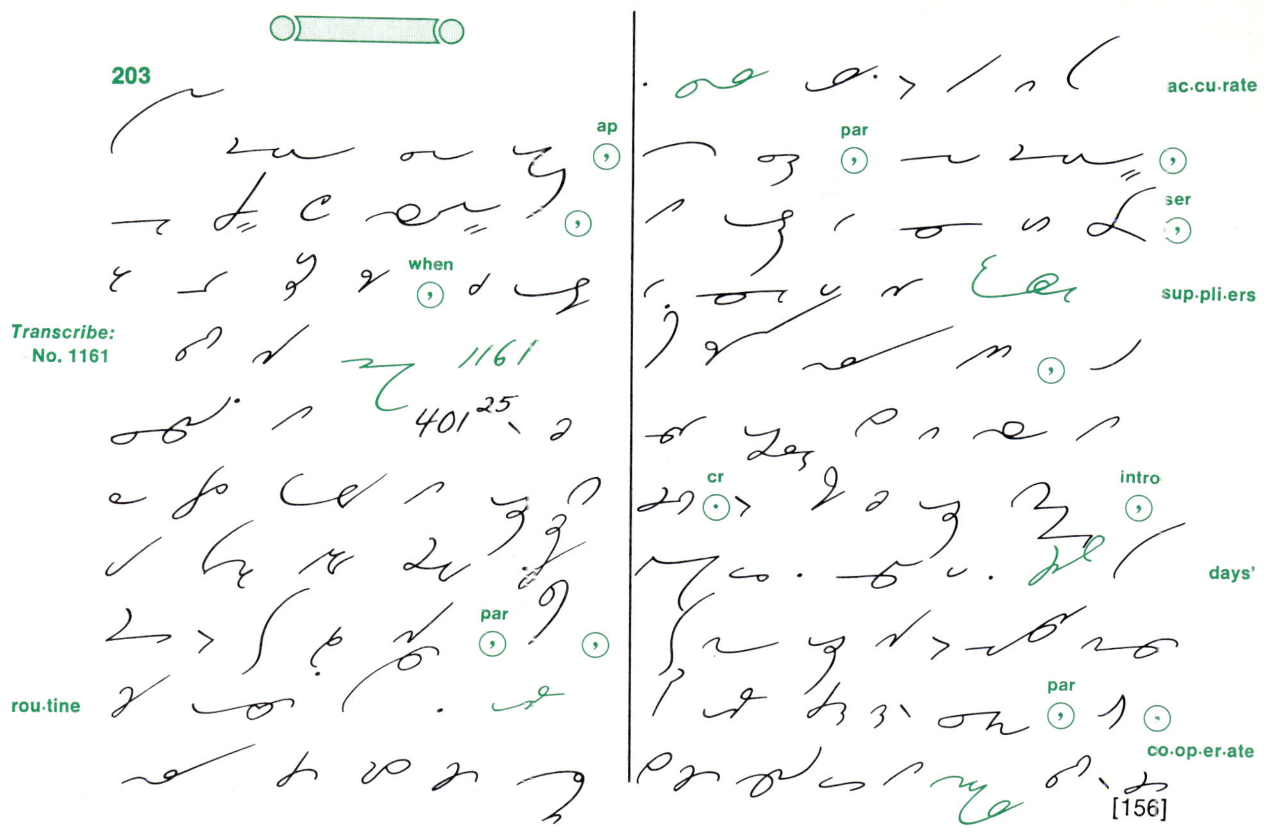

204 Transcription Quiz For you to supply: 8 commas—1 comma *as* clause, 4 commas parenthetical, 2 commas conjunction, 1 comma in a number; 1 semicolon no conjunction; 2 missing words.

[115]

LESSON 24

Warmup For today's warmup, copy the phrase letter on page 125 as rapidly as you can.

Developing Word-Building Power

205 Word Beginnings and Endings

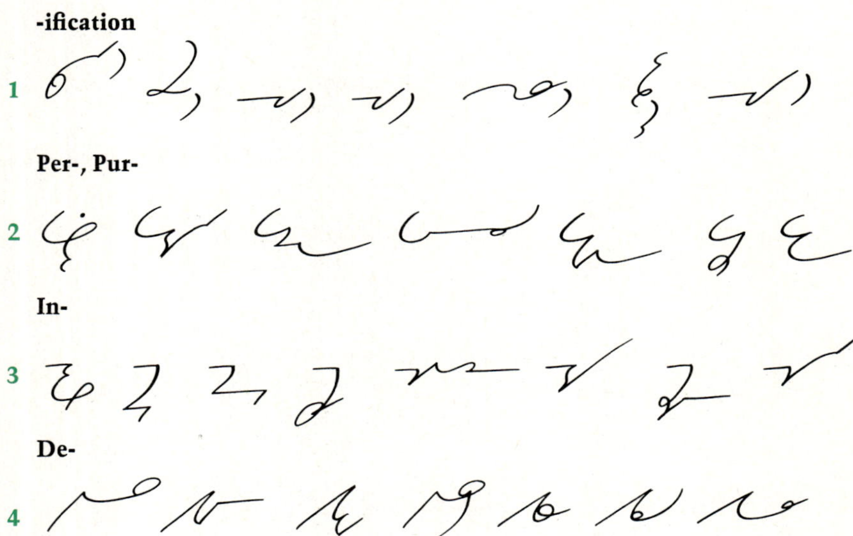

1. *Identification, verification, mortification, notification, gratification, specifications, modification.*
2. *Perhaps, persistent, personal, permanent, perpetual, purchase, purple.*
3. *Inspiration, invention, information, invite, instrument, insisted, investment, instant.*
4. *Delay, department, deposit, derive, desire, depend, deplete.*

Building Transcription Skills

206 TYPING STYLE STUDY time

■ 1 Use figures in expressing time with *o'clock.* (Remember the apostrophe.)

We came at 10 o'clock (not *ten* o'clock).

■ 2 Use figures in expressing time with *a.m.* and *p.m.*

They left at 8:15 a.m. *and returned at* 10:30 p.m.

▶ Note: Type *a.m.* and *p.m.* with small letters and no space after the first period.

■ 3 Spell out time if *a.m., p.m.,* or *o'clock* is not used.

We are open from nine *to* five.

Occasionally these expressions of time will be called to your attention in the margins of the shorthand in the Reading and Writing Practice thus: ***Transcribe:* 9 a.m.**

---

207 Business Vocabulary Builder

frustration Disappointment caused by lack of success.

mortification A sense of humiliation and shame.

persistent Insistently repetitive or continuous.

Reading and Writing Practice

208

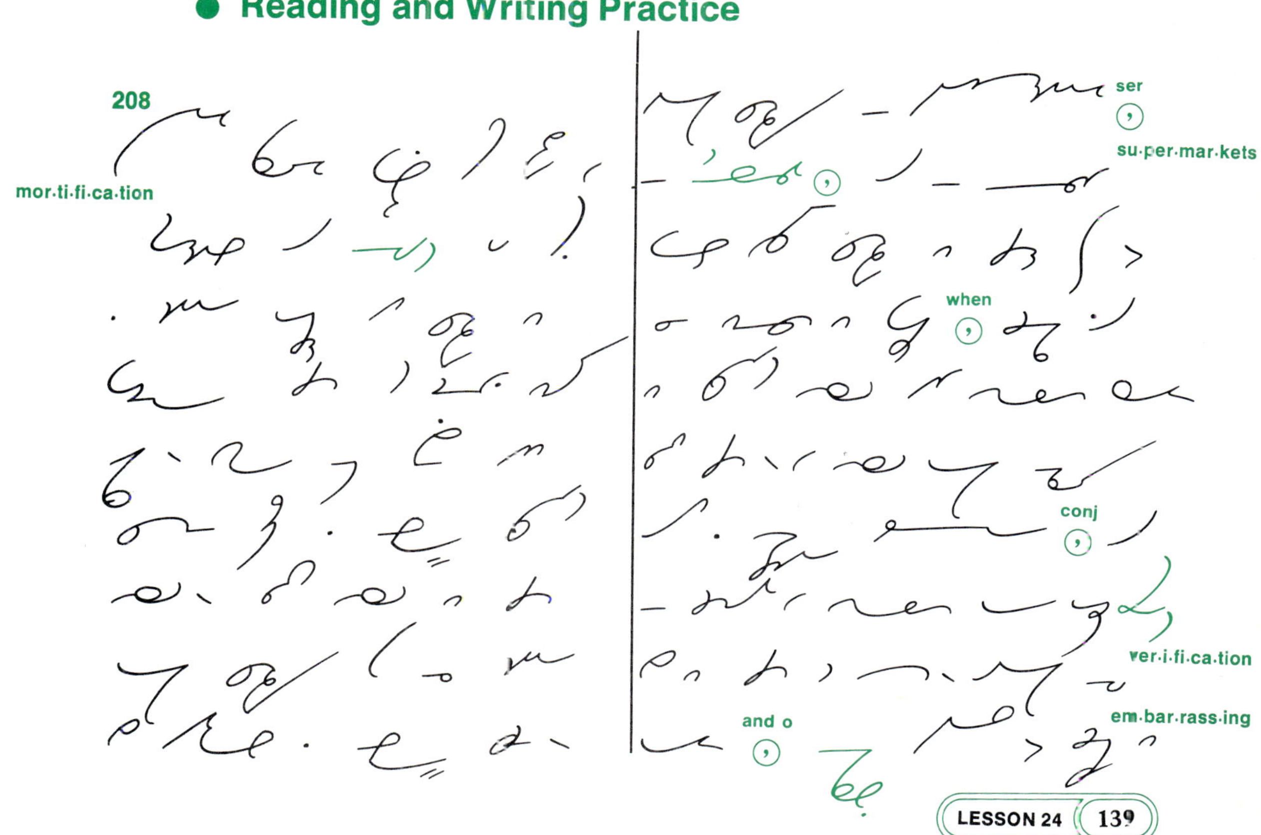

when

di·rec·to·ry

[183]

209

par

con·ve·nience

par

Transcribe:
9 a.m.
5 p.m.

if

intro

[121]

210

as

ap

in·stall·ment

Transcribe:
$300

when

de·pos·it

par

conj

ser

conj

nc

intro

nc

if

555-1181

Transcribe: 10 a.m.

10 4:30 [141]

211

past-due hyphenated before noun

Transcribe: 1161 West 23

ap 1161 23

geo

par

if

if

555-6107 [121]

Transcribe: 9 o'clock

212 Transcription Quiz For you to supply: 6 commas—2 commas parenthetical, 2 commas introductory, 1 comma conjunction, 1 comma *if* clause; 1 semicolon no conjunction; 2 missing words.

555-4107

[137]

Warmup Your warmup for the last time is the phrase letter on page 125. Copy the entire letter as many times as you can and as rapidly as you can in the time available.

Developing Word-Building Power

213 Shorthand Vocabulary Builder

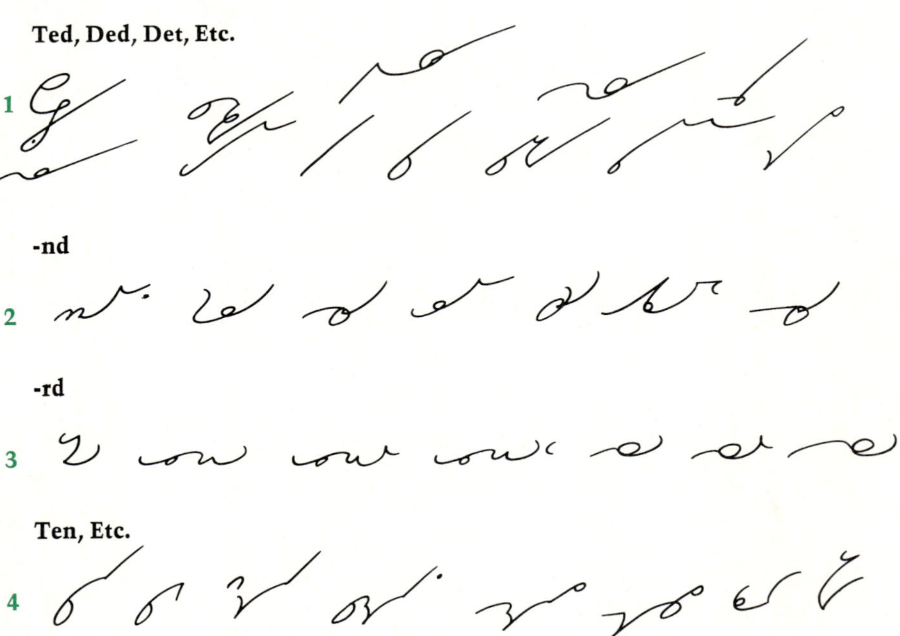

1. *Appreciated, accepted, delighted, graded, needed, credit, auditor, debt, added, adopted, editorial, study.*
2. *Wondering, friend, kind, render, signed, independence, mind.*
3. *Offered, record, records, recordings, card, cards, guard.*
4. *Attend, attention, understand, outstanding, constantly, unfortunately, certain, obtain.*

Building Transcription Skills

214 Business Vocabulary Builder

assume To take on.

auditors Those authorized to examine and verify accounts.

delinquent Overdue in payment.

ledger A book listing the transactions of a business.

Reading and Writing Practice

215

ac·cept·ed

intro

sup·plied

intro

nc

intro

if

[110]

216

sub·mit·ting

Wil·son's

intro

fur·ther

debts

par

when

par

[137]

217

ser

conj

be·lieve

Transcribe:
9 o'clock

ap

of·fered

[115]

218

ap

ours

well-known
hyphenated before noun

when

lose

par

in·de·pen·dent

par

rea·son

de·lin·quent

par

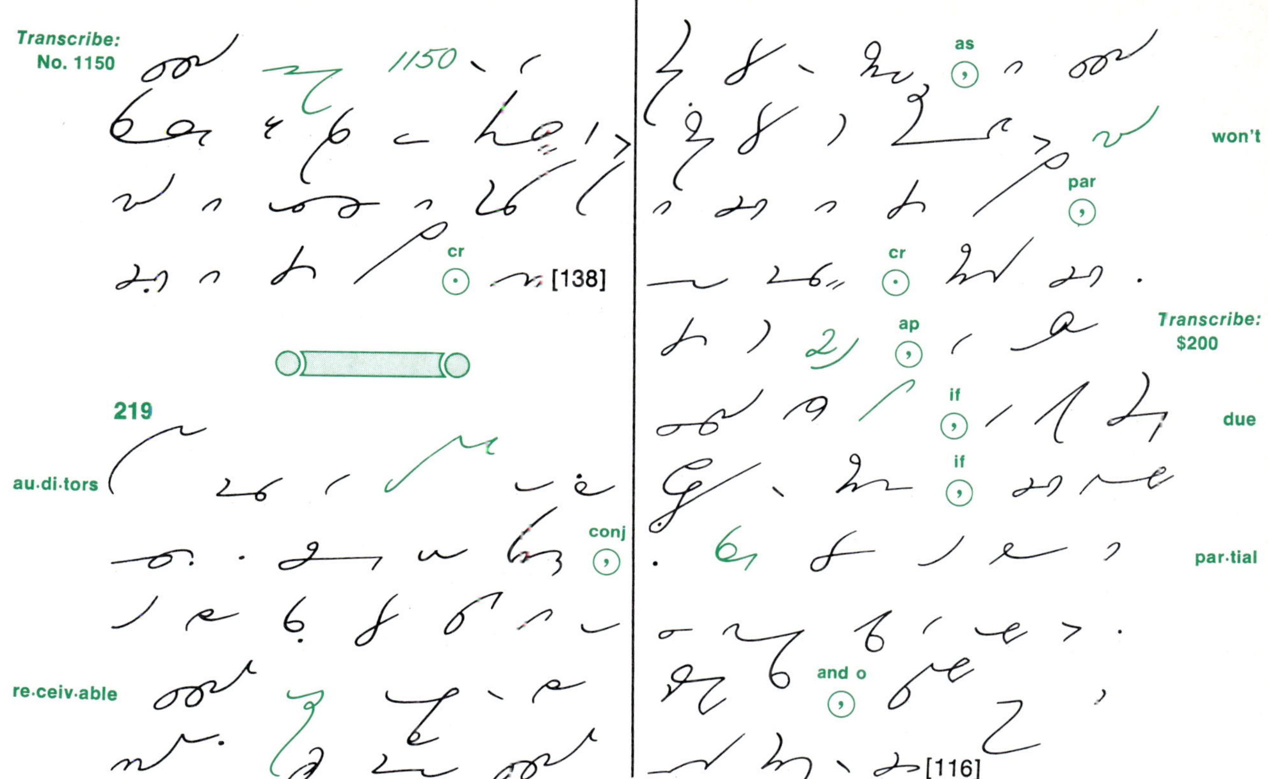

DICTATION TIP ■ **Instructions.**

Allow enough space at the beginning of the letter in your notebook to indicate special instructions about the letter—the number of carbons and who is to get them, any enclosures, and any other pertinent information.

The Secretary on the Job

220 SHH!

Many a

A secretary

[333]

DICTATION TIP ■ **When in Doubt, Ask!**

There will be times when you will have to ask your employer questions, and you should not hesitate to do so. Good judgment will tell you whether it is better to interrupt at the end of a sentence or to wait until the end of the letter to clarify a word, figure, or name that you did not understand. Leave space in your notebook for the missing words, and let the employer finish the train of thought.

CHAPTER

Sales

Almost every business organization in this country makes money by producing some types of goods or services. But once produced, goods and services do not make any money until they are sold. So every company must employ people to sell what it produces. Three major types of sales are: (1) industrial marketing, (2) wholesale marketing, and (3) retail marketing.

Industrial marketing involves selling goods such as raw materials, fabricating parts, and machinery that are used either in the manufacture of other products or to equip factories, utilities, banks, stores, and offices so that their businesses can be carried on. Examples of industrial marketing include a steel company's sale to an automobile manufacturer, a chemical company's sale to a battery manufacturer, and a computer company's sale of data processing equipment to a large supermarket chain. The process of selling finished products to distributors and retailers who will in turn resell them is called wholesale marketing. The sale of products usually in small quantities to individual customers for their personal use is known as retail marketing.

In all areas of marketing, personal selling is a major promotion tool. Personal selling involves an individual's contact with a customer. This contact can be in the form of a face-to-face interview, a telephone conversation, or even a business letter addressed to a specific person.

Selling involves locating prospective customers and getting them to make purchases. Marketing representatives must not only know everything there is to know about the products they are selling, but they must also know a great deal about the customers who will be buying these products. They must be able to determine what customers need and want and then explain how their products or services will satisfy those needs or wants. They must be able to communicate the merits of the products by describing the features of the products, by conveying ideas about how the products can satisfy customer needs, and by furnishing explanations about how the products work. The representatives also must keep their employers informed about what is happening in the marketplace: how customers are receiving a product, how they are using it, what criticisms and compliments they have, and what suggestions they have for improving the product.

The job of a sales department is to provide the sales representatives with as much information as possible about both products and customers, to study and analyze the input from the marketing representatives, and to record and process orders. Without the sales-support staff, the marketing representative's task would be almost impossible to perform.

The sales function is an especially important part of a business because the prosperity of the company depends directly on the amount of goods being sold. The letters in this chapter deal with the various aspects of sales work.

Building Phrasing Skill

221 Phrase Builder

Can you read the 26 phrases in this phrase builder in 30 seconds or less?

Some of

1

One of

2

Ago

3

Hope

4

1. *Some of the, some of them, some of our, some of these, some of that, some of this.*
2. *One of the, one of them, one of these, one of our, one of the most, one of the best.*
3. *Days ago, years ago, months ago, hours ago, minutes ago, weeks ago.*
4. *I hope, I hope that, I hope you can, I hope you will, we hope, we hope you can, we hope you will, we hope you will be.*

222 Warmup Phrase Letter

Can you read the following letter in 40 seconds? Copy it in 1¼ minutes?

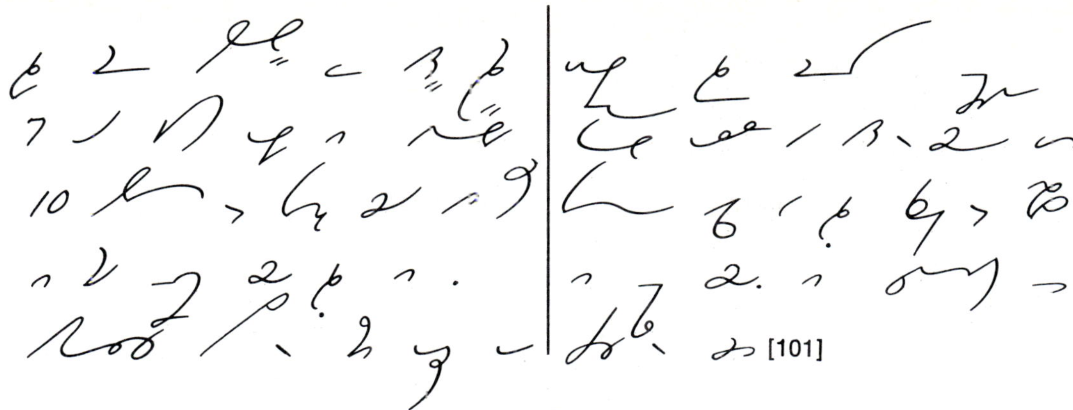

Building Transcription Skills

223 TYPING STYLE STUDY capitalization

Company Names

Divisions in an Organization

■ 1 Capitalize the first letter in the main words of a company name. Capitalize the word *the* only when it is part of the legal name of the organization. (Check the letterhead of the company to be sure.)

I work for The Manufacturing Company of America.

She worked for the First State Bank.

■ 2 Common organizational terms, such as *advertising department, manufacturing division, finance committee* and *board of directors,* are not ordinarily capitalized.

The board of directors *will meet today.*

He works in the advertising department.

She heads the finance committee.

---

224 Business Vocabulary Builder

optimistic Tending to expect a favorable outcome.

depressed Suffering from a period of low general economic activity.

distinguishes Sets above or apart from others.

Reading and Writing Practice

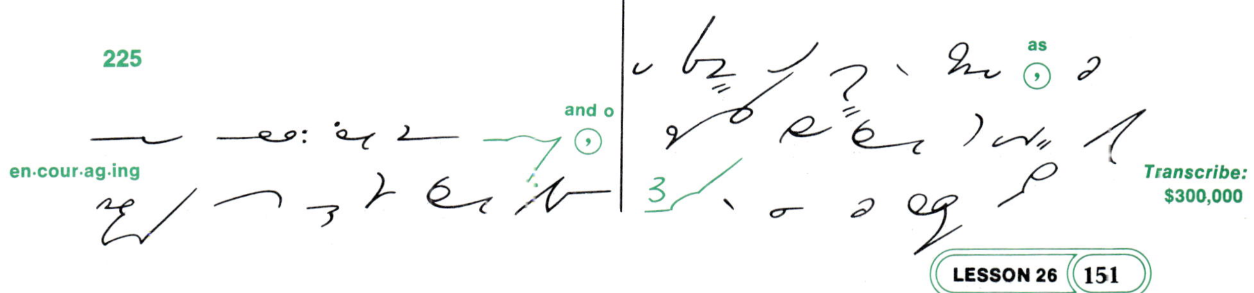

when

op·ti·mis·tic

ap

conj

Transcribe: 33 percent

33,

ex·ceed

staff's

ab

[136]

226

intro

than

25

28 29

ab·sent

27

par

[119]

227

as

ap

bul·le·tin

par

ser

mar·ries

dis·tin·guishes

conj

faith·ful·ly

nc

par

if

[161]

228

conj

re·leased

geo

30,

Transcribe: 30 percent

nonr

achieve·ment

par

[87]

229 For you to supply: 4 commas—3 commas introductory, 1 comma nonrestrictive; 1 semicolon no conjunction; 2 missing words.

Transcription Quiz

[110]

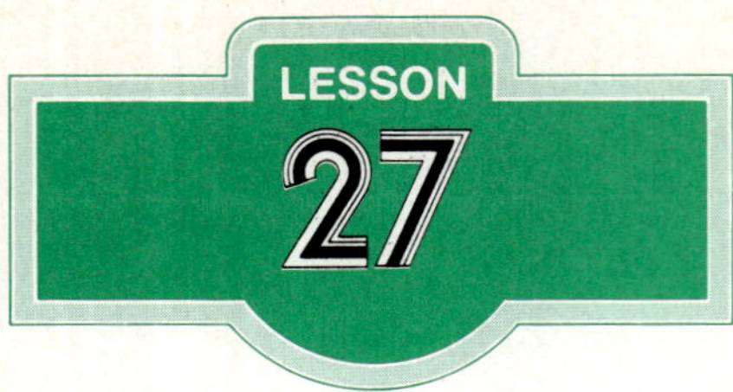

LESSON 27

Warmup Read the first paragraph of the phrase letter on page 150. Then copy that paragraph as many times as you can and as rapidly as possible before your teacher begins the regular class work.

Developing Word-Building Power

230 Brief-Form Chart

Your reading goal for the following 30 brief forms and derivatives: 30 seconds.

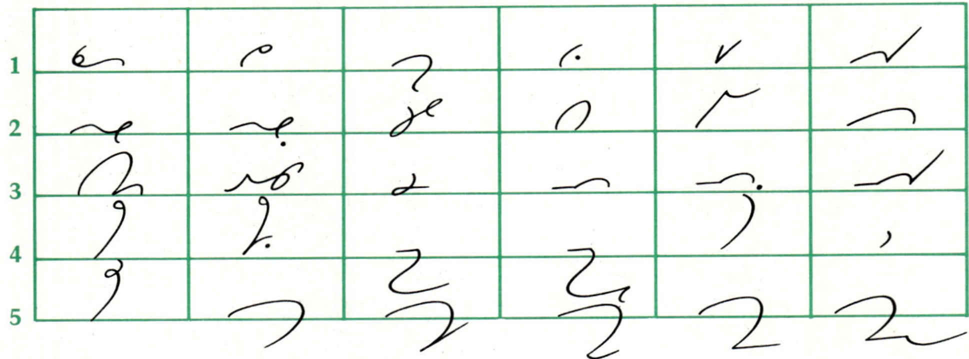

1. *Circular, they, company, thing-think, short, could.*
2. *Correspond-correspondence, corresponding, satisfy-satisfactory, this, Dr., good.*
3. *Difficult, throughout, send, enclose, enclosing, enclosed.*
4. *Ever-every, everything, envelope, envelopes, have, his-is.*
5. *Several, govern, governed, governor, government, governmental.*

231 Geographical Expressions

1

2

1. *Oklahoma City, Fargo, Tulsa, Lincoln, Omaha, Wichita.*
2. *Oklahoma, Kansas, Montana, Nebraska, North Dakota, South Dakota.*

Building Transcription Skills

232 SIMILAR-WORDS DRILL hear, here Sometimes easy words give us difficulty—not because we do not understand them, but because we may be careless in using them. *Hear* and *here* are examples.

hear To gain knowledge of by hearing; to be informed.

I can hear *the record.*

here In this place.

Please be here *at noon.*

---

233 Business Vocabulary Builder

fiscal Financial.

attributes *(noun)* Qualities; characteristics.

Reading and Writing Practice

234 Brief-Form Letter

Can you read this letter in 1¼ minutes? Copy it in 2 minutes?

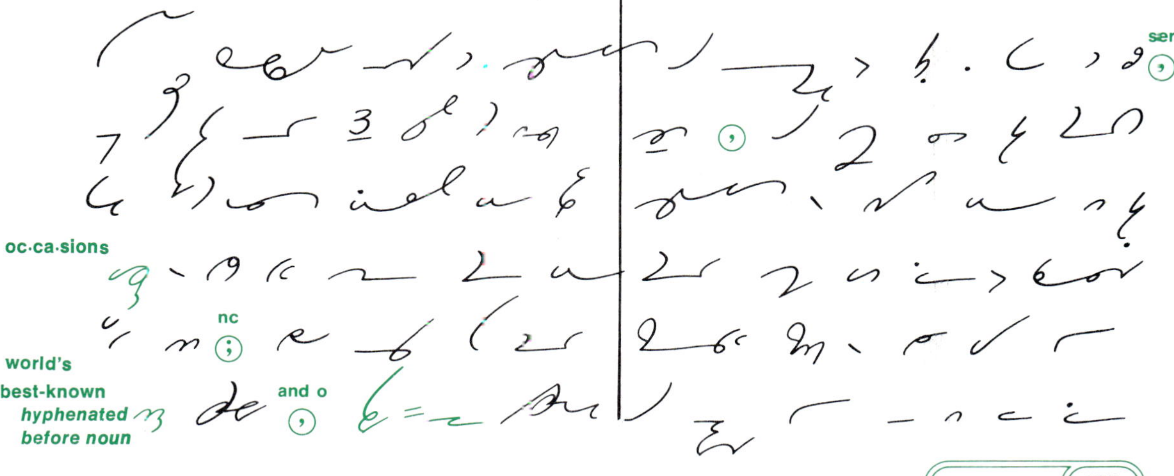

days'

if

if

[152]

235

hear

intro

nonr

ser

here

360

ar·ea

nonr

fis·cal

[119]

236

ea·ger·ly

hear

21

4

par

par

here

geo

par

conj

mu·tu·al

40

4

[125]

237

ac·cept·ed

month's

Transcribe: 1441

1441

geo

ap

when

three-week hyphenated before noun

nonr

worth·while

ap

intro

[133]

238 Transcription Quiz For you to supply: 6 commas—2 commas apposition, 1 comma *as* clause, 1 comma *if* clause, 2 commas parenthetical; 1 semicolon no conjunction; 2 missing words.

18

[106]

Warmup For your warmup use the second paragraph of the phrase letter on page 150. Copy it slowly, then rapidly, and finally in your best shorthand.

Developing Word-Building Power

239 Word Families

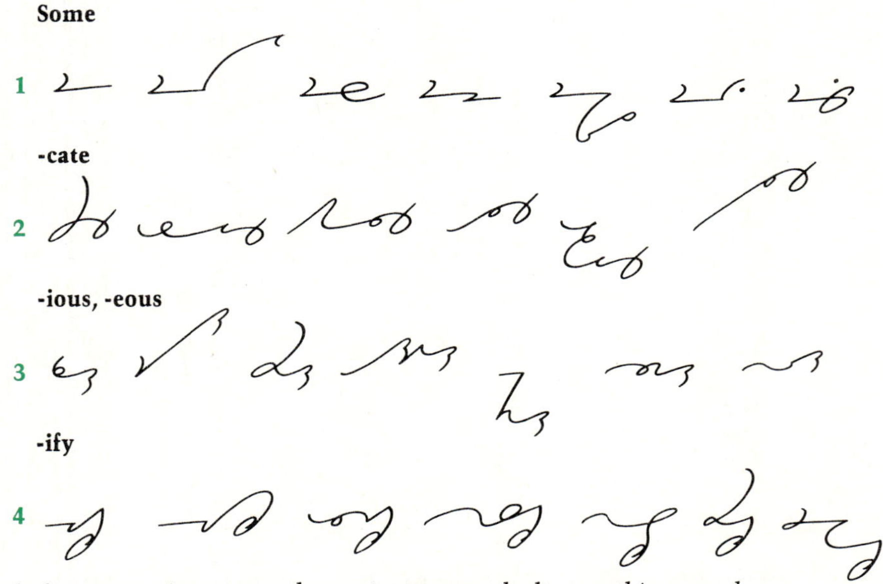

1. *Some, sometimes, somewhere, someone, somebody, something, somehow.*
2. *Vacate, relocate, duplicate, indicate, reciprocate, dedicate.*
3. *Serious, studious, various, industrious, injurious, curious, courteous.*
4. *Notify, modify, rectify, gratify, classify, verify, simplify.*

Building Transcription Skills

240 GRAMMAR CHECKUP possessive with verbal noun

Be very careful when you use a gerund (the *ing* form of a verb used as a noun) following a noun or pronoun; the noun or pronoun takes the possessive case.

Jane's traveling *takes her to many countries.*

I appreciate his taking *the time to help me.*

We will appreciate your letting *us know when the plane is scheduled to leave.*

▶ Note: Be especially careful when the pronoun that precedes the gerund is *your.* If you are not careful, you will transcribe *you* instead of *your.*

---

241 Business Vocabulary Builder

relocate To establish in a new place.

imperative Urgent.

rectify To correct.

compelling Forceful.

Reading and Writing Practice

242

no·ti·fied

prem·ises

ap

intro

as

intro

of·fer·ing

men's

ser

nc

nc

grat·i·fied

[177]

243

em·bar·rass·ing

geo

in·suf·fi·cient

conj

par

par

and o

cour·te·ous

your

nonr

[121]

244

per·son·nel

par

intro

im·per·a·tive

if

conj

bur·den

[140]

com·pel·ling

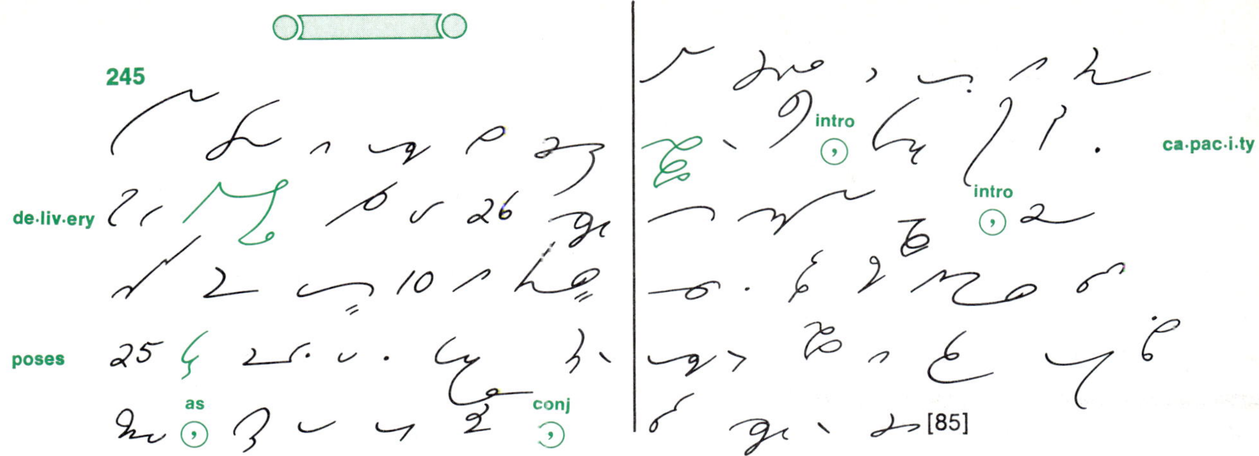

246 Transcription Quiz For you to supply: 7 commas—1 comma *when* clause, 1 comma apposition, 5 commas parenthetical; 2 missing words.

[156]

Warmup For your warmup use the last paragraph of the letter on page 150. Copy the paragraph slowly, then rapidly, and finally in your best shorthand.

Developing Word-Building Power

247 Word Beginnings and Endings

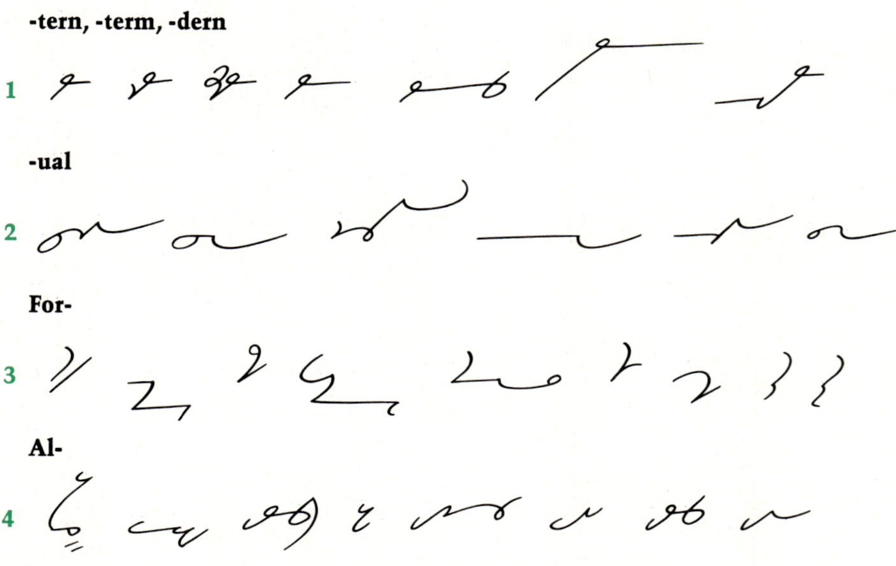

1. *Turn, stern, western, term, terminate, determine, modern.*
2. *Actual, annual, scheduled, manual, mutual, equal.*
3. *Forward, information, effort, performance, formally, forth, comfort, force, forces.*
4. *Albany, almost, alternative, also, altogether, although, alternate, alter.*

Building Transcription Skills

248 COMMON PREFIXES de- A knowledge of the meaning of the most common prefixes is of great value in helping you increase your command of the English language. You have already studied a number of common prefixes; in *Gregg Dictation and Introductory Transcription* you will learn several others.

Read the definition of each prefix carefully and then study the illustrations that follow.

de- down; away from

decrease Go down; grow less.

depress Put down; lower.

depart Go away from.

descend Come down.

detract Take away from.

---

249 Business Vocabulary Builder

agenda A list of things; the program for a meeting.

confirmation Proof; supporting evidence.

prompted Moved to action.

Reading and Writing Practice

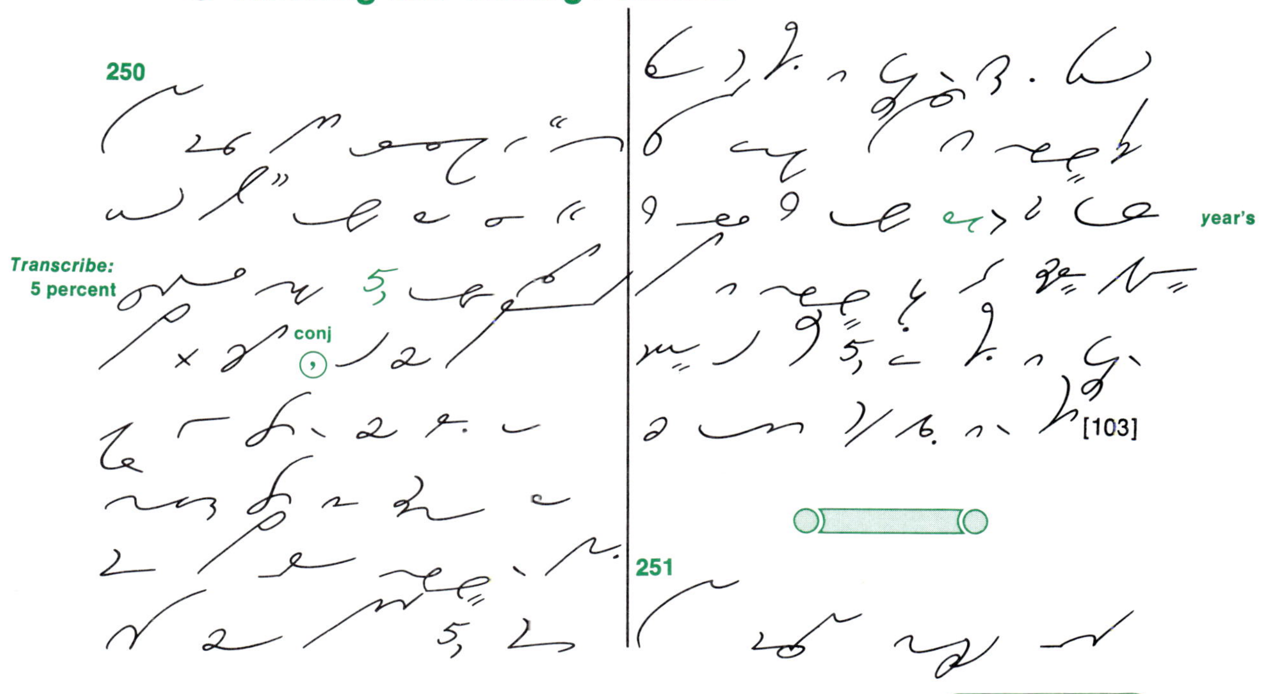

nonr

as

ap

Transcribe:
10 a.m.

trav·el·ers

par

ap

re·ceives

when

if

[153]

252

ap

in·qui·ry

intro

conj

and o

well-known
hyphenated before noun

par

im·pres·sion

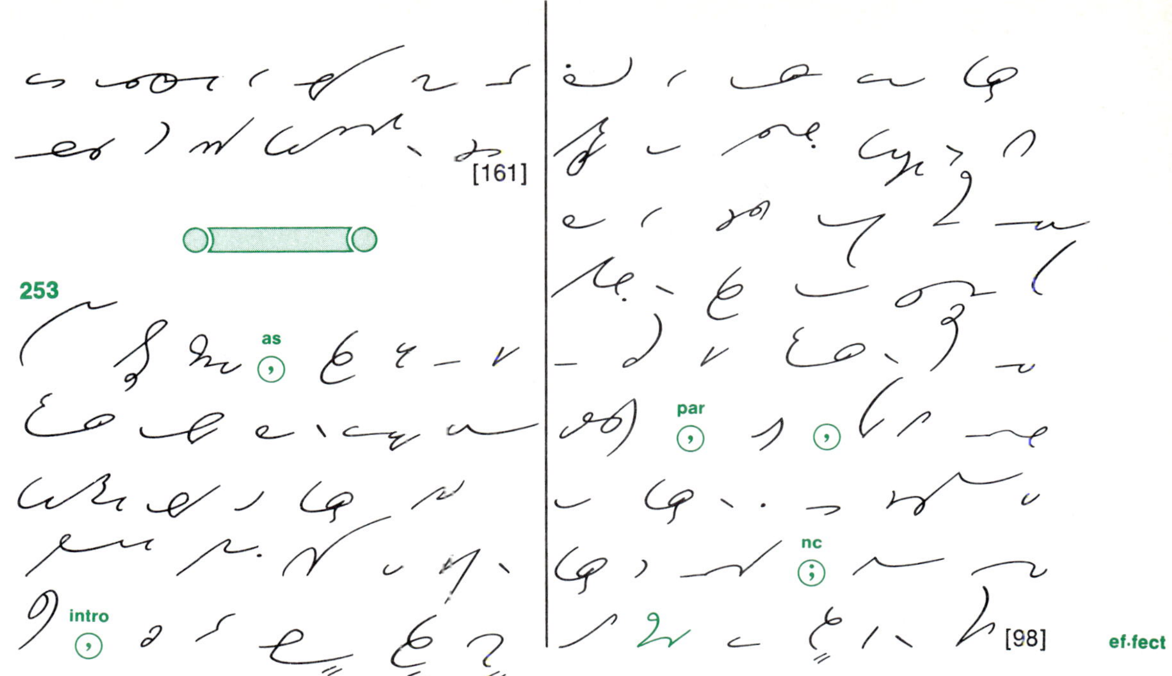

254 Transcription Quiz For you to supply: 4 commas—2 commas conjunction, 1 comma *as* clause, 1 comma introductory; 1 semicolon no conjunction; 2 missing words.

[130]

Warmup Copy the phrase letter on page 150 as rapidly as you can. If there is time, copy it a second time in your very best shorthand.

Developing Word-Building Power

255 Shorthand Vocabulary Builder

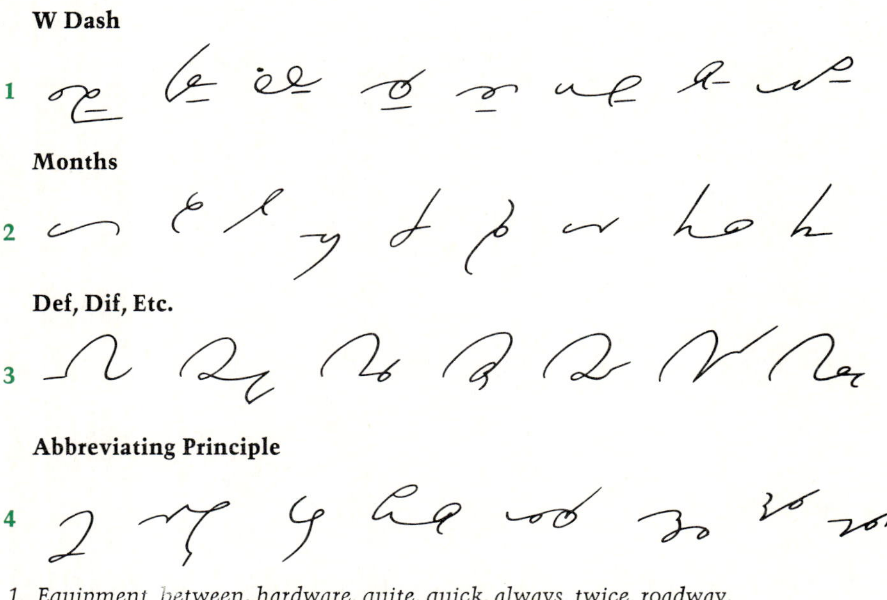

1. *Equipment, between, hardware, quite, quick, always, twice, roadway.*
2. *August, September, December, November, January, February, October, July, June.*
3. *Endeavor, developed, definite, device, divert, dividend, difference.*
4. *Convenient-convenience, contribution, privilege, apologize, required, consequently, substitute, institution.*

Building Transcription Skills

256 Business Vocabulary Builder

apparel Clothing.

revolutionize To change radically.

via By the way of.

Reading and Writing Practice

257

nonr

re·signed

geo

conj

lose

intro

nonr

par

ac·cord

[150]

258

ap

men's

Ma·son's

conj

via

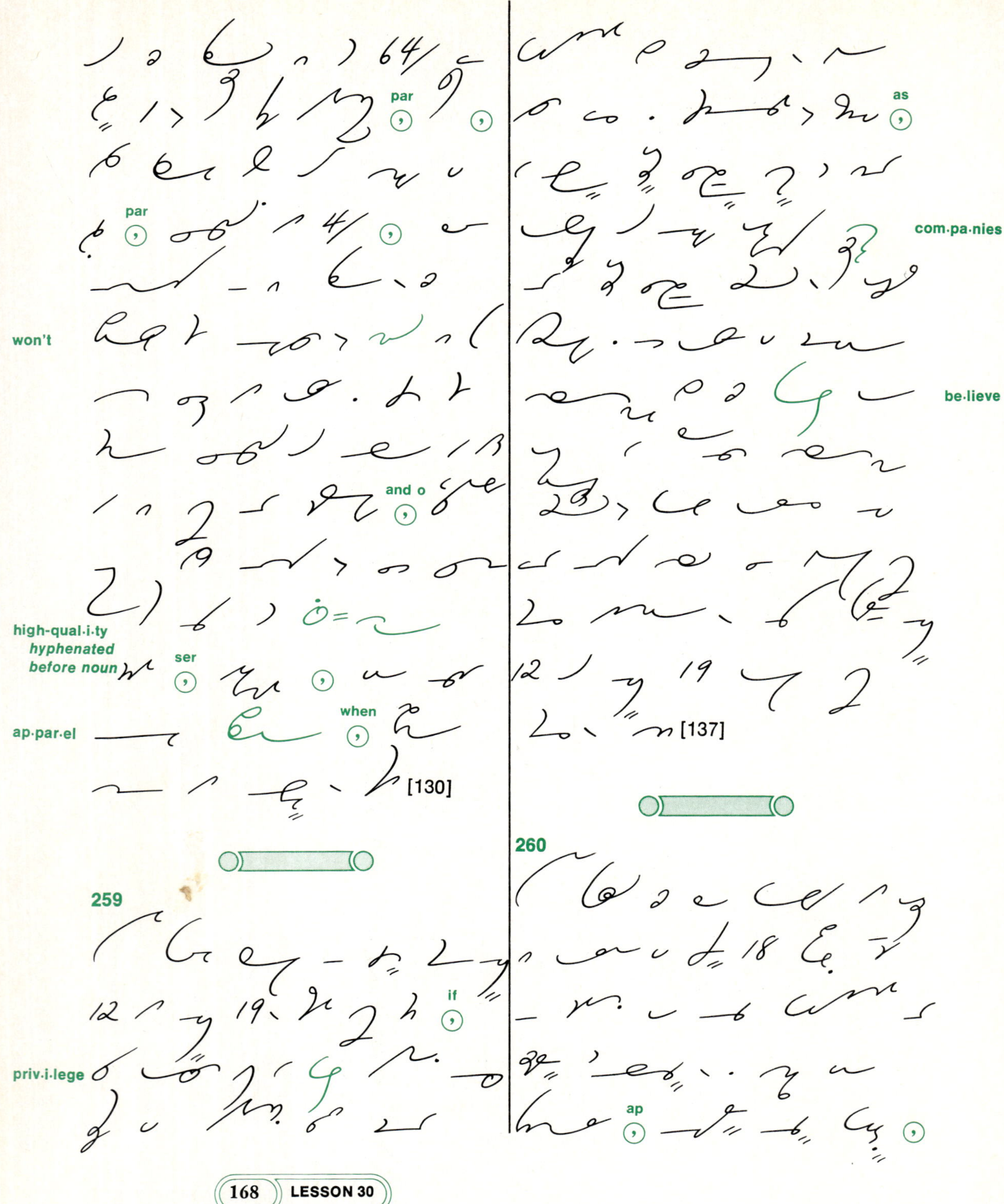

par
par
won't
and o
high-qual·i·ty
hyphenated
before noun
ser
ap·par·el
when
[130]
259
if
priv·i·lege
as
com·pa·nies
be·lieve
[137]
260
ap

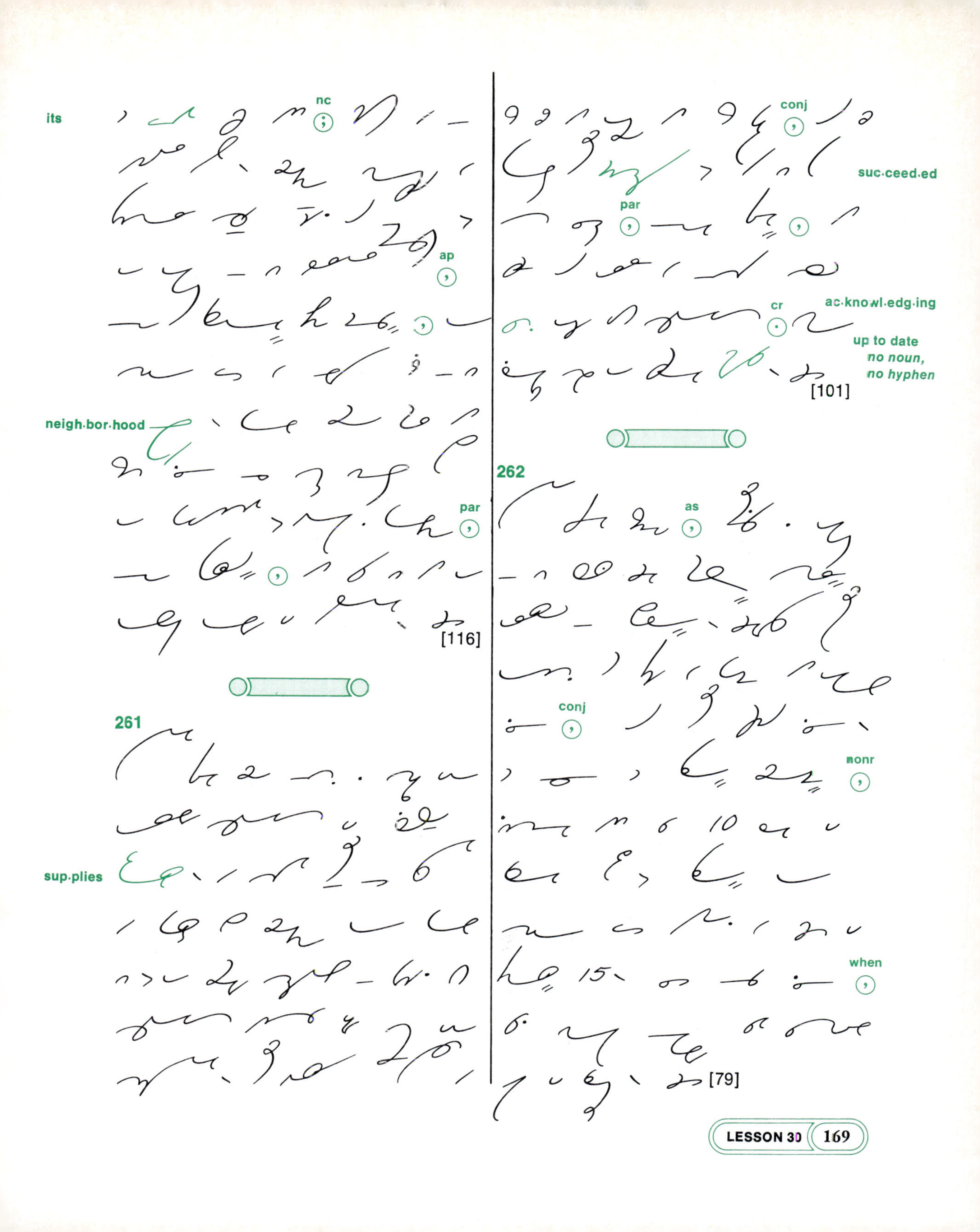

its

nc

ap

neigh·bor·hood

par

[116]

261

sup·plies

conj

suc·ceed·ed

par

cr

ac·knowl·edg·ing

up to date
no noun,
no hyphen

[101]

262

as

conj

nonr

when

[79]

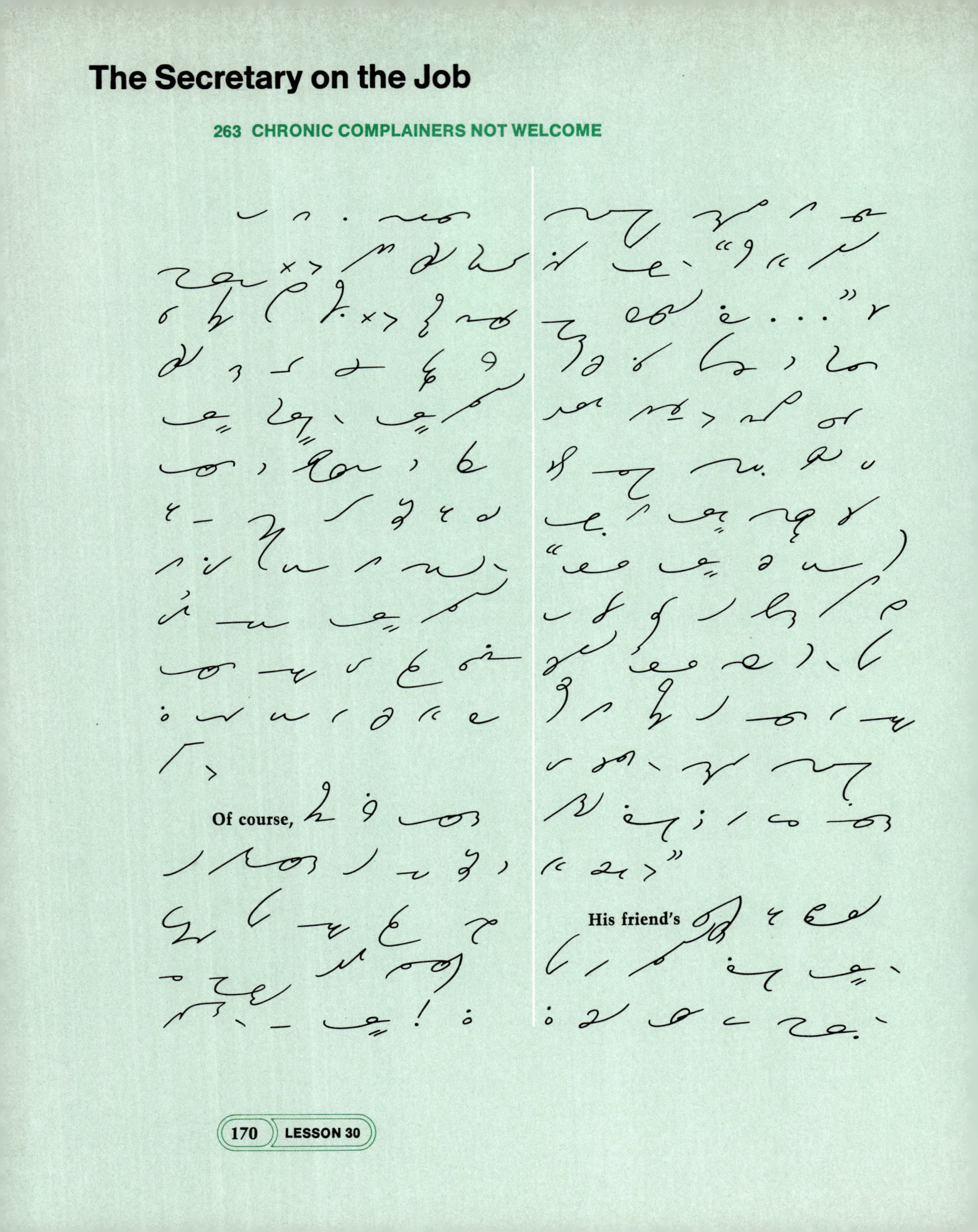

The Secretary on the Job

263 CHRONIC COMPLAINERS NOT WELCOME

Of course,

His friend's

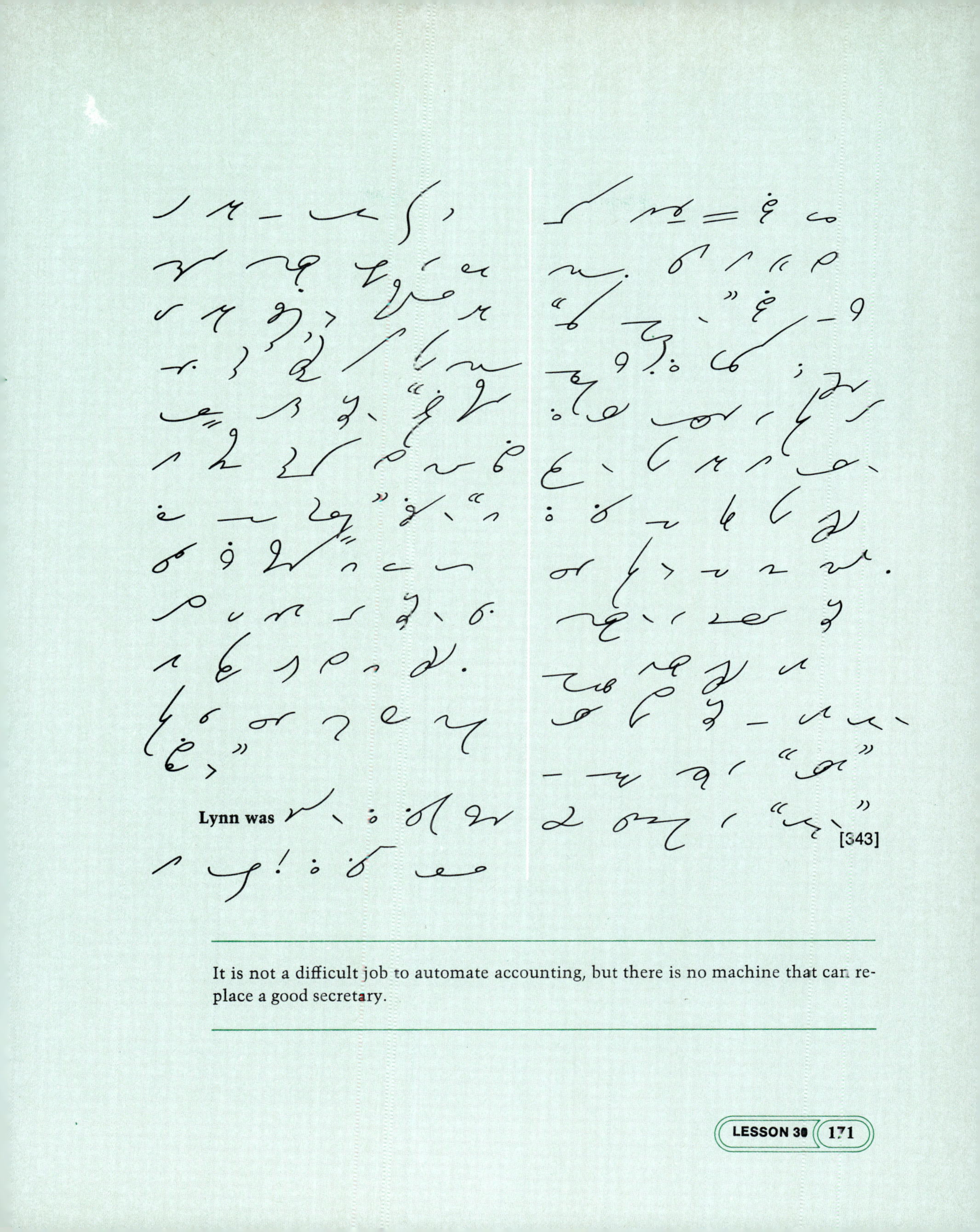

Lynn was

[343]

It is not a difficult job to automate accounting, but there is no machine that can replace a good secretary.

CHAPTER

Retailing

You have been a consumer of goods and services for a number of years. During this time you have been using various types of products such as food, clothing, and luxury items. How and where did you get these products? "I bought them in a store," you will probably answer. Any store that sells merchandise or a service to the final consumer is known as a retail store. Usually when you think of retail stores, you think of them as selling goods. Because it is harder to picture a service, people forget that firms like laundries, beauty shops, and real estate agencies are also retail businesses—they sell a service that they perform for the customer.

Look around your town or city. Retail stores are everywhere, providing you, your family, and your friends with the goods and services you and they want. These wants are different today from what they were only a few years ago because people are constantly changing their style of living. The modern retail store reflects these changes and continues to meet people's new needs.

The first stores in our country were called general stores because they sold a little bit of everything, including such items as groceries, clothing, yard goods, basic drugs, household furnishings, farm tools, and feed for animals. There wasn't much choice in any of these items because the stores were small and there wasn't a very large variety of products available to sell. But once factories began producing more and different products, general stores could not adequately serve either producers or consumers.

Although there are still a few general stores in small country towns, most small stores now concentrate on selling either just one line of goods or a group of related goods. Department stores, supermarkets, discount variety stores, and so on, have replaced the old-time general store in most places. The modern department store carries everything from fine jewelry to lawn mowers. It also provides services such as appliance repair and gift wrapping.

Retailing is not limited to the types of stores just described, of course. The field of retailing also encompasses such businesses as mail-order houses, restaurants, hotels and motels, financial institutions, recreation and tourism businesses, and rental shops.

Retail businesses, whether they sell goods or services, revolve around the customer. The basic difference between a company that sells goods and one that sells services is that the first buys goods for resale while the second concentrates on providing technical skill. Buying, stocking, displaying, and selling merchandise are important functions of the retail store; performing a job is the role of the service business.

Retail operations can be exciting centers of activity, providing opportunities for an attractive career. The letters in this chapter deal with many areas of retail selling.

Building Phrasing Skill

264 Phrase Builder

The following list contains 38 useful business letter phrases. Can you read the entire list in 45 seconds?

Want

1

Been

2

Able

3

To in Phrases

4

1. *I want, I wanted, you want, you wanted, he wants, he wanted, we want, we wanted, if you want.*
2. *I have been, I have not been, we have been, we have not been, you have not been, would have been, should have been, could have been, there have been, to have been.*
3. *Have been able, I have been able, I have not been able, you have been able, we have not been able, to be able, I should be able, may be able, I will be able.*
4. *To be, to have, to see, to sell, to plan, to fly, to put, to find, to check, to blame.*

265 Warmup Phrase Letter

The following 161-word letter is your warmup letter for Chapter 7. Can you read it in 1 minute? Write it in 2 minutes?

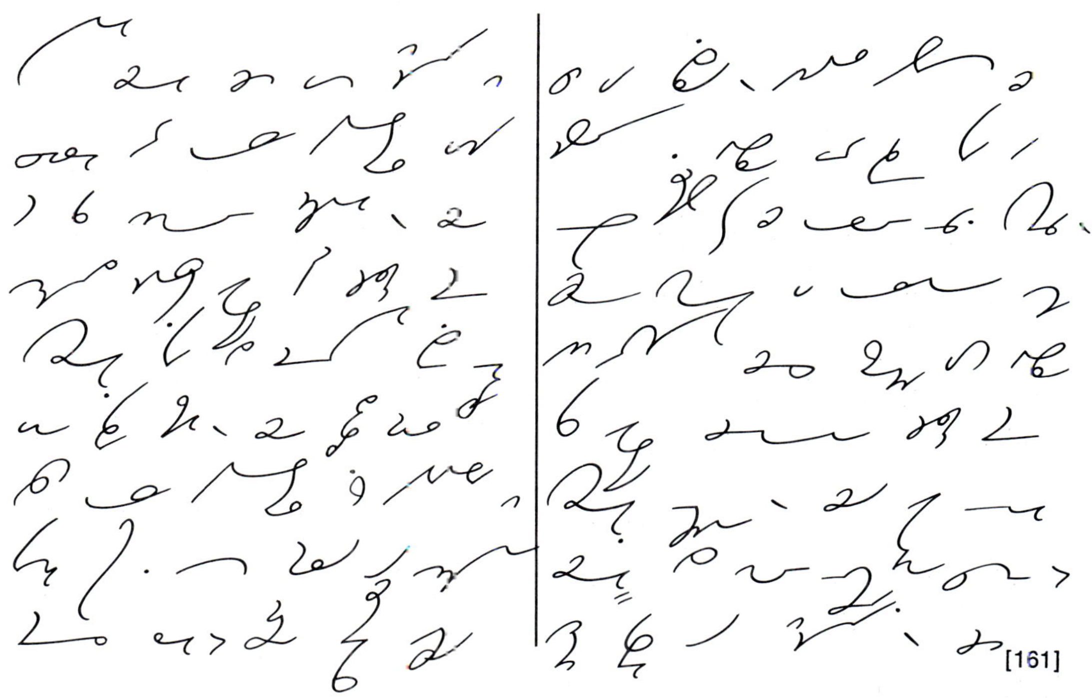

Building Transcription Skills

266 TYPING STYLE STUDY capitalization

Compass Points

Capitalize *north, south, east, west,* etc., only when they designate definite regions or when they are an integral part of a proper name.

I live in the East.

She went to the West Coast.

We are traveling south.

---

267 Business Vocabulary Builder

enviable Highly desirable.

pertinent Relevant; logically associated.

in transit In shipment.

discrepancy Difference.

Reading and Writing Practice

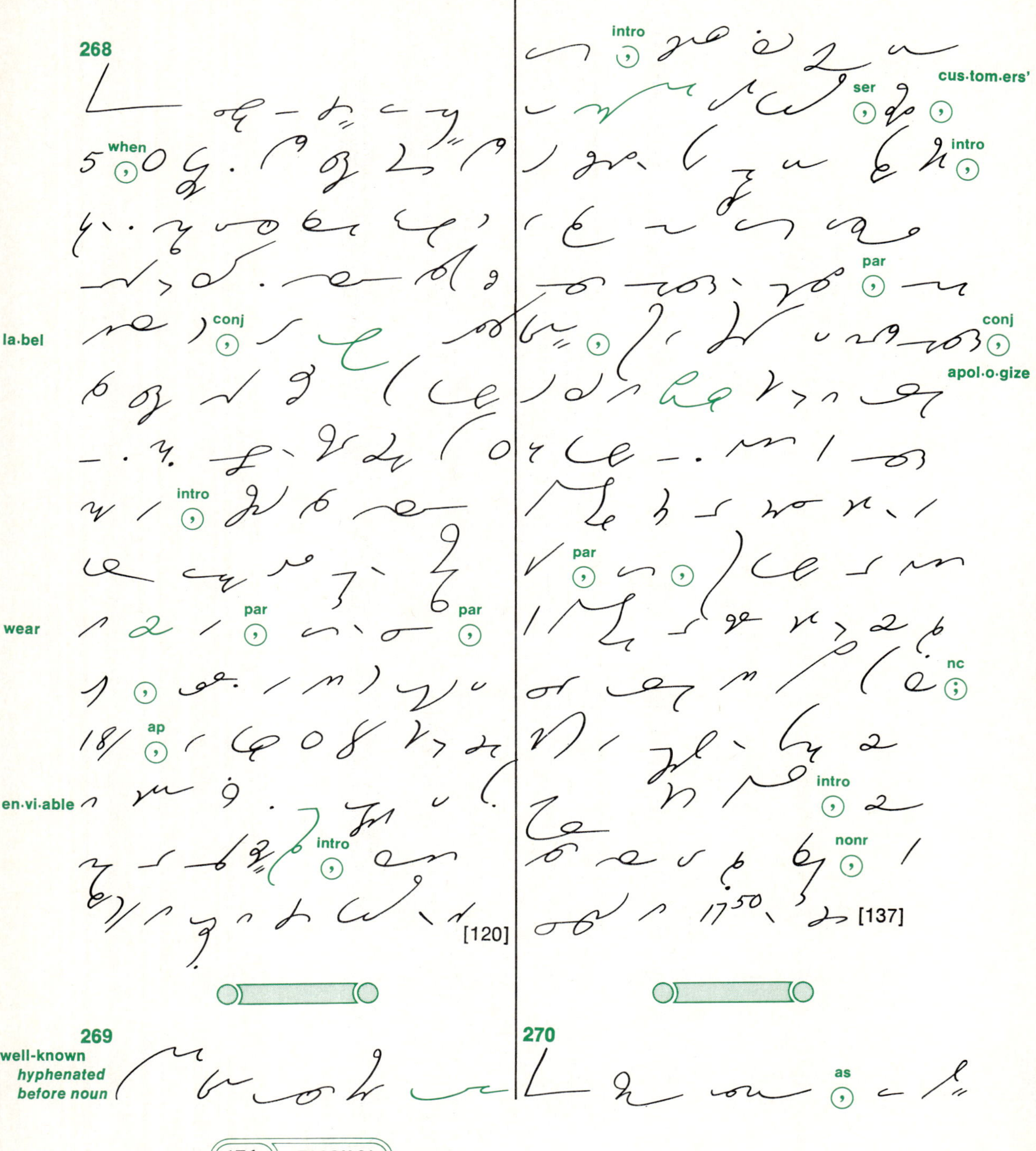

ac·cept

ac·knowl·edg·ing

ware·house

nc

intro

oc·curred

per·ti·nent

conj

if

conj

[118]

[133]

271

272

bi·cy·cle

son's

conj

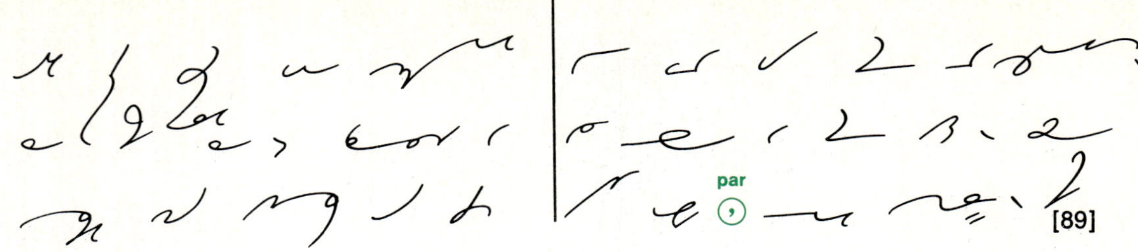

273 Transcription Quiz In the Transcription Quizzes in earlier lessons you have had to supply missing words that were obvious because only one possible word made sense. Hereafter, any one of a number of words will make sense, and it will be up to you to supply the word you think fits best in the sentence.

To illustrate:

Where there has been an omission, any one of the following words would be considered correct: *like, wish, want.* If you decide that the word *like* makes the sentence read most smoothly, you would write in your shorthand notebook thus:

If you like, (, if) we will add your name to our mailing list.

Whatever word you choose, be *sure* that it makes sense in the sentence.

For you to supply: 4 commas—1 comma introductory, 2 commas *if* clause, 1 comma *and* omitted; 2 missing words.

[98]

Warmup Your warmup letter is on page 175. Today let us use a slightly different plan for warming up.

Instead of working with a complete paragraph, let us develop speed on individual sentences by breaking each sentence into several parts and practicing each part separately. For example, this is the way you would practice the first sentence in the letter on page 175.

■ 1 *Write slowly in your best shorthand the group of words, "***Dear Mrs. Wells: We can, of course, understand your annoyance.***"*

■ 2 *Write the same group of words two or three more times, trying to increase your writing speed each time.*

■ 3 *Follow Steps 1 and 2 with the next group of words, "***at the late delivery of your order for six woolen sweaters.***"*

■ 4 *Finally, write the complete sentence in shorthand as rapidly as you can. Follow this procedure with as many sentences as time permits. Your warmup should look something like this in your shorthand notebook:*

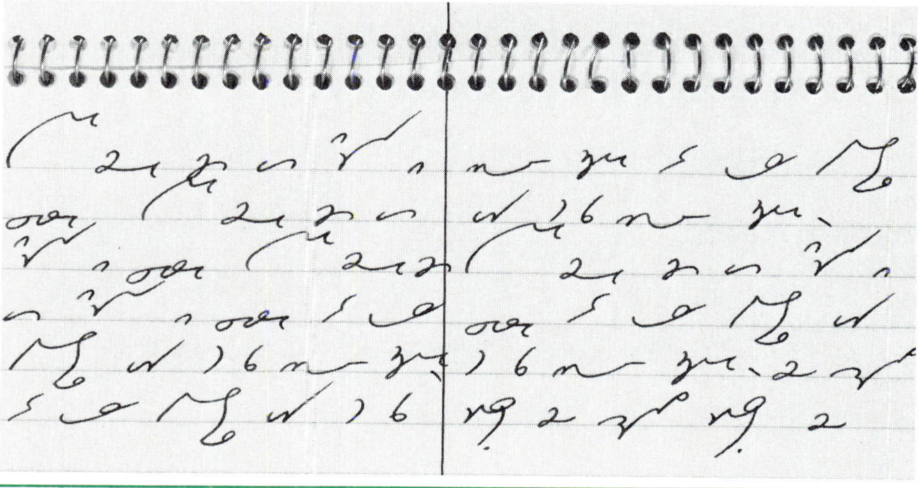

Developing Word-Building Power

274 Brief-Form Chart

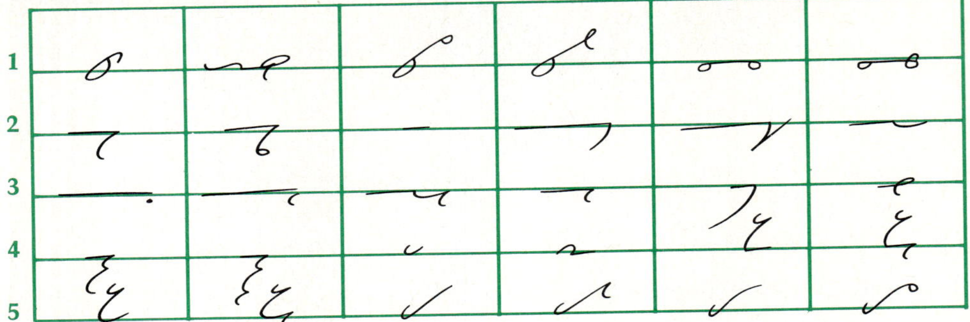

1. Out, recognize, idea, ideas, immediate, immediately.
2. Important-importance, importantly, in-not, manufacture, manufactured, Mr.
3. Morning, mornings, Mrs., Ms., never, next.
4. Newspaper, newspapers, of, one (won), opinion, opinions.
5. Opportunity, opportunities, order, orders, ordinary, ordinarily.

275 Geographical Expressions

1. Detroit, Reno, Rochester, Troy, Bangor, Concord, Montpelier.
2. Michigan, Nevada, New York, Maine, New Hampshire, Vermont, Oregon, Florida.

Building Transcription Skills

276 SIMILAR-WORDS DRILL billed, build

billed (past tense of *bill*) Charged.

We billed *the organization for the supplies they bought.*

build To create or produce; to construct.

Our company will build *the houses in a few months.*

277 Business Vocabulary Builder	**erroneously** Mistakenly.
	overwhelming Overpowering in effect or strength.
	response Reaction.
	alerted Called to a state of readiness.

● Reading and Writing Practice

278 Brief-Form Letter

Can you read this letter in 1 minute? Copy it in 1¾ minutes?

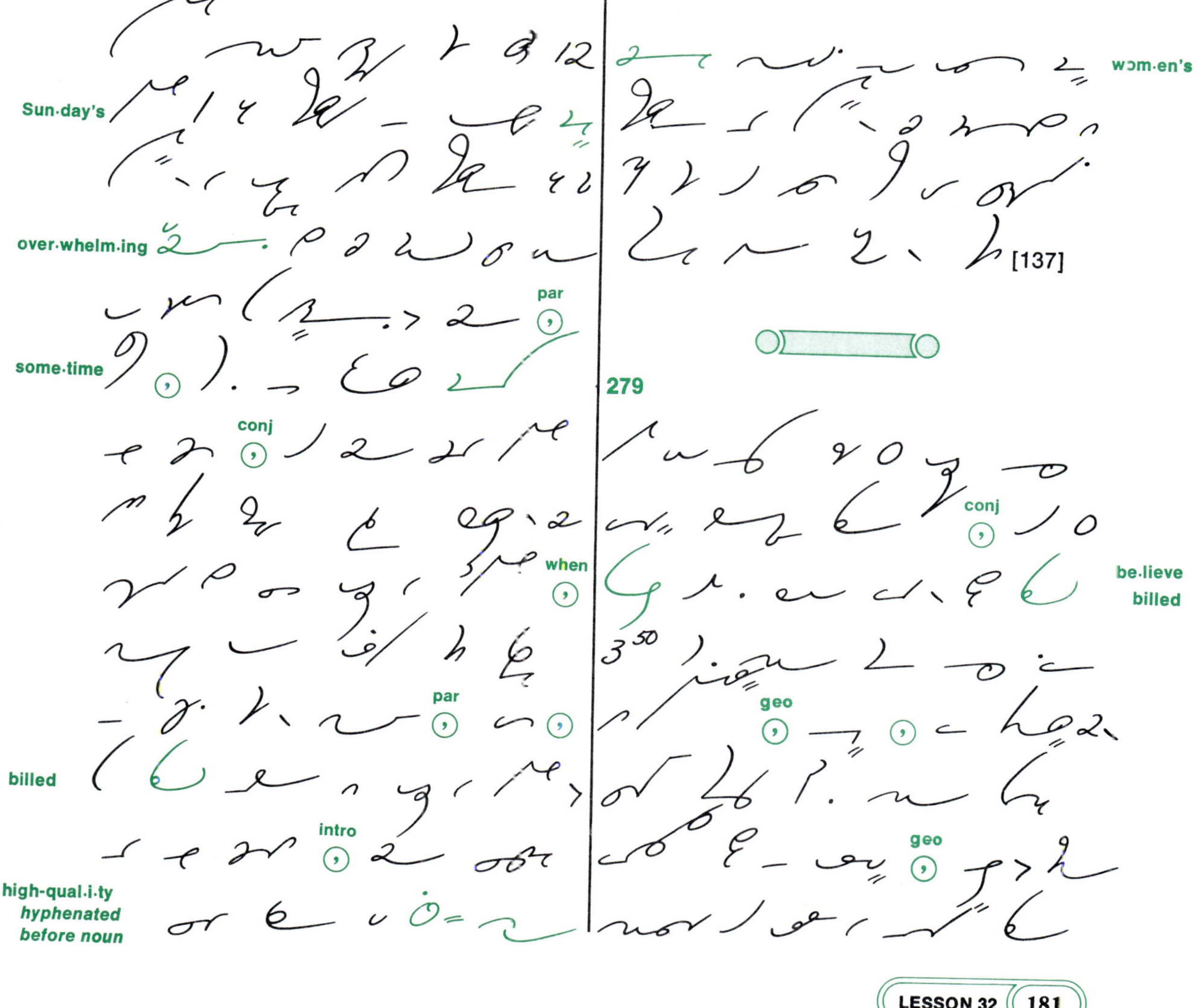

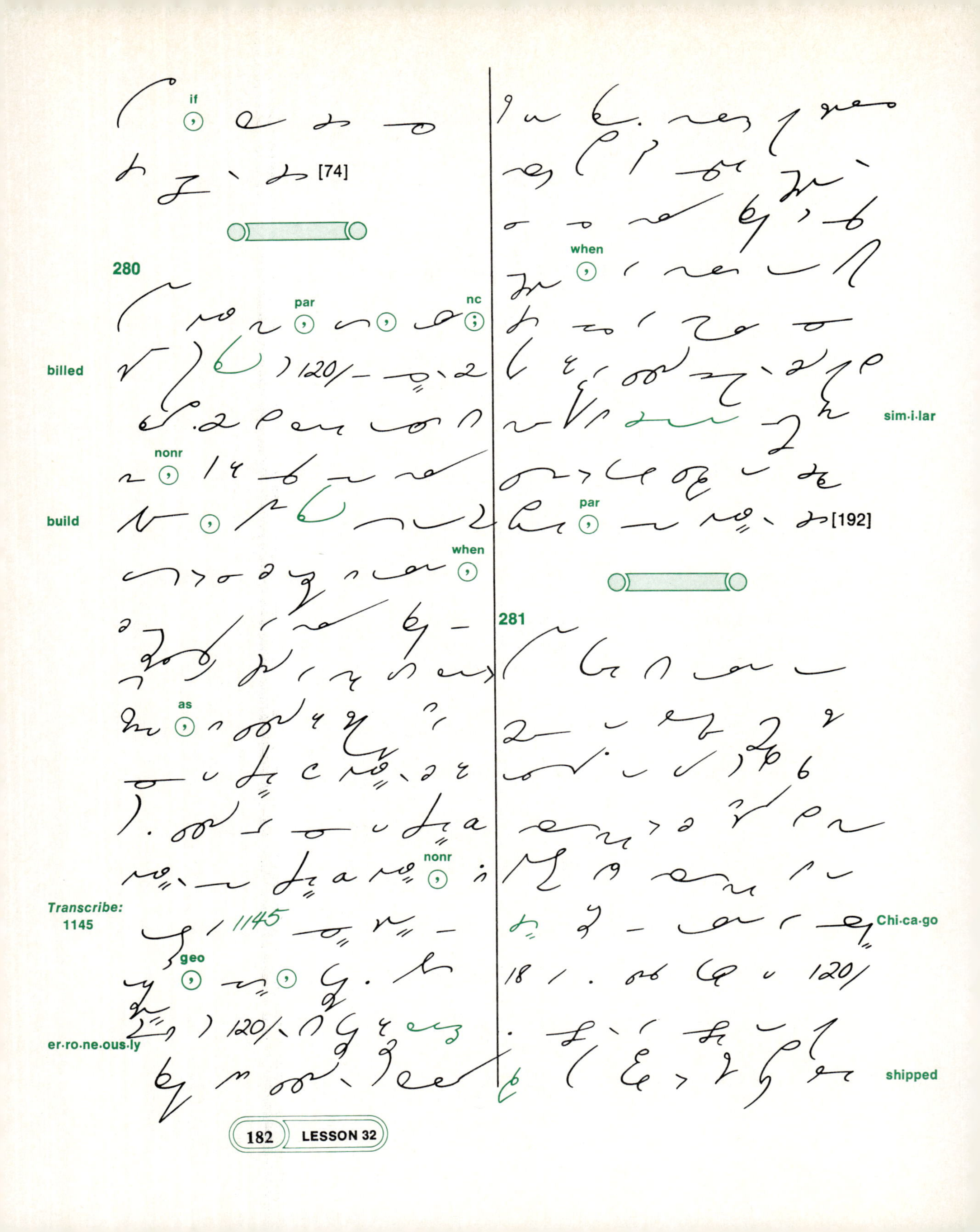

if

[74]

280

par nc

billed

nonr

build

when

as

nonr

Transcribe: 1145

geo

er·ro·ne·ous·ly

when

sim·i·lar

par

[192]

281

Chi·ca·go

shipped

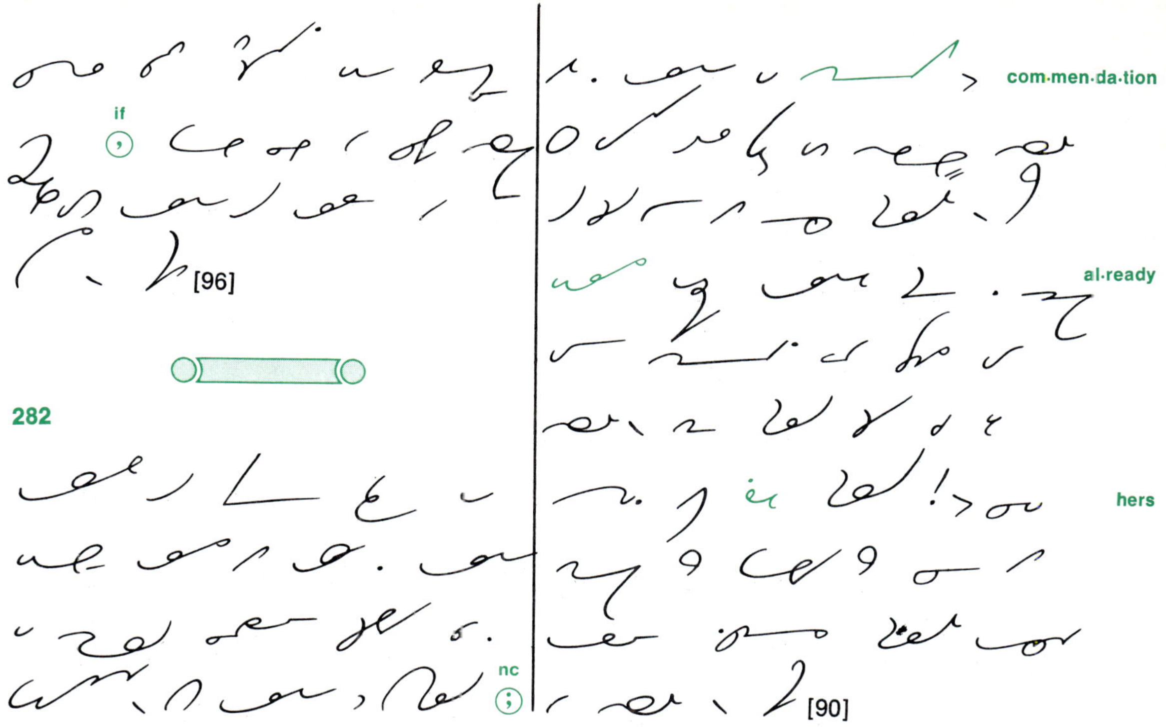

282

283 Transcription Quiz For you to supply: 5 commas—1 comma apposition, 4 commas parenthetical; 1 semicolon no conjunction; 2 missing words.

[114]

LESSON 33

Warmup Your warmup letter is on page 175. Practice the sentences in the second paragraph of the letter, following the steps listed in Lesson 32. Try to increase your writing speed with each repetition.

Developing Word-Building Power

284 Word Families

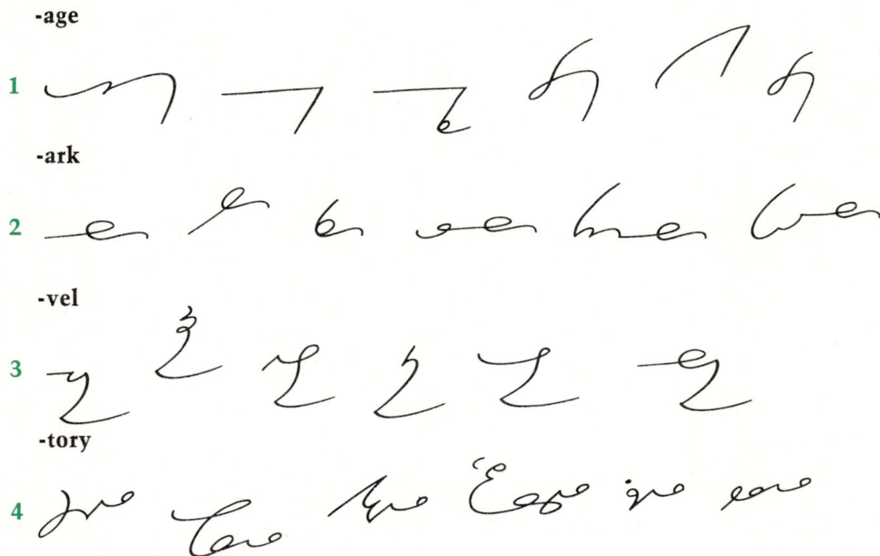

1. *Luggage, manage, manager, baggage, damage, package.*
2. *Mark, dark, park, remark, bookmark, birthmark.*
3. *Novel, swivel, travel, shovel, level, marvel.*
4. *Factory, laboratory, depository, self-explanatory, history, territory.*

Building Transcription Skills

285 SPELLING FAMILIES -cial, -tial Be careful when you transcribe words ending with the sound *shal*; sometimes these endings are spelled *cial*, and other times they are spelled *tial*.

Words Ending in -cial

spe·cial	of·fi·cial	ar·ti·fi·cial
fi·nan·cial	so·cial	ben·e·fi·cial
cru·cial	su·per·fi·cial	com·mer·cial

Words Ending in -tial

es·sen·tial	sub·stan·tial	po·ten·tial
ini·tial	res·i·den·tial	con·fi·den·tial

286 Business Vocabulary Builder

swivel chairs Chairs that pivot.

novel New; unusual.

depository A place where something is put for safekeeping.

Reading and Writing Practice

287

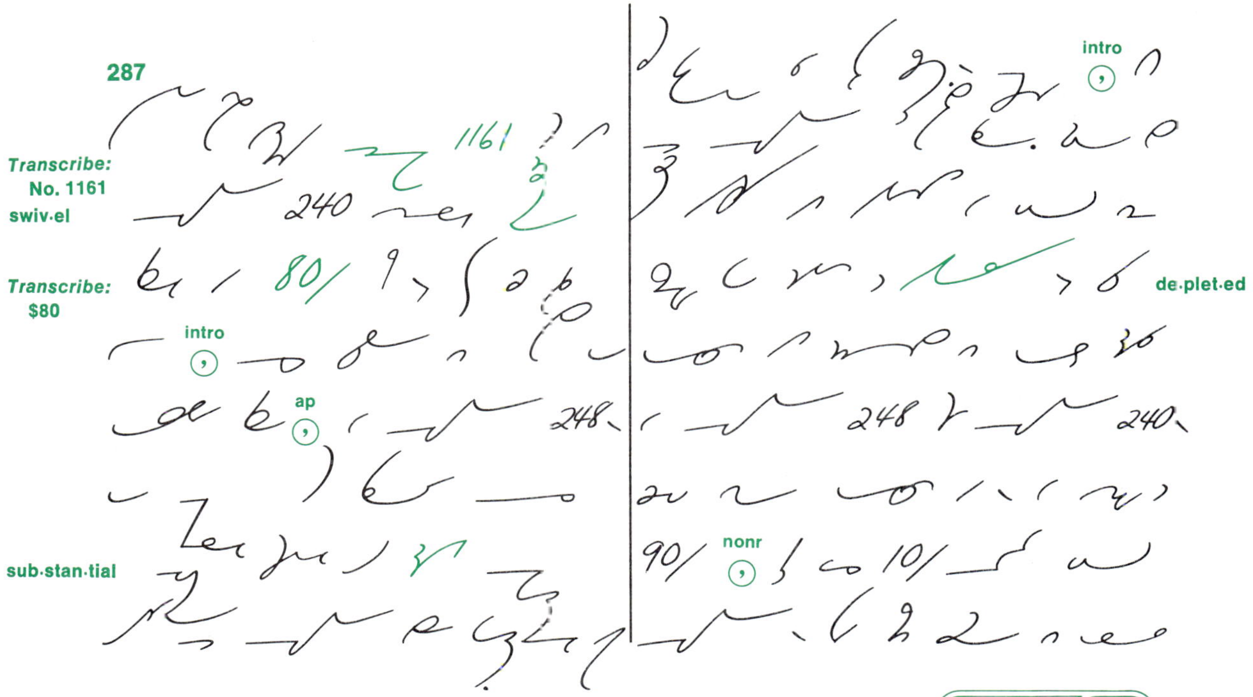

Transcribe: No. 1161

swiv·el

Transcribe: $80

intro

ap

sub·stan·tial

intro

de·plet·ed

nonr

240 if

nc

post·age-paid *hyphenated before noun*

par

[201]

par

and o

suc·cess·ful

ex·er·cise

flaw

[146]

288

dye

conj

lab·o·ra·to·ry

of·fi·cial

when

dyes

es·sen·tial·ly

nc

intro

289

15

pieces

ap

ap

10

re·ceipt

ini·tialed

intro

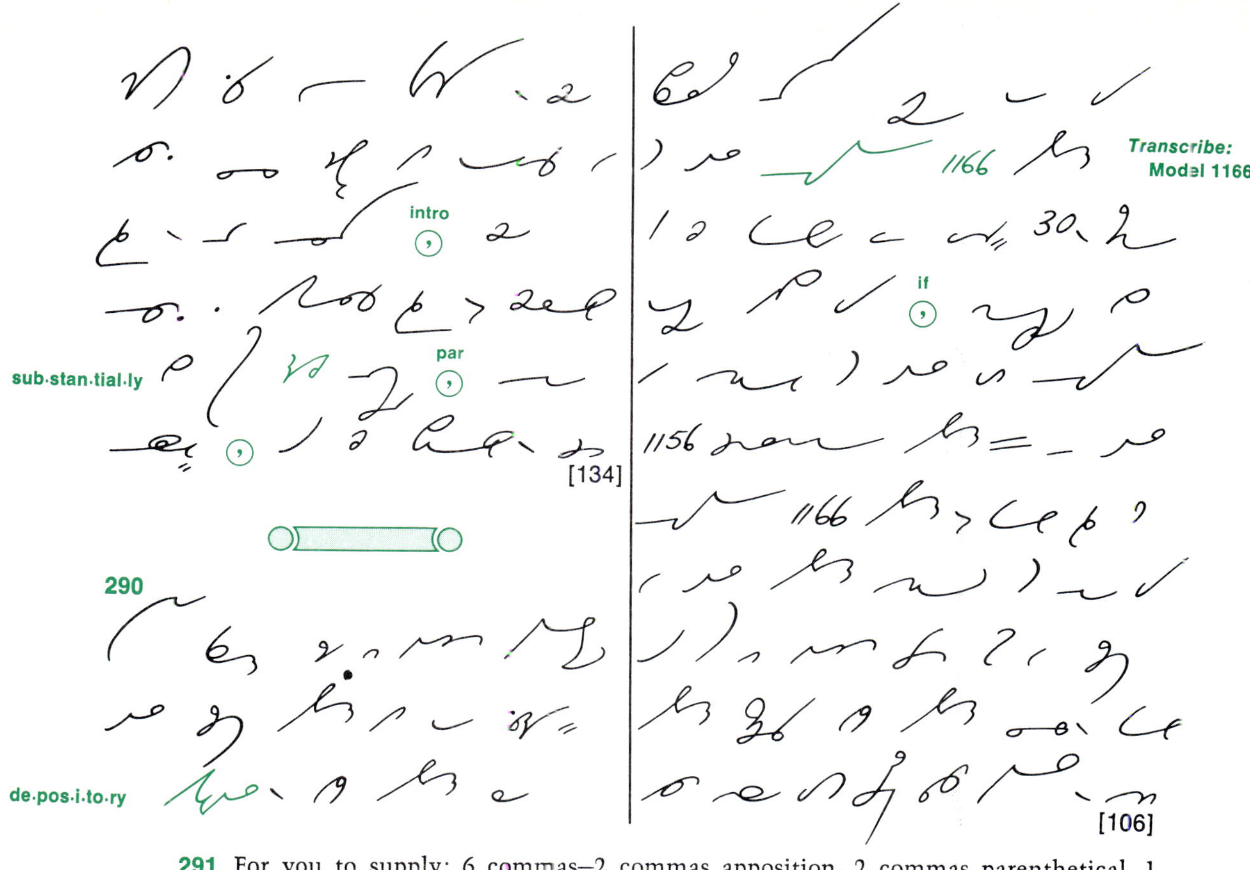

291 Transcription Quiz For you to supply: 6 commas—2 commas apposition, 2 commas parenthetical, 1 comma conjunction, 1 comma introductory; 1 semicolon no conjunction; 2 missing words.

[114]

Warmup Your warmup letter is on page 175. For today, practice the sentence in the third paragraph of the letter, following the steps listed in Lesson 32. Practice the sentence in two parts.

Developing Word-Building Power

292 Word Beginnings and Endings

Be-

1

Sub-

2

-ward

3

Com-

4

1. *Because, become, believe, before, beginnings, betray, beneath, below.*
2. *Subscription, subscribers, substantial, submit, submitted, substance, subway, subside.*
3. *Awkward, eastward, inward, outward, backward, rewarded, forwarded, onward.*
4. *Comfort, complete, complicated, comply, combine, compliment.*

Building Transcription Skills

293 GRAMMAR CHECKUP don't, doesn't

Use *doesn't* in the third person singular, not *don't*.

She doesn't *(not* don't*) want a new job.*

He doesn't *have a private office.*

That doesn't *seem to be reasonable.*

You never hear anyone say, "I doesn't," but you will frequently hear people incorrectly say, "he don't," "she don't," or "that don't." Of course, *you* never make that mistake!

---

294 Business Vocabulary Builder

anticipate To expect; to look forward to.

awkward Hard to handle.

implements Tools.

Reading and Writing Practice

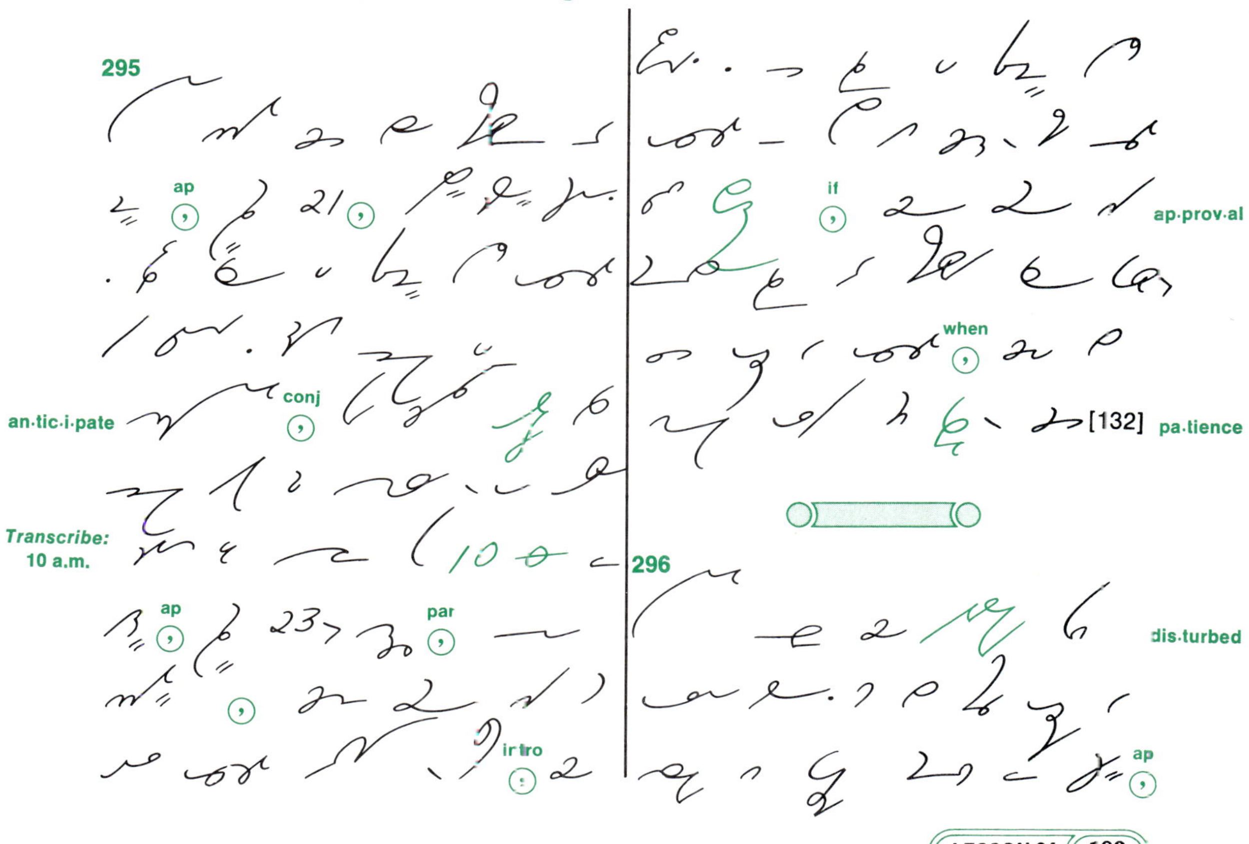

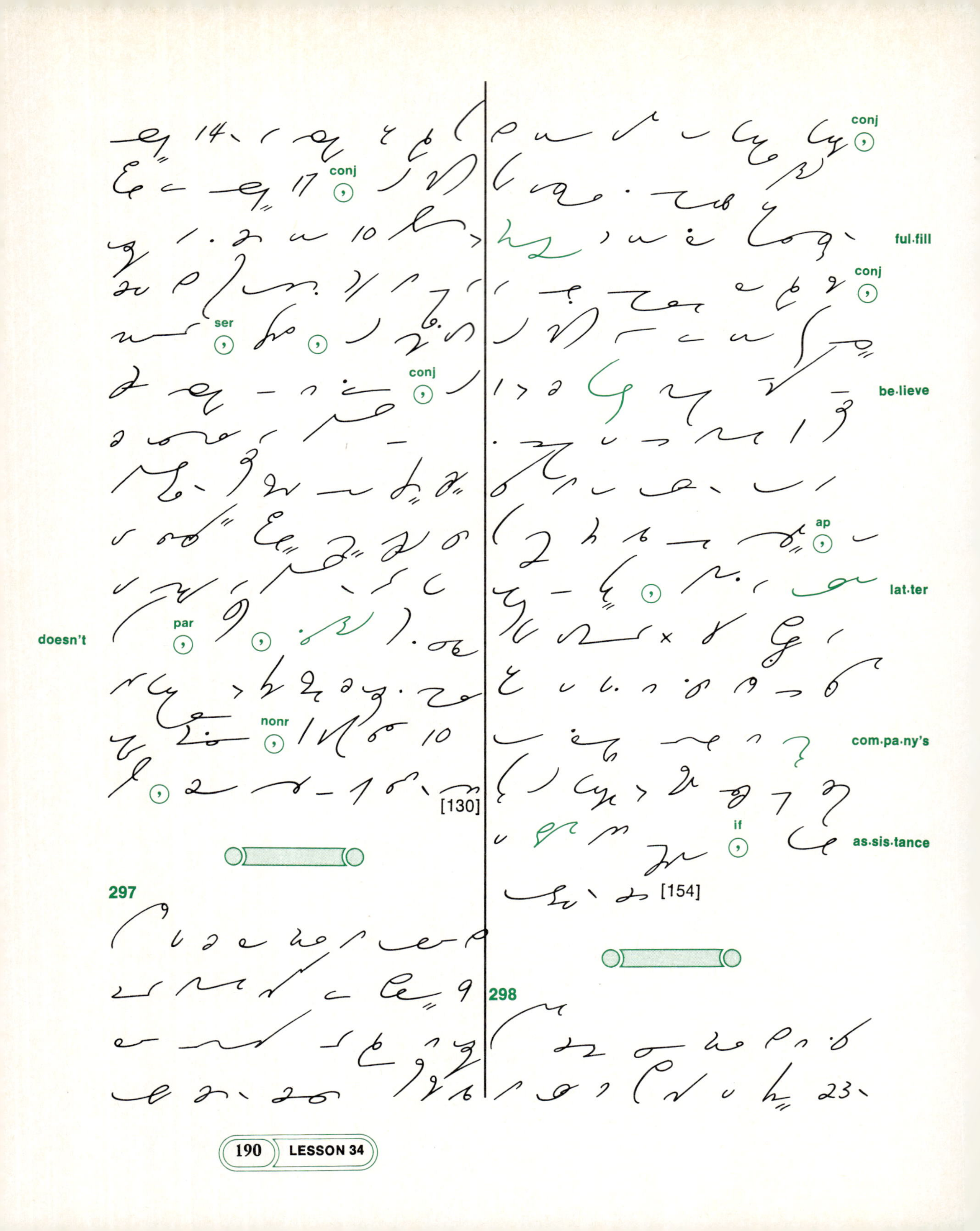

14 conj 17 10

ser conj

doesn't par nonr 10

[130]

conj

ful·fill

conj

be·lieve

ap

lat·ter

com·pa·ny's

if as·sis·tance

[154]

297

298

23

awk·ward

and o

intro

ten-day *hyphenated before noun*

par

tran·sis·tor

nc

than

ap

par

[104]

299

par

in·quir·ies

[78]

300 Transcription Quiz For you to supply: 7 commas—1 comma *as* clause, 4 commas parenthetical, 1 comma *when* clause, 1 comma *and* omitted; 2 missing words.

[112]

Warmup For the last time, the phrase letter on page 175 will be your warmup. Write the entire letter as rapidly as you can.

Developing Word-Building Power

301 Shorthand Vocabulary Builder

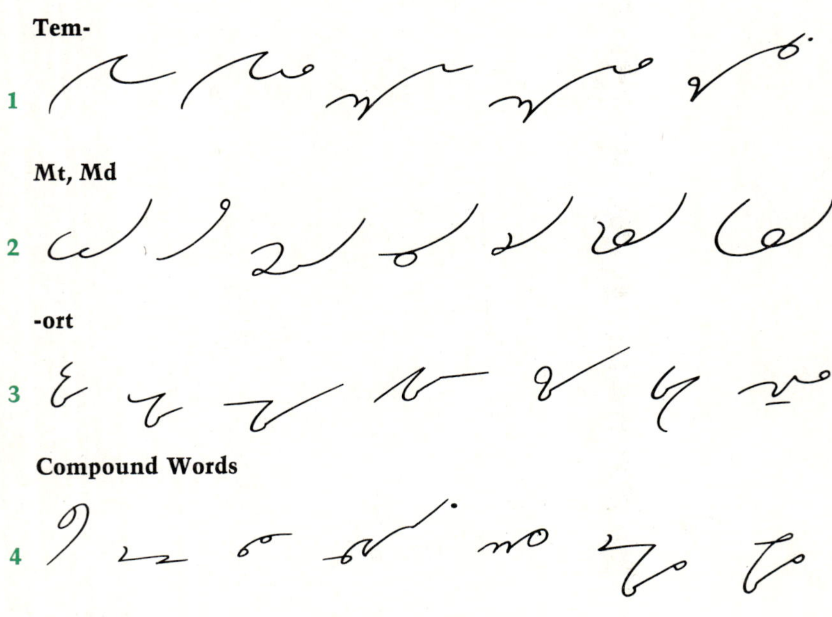

1. *Temple, temporary, customer, customary, estimating.*
2. *Prompt, empty, confirmed, named, seemed, framed, blamed.*
3. *Sport, report, imported, deportment, assorted, portable, quarterly.*
4. *However, someone, within, notwithstanding, worthwhile, somebody, anybody.*

Building Transcription Skills

302 Business Vocabulary Builder

back orders Orders which have been received but on which delivery is delayed.

deportment Behavior.

accommodate Do a favor or service for; oblige.

Reading and Writing Practice

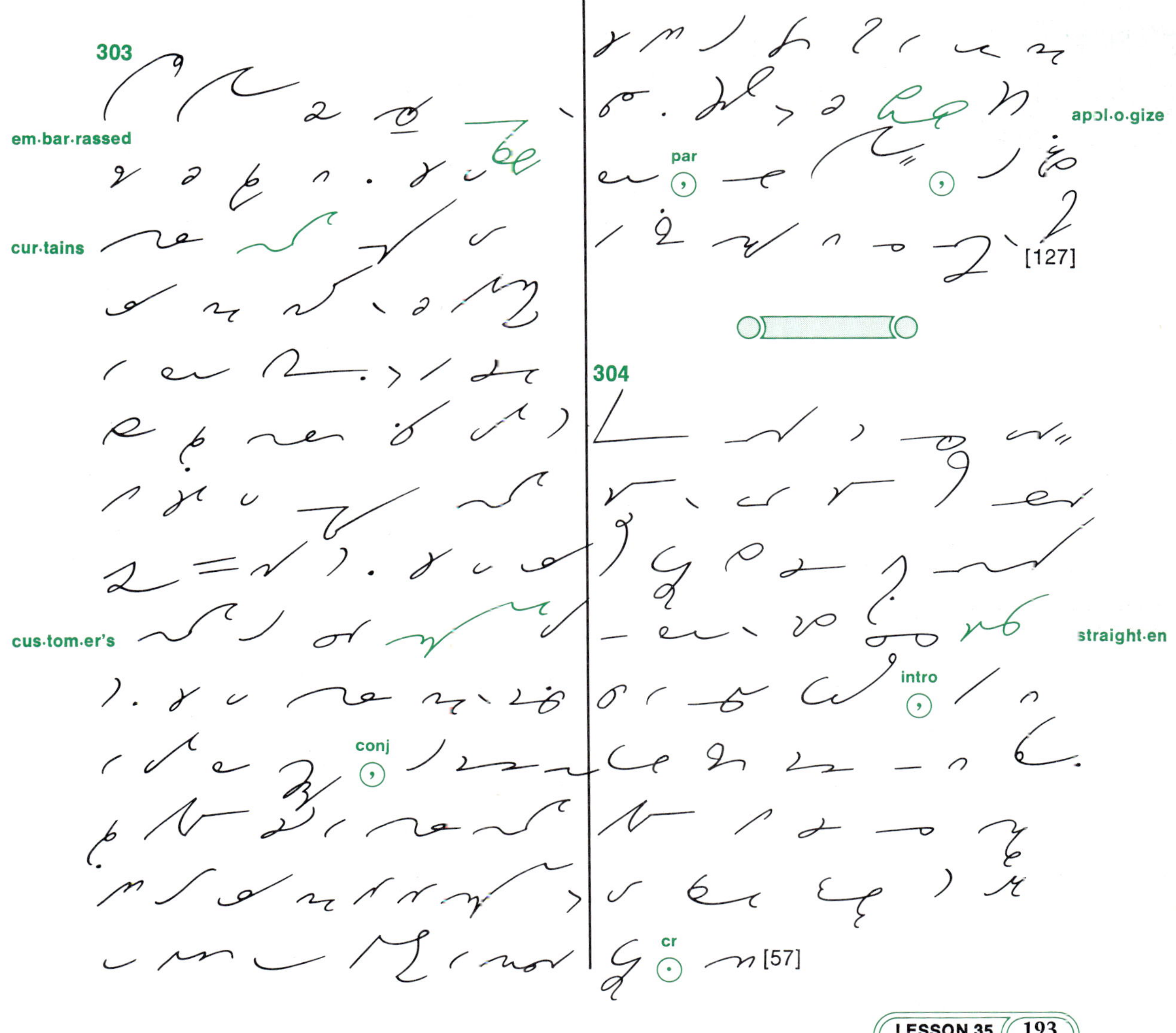

305

nc

par

yours

conj

at·ten·tion

[90]

306

de·port·ment

long-time *hyphenated before noun*

as

ours

and o

cour·te·ous

par

par

intro

ser

[141]

307

Transcribe: No. 1161 Model 18

re·ceipt

conj

tem·po·rar·i·ly

ap

[90]

308

nonr

re·ferred

par

ours

if

intro

[133]

309

ap

ap·praised

of·fered

if

if

[94]

The Secretary on the Job

310 THE THIRTEENTH DOUGHNUT

13 13

13 13

What does this 13

When you 10 15

13

Giving a

[272]

DICTATION TIP ■ **What Is Taken for Granted.**

As a rule, your employer will not give you the address or even the full name of the person that will be sent the letter. The employer will probably say, "This goes to Mrs. Adams," and dictate the letter, omitting the salutation and complimentary closing. This does not mean that your boss wishes these essentials omitted; the assumption is that you do not need to be told.

CHAPTER 8

Insurance

"I'm sure we will sleep a lot easier now," say Mr. and Mrs. J. Smith, "knowing that our possessions are adequately insured." It is comforting to them, as it is to most people, to know that if they lost something valuable, they would be reimbursed by their insurance company. That is the basic purpose of insurance—to protect against financial loss.

When private individuals or businesses buy insurance, they are not buying a piece of merchandise or even a service that they can use right away. They are simply buying a promise that the insurance company will pay them in the future if they suffer a loss. In other words, the people who buy insurance are buying protection. The companies that sell this protection are such an important part of the business scene that today they provide jobs for hundreds of thousands of workers.

Customers for insurance pay an amount that is called a premium for the protection they are buying. They receive a written contract called a policy that spells out exactly what the insurance company promises to do.

The insurance company employs people called actuaries who very carefully figure out what the chances for loss are in a given area for a given amount of time. Then the company sets each premium so that when all the premiums of all its customers are pooled, the insurance company will not only have enough money to pay for the losses that do occur but will also have enough money to cover the expenses of running the business and to make a profit.

There are insurance policies that cover every imaginable kind of loss that anyone could experience, from insurance that farmers can buy in case hail ruins their crops to insurance that beauty-shop owners can buy in case one of the employees seriously damages a customer's hair.

Several basic types of insurance are life insurance, property insurance, liability insurance, and health insurance. People buy life insurance to provide for their families when they die. People buy property insurance to protect things they own such as houses, cars, furniture, and jewelry. People buy liability insurance to protect themselves in case they are responsible for injuring someone or damaging another person's property. The most common form of liability insurance is the kind that covers the owner of a car for the injury to people or damage to their property in case of an accident. People buy health insurance to pay hospital and doctor bills if they become ill.

Insurance companies employ many people in various types of work. They employ agents and sales representatives who run local offices and actually sell insurance policies. They employ many highly trained specialists, including actuaries, financial analysts, lawyers, doctors, public relations and advertising experts, and personnel workers. About half the people employed by insurance companies are office workers, including secretaries, stenographers, typists, clerks, and accountants.

Helping people to protect themselves against possible losses can be a very satisfying career. The letters in this chapter are related to the field of insurance.

Building Phrasing Skill

311 Phrase Builder

Can you read the following phrases in 40 seconds?

About

1

Out of

2

Sure

3

Miscellaneous

4

1. *About the, about this, about that, about that time, about which, about these, about you, about this matter, about them.*
2. *Out of the, out of date, out of the question, out of that, out of stock, out of town, out of these, out of this, out of them.*
3. *To be sure, I am sure, we are sure, you are sure, you may be sure, I will be sure, feel sure.*
4. *To know, to make, to do, to us, let us, let us have, of course, of course it is, your order, you ordered.*

312 Warmup Phrase Letter

The following letter contains 28 useful phrases. How fast can you read it? Write it?

[130]

Building Transcription Skills

313 Business Vocabulary Builder

conflicting Being in opposition.

catastrophes Tragic events.

underwriters Insurers; guarantors.

● Reading and Writing Practice

314

ad·di·tion

intro

when

intro

ser

med·i·cal

intro

safe·guard
fam·i·ly's

par

de·vised

ad·e·quate

ser

Transcribe:
5 percent

conj

par

[199]

315

ma·jor

if

stud·ies

as

Transcribe:
50 percent

conj

intro

sur·vive

in·ter·rup·tion

nonr

tai·lored

and o

well-trained
hyphenated before noun

[147]

316

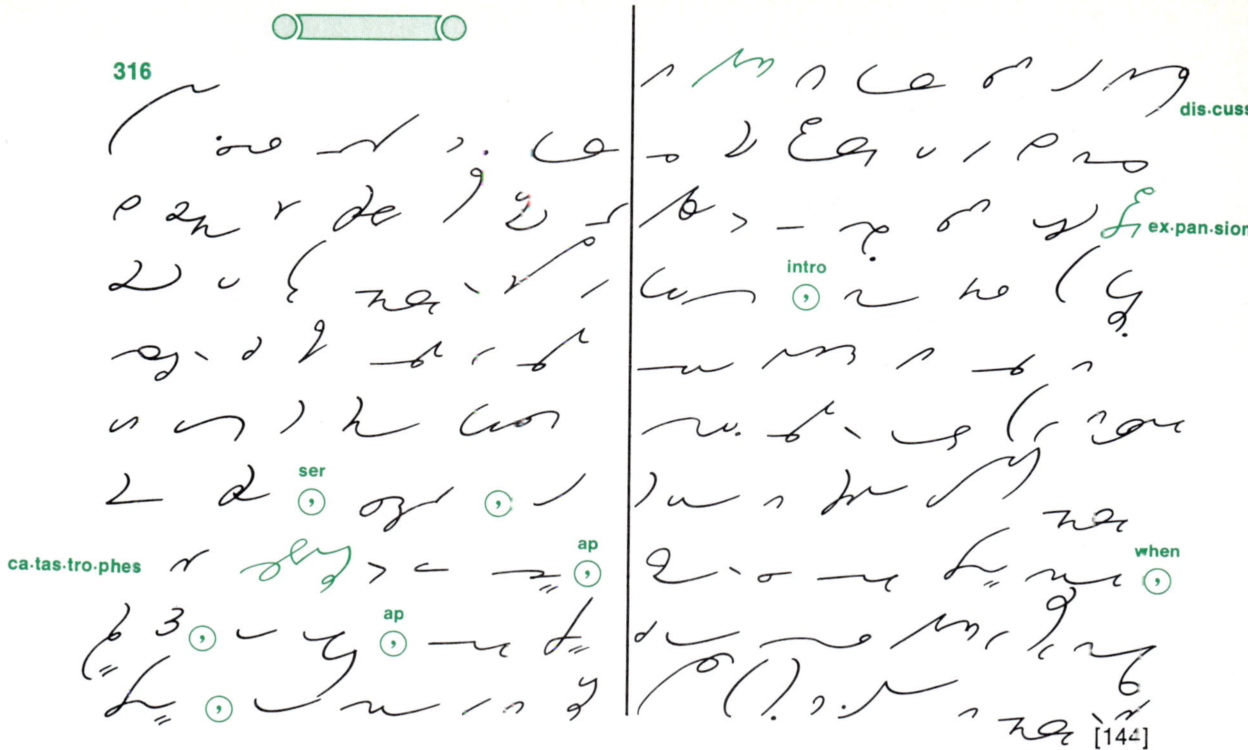

317 Transcription Quiz For you to supply: 3 commas—1 comma parenthetical, 1 comma *if* clause, 1 comma *and* omitted; 1 semicolon no conjunction; 2 missing words.

[104]

Warmup Your warmup letter is on page 201. Warm up on the sentence in the first paragraph, breaking the sentences into two or three convenient parts. Write each part of the sentence three or four times, trying to write faster with each repetition. After you have practiced the sentence in this way, write the entire sentence once in your best shorthand for control.

Developing Word-Building Power

318 Brief-Form Chart

Can you read the brief forms and derivatives in this chart in 30 seconds or less?

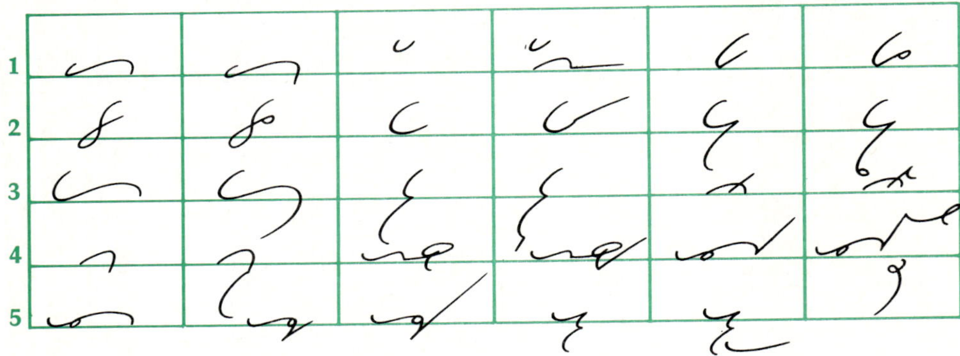

1. *Organize, organization, over, overcome, part, partly.*
2. *Particular, particularly, present, presented, probable, probably.*
3. *Progress, progressive, public, publish-publication, quantity, quantities.*
4. *Question, questionable, recognize, recognized, regard, regardless.*
5. *Regular, request, requested, responsible, responsibility, several.*

319 Geographical Expressions

1

2

1. *Juneau, Honolulu, St. Louis, Kansas City, Jefferson City.*
2. *Alaska, Hawaii, Missouri, Wyoming, America, American.*

Building Transcription Skills

320 SIMILAR-WORDS DRILL scene, seen

scene A setting; a place.

It was a beautiful scene.

seen Past participle of *see.*

I have seen *the report.*

321 Business Vocabulary Builder

fringe benefit An employment benefit, such as retirement, granted by an employer that involves a money cost without affecting basic wage rates.

divest To rid; to free.

fatal Deadly; causing death.

Reading and Writing Practice

322 Brief-Form Letter

Can you read the following letter in 1¼ minutes? Write it in 2 minutes?

if

to·day's

par

seen

well-trained hyphenated before noun

ṅc

when

safe·guard

conj

[184]

323

ap

intro

geo

Route

par

fa·tal

intro

and o

scene

intro

grate·ful

Worth's

[164]

324

par

em·ploy·ees

when

nonr

com·pa·nies

conj

ad·van·tages

[145]

di·vest

intro

nonr

Transcribe: 1116 Fifth Avenue

geo

par

en·trust·ing

[144]

325

as

326

intro
cig·a·rettes if
pre·mi·um
if

[100]

327

de·scribes
al·ready
intro

[60]

328 Transcription Quiz For you to supply: 7 commas—1 comma conjunction, 1 comma *if* clause, 2 commas parenthetical, 1 comma apposition, 2 commas series; 2 missing words.

[128]

Warmup For your warmup today, practice the sentence in the second paragraph of the letter on page 201. Break the sentence into as many parts as you feel desirable.

Developing Word-Building Power

329 Word Families

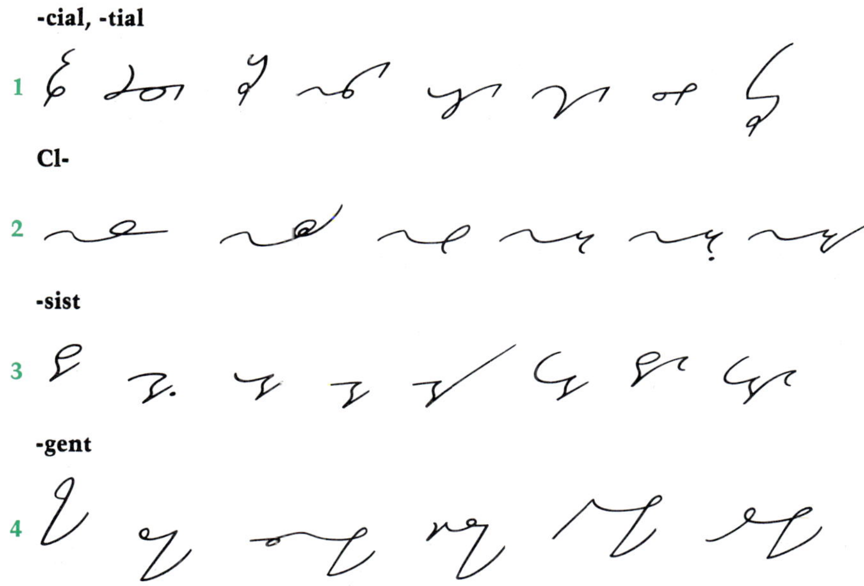

1. *Special, financial, official, credential, residential, confidential, initial, beneficial.*
2. *Claim, client, class, close, closing, closed.*
3. *Assist, consisting, resist, insist, insisted, persist, assistance, persistence.*
4. *Agent, urgent, negligent, stringent, diligent, intelligent.*

Building Transcription Skills

330 SPELLING FAMILIES -cal, -cle Whenever you transcribe a word ending with the sound *kle,* be careful; it may be spelled *cal* or *cle*. Here are examples of each ending.

Words Ending in -cal

pe·ri·od·i·cal	**ver·ti·cal**	**chem·i·cal**
crit·i·cal	**po·lit·i·cal**	**med·i·cal**
log·i·cal	**mu·si·cal**	**sur·gi·cal**

Words Ending in -cle

ar·ti·cle	**mir·a·cle**	**bi·cy·cle**
par·ti·cle	**spec·ta·cle**	**ve·hi·cle**

---

331 Business Vocabulary Builder

appraise Evaluate the worth of.

probe Investigate thoroughly.

negligent Careless; neglectful.

medicare A government program of medical care for the aged.

Reading and Writing Practice

332

whole·sale

ser

rise

bank·rupt·cy

crit·i·cal

par

when

bank·rupt

ap

nc

intro

and o

well-trained *hyphenated before noun*

re·ceiv·able

[144]

[146]

555-1818

333

com·pa·nies

par

loss-pre·ven·tion *hyphenated before noun*

intro

ap·praise

conj

ex·plo·sions

ser

334

ser

65

med·i·cal

sur·gi·cal

se·nior

nonr

if

ris·ing

par

[138]

335

crit·i·cal·ly

ve·hi·cle

bi·cy·cle

if

de·signed

de·scribed

nonr

intro

[115]

336

par

world's

tai·lor

com·pa·ny's

choose

yours [117]

337

fam·i·ly's

ser

pleas·ant

conj

if

(8) 411-1161 [140]

338 **Transcription Quiz** For you to supply: 4 commas—1 comma *as* clause, 1 comma introductory, 2 commas parenthetical; 2 missing words.

11811

[110]

LESSON 39

Warmup Today, warm up on the sentences in the third paragraph of the phrase letter on page 201. Before beginning, turn to page 179 and reread the instructions given there for warming up.

Developing Word-Building Power

339 Word Beginnings and Endings

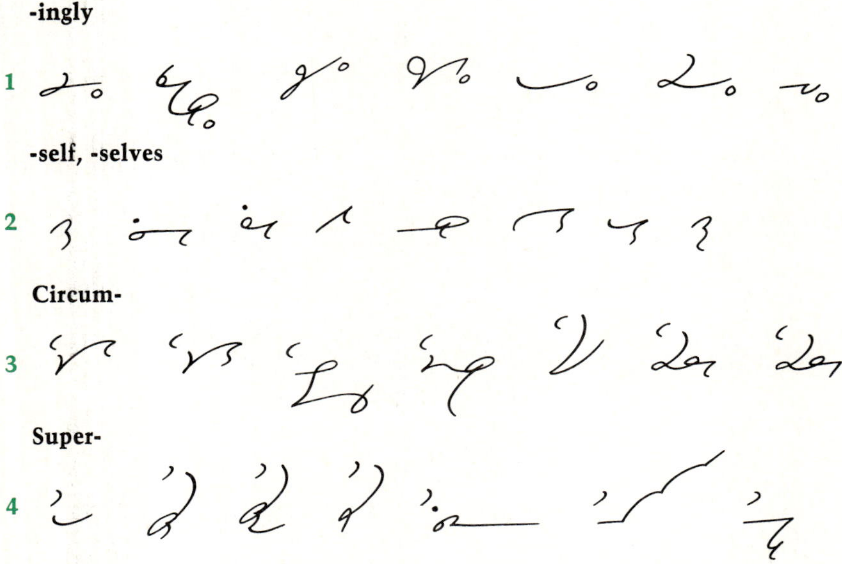

-ingly

-self, -selves

Circum-

Super-

1. *Seemingly, surprisingly, exceedingly, astonishingly, willingly, feelingly, knowingly.*
2. *Yourself, himself, herself, itself, myself, themselves, ourselves, yourselves.*
3. *Circumstance, circumstances, circumnavigate, circumscribe, circumvent, circumference, circumferential.*
4. *Superior, supervise, supervisor, supervision, superhuman, superintendent, superimpose.*

Building Transcription Skills

340 GRAMMAR CHECKUP than, as

You can determine which pronoun to use after *than* or *as* by mentally adding the words that make a complete phrase or clause.

I prefer to buy from you rather than him. *(rather than* buy from him*)*

Ann can do the work as easily as I. *(*can do the work*)*

No one knows your qualifications better than I. *(better than* I know your qualifications*)*

---

341 Business Vocabulary Builder

heirs Those who inherit property.

lapse To become void or ineffective.

fund *(verb)* To finance.

deceased Dead.

Reading and Writing Practice

342

if

loss

part·ner's heirs

if

than

conj

par

de·ceased

when

[149]

343

dil·i·gent·ly

conj

ad·just

if

guar·an·teed

conj

if

ap

years'

10

than

[210]

344

ser

sur·vive

in·ter·rup·tion

sta·bil·i·ty

and o

if

555-1181

[127]

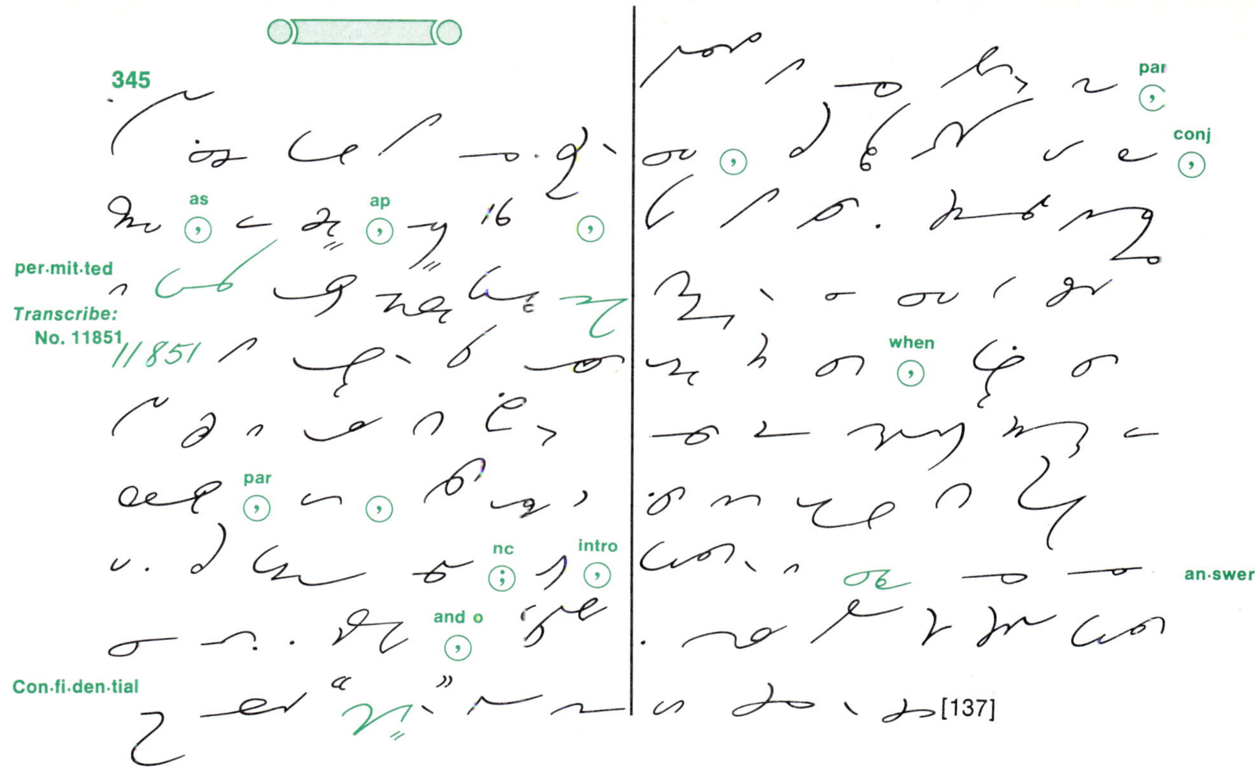

346 Transcription Quiz For you to supply: 7 commas—2 commas parenthetical, 2 commas nonrestrictive, 1 comma conjunction, 2 commas introductory; 2 missing words.

[133]

Warmup For the last time you will use the letter on page 201 for your warmup. Warm up in the same way as you did in the preceding lessons of this chapter.

Developing Word-Building Power

347 Shorthand Vocabulary Builder

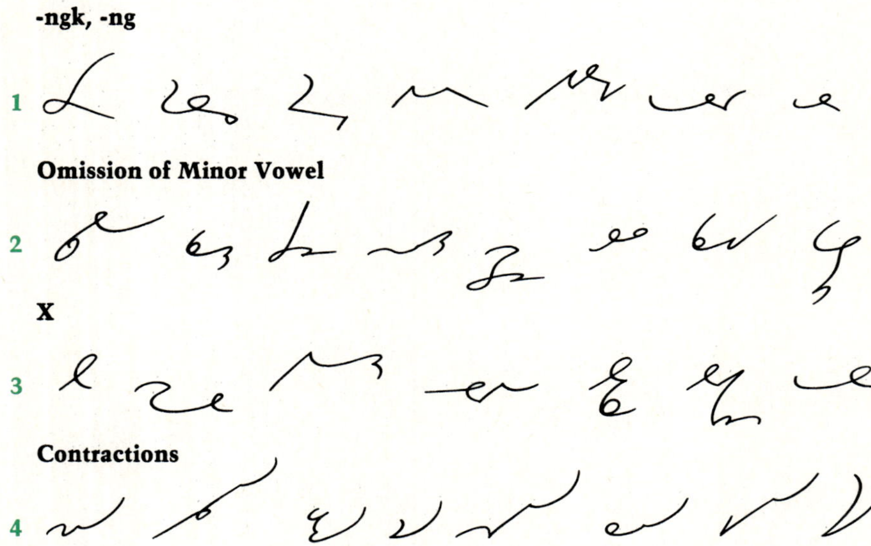

1. *Bank, frankly, function, trunk, distinguished, length, ring.*
2. *Ideal, serious, genuine, courteous, companion, theory, period, previous.*
3. *Tax, complex, deluxe, mixture, taxpayer, textbook, lax.*
4. *Won't, didn't, wasn't, isn't, couldn't, weren't, shouldn't, haven't.*

Building Transcription Skills

348 Business Vocabulary Builder

complex Complicated.

term life insurance Insurance on a person's life for a specific length of time.

deluxe Luxurious; elegant.

chore Hard or disagreeable job.

Reading and Writing Practice

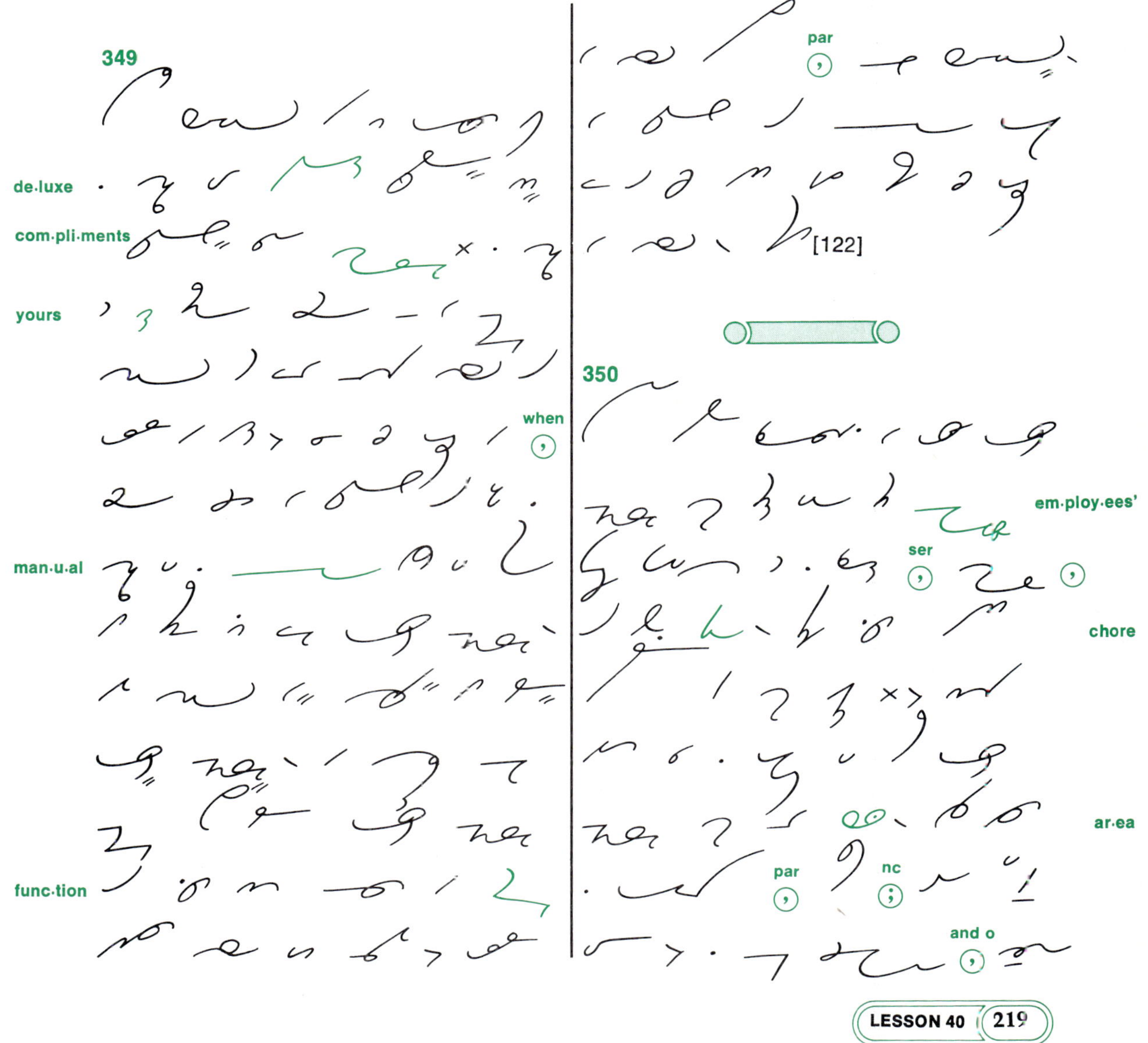

nonr

choos·ing

ser

prof·it-shar·ing
hyphenated before noun

conj

knowl·edge

if

cou·pon

[168]

351

ap

daugh·ter

intro

wed·ding

years'

pre·mi·ums

intro

too

lapse

conj

praise

son-in-law [181]

[140]

352

di·rec·tors

intro

as

Transcribe: January 2, 1975,

ap

conj

ap

com·pli·men·ta·ry

par

if

353

intro

64-page hyphenated before noun

yours

and o

easy-to-un·der-stand *hyphenated before noun*

intro

nc

intro

conj

[104]

The Secretary on the Job

354 WHY MILDRED ANDERSON LOST HER JOB

5:30

Mildred felt

The employer

Perhaps

She made

[350]

Transcription on the Typewriter

If you have practiced taking dictation regularly and have kept up with your assignments on a daily basis, your skill has probably grown to the point that you are ready to transcribe letters on the typewriter.

Making the transition from transcribing in longhand to transcribing on the typewriter can be easy and simple if you remember a few basic things. Do not expect your first attempt to transcribe on the typewriter to produce mailable letters. Your first few tries will probably be typing easy, familiar letters from the shorthand plates in your textbook. At this stage, you should pay little attention to letter form, typing style, or typographical errors. The main thing is simply to type all of the material in the letter.

When you can transcribe the notes in your textbook easily and quickly on your typewriter, your teacher will probably introduce transcription from your homework notes or from material dictated in class.

As your skill develops further, your teacher will likely add the other elements of transcription one at a time—typing in letter form, correcting errors, producing mailable copy, and so on.

It is very important in transcription to keep your work station properly organized. You should select a place to keep your textbook, your typewriter paper, your pen, and any other supplies which you will need. If these things are always in the same place, you will be able to find them easily.

When you are taking dictation for transcription, it is a good idea to date each page of your notebook in the bottom right corner. In this way, you will be able to find your shorthand notes quickly if you should need them for future reference. After you have transcribed a letter, you should draw a diagonal line through the notes. This will tell you at a glance that you have finished transcribing that particular letter.

As you take dictation for transcription, keep in mind that producing mailable letters is your final goal, but that transcription skill grows slowly—a little every day. Do not demand perfection of yourself in the early stages, but do demand that your work improve slightly each day. By the end of the term, you should be able to produce business letters from your own shorthand notes that a business executive would be happy to sign!

CHAPTER

Publishing

Every time you read a book, magazine, or newspaper, you are using a product of the publishing industry—a very diverse and exciting business. Although periodical publishing differs somewhat from book publishing, similar steps are followed to produce a book or a magazine. The editorial staff is responsible for coordinating the activities of writers, illustrators, photographers, designers, typesetters, printers, and many others to produce the final product.

Have you ever wondered how the printed material you read every day comes into being? A new publication goes through a number of basic steps before it can be made available to the public. In order to show you how the process works, we will use a book for an example. Keep in mind that the process, with a few alterations, is similar for almost all types of printed matter.

First, of course, a book must be written. An author develops the idea for a book on paper and submits this manuscript—usually typewritten—to a publisher with the hope that the publisher will accept it. If the publisher likes it and thinks the public will too, a contract is drawn up specifying the royalties—the amount of money per copy sold that the author will receive. The more copies sold, the more money both the author and publisher will make.

The manuscript is then assigned to an editor who is responsible for making sure that all the author's facts are accurate and for checking to see that the spelling, punctuation, and grammar are correct.

Once the editing is completed, the manuscript goes to a book designer who works closely with the editor in deciding what typeface will be used, how the book will be illustrated—photographs, drawings, charts, and so on—and finally what the cover will be. The designer is responsible for how the book will look.

Next, the manuscript goes to the compositor, who sets it in type. The compositor first sends galleys to the publisher. They are proofread by both the editor and author. The corrected galleys are returned to the compositor, who makes the changes and sends them back to the editor for checking. Once approved by the publisher, the typeset material is arranged into pages with illustrations in place and is ready to go to the printer to be printed and bound.

A secretary in the publishing field is involved in all these phases. As a book proceeds from raw manuscript through the final phases of production, the secretary may be involved in proofreading, checking facts and figures, reminding authors that their corrections are due, inserting corrections into a master set of galleys, and generally being an invaluable coordinator of many details. As in so many other areas, teamwork is vital to the production of a book or a magazine, and the secretary is an important member of the team.

This chapter provides reading and dictation material that is directly related to publishing activities. These letters should give you a taste of the stimulating, creative atmosphere that characterizes this very exciting industry.

AV GUIDE

American Home

ENCOUNTER

ARCHERY WORLD

Design

Business W

FLYING

Sunset

HIGH FIDELITY

Saturday Review

Radio-Electr

TENNIS

HIGH FIDELITY

ANALYTICAL CHEMISTRY

Ocea

Newsweek

JUSTICE ON TRIAL

Building Phrasing Skill

355 Phrase Builder

Reading goal: 50 seconds.

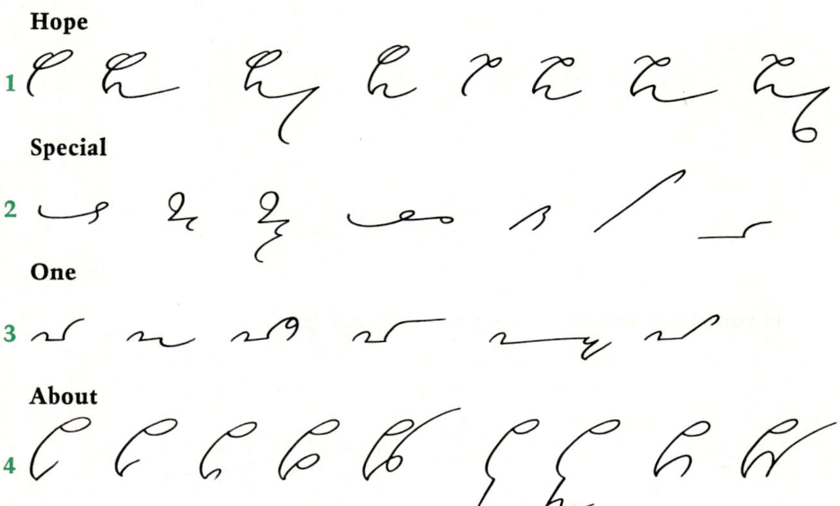

1. *I hope, I hope you will, I hope you will be, I hope you are, we hope, we hope you are, we hope you will, we hope you will be able.*
2. *Let us, as soon as, as soon as possible, let me, to us, to do, more than.*
3. *One of the, one of our, one of these, one of them, one of the most, one or two.*
4. *About it, about the, about your, about that, about that time, about which, about which you are, about this, about this time.*

356 Warmup Phrase Letter

The following 101-word letter contains 31 phrases. How fast can you read it? Copy it?

[101]

Building Transcription Skills

357 TYPING STYLE STUDY short letters In this lesson you will learn how to place short letters of approximately 100 words by judgment. Following you will see a short letter as it was written in shorthand and transcribed. The transcript was typed on a machine that had elite (small) type.

The shorthand required a little more than half a column in the notebook. When a letter takes about half a column in your notebook, you should do these things:

- **1** Set your typewriter for a 2-inch left margin and a 2-inch right margin.
- **2** Insert a sheet of letterhead paper.
- **3** Type the date on the third line below the last line of the printed letterhead, beginning at the horizontal center of the page.
- **4** Begin the address at the left margin about 10 lines below the date. (If you use a machine with pica (large) type, begin 8 lines below the date.)

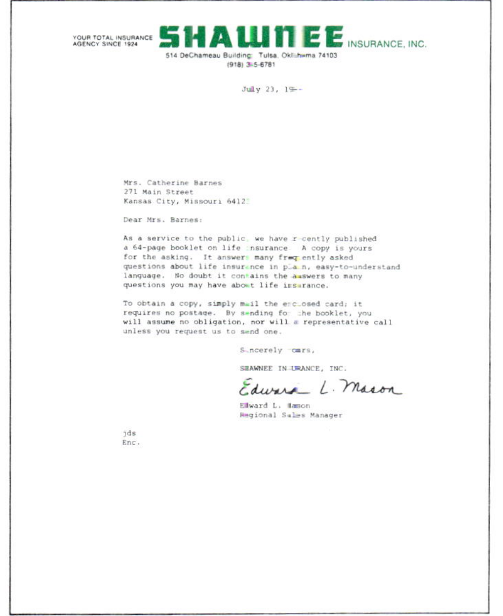

YOUR TOTAL INSURANCE AGENCY SINCE 1924 **SHAWNEE** INSURANCE, INC.
514 DeChameau Building Tulsa, Oklahoma 74103
(918) 3[illegible]5-6781

July 23, 19--

Mrs. Catherine Barnes
271 Main Street
Kansas City, Missouri 6412[illegible]

Dear Mrs. Barnes:

As a service to the public, we have recently published a 64-page booklet on life insurance. A copy is yours for the asking. It answers many frequently asked questions about life insurance in plain, easy-to-understand language. No doubt it contains the answers to many questions you may have about life insurance.

To obtain a copy, simply mail the enclosed card; it requires no postage. By sending for the booklet, you will assume no obligation, nor will a representative call unless you request us to send one.

Sincerely yours,

SHAWNEE INSURANCE, INC.

Edward L. Mason

Edward L. Mason
Regional Sales Manager

jds
Enc.

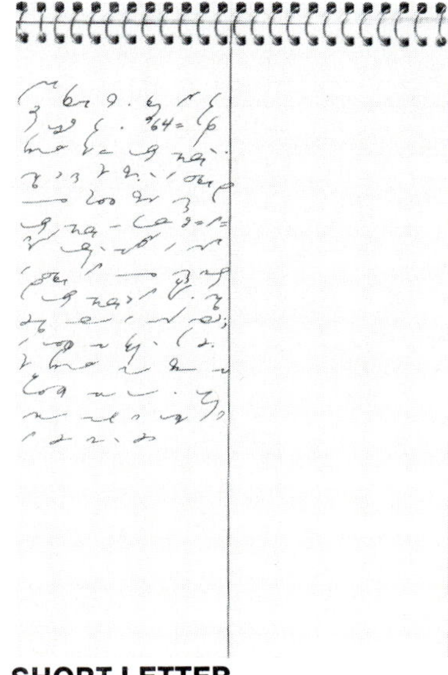

SHORT LETTER

358 Business Vocabulary Builder

era A particular or special period of time.

ample Sufficient.

perturbed Disturbed; upset.

Reading and Writing Practice

359

be·lieve

es·pe·cial·ly

era

ap

ap

and o

ap

if

post·age-paid
hyphenated before noun

[137]

360

as

ap

conj

am·ple

when

par

ad·di·tion·al

cr

[101]

361

ap

conj

fur·ther

if

nc

cus·tom·ers'

[77]

362

ap

ba·sis

conj

intro

per·turbed

intro

conj

[104]

363

ap

re·ceiv·ing

par

par

post·al

if

pa·tience [118]

364

ap

Chil·dren's

cr

[74]

365 Transcription Quiz For you to supply: 7 commas—2 commas apposition, 2 commas series, 1 comma conjunction, 2 commas parenthetical; 1 semicolon, no conjunction; 2 missing words.

[115]

Warmup Your warmup letter today is on page 228. Continue to follow the warmup plan that you used in Chapter 7, breaking each sentence into parts, writing each part several times as rapidly as possible, and finally writing the complete sentence. Use the first paragraph today.

Developing Word-Building Power

366 Brief-Form Chart

Reading goal: 25 seconds.

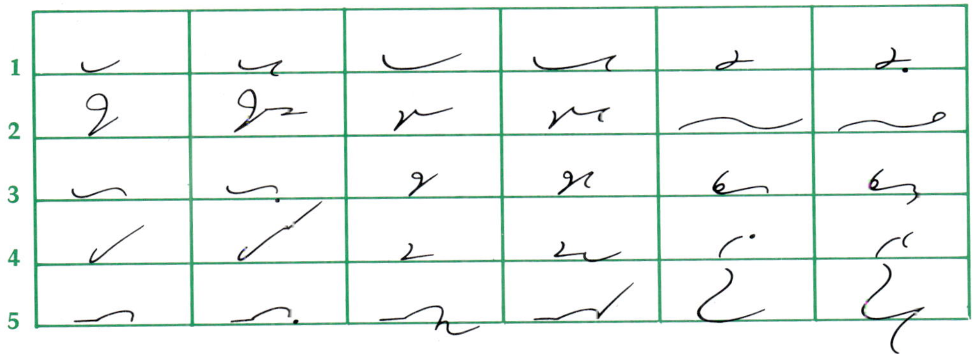

1. *Are-our-hour, hours, will-well, wills, send, sending.*
2. *After, afternoon, street, streets, glad, gladly.*
3. *Work, working, yesterday, yesterdays, circular, circulars.*
4. *Order, ordered, soon, sooner, thank, thanks.*
5. *Enclose, enclosing, enclosure, enclosed, value, valuable.*

367 Geographical Expressions

1

2

1. *Pittsburgh, Trenton, Camden, Paterson, Springfield, Harrisburg.*
2. *New Jersey, California, Pennsylvania, New York, Texas, United States, England, English.*

Building Transcription Skills

368 COMMON PREFIXES con-

con- together; with.

confer Talk with.

consented Agreed with.

conventional That which agrees with accepted standards.

convene Come together.

convention Meeting of people together.

---

369 Business Vocabulary Builder

emeritus Retired from office or position.

psychology The science of behavior.

detailed *(adjective)* Thorough; complete.

Reading and Writing Practice

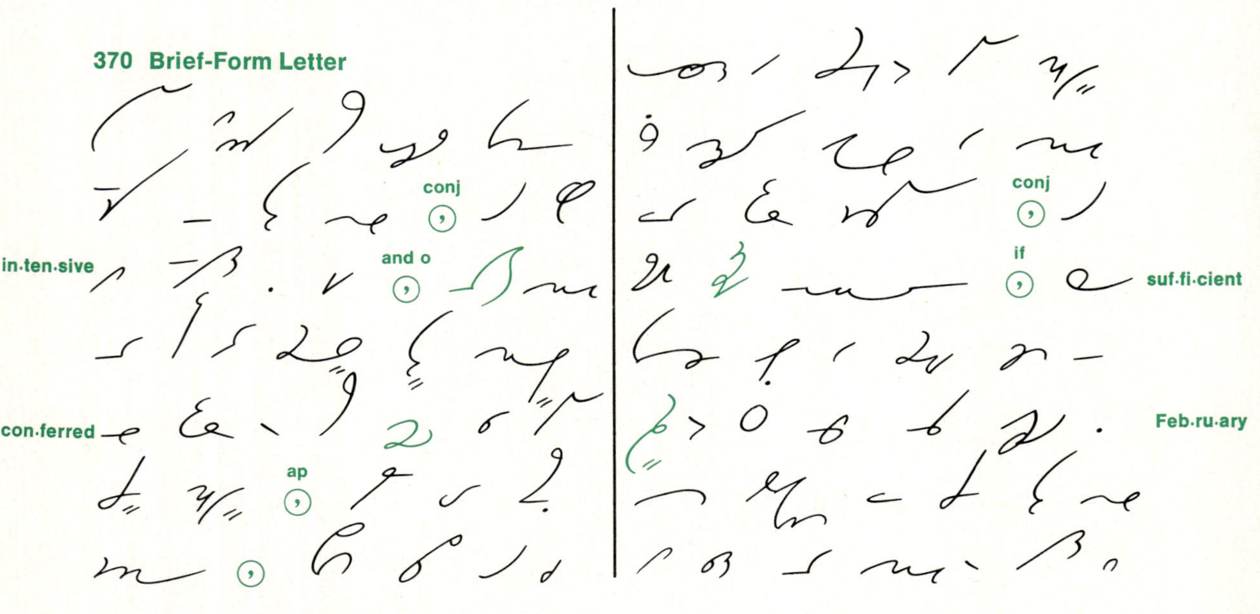

if

geo

ap

[148]

371

be·lieve

ap

as·so·ci·ate

ap

nc

psy·chol·o·gy

par

when

[207]

372

edi·tion

nonr

intro

intrc

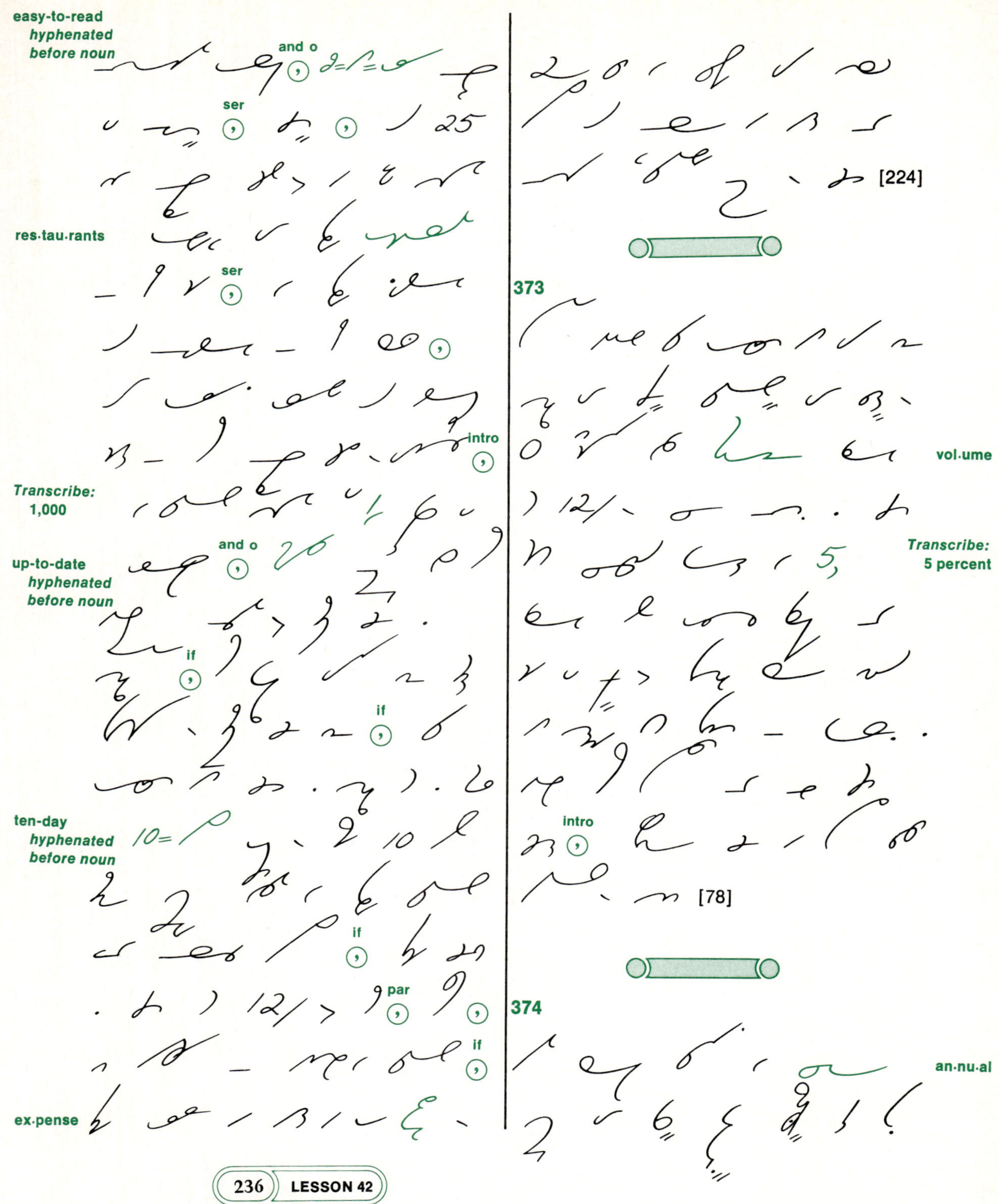
easy-to-read
hyphenated
before noun
and o
ser
ser
res·tau·rants
intro
Transcribe:
1,000
up-to-date
hyphenated
before noun
and o
if
if
ten-day
hyphenated
before noun
if
par
if
ex·pense
[224]
373
vol·ume
Transcribe:
5 percent
intro
[78]
374
an·nu·al

conj

ser

ap ser

cr

intro

[77]

375

geo

ser ap

ser

ap

Transcribe:
$20
ho·tel's

as

[83]

376 Transcription Quiz For you to supply: 6 commas—2 commas apposition, 2 commas conjunction, 2 commas *if* clause; 2 missing words.

[127]

Warmup Your warmup letter today is on page 228. Warm up on the sentence in the second paragraph, breaking it into convenient groups.

Developing Word-Building Power

377 Word Families

-book

1

Pre-

2

-val, -vel

3

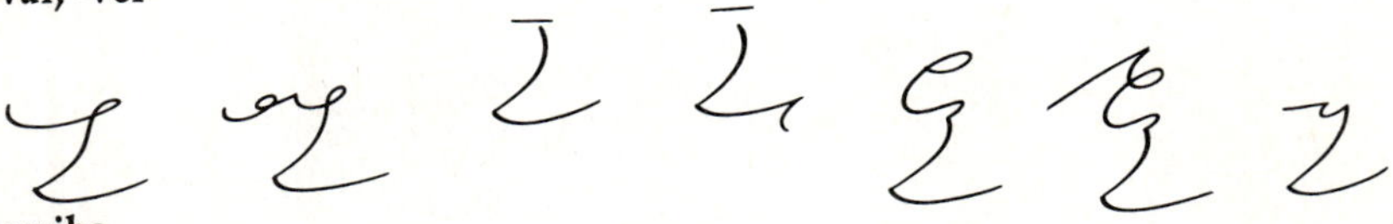

-scribe

4

1. *Book, textbook, handbook, workbook, notebook, yearbook.*
2. *Prepare, preliminary, prefer, preserve, predict, presume.*
3. *Level, retrieval, interval, intervals, approval, disapproval, novel.*
4. *Subscribe, subscribed, inscribe, prescribes, transcribe, describe, described.*

Building Transcription Skills

378 SPELLING FAMILIES des-, dis- People sometimes pronounce the word beginning *des* and *dis* alike in such words as *despite* and *discuss*. Therefore, pronunciation will not help to give you the correct spelling of words beginning with these similar sounds. Study the following list carefully and be sure that you can spell each of the words correctly.

Words Beginning With Des-

de·signed	**des·per·ate**	**de·sert**
de·scribed	**de·spon·dent**	**des·ti·tu·tion**
de·spite	**des·sert**	**de·stroy**
de·scribe	**de·sign**	**de·scrip·tion**

Words Beginning With Dis-

dis·ap·point·ed	**dis·charge**	**dis·pense**
dis·con·tin·ue	**dis·cour·age**	**dis·close**
dis·cern	**dis·cre·tion**	**dis·pel**
dis·cov·er	**dis·count**	**dis·par·age**

---

379 Business Vocabulary Builder

milestone An important event or turning point.

computer input and output The information put into a data processing system and the information produced by it.

retrieval The process of regaining information.

Reading and Writing Practice

380

pro·gram·ming

ap

func·tions

prin·ci·ples

re·triev·al

and o

al·most

conj

if

[117]

381

ap

lan·guages
sep·a·rate

intro

teach·er's

stu·dent's

and o

com·pre·hen·sive

if

[130]

382

cr

as

role

if

pre·lim·i·nary

[93]

383

chil·dren's

chose

conj

par

in·ter·me·di·ate

eight-year-old *hyphenated before noun*

cr

when

choose

[128]

384

de·scribed

par

dis·ap·point·ed

[91]

385

mile·stone

ac·cept·ing

well-in·formed *hyphenated before noun*

conj

ser

up-to-date *hyphenated before noun*

intro

[156]

386 Transcription Quiz For you to supply: 6 commas—2 commas introductory, 1 comma apposition, 1 comma conjunction, 2 commas parenthetical; 2 missing words.

[103]

Warmup Your warmup letter is on page 228. Practice the sentences in the usual manner.

Developing Word-Building Power

387 Word Beginnings and Endings

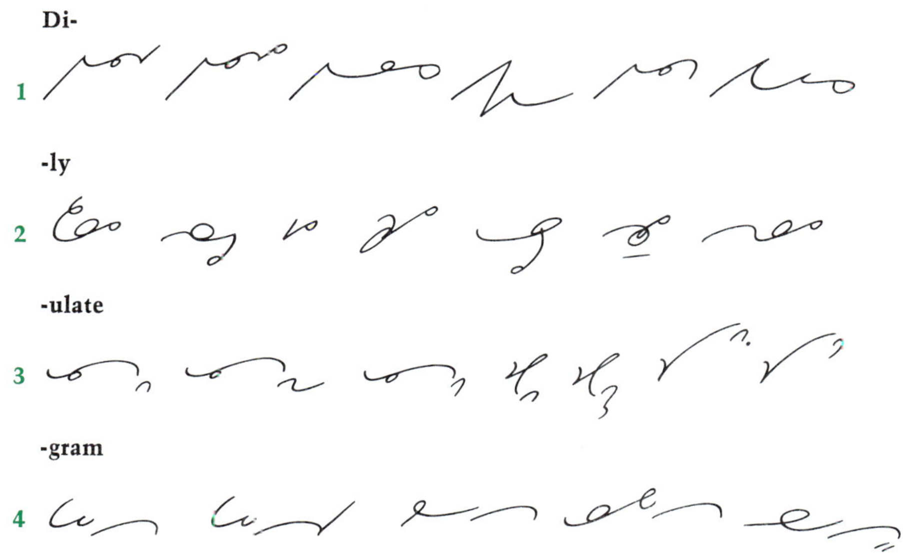

1. *Direct, directly, dilemma, digital, direction, diploma.*
2. *Separately, carefully, shortly, widely, lively, quietly, greatly.*
3. *Regulate, regulator, regulation, stipulate, stipulations, stimulating, stimulates.*
4. *Program, programmed, telegram, radiogram, Mailgram.*

Building Transcription Skills

388 SIMILAR-WORDS DRILL through, though, thought

through From one point to another.

I took a few minutes to look through *the proofs.*

though In spite of; however.

I hope, though, *you will speak on the subject of government regulations.*

thought Past tense of *think.*

I thought *of a new plan.*

---

389 Business Vocabulary Builder

exceptional Uncommon; superior.

catered Food service provided for.

precisely Exactly.

Reading and Writing Practice

390

weeks'

thought

if

pe·ri·od·i·cals

[130]

391

nc

precise·ly

conj

nonr

par

[79]

392

sep·a·rate·ly

pro·ce·dures

cr

intro

af·fect

as

nc

[106]

393

re·ceived

conj

through

conj

[57]

394

conj

ser

ap

ser

geo

ses·sion

par

though

par

ef·fect
gov·ern·men·tal

[121]

395

year's

ap

ser

au·di·ence

when

[100]

396

ap

cease

ar·eas

sore·ly

intro

par

116-1181 [132]

397 Transcription Quiz For you to supply: 8 commas—2 commas apposition, 2 commas series, 2 commas conjunction, 1 comma introductory, 1 comma *if* clause; 2 missing words.

3 4 5

150

[147]

Warmup As your final warmup for this chapter, make as many complete copies of the phrase letter on page 228 as time permits. Write as rapidly as you can, but be sure your notes are readable.

Developing Word-Building Power

398 Shorthand Vocabulary Builder

Ow

1

Ī

2

O

3

Ol

4

1. *Frowns, pounding, houses, ounce, brown, round, sounding, mount.*
2. *Style, writing, delighted, isolation, arrival, drive, mile.*
3. *Token, local, door, know, more, ignore, store.*
4. *All, small, fall, call, ball, tall.*

Building Transcription Skills

399 Business Vocabulary Builder

thought-provoking Causing concentration; interesting.

honorarium A payment or reward in recognition of services.

isolation State of being alone.

token Something that serves as a symbol.

Reading and Writing Practice

400

an·nu·al

if ,

la·pel

ser ,

screen ,

au·di·ence

intro ,

[108]

401

ap ,

ex·cel·lent

nonr ,

au·di·to·ri·um

ser ,

,

if ,

as ,

[130]

402

thought-pro·vok·ing *hyphenated before noun*

and o

intro

hon·o·rar·i·um

nc

par

[93]

403

ap

Tren·ton's

ap

15

an·ni·ver·sa·ry

conj

one-fam·i·ly *hyphenated before noun*

50,

Transcribe: 50,000

intro

to·ken

intro

15

[139]

404

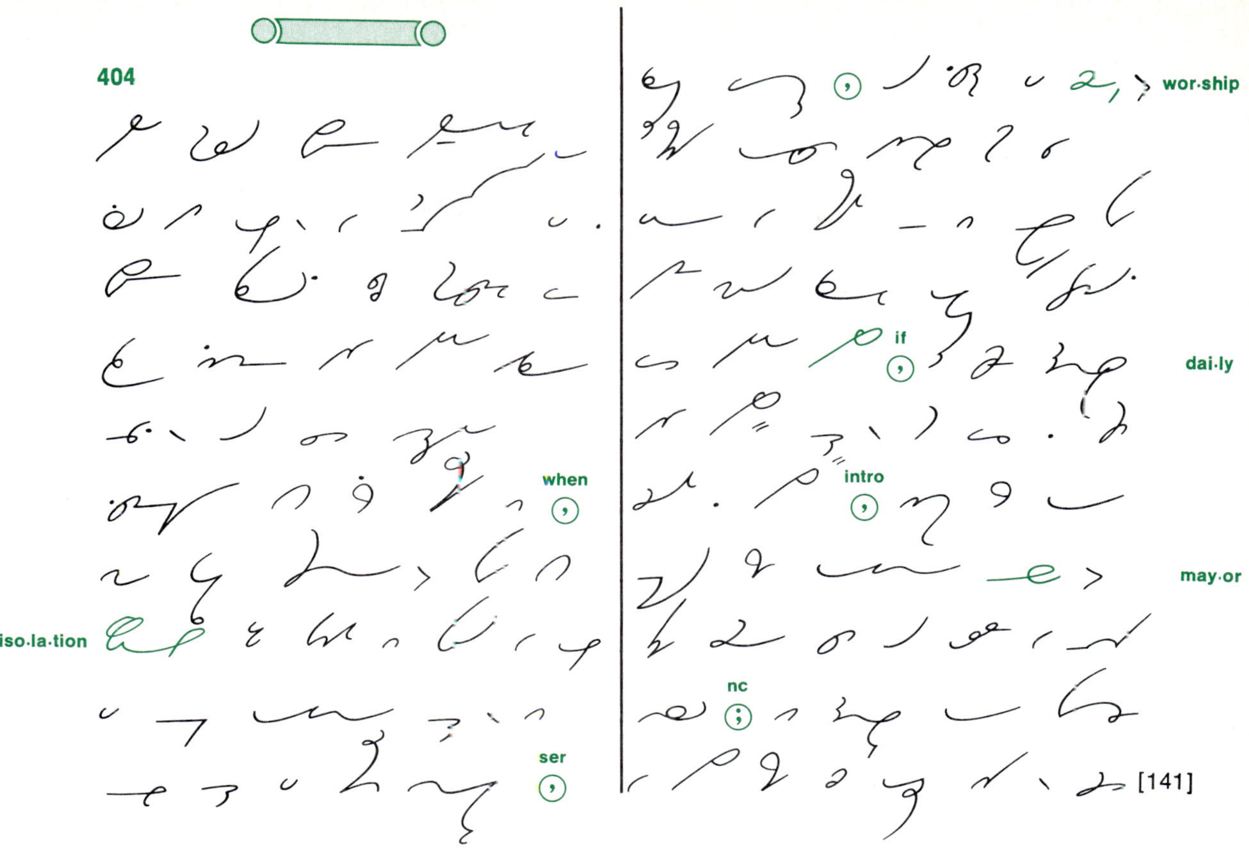

Don't be discouraged if your first job in business is not one of major importance; few people actually start at the top. However, a good worker will soon advance to a position of greater responsibility.

The Secretary on the Job

405 THE PERSON WHO NEVER MAKES A MISTAKE

There are

There are

4

10

Some letters

2.50

Your employer

15

[393]

CHAPTER

Government

If you were asked the question, "Who is the largest employer in the United States?" what would you answer? Well, believe it or not, the answer is the United States. That's right; the largest employer in the nation is the government. The federal government employs over 5 million people, and state and local governments employ nearly 14 million people, making a total of approximately 19 million people in government service occupations.

Who most often comes to mind when you think about government employees? Perhaps you might think of the President of the United States. Or you might think of senators, members of Congress, governors, and mayors. But obviously there are not 19 million people in these jobs. Elected officials are only a fraction of the people who work for federal, state, and local governments.

The largest single category of government employees is in the public education systems. All public school teachers, administrators, and other school workers are government employees; in most cases, they are employees of local governments. All the people in the U.S. Postal Service and the U.S. Armed Forces—the U.S. Army, Navy, Air Force, Marine Corps, and Coast Guard—are federal government employees.

Governments, like all large organizations, also depend on office work in order to function. They need office supervisors, clerical workers, accountants, bookkeepers, secretaries, stenographers, machine operators, and data processing specialists.

As an employer, the government probably offers the widest variety of fields in which to work of any business organization in the country. The range of opportunities for the civil service secretary is huge—and all secretaries who work for the government at any level come under the Civil Service Commission. Civil service secretaries may work in Washington, D.C., in almost any city across the country, or in any one of more than 300 government posts all over the world. Secretaries may be part of NASA, the Peace Corps, VISTA, the Bureau of Indian Affairs, the Department of State, the FBI, or the CIA; and the list goes on and on. In addition, there are many similar opportunities for secretaries in state and local governments.

To be hired as a civil service secretary, the applicant must pass a shorthand examination and a typing test. In addition, each applicant is also given a general aptitude test covering such areas as English, spelling, and current information; a test on alphabetizing; and another on math. An applicant who has passed these tests is eligible for employment.

There are so many different occupational fields in government that there is something to suit any special interest or preference you may have. And since government, by definition, is where influence resides and decisions are made affecting millions of people, it can be a very exciting area to work in. The letters in this chapter are related to government work.

Building Phrasing Skill

406 Phrase Builder

Reading goal: 50 seconds.

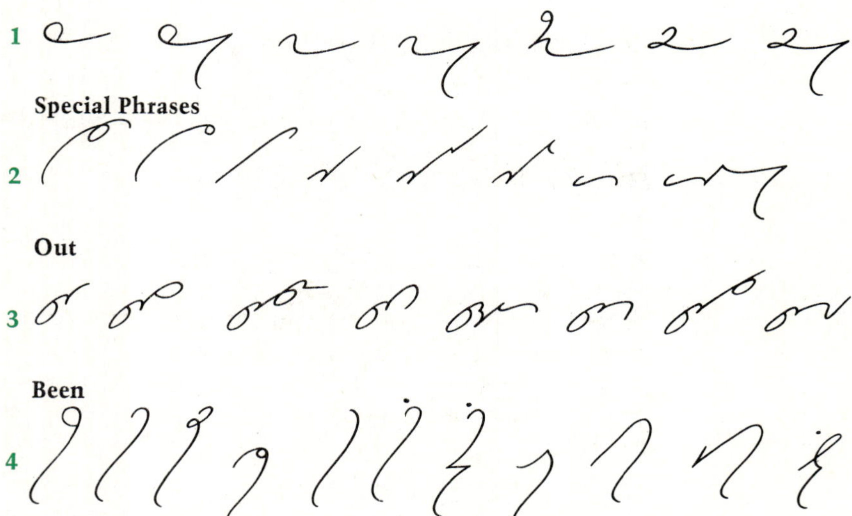

1. *I will, I will be, you will, you will be, if you will, we will, we will be.*
2. *To make, to me, to do, your order, you ordered, your orders, of course, of course it will be.*
3. *Out of the, out of that, out of town, out of this, out of stock, out of the question, out of date, out of court.*
4. *I have been, you have been, we have been, they have been, have been, who have been, who have not been, there have been, would have been, should have been, it has been.*

407 Warmup Phrase Letter

This is your warmup letter for Chapter 10. How fast can you read it? Copy it?

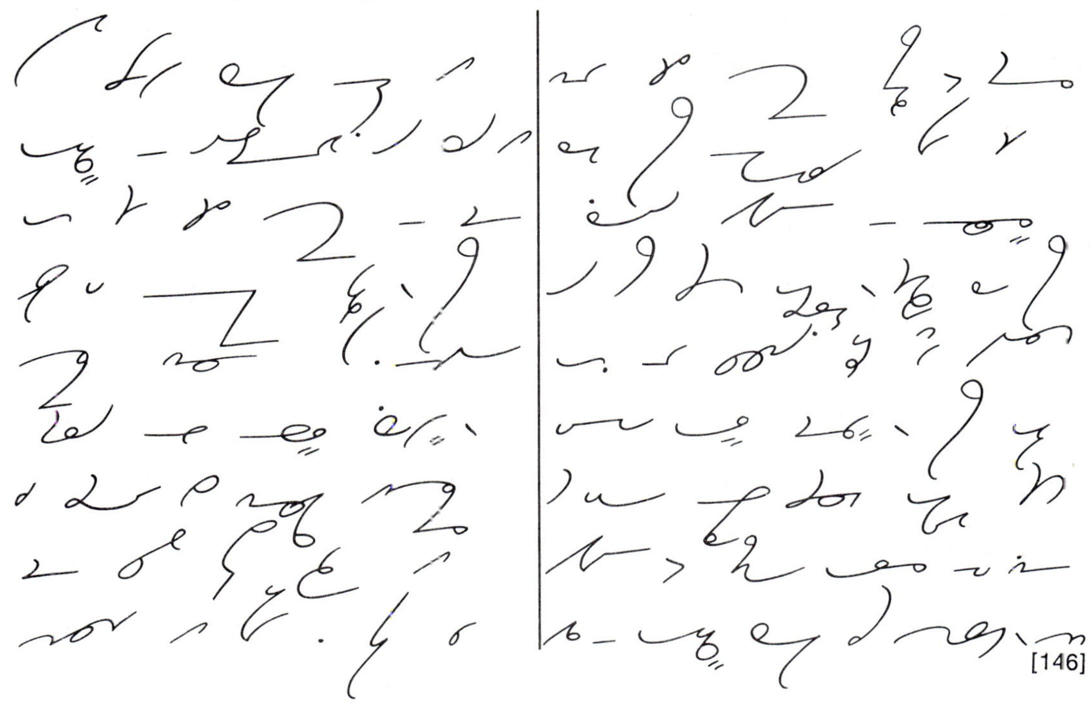

Building Transcription Skills

408 Business Vocabulary Builder

extinguish Cause to cease burning; put out.

intersection A place or area where two or more streets come together.

reprehensible Deserving censure.

confined Restricted to certain limits or borders.

Reading and Writing Practice

409

Coun.cil

intro

conj

and o

conj

fright·en·ing

won't

when

ser

par

cr

[114]

410

town's

ap

par

well-or·ga·nized
hyphenated before noun

[119]

411

intro

oc·curred

lo·cal

conj

scene

ex·tin·guish

nonr

intro

min·utes'

par

smoth·er

nc

[174]

412

dis·turb·ing

re·ferred

rep·re·hen·si·ble

par

[86]

413 **Transcription Quiz** For you to supply: 6 commas—1 comma *as* clause, 2 commas conjunction, 2 commas introductory, 1 comma *if* clause; 2 missing words.

[141]

Warmup Your warmup letter is on page 257. Copy as much of the letter as time permits. Write as rapidly as you can, but be sure that your shorthand is readable.

Developing Word-Building Power

414 Brief-Form Chart

Reading goal: 25 seconds.

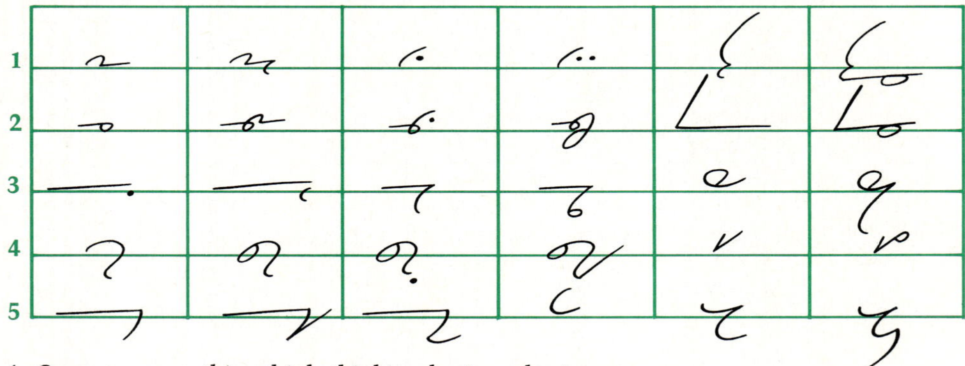

1. *One-won, once, thing-think, thinking, business, businessman.*
2. *Any, anyone, anything, anyway, gentlemen, gentleman.*
3. *Morning, mornings, important-importance, importantly, where, whereby.*
4. *Company, accompany, accompanying, accompanied, short, shortly.*
5. *Manufacture, manufactured, manufacturer, present, represent, representative.*

415 Geographical Expressions

1. *Spokane, Provo, Cleveland, Cincinnati, Lynn, Salem, Cambridge.*
2. *Washington, Utah, Hawaii, Illinois, Ohio, Massachusetts, Montana.*

Building Transcription Skills

416 SPELLING FAMILIES y changed to i in words

In the following words *y* is changed to *i* in the past tense and in the *s* form.

ap·ply	**ap·plied**	**ap·plies**
im·ply	**im·plied**	**im·plies**
com·ply	**com·plied**	**com·plies**
re·ply	**re·plied**	**re·plies**
re·ly	**re·lied**	**re·lies**

---

417 Business Vocabulary Builder

laudable Worthy of praise; commendable.

attribute *(verb)* To designate; to explain by stating a cause.

appropriation Money set aside by formal action for a specific use.

convey To communicate by statement or appearance.

Reading and Writing Practice

418 Brief-Form Letter

sen·a·tor

as

va·ri·ety

conj

intro

Salt Lake City

conj

ap

nonr

intro

dis·trict's

ser

par

[231]

de·vel·op
first-class
hyphenated before noun

nc

intro

[145]

419

ap·pro·pri·a·tion

intro

mod·el

intro

as

intro

420

geo

when

conj

and o

well-main·tained
hyphenated before noun

intro

ser

pol·lu·tion
traf·fic

par

and o

at·mo·sphere

par

may·or

par

your

[180]

421

geo

clean-up *hyphenated before noun*

intro

vol·un·tari·ly

intro

intro

en·dorse·ment

pub·lic·i·ty

if

[234]

422

laud·able

conj ,

geo ,

city-wide *hyphenated before noun*

par ,

rec·og·ni·tion

intro ,

[144]

423 Transcription Quiz For you to supply: 3 commas—1 comma *as* clause, 2 commas conjunction; 2 missing words.

[130]

Warmup Your warmup letter is on page 257. This time, write as many copies of the first paragraph as time permits. Strive to increase your speed with each writing.

Developing Word-Building Power

424 Word Families

-fund

1

-tment

2

-tional

3

-or

4

1. *Fund, refund, refunds, refunded, fundamental, fundamentally.*
2. *Investment, treatment, adjustment, statement, deportment, department.*
3. *National, nationally, vocational, conditional, traditional, traditionally.*
4. *Floor, nor, or, door, more, pour, soar, tore.*

Building Transcription Skills

425 COMMON PREFIXES re-

re- as a prefix, *re-* means *back* in many words.

refund To pay back funds.

repay To pay back.

reserve To hold back.

recline To lie back.

---

426 Business Vocabulary Builder

frugal Thrifty.

deficit Shortage.

resolve Determine.

Reading and Writing Practice

427

ea·ger·ly

intro

if

al·lows

fru·gal

nc

when

[78]

428

it's

if

conj

fair·ly

if

fig·ur·ing

and o

well-trained *hyphenated before noun*

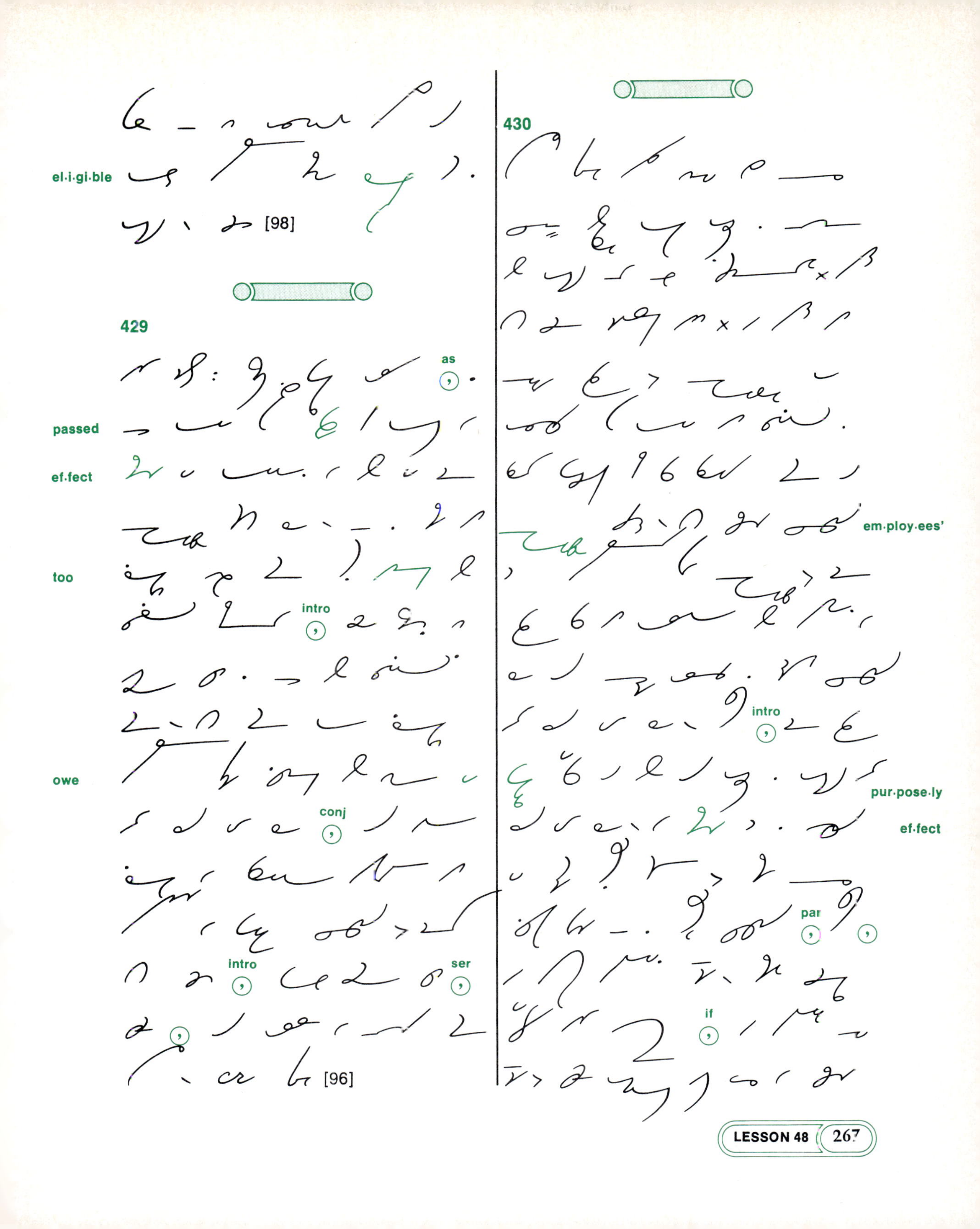

el·i·gi·ble

[98]

429

as

passed

ef·fect

too

intro

owe

conj

intro

ser

[96]

430

em·ploy·ees'

intro

pur·pose·ly

ef·fect

par

if

owe

[176]

431

if

too

de·plete

if

def·i·cit

if

de·pos·i·tor

intro

conj

[116]

432 **Transcription Quiz** For you to supply: 7 commas—1 comma *as* clause, 2 commas parenthetical, 1 comma introductory, 2 commas nonrestrictive, 1 comma apposition; 2 missing words.

[120]

Warmup Your warmup letter is on page 257. Make as many copies of the second paragraph as you can in the time available. If you write a poor outline, don't stop to cross it out and rewrite it; just keep on writing.

Developing Word-Building Power

433 Word Beginnings and Endings

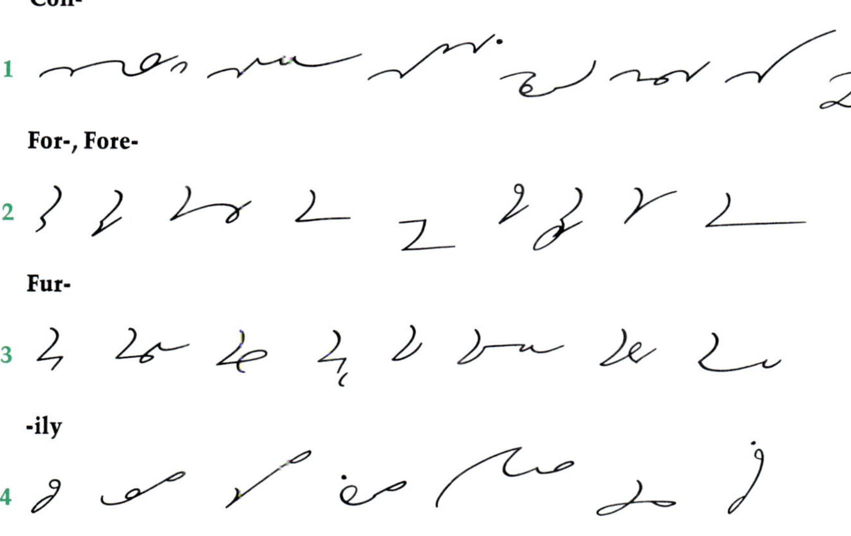

1. *Congratulate, control, conducting, concerned, connect, condemn, confer.*
2. *Force, forced, forget, form, inform, effort, foresight, fortune, foremen.*
3. *Furnish, furniture, furnace, furnishings, further, furthermore, furthest, furlough.*
4. *Easily, readily, steadily, heartily, temporarily, family, heavily.*

Building Transcription Skills

434 SIMILAR-WORDS DRILL site, sight, cite

site *(noun)* A location.

The site *for the new building is in the center of the city.*

sight *(noun)* Vision; view.

The first snow was a beautiful sight.

cite *(verb)* To quote; to refer to.

Did you cite *the source of the quotation?*

---

435 Business Vocabulary Builder

emissions Substances, such as smoke, discharged into the air.

revitalize To give new life or vigor to.

valuation The estimated or determined market value of a thing.

Reading and Writing Practice

436

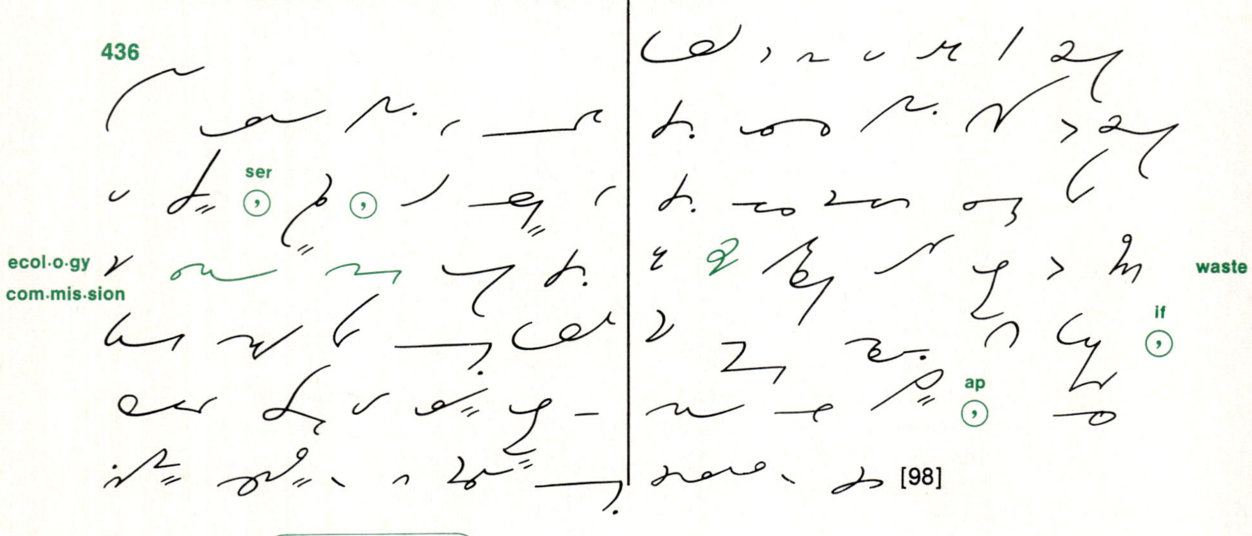

437

as

met

than

conj

ser

[114]

438

as

shop·ping

conj

sub·urbs

cite

conj

ar·ea's

site

when

re·vi·tal·ize

[160]

439

val·u·a·tion

Transcribe: 1515

as

Transcribe: 15 percent

than

if

[88]

intro

intro

intro

ad·di·tion

conj

intro

raised

nonr

Transcribe: $40,000

up-to-date hyphenated before noun

[105]

440

Transcribe: 1416

441 **Transcription Quiz** For you to supply: 3 commas—2 commas introductory, 1 comma *if* clause; 1 semicolon, no conjunction; 2 missing words.

[107]

Warmup Your warmup letter is on page 257. Write the third paragraph as rapidly as you can; then make a copy of the entire letter in your best shorthand.

Developing Word-Building Power

442 Shorthand Vocabulary Builder

Ah, Aw

1

Md

2

Omission of Short U

3

Tern, Term, Etc.

4

1. *Awareness, aware, away, awake, awoke, award, ahead, await.*
2. *Formed, reformed, named, seemed, blamed, deemed, dreamed.*
3. *Sum, summer, run, much, front, budget, luncheon.*
4. *Term, determined, turn, return, modern, southern, thermometer.*

Building Transcription Skills

443 Business Vocabulary Builder

restructure To change the organization of something.

reform *(verb)* To change for the better.

controversial Causing differing opinions.

Reading and Writing Practice

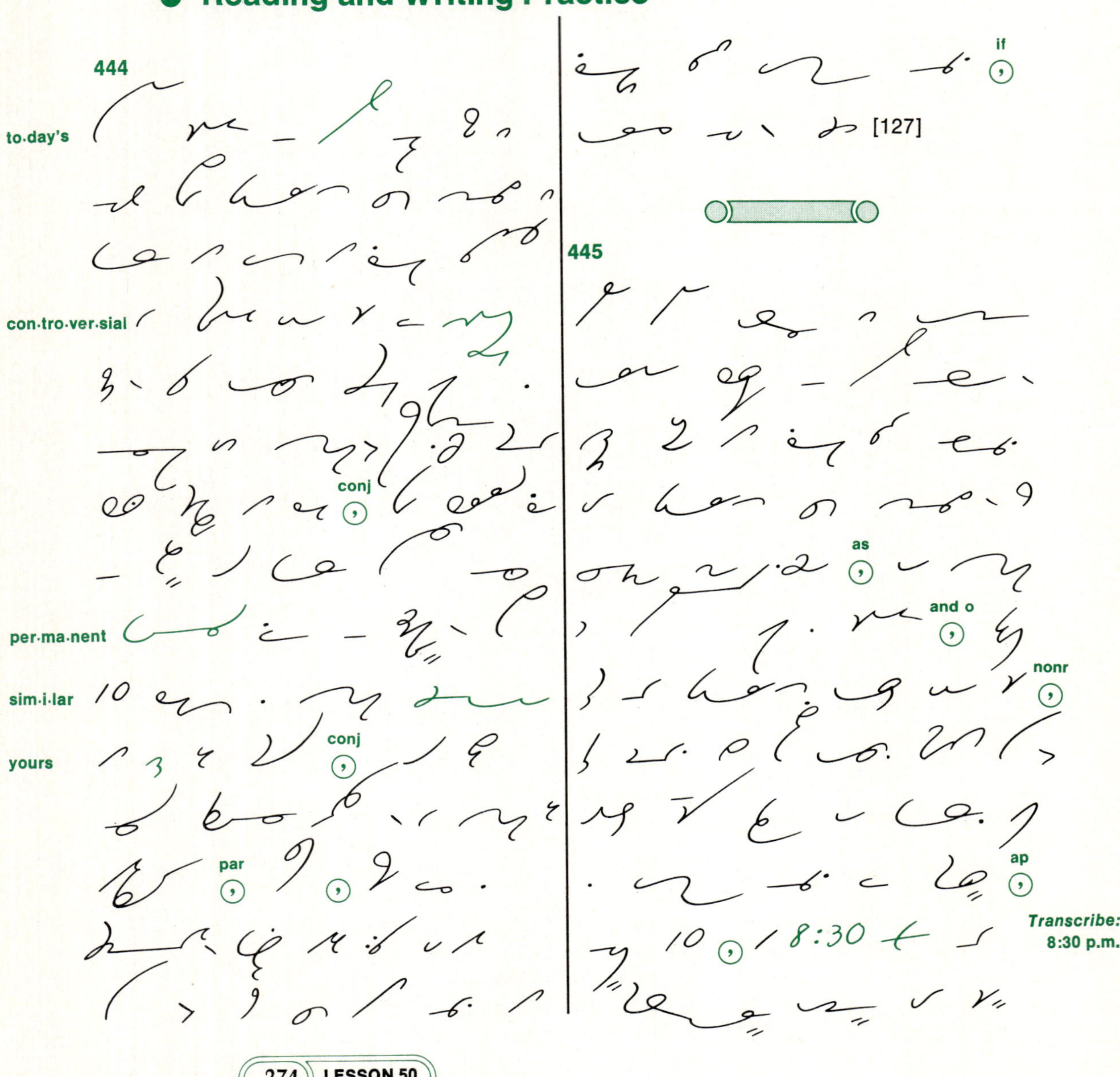

[108]

when

[128]

446

as

polls

four-year *hyphenated before noun*

ser

if

[116]

447

if

conj

dis·sat·is·fied

intro

re·struc·ture

nc

conj

The Secretary on the Job

448 TELEPHONE TECHNIQUE FOR THE SECRETARY

"Hello."
"May I ask who is speaking, please?"
"This is Kay Johnson."
"Is this Mr. Hoffman's office?"
"Yes, it is."
"May I speak to him please? This is J. W. Jackson of the Arnold Products Corporation."
"Just a moment, I'll see if he is in."

20

Knowing how

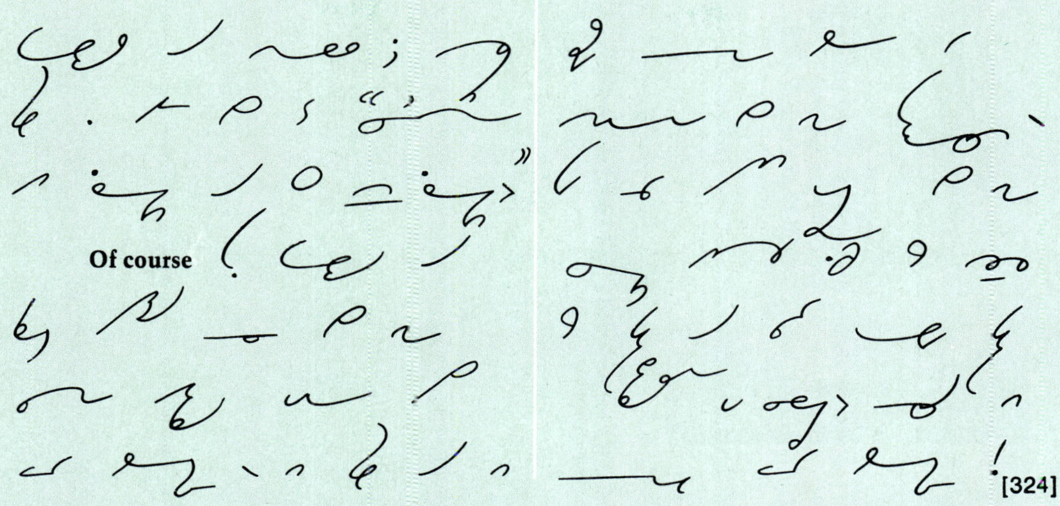

TRANSCRIPTION TIPS

- **Verify.**

Verify the spelling and initials of every name you type by checking the original correspondence, files, mailing lists, telephone book, or as a last resort, your employer. The important thing is GET IT RIGHT!

- **Don't Divide.**

Avoid dividing names, places, or figures at the end of a line.

- **Hold That Filing.**

Do *not* file carbon copies until the originals have been signed—there may be changes made on the originals that should appear on the carbon copies. Naturally, if the original must be retyped, a new carbon copy would be made.

- **Photocopies.**

Making a photocopy of a letter can be a lifesaver at times; however, most employers agree that photocopying should not always replace the carbon copy.

CHAPTER 11

Banking

Banks are business organizations that handle people's money. They are in business to make money by charging fees for many services that relate to money. A bank is a safer place to keep money than is a mattress or an old sock. In return for putting money in a bank, people receive different types of services.

Depositors can put money in checking accounts that offer safety for their funds as well as offer checks with which to pay for purchases. A check is a written order from a customer to the bank to pay a specified sum of money to a designated recipient. Checking accounts also give the depositors receipts for their payments in the form of canceled checks and monthly statements of their financial balances. Some banks charge fees for these services, while others do not.

Banks also enable customers to deposit money in savings accounts. Money in savings accounts earns interest during the time it is left there. Thus depositors can keep their money safe and also have it grow. In addition, they can withdraw all or part of their money from a savings account at any time.

Banks do much more than receive deposits, handle checks, and pay interest. Since banking is a business, profits are the objective of most banking operations. Banks seek profits through lending and investing the funds placed at their disposal and earning interest on these loans and investments. Interest charged on loans is their primary source of income. Banks loan money to both individuals and businesses. People may borrow money to finance the purchase of large items, such as appliances or automobiles, or to finance their education or a trip. Banks also make mortgage and property improvement loans available. They make loans to businesses for many reasons, including building a plant or meeting a payroll.

Economic activity could not survive without a continuing flow of money and credit. The economy of this country depends on the efficient operation of complex and delicately balanced systems of money and credit. Banks are an indispensable element in these systems. They provide the bulk of the money supply as well as the primary means of facilitating the flow of credit. They play a major role in maintaining the financial well-being of the nation.

The letters and memorandums in this chapter represent the type of material you will take from dictation if you decide to enter the field of banking.

MONEY
$2000
MONEY
$2000
$2000
MONEY
$2000
MONEY
MONEY
MONEY
$2000
$2000
MONEY

Building Phrasing Skill

449 Phrase Builder

Can you read the following four groups of phrases in 55 seconds?

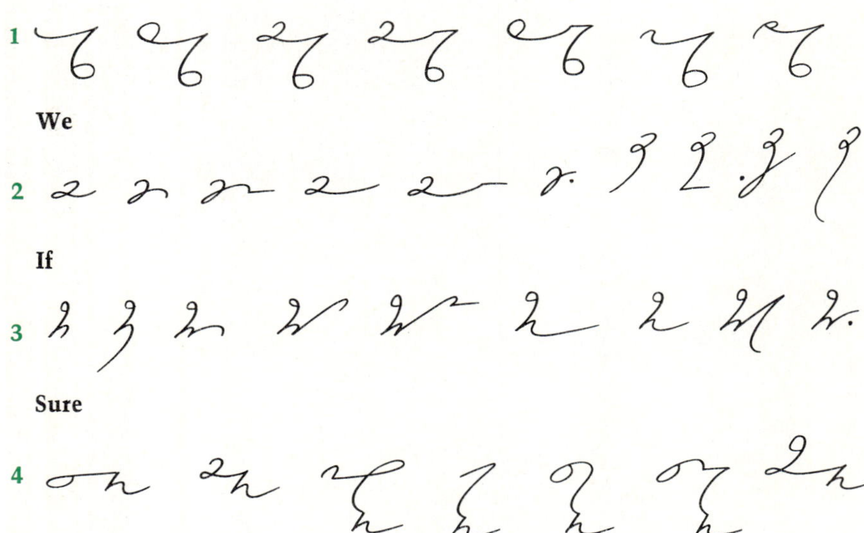

1. *Will be able, I will be able, we will be able, we will not be able, I will not be able, you will be able, they will be able.*
2. *We are, we can, we cannot, we will, we will not, we think, we have, we have not, we have had, we have been.*
3. *If you, if you have, if you can, if you do, if you do not, if you will, if you are, if you would be, if you think.*
4. *I am sure, we are sure, you may be sure, to be sure, I can be sure, I cannot be sure, I feel sure.*

450 Warmup Phrase Letter

Your warmup letter contains 104 words. Can you read it in 35 seconds? Copy it in 70 seconds?

[104]

Building Transcription Skills

451 Business Vocabulary Builder

vault A compartment for the safekeeping of valuables.

possession Having or taking into control; ownership.

interior Lying within the limits; inner.

Reading and Writing Practice

452

as

nonr

nc

intro

ap

[100]

453

Transcribe:
$6,000

well-trained
hyphenated before noun

par

[84]

454

con·ve·nience

it's

if

intro

bank's

when

wor·ry

in·te·ri·or

conj

50

of·fered

intro

its

and o

ser

[164]

455

when

intro

ap·pli·ca·tion

when

[68]

456

and o

em·ploy·er

per·son·al

[107]

457 **Transcription Quiz** For you to supply: 5 commas: 1 comma *if* clause, 2 commas series, 1 comma *when* clause, 1 comma introductory; 2 missing words.

[117]

Warmup Your warmup letter is on page 281. Practice the sentences in the first paragraph, breaking each sentence into several parts and writing each part as rapidly as you can.

Developing Word-Building Power

458 Brief-Form Chart

On your first reading of the following brief forms, read the rows across from left to right. On your second reading, read *down* each column. Do you read the brief forms and derivatives as rapidly when you read them down as when you read them across from left to right? Your goal on the first reading: 25 seconds.

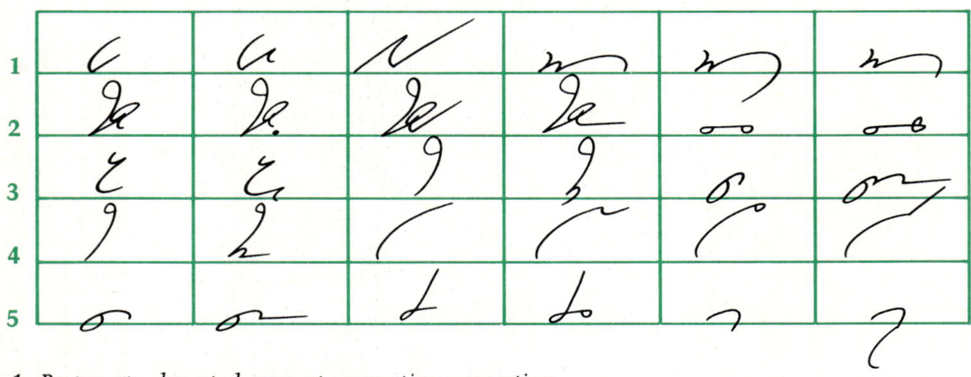

1. *Part, parts, departed, suggest, suggestive, suggestion.*
2. *Advertise, advertising, advertised, advertisement, immediate, immediately.*
3. *Opportunity, opportunities, advantage, advantageous, out, outcome.*
4. *Ever-every, everyone, time, timer, timely, timed.*
5. *Acknowledge, acknowledgment, general, generally, question, questionable.*

459 Geographical Expressions

1

2

1. *Maryland, Delaware, Indiana, Connecticut, Maine, New Hampshire, Vermont.*
2. *Europe, European, Asia, Asian, Africa, African, Australia, Australian.*

Building Transcription Skills

460 TYPING STYLE STUDY average letters By this time you should be able to place a short letter by judgment. You will now learn to place an average-length letter (one that contains about 150 words).

If you write shorthand similar in size to that which appears in this book, you will require almost an entire column in your notebook for an average letter.

When a letter takes approximately one column in your notebook, you should do three things:

■ 1 Set the margin stops on the typewriter for a 1½-inch margin at the left and a 1½-inch margin at the right.

■ 2 Type the date a double space (one blank line) below the last line of the letterhead.

■ 3 Start the address eight lines (seven blank lines) below the date. If your typewriter has pica (large) type, start the inside address on the sixth line below the date.

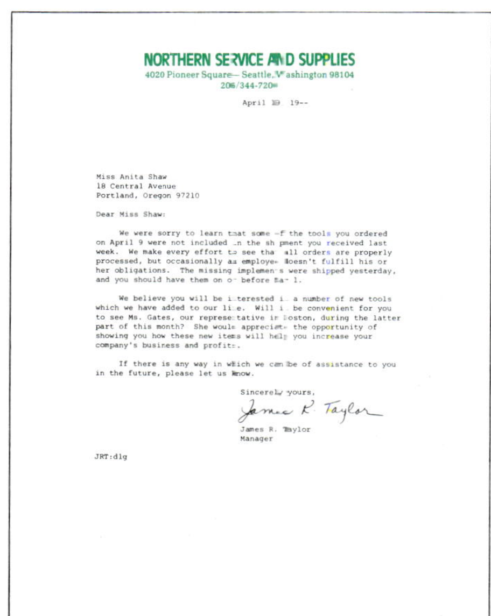

NORTHERN SERVICE AND SUPPLIES
4020 Pioneer Square—Seattle, Washington 98104
206/344-720[illegible]

April [illegible], 19--

Miss Anita Shaw
18 Central Avenue
Portland, Oregon 97210

Dear Miss Shaw:

We were sorry to learn that some of the tools you ordered on April 9 were not included in the shipment you received last week. We make every effort to see that all orders are properly processed, but occasionally an employee doesn't fulfill his or her obligations. The missing implements were shipped yesterday, and you should have them on or before May 1.

We believe you will be interested in a number of new tools which we have added to our line. Will it be convenient for you to see Ms. Gates, our representative in Boston, during the latter part of this month? She would appreciate the opportunity of showing you how these new items will help you increase your company's business and profits.

If there is any way in which we can be of assistance to you in the future, please let us know.

Sincerely yours,

James R. Taylor

James R. Taylor
Manager

JRT:dlg

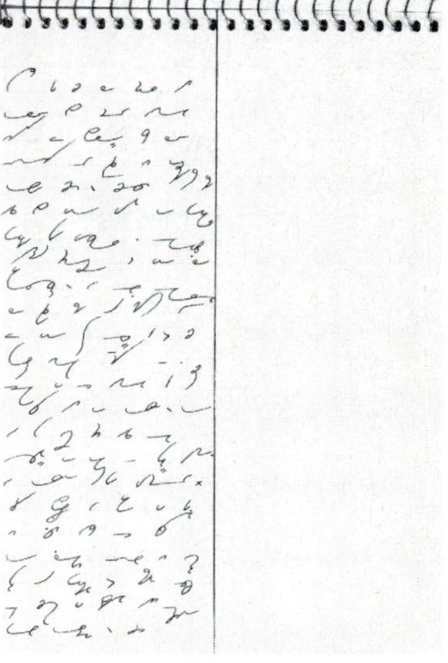

AVERAGE-LENGTH LETTER

461 Business Vocabulary Builder

peers Equals; of equal standing with each other.

intriguing Engaging interest; fascinating.

varied *(adjective)* Having numerous forms or types; diverse.

Reading and Writing Practice

462 Brief-Form Letter

463

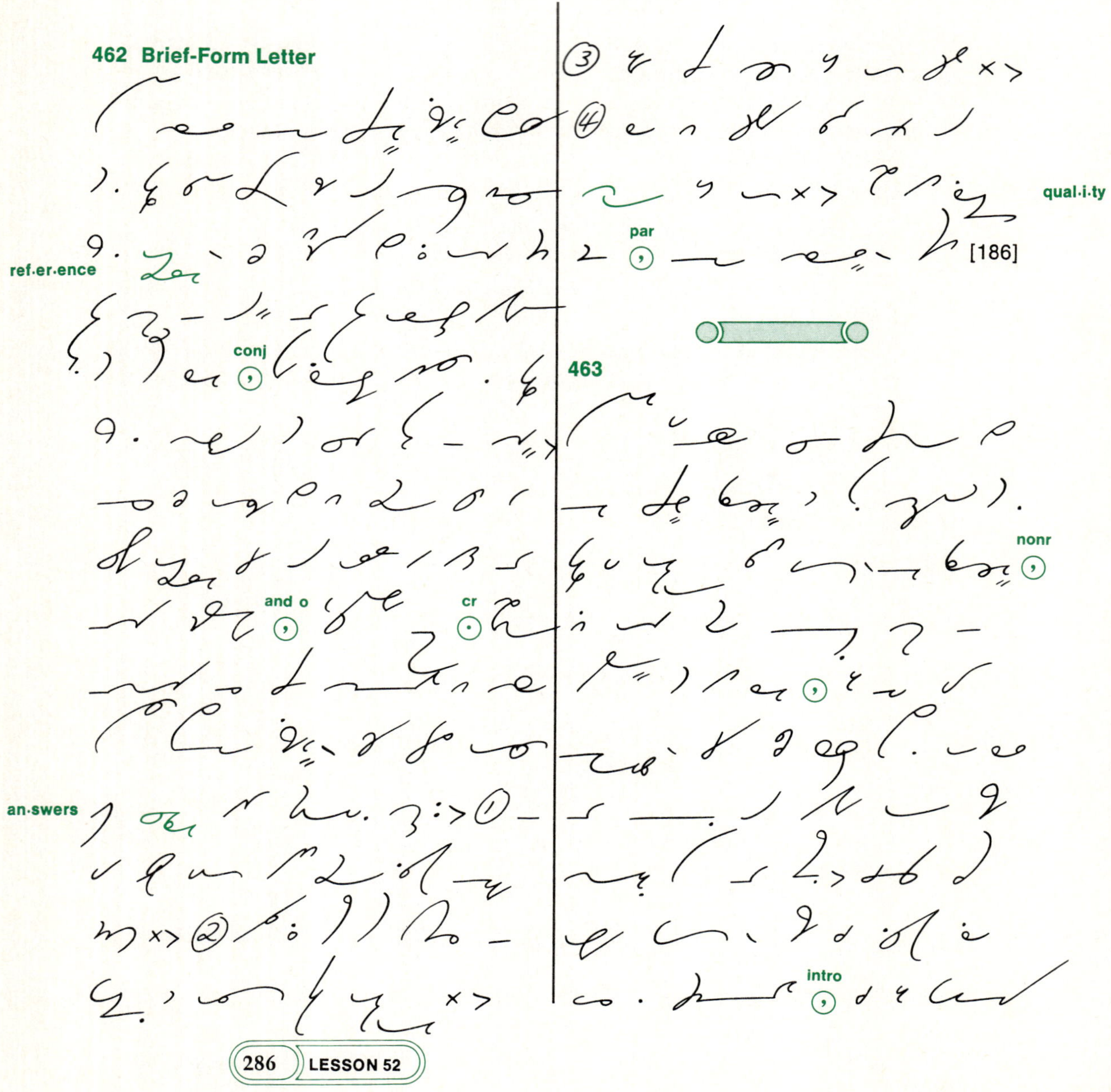

peers

when

[177]

464

in·qui·ry

equal

and o

ser

edi·tions

ap·pli·cants

per·ti·nent

per·son·nel

intro

re·ferred

[207]

465

ac·knowl·edge

Eu·ro·pe·an

par

usu·al·ly

com·pa·ny's

be·gin·ning

full-time
hyphenated before noun

[141]

466

in·trigu·ing

[77]

467 Transcription Quiz For you to supply: 7 commas—2 commas introductory, 1 comma parenthetical, 1 comma *and* omitted, 2 commas series, 1 comma *as* clause; 2 missing words.

[135]

Warmup Your warmup letter is on page 281. Use the sentence in the second paragraph for your warmup today. Break it into convenient parts. Practice writing each part several times as rapidly as you can.

Developing Word-Building Power

468 Word Families

St-

1

Pr-

2

-br

3

-place

4

1. *Still, stolen, stop, style, stray, stream, string.*
2. *Proof, pride, praise, provide, protect, prime, promote.*
3. *Branch, brook, break, broke, brace, labor, member.*
4. *Place, replace, replaced, misplace, misplaced, displace, displaces.*

Building Transcription Skills

469 SPELLING FAMILIES -ious, -eous In most words the sound *e-us* is spelled *ious,* but in some words it is spelled *eous.* Stop and think before you transcribe any word which has this sound.

Words Ending in -ious

se·ri·ous	de·vi·ous	gra·cious
var·i·ous	pre·vi·ous	con·scious
in·dus·tri·ous	cu·ri·ous	cau·tious

Words Ending in -eous

cour·te·ous	spon·ta·ne·ous	cou·ra·geous
ad·van·ta·geous	mis·cel·la·neous	si·mul·ta·neous

---

470 Business Vocabulary Builder

per annum Per year; yearly.

compounded Interest paid on both the accrued interest and the principal.

teller A member of a bank's staff concerned with the direct handling of money received or paid out.

Reading and Writing Practice

471

ad·vice

if

nc

trav·el·er's

as

los·ing

se·ri·ous

when

cit·ies

conj

cour·te·ous

if

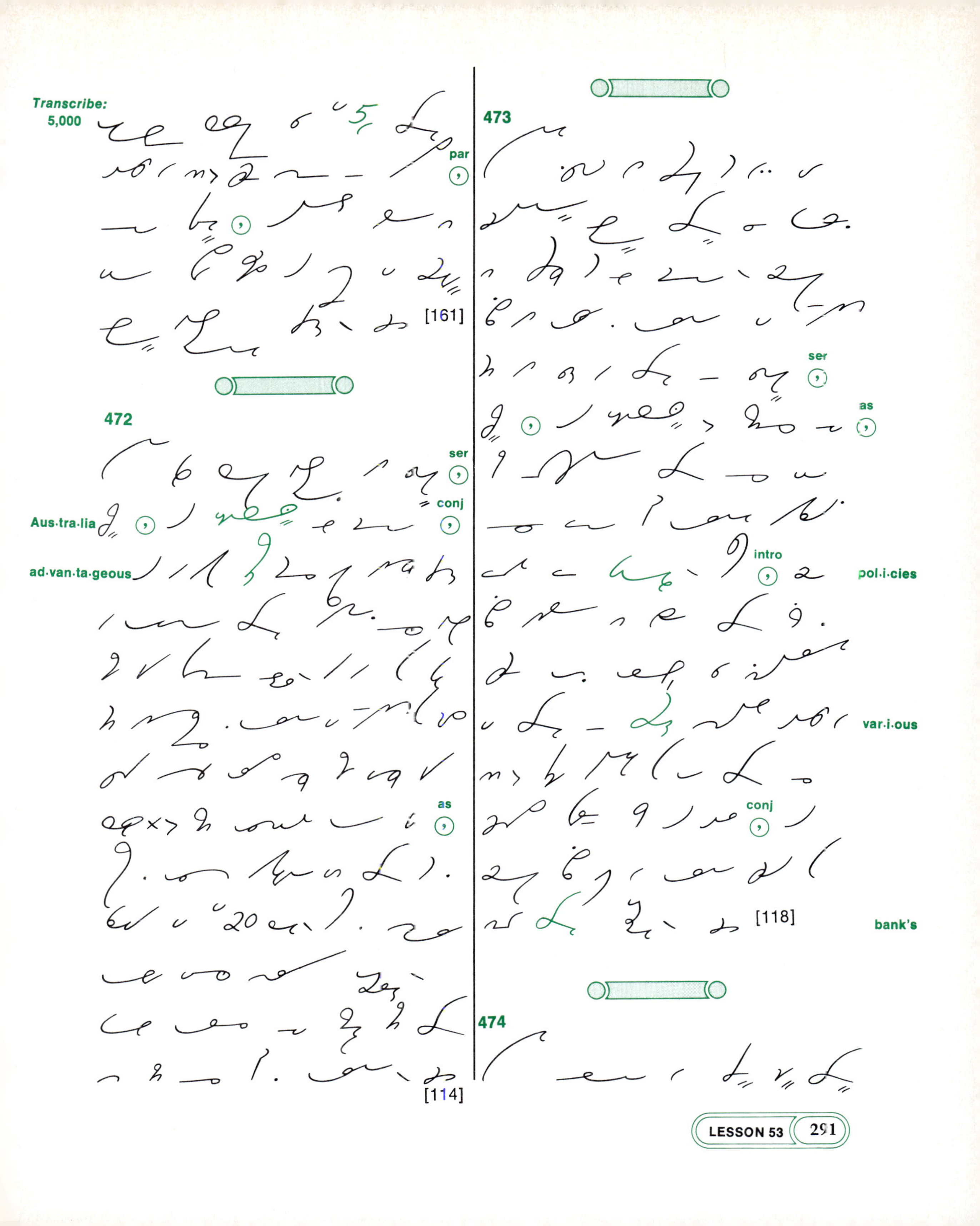

Transcribe: 5,000

par

[161]

472

ser

Aus·tra·lia

conj

ad·van·ta·geous

as

[114]

473

ser

as

intro

pol·i·cies

var·i·ous

conj

[118]

bank's

474

its

day-of-de·pos·it
day-of-with·draw·al
hyphenated before noun

and o

if

intro

ser

[103]

475 For you to supply: 6 commas—2 commas introductory, 2 commas apposition, 1 comma *as* clause, 1 comma *and* omitted; 2 missing words.

Transcription Quiz

[149]

Warmup Your warmup letter is on page 281. Practice the sentences in the last paragraph. Remember, when you write an outline that is not to your liking, don't stop to scratch it out—keep on writing.

Developing Word-Building Power

476 Word Beginnings and Endings

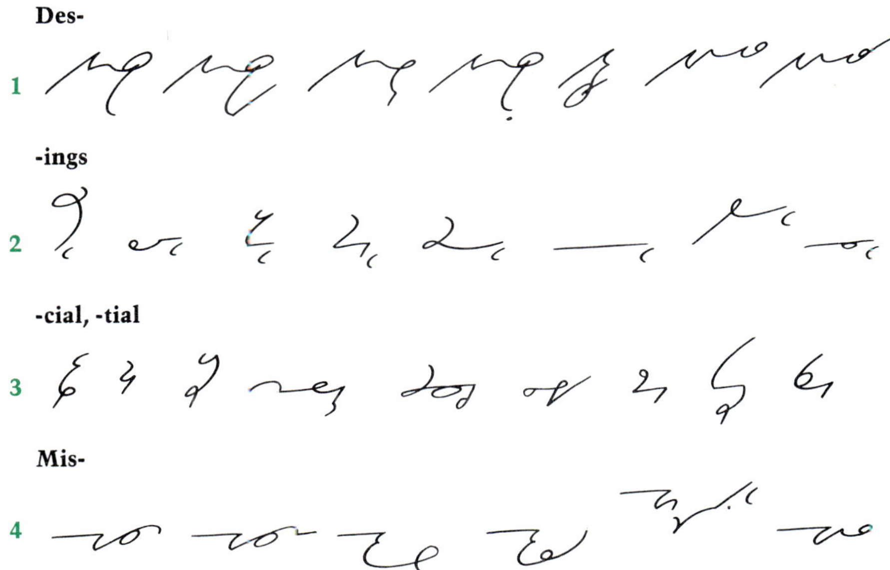

1. *Describe, described, description, describing, despite, destroy, destroyed.*
2. *Savings, earnings, openings, furnishings, feelings, mornings, dealings, meanings.*
3. *Special, social, official, commercials, financially, initialed, essential, beneficial, partial.*
4. *Mistake, mistaken, misplace, misprint, misunderstandings, mystery.*

Building Transcription Skills

477 COMMON PREFIXES ex-

ex- in many English words *ex-* stands for *out.*

expansion Spreading out.

export Send out of the country.

expire Die out; come to an end.

exclusive Leaving out all others.

exempt Left out.

exhaust To tire out; to run out of.

---

478 Business Vocabulary Builder

pursuits Activities that one engages in.

resume To start again.

resolution A decision or declaration.

currency Coins, government notes, etc. in circulation as a medium of exchange.

Reading and Writing Practice

479

as

conj

rea·sons

conj

cr

[117]

480

char·ac·ter

par

[84]

481

if

de·scribed
four-page
hyphenated before noun

el·i·gi·ble

pre·mi·um

intro

won't

555-1701

cr

par

[153]

482

oc·ca·sion

Com·mer·cial

ex·pan·sion

com·pa·ny's

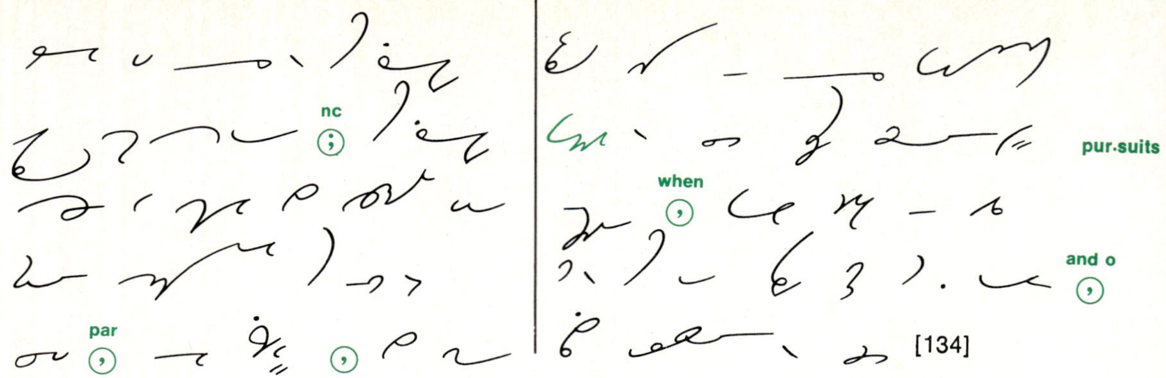

483 Transcription Quiz For you to supply: 4 commas—1 comma nonrestrictive, 1 comma introductory, 2 commas parenthetical; 2 missing words.

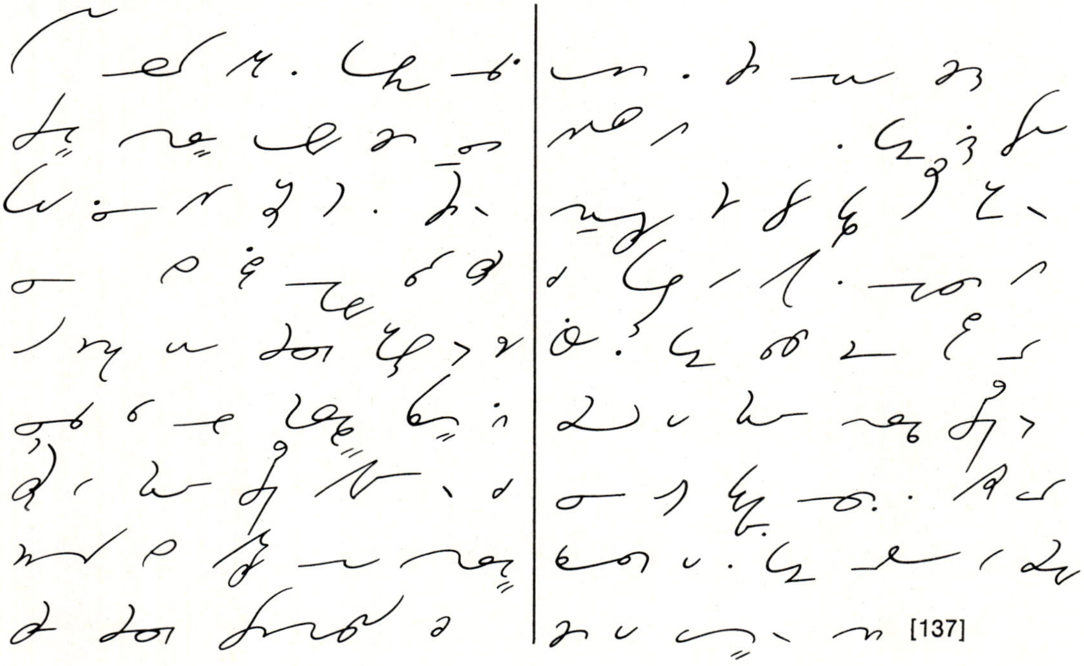

[137]

It is always a good idea to help other office personnel whenever you have time. Co-operation is the key to an efficiently run office.

Warmup Your warmup letter is on page 281. Write one complete copy of the letter. Write it in your best shorthand.

Developing Word-Building Power

484 Shorthand Vocabulary Builder

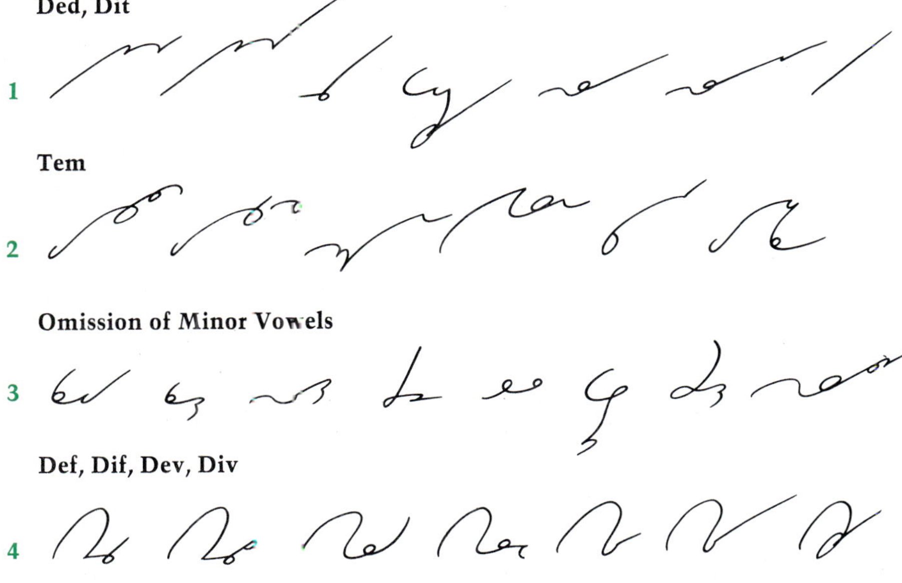

1. *Deduct, deducted, needed, provided, credit, credited, debt.*
2. *Automatic, automatically, customer, temperature, attempt, automobile.*
3. *Period, serious, courteous, genuine, theory, previous, various, graduate.*
4. *Definite, definitely, different, difference, devote, devoted, divide.*

Building Transcription Skills

485 Business Vocabulary Builder

incentive Something that incites; motive.

venture *(noun)* An undertaking; a business enterprise.

verifying Establishing truth or accuracy.

authorizing Giving power to.

Reading and Writing Practice

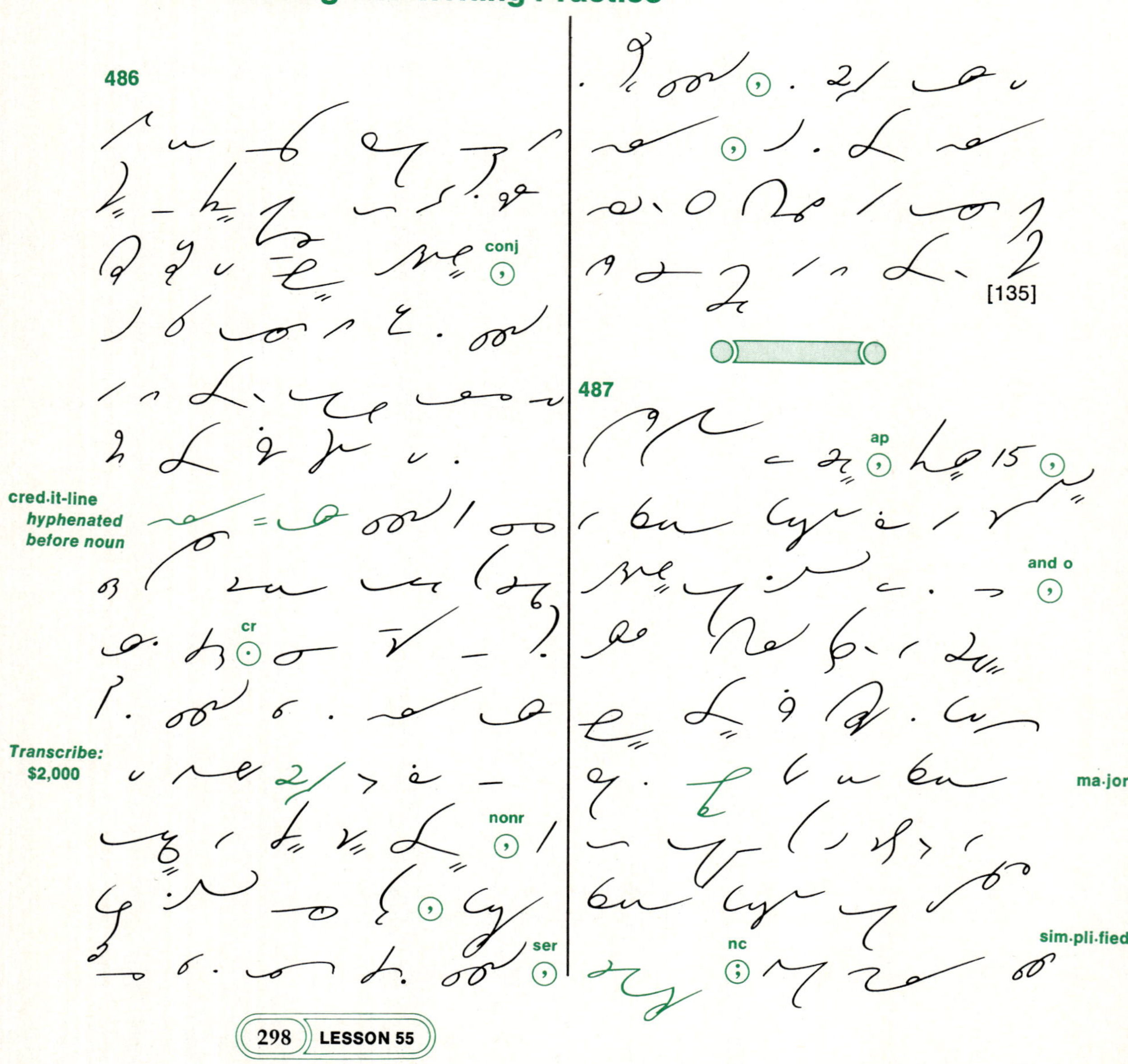

is·su·ance

intro

em·ploy·ee's

in·cen·tive

intro

par

[184]

488

as

ap

its

per·son·al·ly

prompt·ly

conj

ver·i·fy·ing

intro

al·ready

conj

intro

in·ci·den·tal·ly

when

[161]

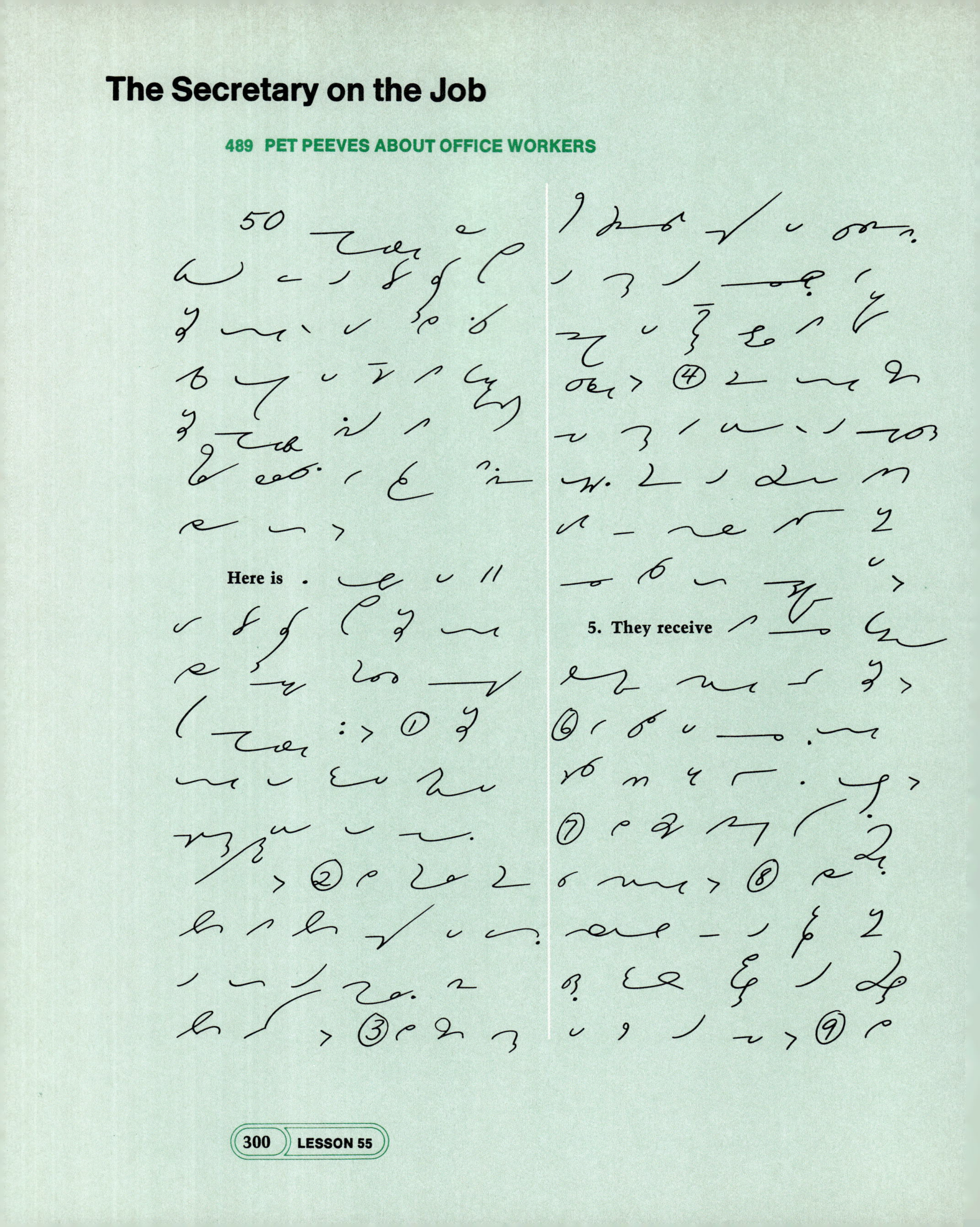

The Secretary on the Job

489 PET PEEVES ABOUT OFFICE WORKERS

50

Here is

5. They receive

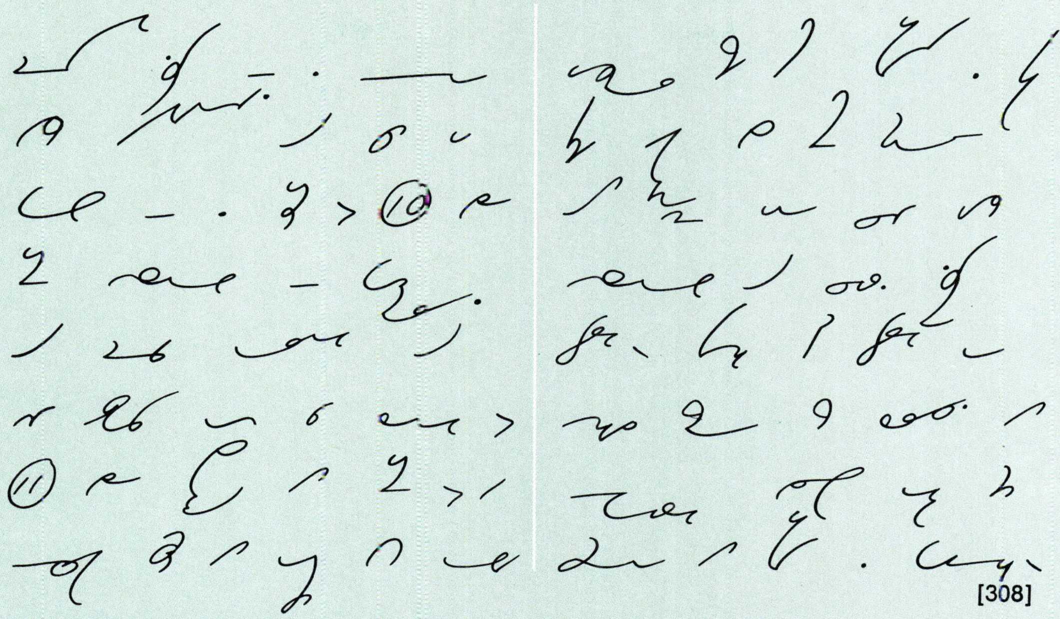

In order to obtain your major objectives, you must set small goals for yourself. Check often to be sure that you are meeting these small goals, and the major objectives will take care of themselves.

CHAPTER

12 Services

It is said that food, clothing, and shelter are the three basic human needs. This may be true, but there are other needs that are almost as important. There is knowledge, for example, and physical safety, personal advice, and protection under the law. There are more than 20 million people in this country who help look after needs like the ones mentioned above, and they are often put into the category of public and social service workers.

The Department of Labor has predicted that the greatest career potential in the remainder of the twentieth century lies in the service occupations. This is a term that loosely covers a very broad range—from organized religious groups to philanthropic foundations to private and public welfare agencies.

Service employees may be found working in a wide variety of places—in a temporary shelter for children, a recreation center for senior citizens, the national headquarters of a service club, or a city welfare office, among many others.

All service jobs have one thing in common: they are involved in helping people. Social workers aid the poor, the undereducated, the elderly, and others in need of help. Professional counselors help others to build a satisfactory future for themselves. Religious leaders guide and advise the people they serve. Police officers and fire fighters are in the business of safeguarding people's rights, property, and lives. Fund raisers and workers in nonprofit organizations help to raise money and to set up programs to help people in trouble, to guide youngsters, to build new and better educational facilities and fund scholarships, to help protect the environment, and to support cultural institutions such as museums, libraries, and symphony orchestras; the list is almost endless.

Service work is highly people-oriented, and employees in this field must develop a strong regard for the rights and dignity of others, not just a superficial liking for people. This type of work offers a combination of satisfying rewards and challenging duties. Service workers derive a tremendous sense of satisfaction from dealing personally with people who need help and from meeting vital human needs in an increasingly impersonal world.

The letters in this chapter are similar to ones you might send or receive in a service organization.

Building Phrasing Skill

490 Phrase Builder

Your reading goal: 55 seconds.

To in Phrases

1

Thank

2

Of

3

From

4

1. *To be, to have, to see, to sell, to pay, to begin, to plan, to join.*
2. *Thank you, thank you for, thank you for the, thank you for this, thank you for your, thank you for your order, I thank you, we thank you.*
3. *Of the, of this, of that, of them, of which, of your, of my, of our, of these.*
4. *From you, from the, from that, from our, from which, from that time, from us.*

491 Warmup Phrase Letter

The following 170-word letter contains 24 phrases. Can you read it in 55 seconds? Copy it in 1¾ minutes or less?

[170]

Building Transcription Skills

492 Business Vocabulary Builder

radius The distance from the center to the edge of a circle.

territorial Nearby; regional.

preceding Previous; prior.

Reading and Writing Practice

493

ap

ac·quir·ing

Transcribe: $10,000

when

and o

mod·ern

intro

fee

intro

Transcribe:
5 percent

com·mer·cials

par

if

[238]

suc·cess·ful·ly

50-mile
hyphenated before noun

past

nonr

as

vi·o·la·tion

conj

[136]

494

495

to·day's

saw

re·ferred

conj

par

if

if

nc

[134]

496

Transcribe: 5 percent

pre·ced·ing

intro

[114]

497

cop·ies

ap

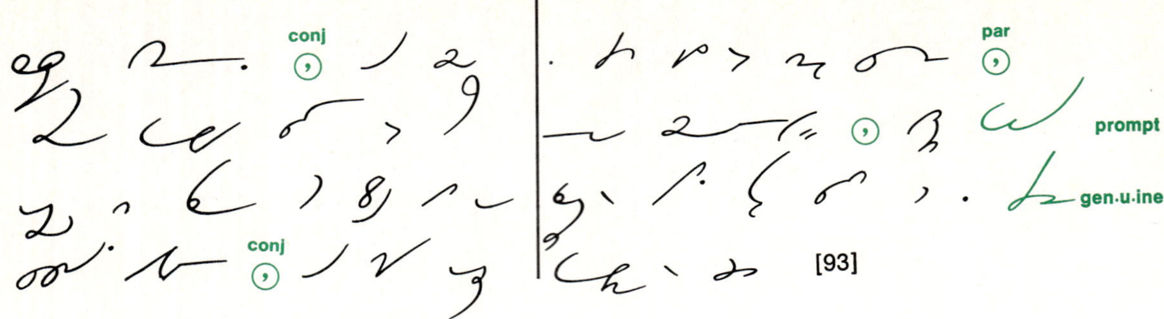

498 Transcription Quiz For you to supply: 7 commas—3 commas series, 2 commas parenthetical, 1 comma introductory, 1 comma in a number; 2 missing words.

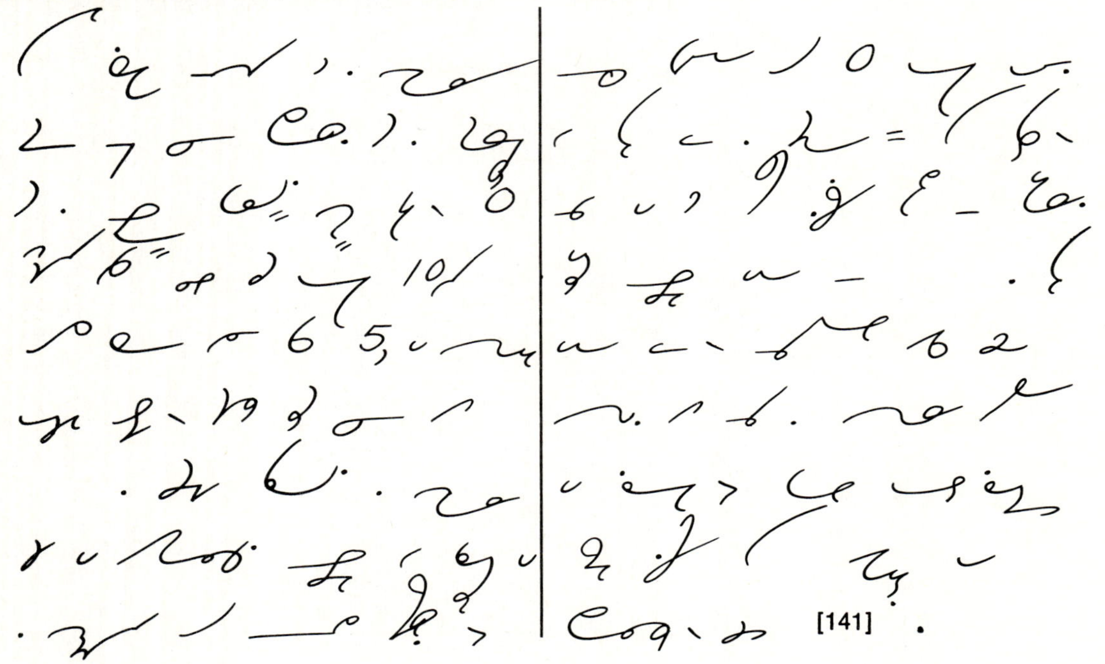

Most busy executives do not have time to read every piece of correspondence that leaves their office. The secretary who can type letters that can be signed with confidence is valuable indeed.

Warmup The letter on page 304 is your warmup letter for today. Write rapidly as much of the letter as time permits.

Developing Word-Building Power

499 Brief-Form Chart

Read the brief forms and derivatives in each row of the following chart from left to right; then read down each column. Can you read them down as rapidly as you can read them across? Your reading goal: 25 seconds.

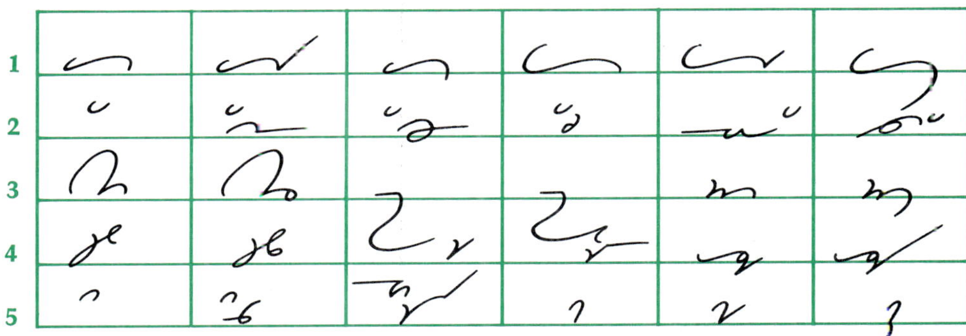

1. *Organize, organized, organization, progress, progressed, progressive.*
2. *Over, overcome, overcame, oversee, moreover, takeover.*
3. *Difficult, difficulty, envelope, envelopes, success, successful.*
4. *Satisfy-satisfactory, satisfactorily, state, statement, request, requested.*
5. *Under, underneath, misunderstand, wish, wished, wishful.*

500 Geographical Expressions

1

2

1. *San Antonio, El Paso, Odessa, Tucson, Tampa, Orlando.*
2. *Texas, New Mexico, Arizona, Mississippi, Colorado, Florida, Georgia.*

Building Transcription Skills

501 TYPING STYLE STUDY mailability

A letter is usually judged not on the number of errors it contains, not on the number of erasures it has, and not on any other *one* aspect. Rather, it is judged as a *whole* for *mailability*.

Mailability simply means this: A business executive is willing to sign it and mail it to a customer or other recipient.

To judge your letters for mailability, you should do these things:

■ 1 Check to see if the content is accurate. It is not always necessary to follow the dictator's words verbatim. What is important, however, is to follow the meaning exactly.

■ 2 Check to see if the letter has a good appearance. A letter may be accurate in nearly every detail but be so unattractively arranged on the page that a business executive would not be willing to sign it. If your letter is too high or too low or if the margins are obviously uneven, it will create a bad impression.

■ 3 Check to see that any errors have been corrected neatly. Sometimes you will make an error in transcription which you can correct easily. Take the time and effort to make the correction as neat as possible. And, of prime importance, be sure that if you do make an error, it *is* corrected.

---

502 Business Vocabulary Builder

ethical Conforming to accepted professional standards of conduct.

extension Projection; an addition to.

conflict of interest A conflict between the private interests and the responsibilities of a person in a position of trust.

● Reading and Writing Practice

503 Brief-Form Letter

ser

its

eth·i·cal

conj

ser

ac·cept·ing

char·ac·ter·is·tic

[158]

504

ap

ap

guide·lines

intro

ser

ap

busi·nesses

de·vel·op

[118]

505

old-fash·ioned

if

equipped

sore·ly

intro

re·mod·el·ing

intro

555-1181 [227]

dis·sat·is·fied

when

506

as

brand-new

intro

Mis·sis·sip·pi

and o

un·in·ter·rupt·ed

re·lo·cate

ser

intro

month's

Coun·cil

intro

nc

raise

conj

intro

Feb·ru·ary

[163]

507 **Transcription Quiz** For you to supply: 4 commas—1 comma conjunction, 1 comma introductory, 2 commas parenthetical; 1 period courteous request; 2 missing words.

[117]

LESSON 58

Warmup Your warmup letter is on page 304. Break the sentences in the first paragraph into convenient groups, and write each group several times as rapidly as possible.

Developing Word-Building Power

508 Word Families

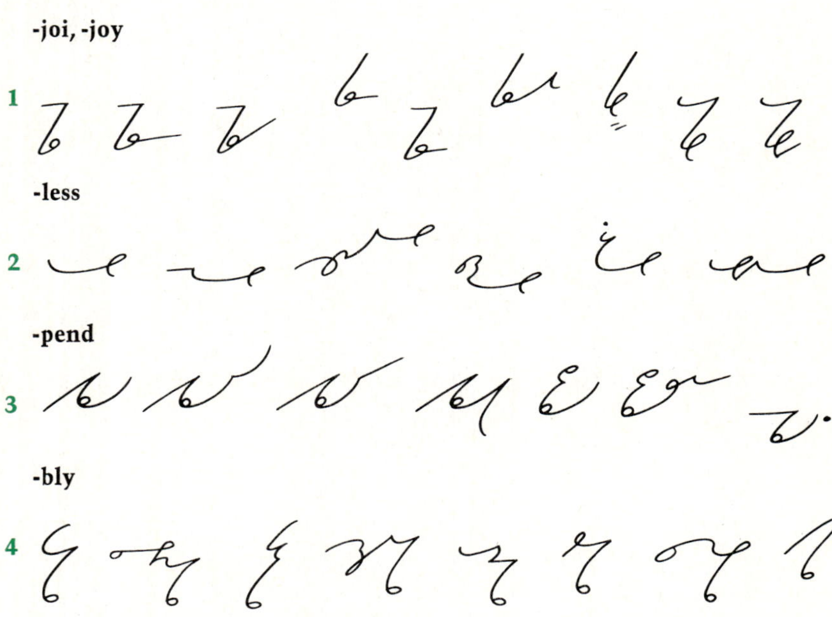

1. *Enjoy, enjoyment, enjoyed, join, enjoin, joints, Joyce, rejoice, rejoiced.*
2. *Less, unless, countless, useless, hopeless, restless.*
3. *Depend, dependent, depended, dependable, expend, expenditure, impending.*
4. *Probably, immeasurably, possibly, considerably, reasonably, terribly, agreeably, doubly.*

Building Transcription Skills

509 COMMON PREFIXES im-

im- in many English words *im-* means *not*.

impossible Not possible.

immeasurable Not measurable.

improbable Not probable.

imperfect Not perfect.

impolite Not polite.

impatient Not patient.

---

510 Business Vocabulary Builder

auxiliary Organization which offers or provides help to another.

epidemic An outbreak; sudden spread of disease.

corps A group of persons associated together for a common cause.

Reading and Writing Practice

511

un·fore·seen

intro

cit·i·zens

up-to-date *hyphenated before noun*

and o

corps

ser

pa·tients

hours'

if

cr [162]

[127]

512

im·mea·sur·ably

conj

par

intro

or·ga·ni·za·tion·al

nonr

513

par

role

ac·cu·rate

conj

rolls

150

par

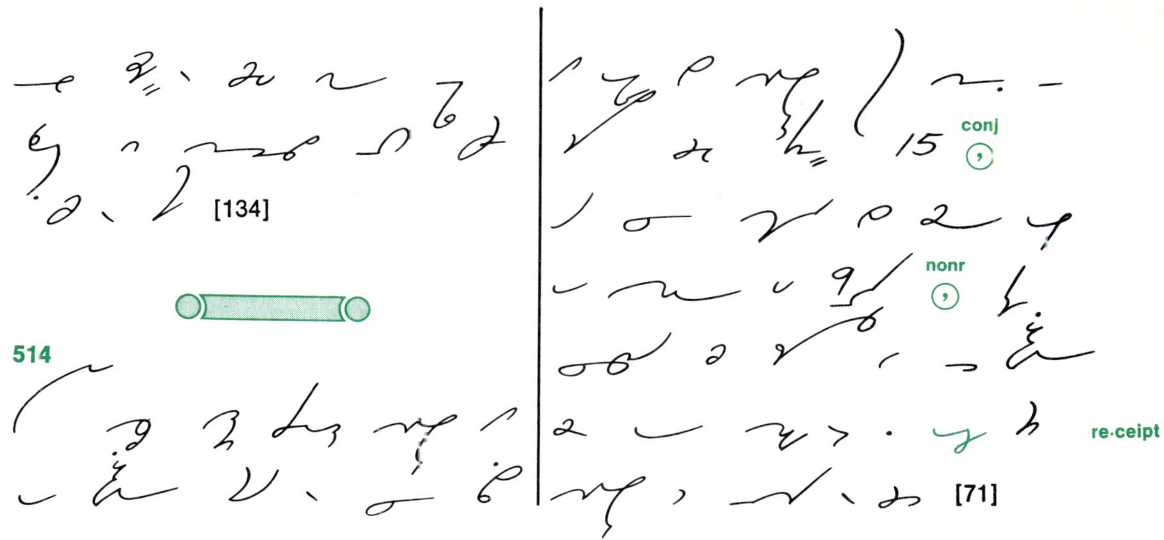

515 Transcription Quiz For you to supply: 7 commas—1 comma *if* clause, 1 comma *as* clause, 2 commas apposition, 2 commas series, 1 comma parenthetical; 2 missing words.

[153]

Warmup Your warmup letter is on page 304. Break the sentences in the second paragraph into convenient groups, and write each group several times as rapidly as possible.

Developing Word-Building Power

516 Word Beginnings and Endings

Re-

1

Sub-

2

-lity, -lty

3

-ther

4

1. *Reception, recently, respect, reply, reserve, reservation, reported.*
2. *Subscribe, subscriber, subscribed, suburb, subdivision, sublet, subway, substandard.*
3. *Dependability, reliability, personality, quality, penalty, faculty.*
4. *Other, rather, neither, either, mother, father, altogether, leather.*

Building Transcription Skills

517 SIMILAR-WORDS DRILL choose, chose

choose To select.

He did not choose *to go.*

chose (past tense of *choose*) Selected.

She chose *several new books yesterday.*

---

518 Business Vocabulary Builder

intervals Spaces of time between events; pauses.

random Lacking a definite plan or pattern.

apportioned Divided and shared according to a plan.

technicians Specialists with practical knowledge of a subject.

Reading and Writing Practice

519

re·cep·tion

when

intro

choose

par

than

in·flu·ence

[158]

520

chose

conj

sur·vey

ap

and o

com·pa·nies

conj

if

com·plete

conj

[210]

521

com·pa·ny's

view·ing

[74]

522

ap

as

ap·por·tioned

15-min·ute *hyphenated before noun* 15=

in·ter·vals

when

5

15=

if

5

if

555-3587

nonr

toll-free *hyphenated before noun*

intro

ser

par

[201]

523

as

15

15=

spon·sor·ing

WQAT

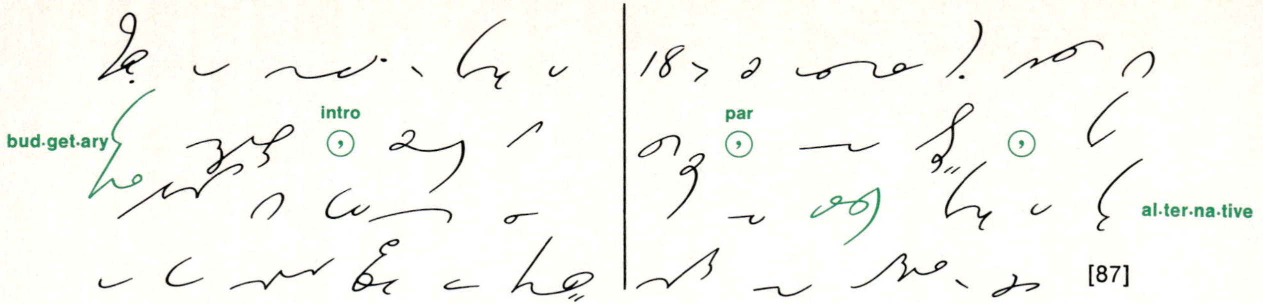

524 Transcription Quiz For you to supply: 7 commas—2 commas introductory, 2 commas conjunction, 2 commas series, 1 comma *if* clause; 1 semicolon, no conjunction; 2 missing words.

555-7879

[217]

Warmup Your warmup letter is on page 304. Copy the entire letter in your best shorthand.

Developing Word-Building Power

525 Shorthand Vocabulary Builder

1. *Quite, between, Broadway, roadway, equipped, liquid, quit.*
2. *Consultation, result, ultimately, insult, adult, culminate, culture.*
3. *Demonstrate, demonstrating, freedom, demand, demanding, seldom.*
4. *Attend, bulletin, competent, consistent, Newton, tonight, tentative.*

Building Transcription Skills

526 Business Vocabulary Builder

consultation A conference.

competent Capable.

floral Having to do with flowers.

Reading and Writing Practice

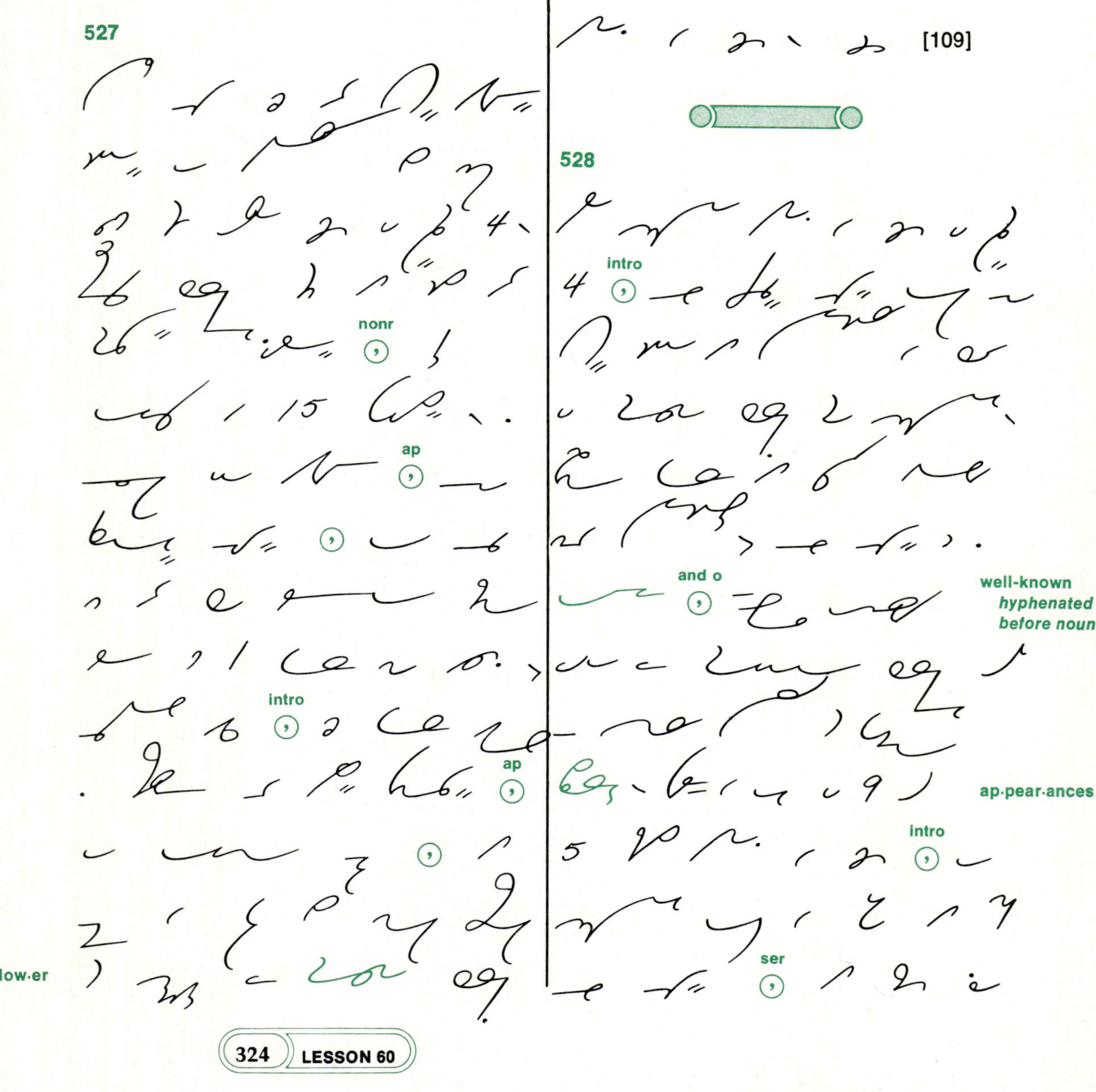

ad·vice

one-of-a-kind *hyphenated before noun*

and o

conj

na·tion's

[155]

529

geo

en·joy·able

intro

per·ma·nent

as

if

[96]

530

sched·ule

when

intro

in·quired

conj

nonr

par

par

[118]

The Secretary on the Job

531 GOOD WORK HABITS WIN PROMOTION

Frank soon

Frank began

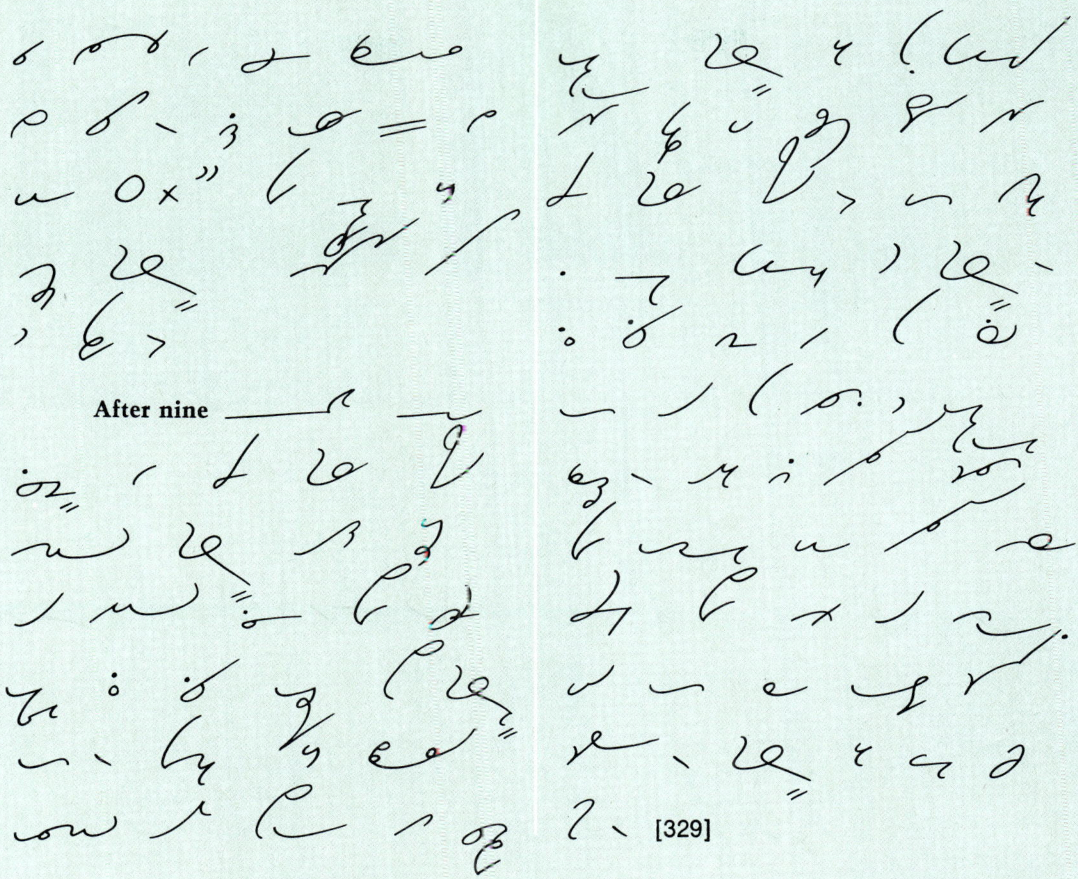

It goes without saying that a secretary must be able to type well and take dictation rapidly and accurately. These skills are basic and absolutely essential for success in the modern business world.
Philip S. Pepe

PART

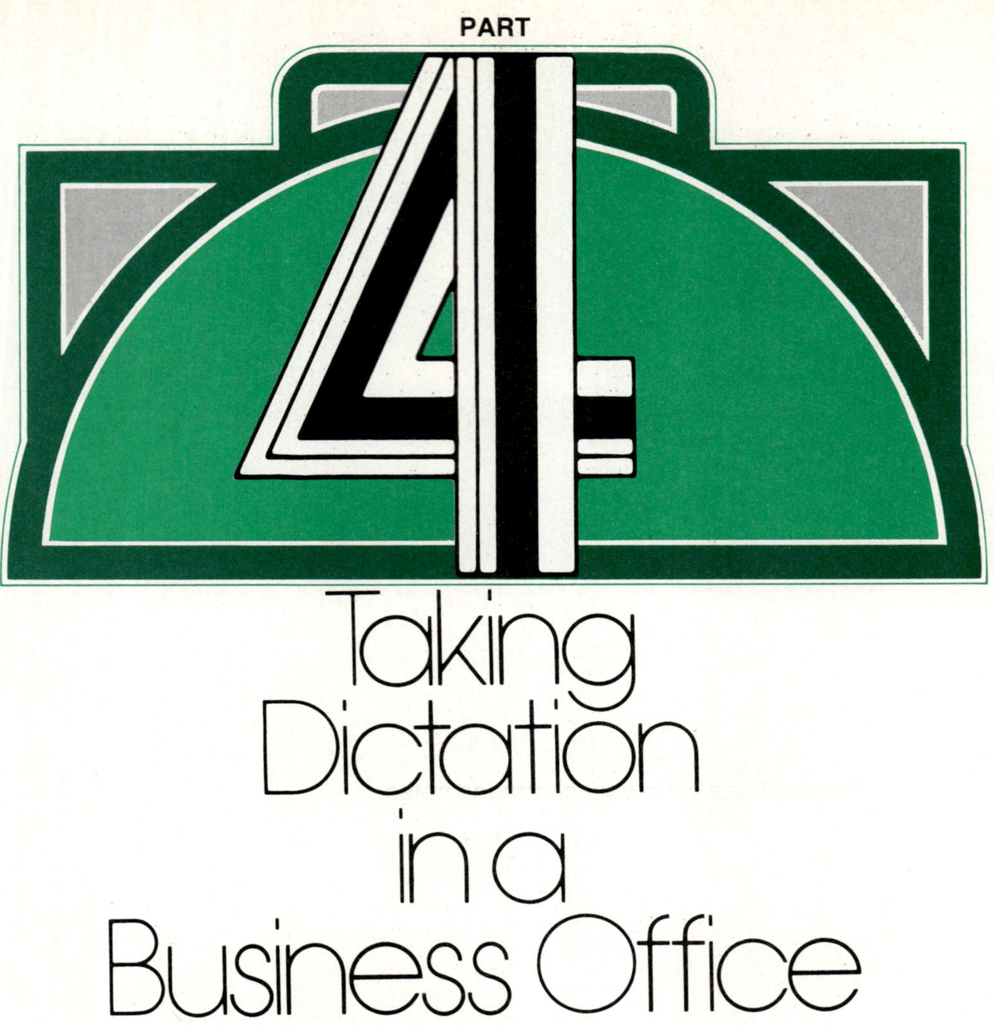

Taking Dictation in a Business Office

Could you take a letter from a dictator if you were called upon to do so? If you have been reading and copying each lesson every day, you probably could, provided the letter was not too difficult or was not dictated too fast.

You would, however, find the dictation of an executive a little different from the dictation that you have probably been taking in class. In class, your teacher's task has been to develop your shorthand speed as rapidly as possible. Your teacher knows that the best way to do this is to have you practice under the most favorable conditions. That is why the dictation has been smooth and even, with every word spoken clearly and distinctly.

Your teacher knows that when you are striving to increase your speed, your attention should be completely occupied with writing and should not be distracted by problems of hearing. Furthermore, your teacher has probably timed most of your dictation, as that is the only way your skill development can be determined.

OFFICE-STYLE DICTATION

Business executives, however, are not concerned with developing your speed; they assume that you have the necessary skill to take down what they say. Their dictation will not always be smooth; in fact, it may on occasion be choppy—sometimes fast, sometimes slow. They may slur some words. What is more, they may sometimes change their mind about a word or phrase and substitute another that expresses more clearly what they want to say. They may delete, insert, or even transpose words.

You will quickly become accustomed to this type of office-style dictation if you have sufficient shorthand speed. The more speed you possess, the easier office-style dictation will be for you. Therefore, strive to build your shorthand speed to the highest point possible; you will always be glad that you did!

In the following lessons you will become familiar with some of the problems you will meet when you take office-style dictation. You will be given suggestions on how to deal with each problem and shown how to handle it in your shorthand notes.

INSTRUCTIONS DURING DICTATION

Dictators will not only make deletions, insertions, and transpositions during dictation, but they may also ask you, right in the middle of a sentence, to check a date or an amount or the spelling of a name. When this happens, the easiest way to indicate the instructions in your notes is to write in shorthand the word *check* in parentheses, close to the item to be checked. The dictator may say:

We had a call from your representative, Ms. Small, or was her name Hall? Please check that.

This will appear in your notes as follows:

Then before you transcribe, you will go to previous correspondence, the files, or any other source from which you can obtain the necessary information and "check."

CHAPTER

13

Recreation

One thing certain about Americans is that they like to have fun. Every weekend, every evening, Americans by the millions go off to places where they can play, enjoy themselves, and be entertained. Because the public has such a variety of tastes, there are hundreds of different kinds of amusement and recreation facilities in the United States, running the gamut from A to Z—amusement parks to zoos—including everything from camping to stamp collecting.

Recreation facilities vary in size from national parks covering more than a million acres to small vacant lots that serve as neighborhood ball parks. Indoor centers range from large clubhouses with 15 or 20 major activities to small rooms in churches or schools, large enough for only a game table or for small group meetings.

Many public organizations include recreation as one of their functions and provide one or more recreational facilities. Federal, state, and local governments all have recreational agencies, committees, commissions, or departments. Schools, both public and private, sponsor numerous recreation programs and provide leadership for these activities both within the curriculum and on an extracurricular basis. Religious organizations have youth groups, and many local congregations provide recreational facilities for their members and neighbors. Many business and labor groups have recreational centers. Neighborhood centers exist under a variety of auspices: civic clubs, veterans' organizations, parent-teacher associations, and various social agencies. The array of facilities in large communities requires coordination, often through a council of social agencies.

Commercial recreation, which is operated to make a profit, encompasses several industries including the theater, amusement parks, movie theaters, radio and television, and professional sports.

Recreational activities are really anything that people do to relax and enjoy themselves. Whether by participating or just watching, Americans spend much time and money on recreation, and a number of industries are involved in providing the facilities and equipment used to fill leisure time. The letters in this chapter concern the recreation field.

Building Phrasing Skill

532 Phrase Builder

Reading goal: 50 seconds.

As

1

Have

2

At

3

There

4

1. *As you, as you know, as you have, as you can, as well, as you will see, as the, as long, as it will be.*
2. *I have, I have not, you have, you have not, we have, we have not, they have, they have not, we should have, to have, I will have.*
3. *At the, at the time, at that, at this, at this time, at these, at which time, at last.*
4. *There is, there are, there are not, there will, there will be, there will not be, there might, there has been.*

533 Warmup Phrase Letter

Can you read your warmup letter for Chapter 13 in 40 seconds or less? Copy it in 1⅓ minutes?

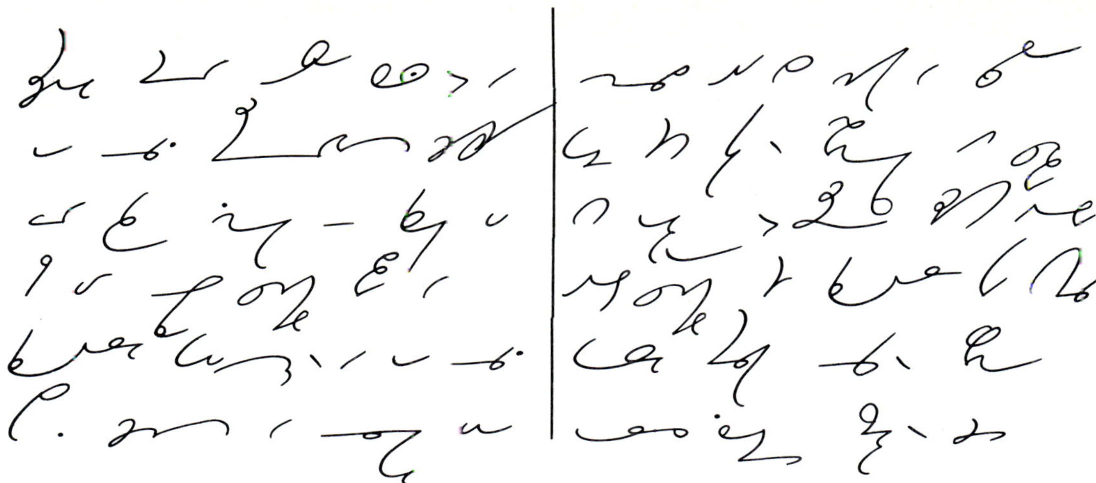

Building Transcription Skills

534 OFFICE-STYLE DICTATION short deletions

An executive will occasionally decide to delete—take out—a word or phrase or even a sentence that has been dictated. The dictator might say:

I have a large, well-designed office—take out **large**.

To indicate that *large* should be deleted, simply strike a heavy downward line through the word, thus:

Sometimes the executive may simply repeat the sentence without the word or phrase that should be omitted.

I have a large and well-designed office—no, **I have a well-designed office**.

To indicate the deletion, you would strike out in your notes not only the word *large* but the *and* as well.

If only a word or short expression is to be taken out, use a heavy downward line; if several words are to be taken out, use a wavy line.

I have a large office—oh, scratch it out.

In your notes you would show this deletion thus:

Illustration of Office-Style Dictation

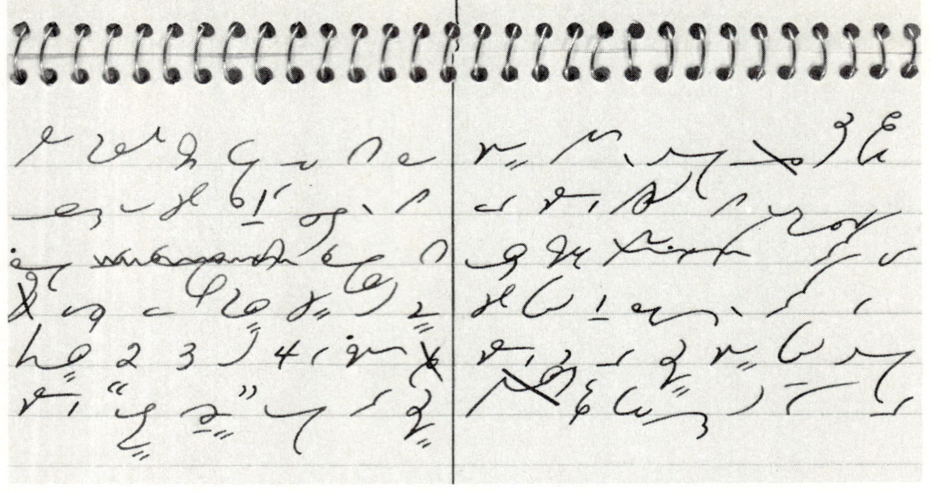

535 Business Vocabulary Builder

berth Place where a ship is docked.

vicinity Nearby area; neighborhood.

unprecedented Without similar pattern in the past.

● Reading and Writing Practice

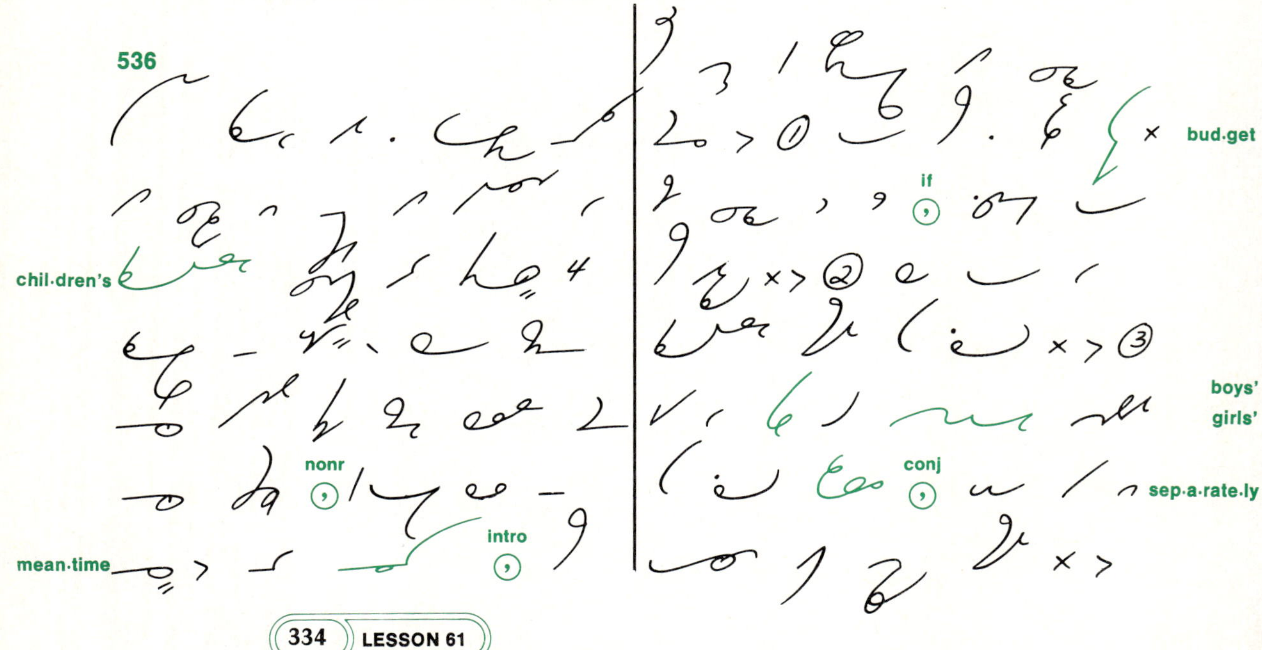

when

[119]

537

as

city's

oc·ca·sion

intro

ser

ap

ser

ex·hib·its

birth

berth

intro

ad·ja·cent

three-day
hyphenated before noun

state's

conj

[154]

guid·ed

538

ser

berthed

and o

intro

sim·i·lar

year's

if

nc

grate·ful·ly

[104]

539

33

Phoe·nix

nip·py

intro

when

intro

bal·my

intro

ap

[133]

540 Supply the necessary punctuation and the missing words.

Transcription Quiz

15

[114]

Warmup Your warmup letter is on page 332. Write the first paragraph as rapidly as you can and as often as you can in the time you have available.

Developing Word-Building Power

541 Brief-Form Chart

Reading goal: 20 seconds

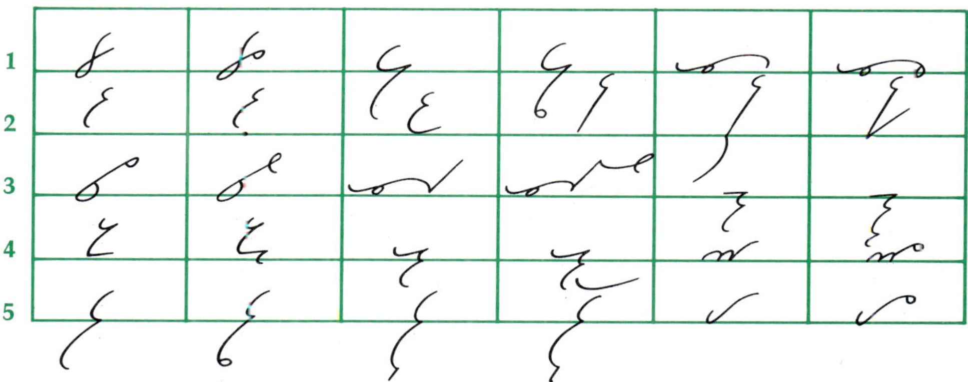

1. *Particular, particularly, probable, probably, regular, regularly.*
2. *Speak, speaking, speaker, subject, subjective, subjected.*
3. *Idea, ideas, regard, regardless, newspaper, newspapers.*
4. *Opinion, opinions, responsible, responsibility, worth, worthy.*
5. *Public, publicly, publish-publication, publishes-publications, ordinary, ordinarily.*

542 Geographical Expressions

1. *Greenville, Nashville, Knoxville, Louisville, Bronxville, Brownsville, Crawfordsville.*
2. *Michigan, Nebraska, Alabama, Alaska, Minnesota.*

Building Transcription Skills

543 SPELLING FAMILIES -an, -en, -on Words ending with the letter *n* preceded by *a, e,* or *o* have always been a source of spelling difficulty for stenographers. Here are a number of words with these endings.

Words Ending in -an

ur·ban	**met·ro·pol·i·tan**	**slo·gan**
sub·ur·ban	**vet·er·an**	**or·phan**

Words Ending in -en

bur·den	**tak·en**	**of·ten**
cit·i·zen	**less·en**	**fas·ten**

Words Ending in -on

rea·son	**aban·don**	**car·ton**
per·son	**par·don**	**cot·ton**

---

544 Business Vocabulary Builder

disrupt To put into disorder.

magnitude Great size or extent.

nuisance Something unpleasant or obnoxious.

prevailing Generally current; common.

Reading and Writing Practice

545 Brief-Form Letter

morn·ing's

sub·ur·ban

conj

if

traf·fic

nonr

usu·al·ly

crowd·ed

and o

ag·gra·vat·ing

par

Coun·cil

[154]

[135]

546

547

rea·sons

amuse·ment

as

com·mu·ni·ty

un·em·ploy·ment

conj

Transcribe:
2 percent

par

re·luc·tant

dis·cour·age

mag·ni·tude

if

first-class
hyphenated before noun

nui·sance

[152]

548

shop·ping

geo

if

par

pre·vail·ing

dis·rupt

intro

if

ser

[117]

549

as

site

sta·di·um

conj

of·ten

aban·don

in·ten·si·fied

ap

Transcribe: 8 p.m.

intro

when

nc

at·tempt

[193]

550 Supply the necessary punctuation and the missing words.

Transcription Quiz

[142]

Warmup Your warmup letter is on page 332. Write the second paragraph as rapidly as you can and as often as you can in the time you have available.

Developing Word-Building Power

551 Word Families

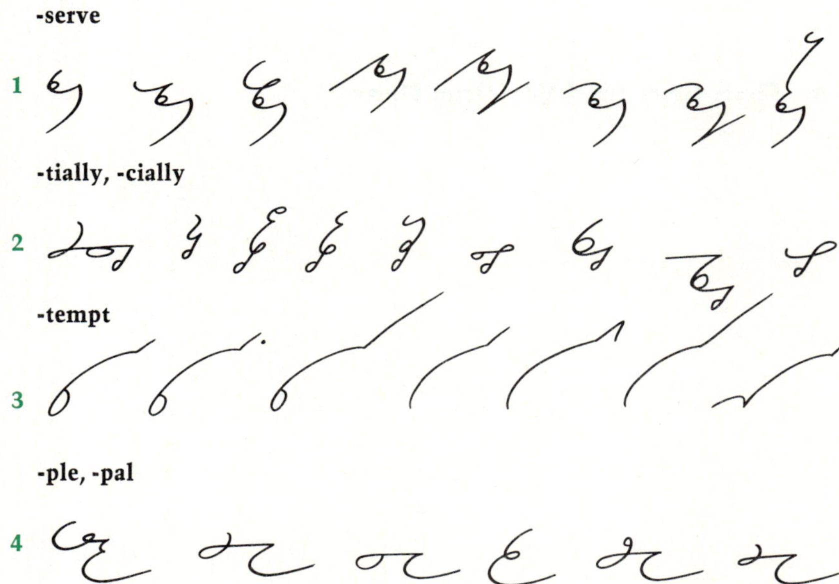

1. *Serve, reserve, preserve, deserve, deserved, conserve, conserved, observe.*
2. *Financially, socially, especially, specially, officially, initially, partially, impartially, racially.*
3. *Attempt, attempting, attempted, tempt, temptation, tempted, contempt.*
4. *Principal, sample, ample, people, example, simple.*

Building Transcription Skills

552 SIMILAR-WORDS DRILL access, excess

access Availability; ability to make use of.

We have access *to the park.*

excess Too much; extra.

The excess *money will be used for a new park.*

---

553 Business Vocabulary Builder

issuance Act of putting forth or sending out.

renovation Restoring; remodeling.

premier Beginning; opening.

Reading and Writing Practice

554

mu·si·cal

the·ater

if

prin·ci·pal

three-month
hyphenated before noun

pre·mier

conj

par

ap

Transcribe:
8 p.m.
$200,000

if

[140]

555

spon·sor·ing

ap

fi·nan·cial·ly

par

[79]

556

ap

polls

au·tho·rize

as

nonr

and o

well-kept
hyphenated before noun

ex·ist·ing

nc

[111]

557

ap

as

am·ple

cit·i·zens'

ex·cess

nc

nc

intro

ac·cess

ma·jor

intro

ser

when

cr

[210]

558

bro·chure

beau·ti·ful

conj

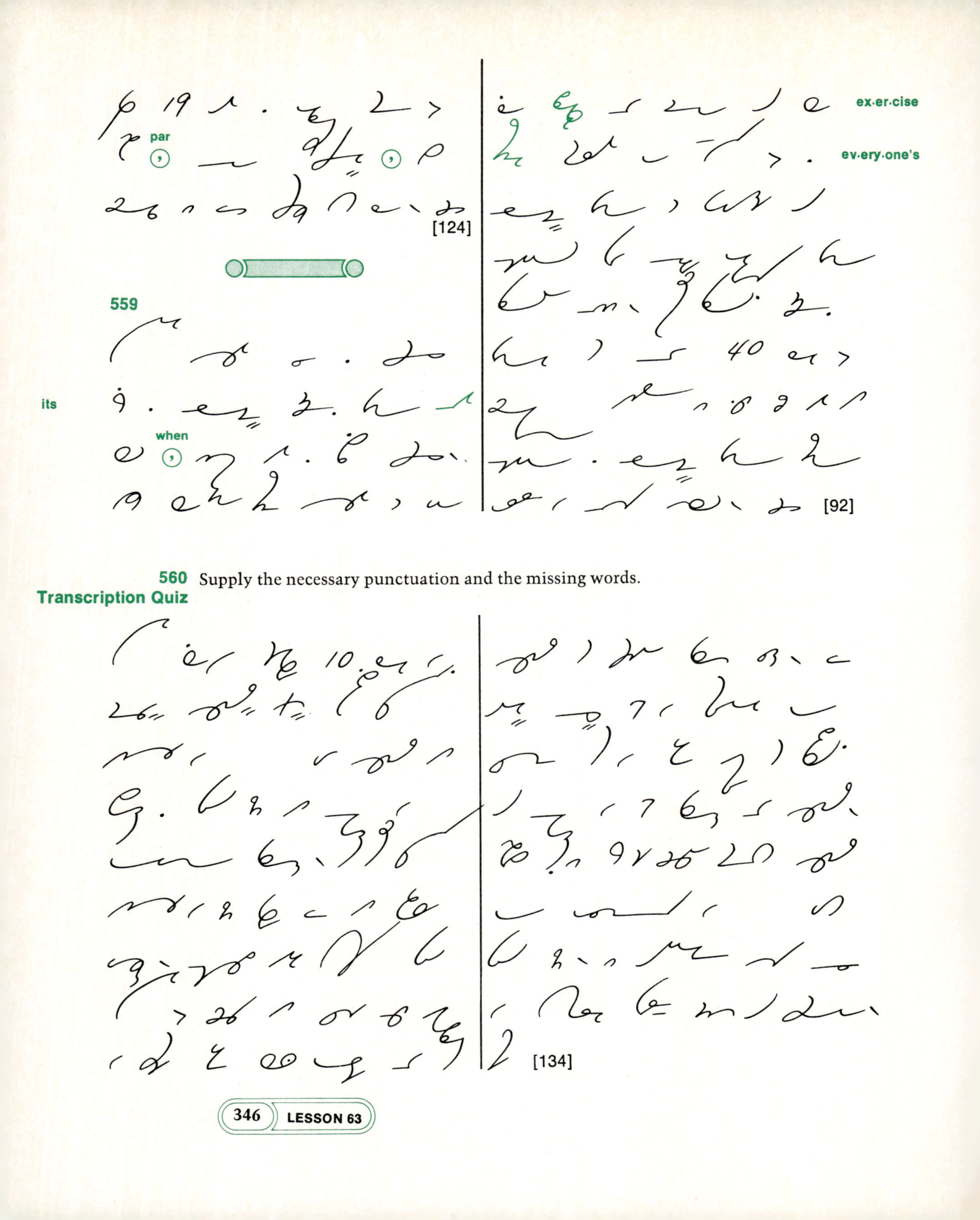

ex·er·cise

par

ev·ery·one's

[124]

559

its

when

[92]

560 Supply the necessary punctuation and the missing words.

Transcription Quiz

[134]

Warmup Your warmup letter is on page 332. Write the last paragraph of the letter as rapidly as you can and as often as time permits.

Developing Word-Building Power

561 Word Beginnings and Endings

Per-

1

Enter-, Entr-

2

-ure

3

-hood

4

1. *Performance, perfect, permit, perplex, personal, personally.*
2. *Entertaining, entertainment, entered, enterprising, entrance, entrances, entrancingly, entrant.*
3. *Feature, future, procedure, nature, lecture, figure, failure.*
4. *Neighborhood, manhood, childhood, womanhood, parenthood, girlhood, boyhood.*

Building Transcription Skills

562 COMMON PREFIXES en-

en- in the English language the prefix *en-* often means *into* or *within*.

- **enclose** To place within a container.
- **enter** To go in.
- **entrance** A way in.
- **enact** To make into law.
- **enroll** To register in.

---

563 Business Vocabulary Builder

cultural Pertaining to knowledge, art, etc.

affiliate *(noun)* A company effectively controlled by or associated with another.

repertory The stock of songs, plays, operas, or other pieces that a company is prepared to perform.

Reading and Writing Practice

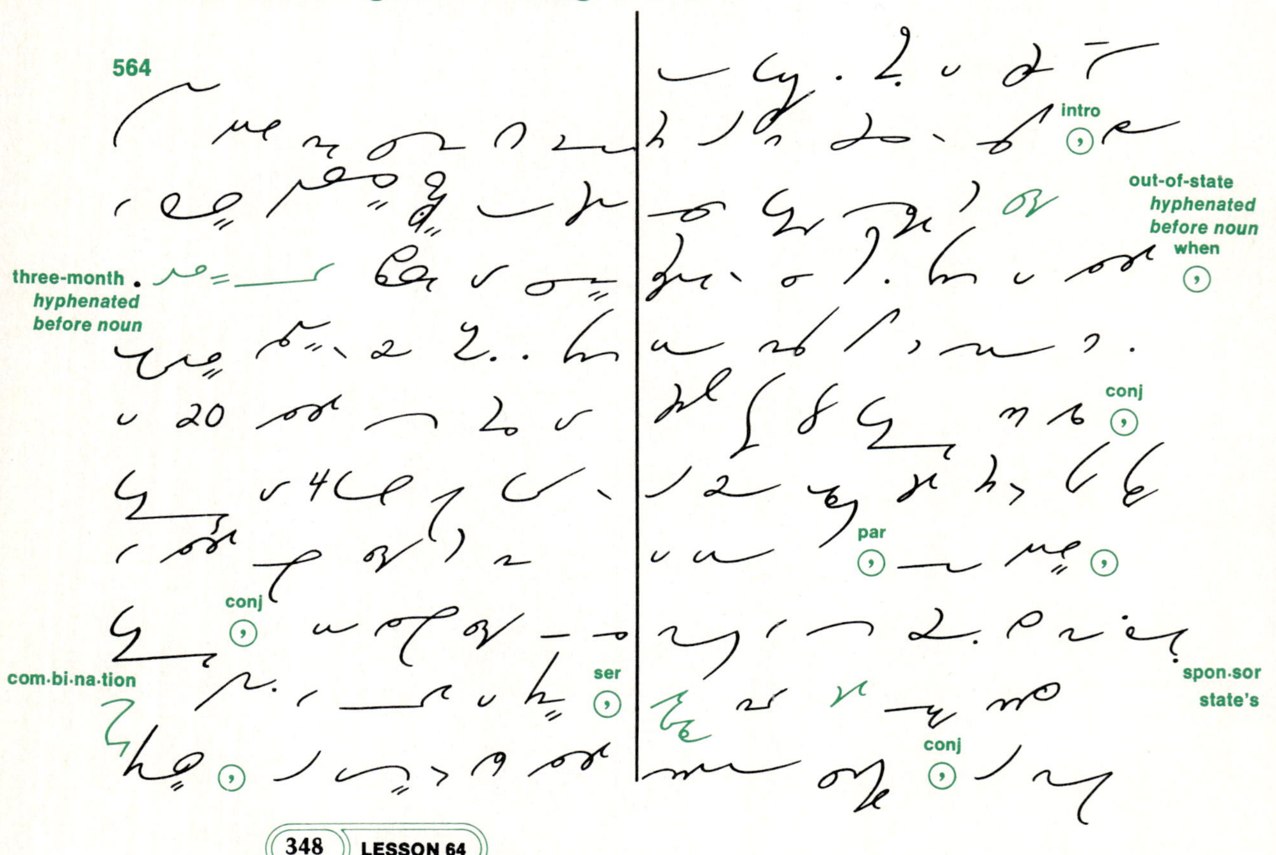

its

intro

ap

Transcribe:
25 percent

[202]

565

as

ser

conj

intro

pri·or

conj

intro

Transcribe:
10 a.m.
4 p.m.

nc

and o

[157]

566

intro

geo

tap·ing

ser

cr

study·ing

conj

[119]

567

intro

dai·ly

nonr

10

[113]

568

Any·one

as

conj

al·ways

bought

in·trigued

intro

prac·ti·cal

par

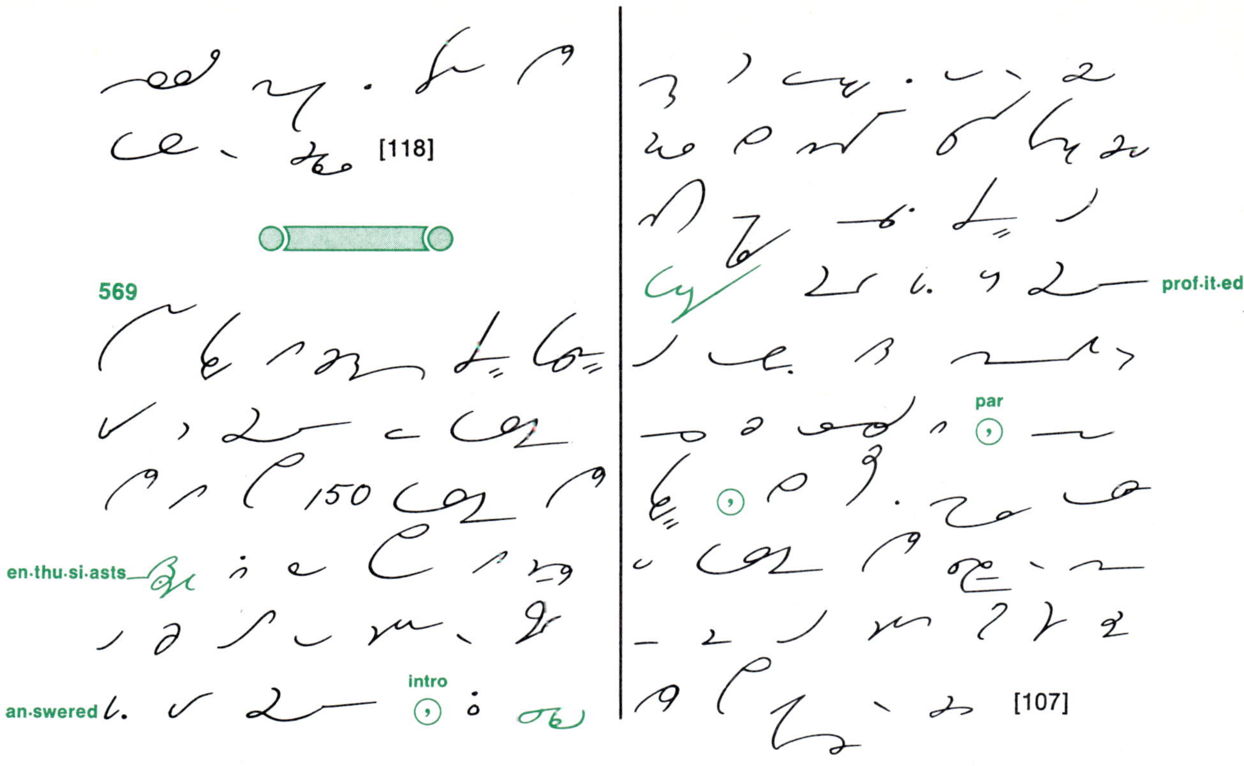

570 Supply the necessary punctuation and the missing words.

Transcription Quiz

[129]

Warmup For the final time, the letter on page 332 will be your warmup letter. Copy as much of the letter as time permits in your best shorthand.

Developing Word-Building Power

571 Shorthand Vocabulary Builder

Men

1

-tition, -tation

2

-ngk

3

-rd

4

1. *Men, meant, mention, women, amend, recommend.*
2. *Station, admission, recommendations, addition, permission, combination, commutation.*
3. *Blank, banquet, frank, frankly, rank, sink, bank.*
4. *Guard, garden, Gardner, third, hired, toward, tired.*

Building Transcription Skills

572 Business Vocabulary Builder

admission A fee paid at or for entrance to a place.

admittance Permission to enter a place.

fair *(noun)* An exhibition usually with accompanying entertainment.

coliseum A large building for public entertainment.

Reading and Writing Practice

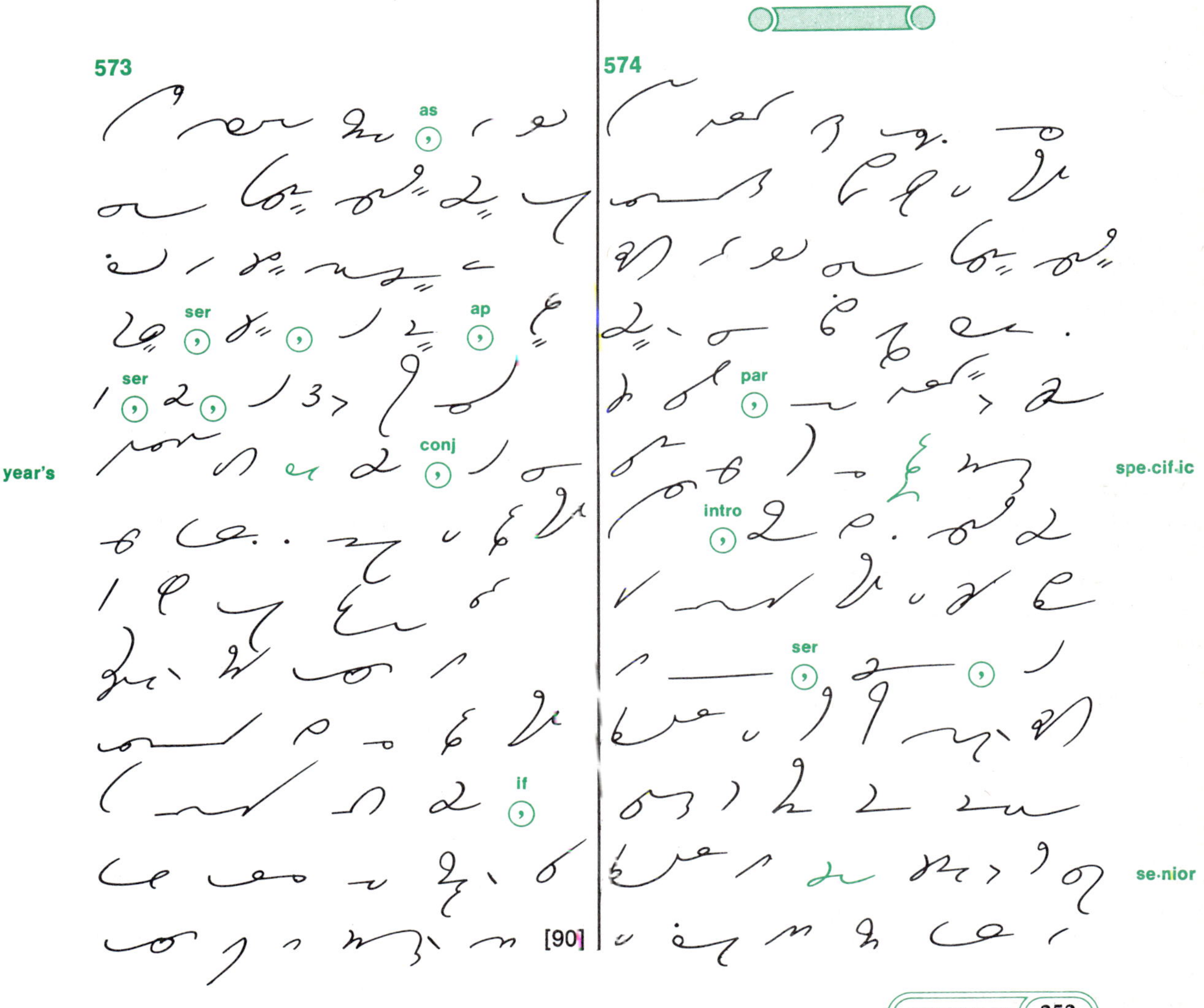

if [101]

575

to·day's

fair

ser

intro

nc

year's

conj

and o

ad·mis·sion

ser

cr

fare

intro

[123]

576

in·qui·ry

when

conj

chil·dren's

ser

nonr

round-trip *hyphenated before noun*

nc

[142]

577

yes·ter·day's

ap

spon·sor
fi·es·ta

conj

cr

[95]

578

if

intro

ef·fect

45%

ocean

con·ve·nient

[100]

579

al·ready

[38]

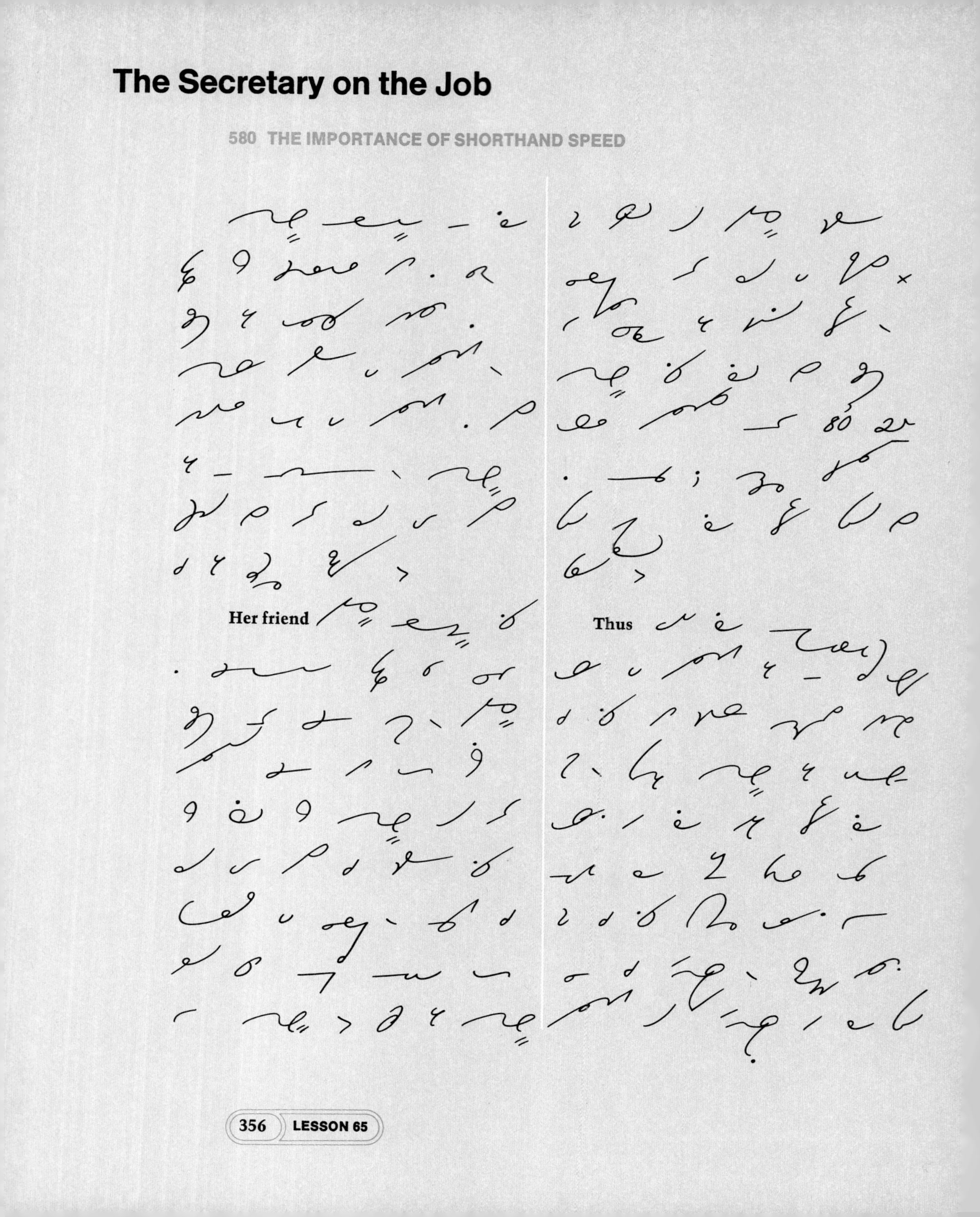

The Secretary on the Job

580 THE IMPORTANCE OF SHORTHAND SPEED

Her friend

Thus

[332]

She had .

The best way to prepare for promotion is to do the very best job possible on the work you are doing right now. Good performance in the current position places the secretary in a position for advancement.

Food and Agriculture

Do you know how much food you eat in a year? If you are an average eater, you eat about three-quarters of a ton of food in one year. Multiply that by the approximately 3½ billion people in the world today and the result is astounding. Feeding the world is big business, and it requires many people who have backgrounds in such diverse areas as agriculture, geology, business management, and veterinary medicine, to name just a few. The business of providing food for people is known as agribusiness, which includes everyone who works to grow, process, and distribute products that we eat.

The business of providing food begins with producers, more commonly known as farmers and ranchers. They grow the crops, raise the animals, and produce the dairy products that eventually wind up in our refrigerators and on our tables.

Today, fewer farmers are producing more agricultural products on much larger farms than ever before. Running a big farm requires not only a knowledge of agriculture but business and mechanical skills as well. Machinery is now doing much of the work that people used to do by hand or with simple tools. Chemicals are being used to fertilize the soil, to control insects, and to prevent and cure diseases of both crops and animals. In addition, agricultural products are being moved from the farm to the processing plants and on to the consumer in better and quicker ways.

Very few agricultural products reach the consumer in the same form as they left the farm or the ranch. Most food products are processed or changed in some way so that they can be sold for daily use. Vegetables and fruit are often canned or frozen. Cattle and other meat-producing animals are cut up and packaged and sometimes even cooked or canned. Wheat and other grains are ground into flour or made into food—bread, cookies, crackers, cake mixes, and so on. After being processed, food products must be distributed and transported to stores where consumers can buy them.

In addition to those people who actually handle food products—the farmers, processors, and distributors—there are hundreds of others who are involved in the field of agribusiness. Farms cannot run without farm supplies, such as seed, animal feed, and fertilizer. Farms also need equipment, including plows, tractors, and harvesters, all of which use petroleum products, such as gasoline, oil, and diesel fuel. Botanists, biologists, and veterinarians are constantly looking for new and better ways to raise crops and animals.

The business of making food available for people to eat is probably much bigger and more complex than many people realize. The letters in this chapter concern the field of agribusiness.

Building Phrasing Skill

581 Phrase Builder

Reading goal: 50 seconds.

On

1

In

2

Want

3

With

4

1. *On the, on that, on that date, on time, on our, on which, on it, on your.*
2. *In the, in that, in that time, in our, in the future, in which, in which it is, in these, in this.*
3. *I want, you want, we want, if you want, we wanted, they want, he wants, who wants.*
4. *With the, with that, with you, with our, with us, with which, with these, with them, with this.*

582 Warmup Phrase Letter

This is your warmup phrase letter for Chapter 14. Read it and copy it as rapidly as you can.

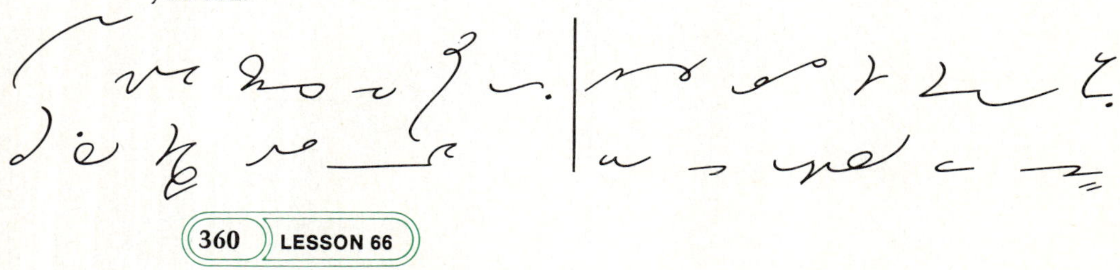

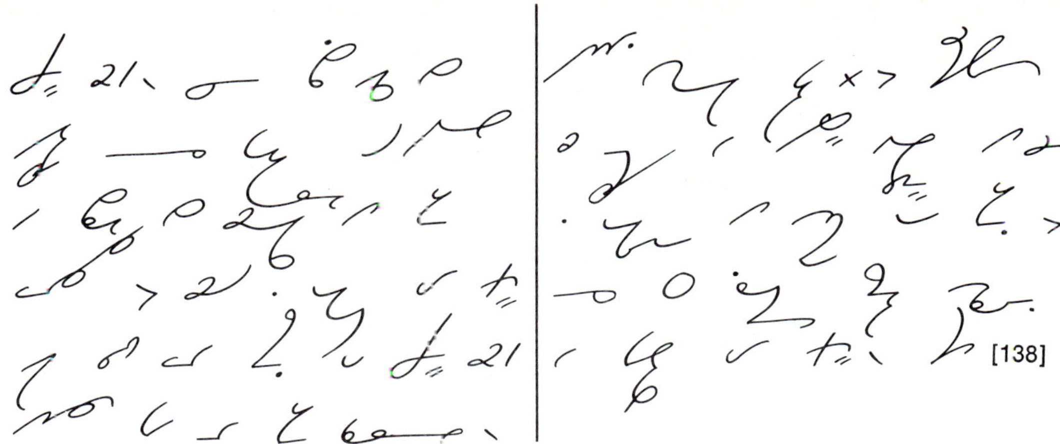

Building Transcription Skills

583 OFFICE-STYLE DICTATION short insertions and changes Sometimes a dictator may decide to change a word or phrase after completing a sentence.

I want to buy a cheap calculator—change **cheap** *to* **inexpensive**.

You would indicate this change in your notes thus:

Sometimes the dictator may wish to insert a word or a phrase in a sentence.

I want to buy an inexpensive calculator—make that **small and** *inexpensive calculator.*

You must be alert so that you can quickly find the point at which the addition is to be made. When you find the point, insert the word or phrase with a caret, just as you would in longhand, thus:

Illustration of Office-Style Dictation

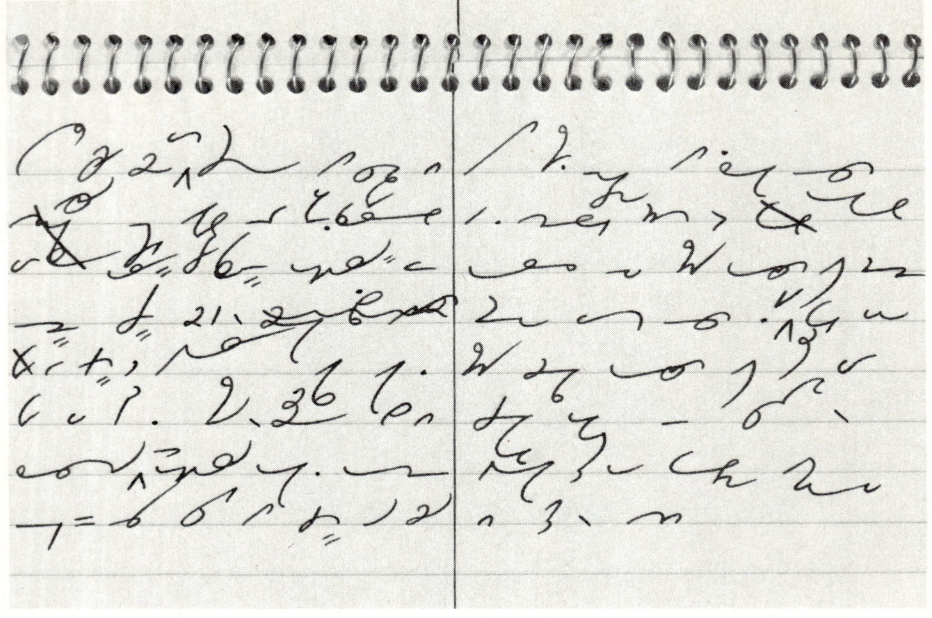

---

584 Business Vocabulary Builder

elegant Of high quality; splendid.

variance A license to do something contrary to the usual rule.

ordinance A law set forth by a governmental authority.

dignitaries Those who possess high rank or hold positions of honor.

Reading and Writing Practice

585

par

ac·cept

ap

and o

wel·come

conj

much-need·ed *hyphenated before noun*

cr

[137]

586

as

dig·ni·tar·ies

ser

for·ward

Chi·ca·go's

[81]

587

intro

re·al·ized

nc

intro

intro

vari ance

curb

nonr

when

[129]

588

of·ten

ap·pe·tiz·ing

intro

ful·filled

ap

nonr

par

steaks

intro

poul·try

intro

ac·com·mo·date

[138]

589 **Transcription Quiz** Supply the necessary punctuation and the missing words.

[118]

Warmup Your warmup letter is on page 360. Write the first paragraph of that letter as rapidly as you can and as often as you can in the time available.

Developing Word-Building Power

590 Brief-Form Chart

Your reading goal: 20 seconds.

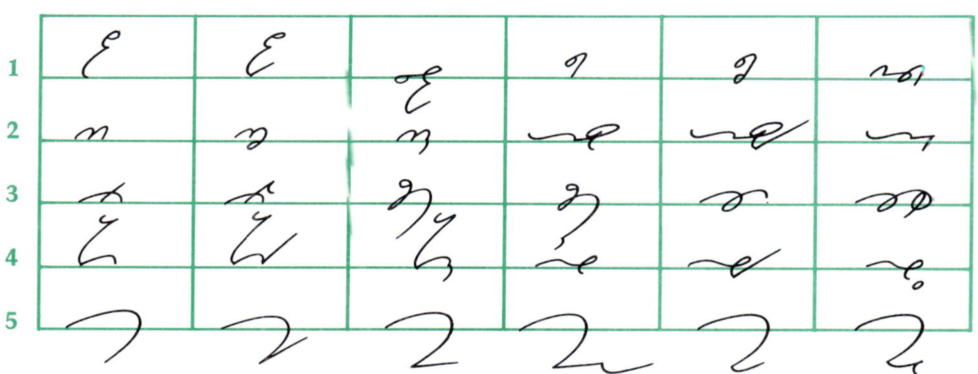

1. *Experience, experienced, inexperienced, usual, usually, unusual.*
2. *World, worldly, world's, recognize, recognized, recognition.*
3. *Quantity, quantities, executive, executives, character, characterize.*
4. *Object, objected, objects, correspond-correspondence, corresponded, correspondingly.*
5. *Govern, governed, government, governmental, governor, governors.*

591 Geographical Expressions

1

2

1. *Bennington, Burlington, Lexington, Washington, Huntington, Wilmington.*
2. *Arkansas, Kentucky, North Carolina, Montana, America, American, United States.*

Building Transcription Skills

592 SPELLING FAMILIES -ant, -ent

Be sure that when you transcribe a word with the sound *ent* you spell it correctly. Some words are spelled *ant*; some *ent*.

Words Ending in -ant

res·tau·rant	**ig·no·rant**	**ser·vant**
ap·pli·cant	**war·rant**	**ac·coun·tant**
pleas·ant	**re·luc·tant**	**sig·nif·i·cant**

Words Ending in -ent

com·pe·tent	**su·per·in·ten·dent**	**de·pen·dent**
res·i·dent	**pres·i·dent**	**ac·ci·dent**
ev·i·dent	**stu·dent**	**in·ci·dent**

593 Business Vocabulary Builder

placard A notice posted in a public place; poster.
vita A brief autobiographical sketch.
violation An infringement of the rules.

Reading and Writing Practice

594 Brief-Form Letter

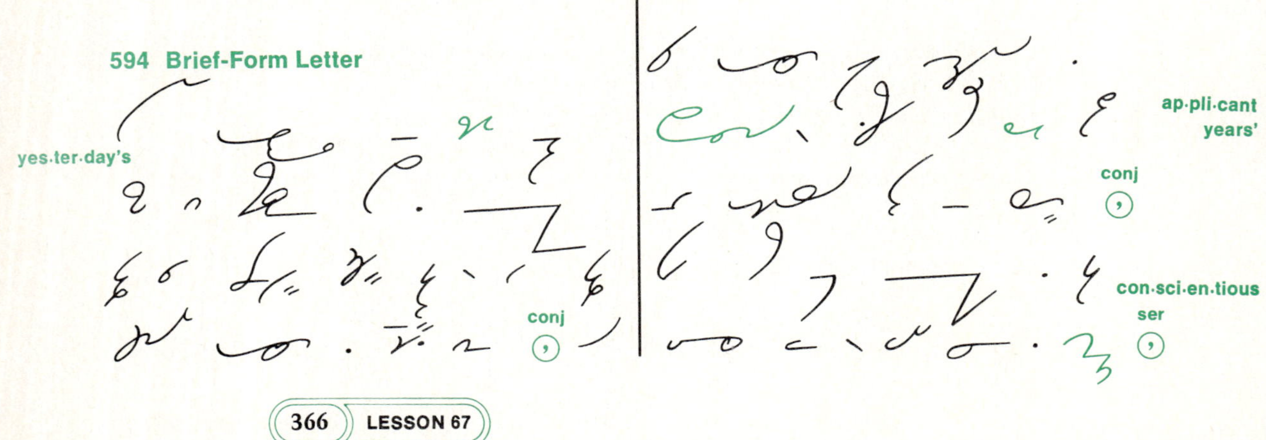

intro

vi·ta

when

[115]

595

if

Bur·ling·ton's

when

nc

Eu·rope

intro

intro

pleas·ant

if

[162]

596

cou·pons

Transcribe:
$8

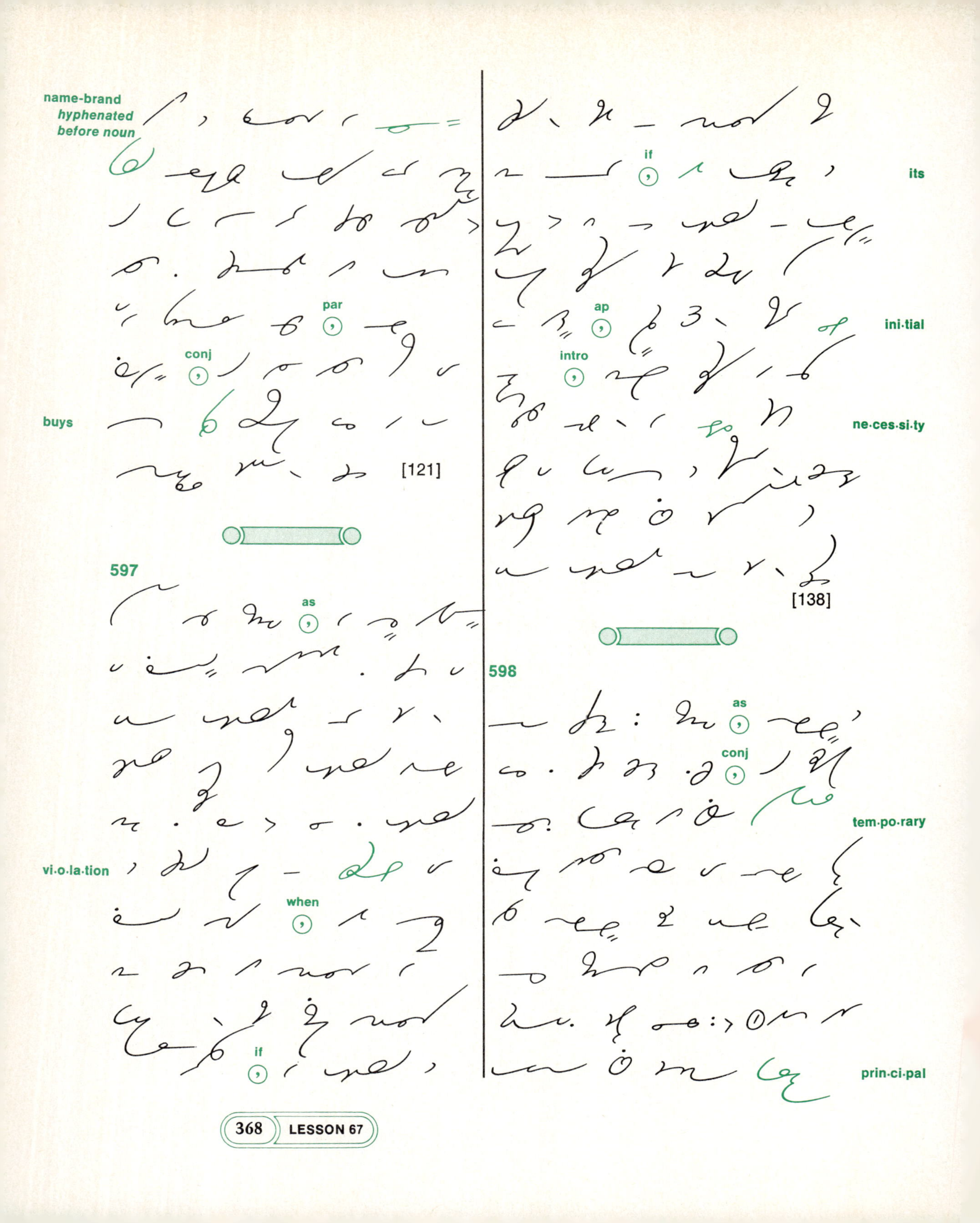

name-brand *hyphenated before noun*

buys

par

conj

[121]

597

as

vi·o·la·tion

when

if

if

its

ap

ini·tial

intro

ne·ces·si·ty

[138]

598

as

conj

tem·po·rary

prin·ci·pal

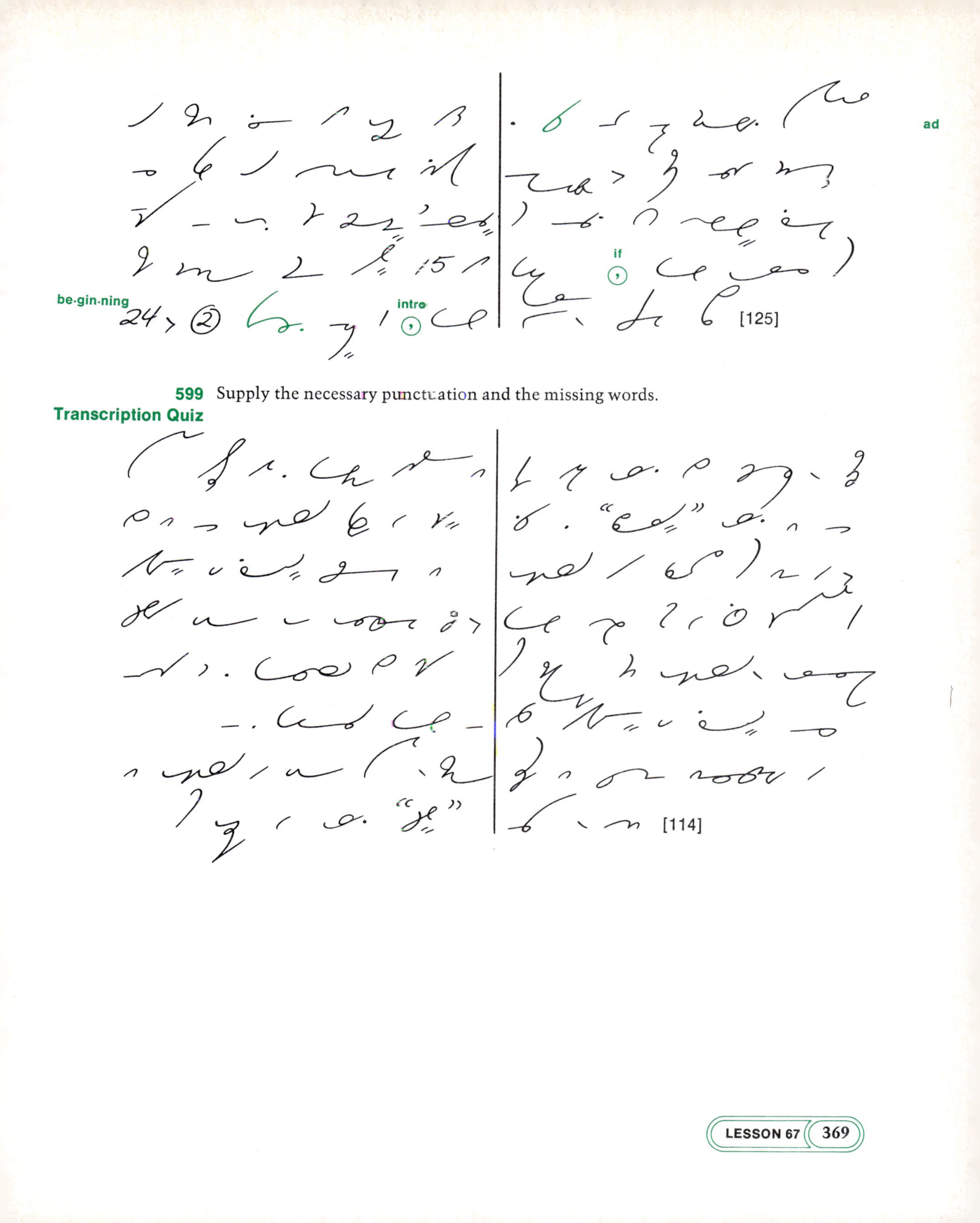

ad

if

be·gin·ning

intro

[125]

599 Supply the necessary punctuation and the missing words.

Transcription Quiz

[114]

Warmup Your warmup letter is on page 360. Copy the second paragraph of this letter as rapidly as you can and as often as you can.

Developing Word-Building Power

600 Word Families

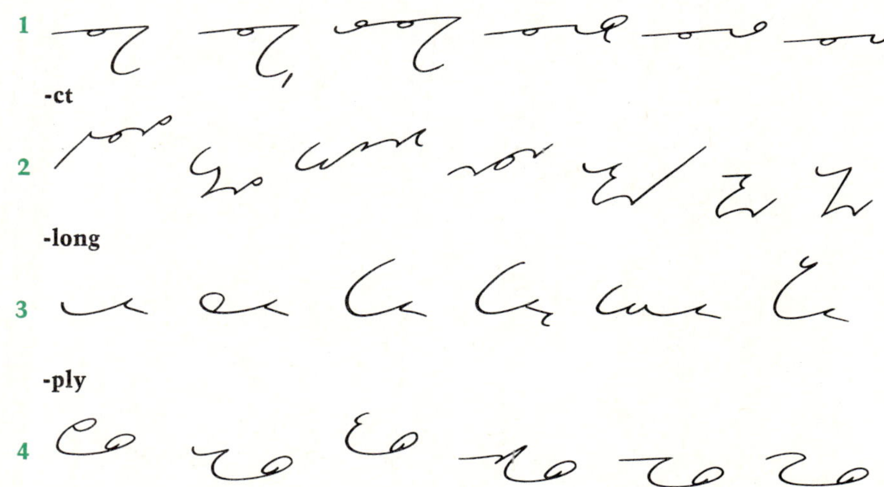

1. *Member, membership, remember, memorize, memory, memorandum.*
2. *Directly, perfectly, products, contact, respected, inspect, reject.*
3. *Long, along, belong, belongs, prolong, oblong.*
4. *Apply, reply, supply, multiply, imply, comply.*

Building Transcription Skills

601 COMMON PREFIXES co-

co- means *with; together; jointly.*

cooperate To work together.

cooperative *(noun)* A group of people working together for a common interest.

coordinate To be able to work together smoothly.

coinsurance Joint assumption of risk with another.

---

602 Business Vocabulary Builder

minimum The least quantity.

wholesale Relating to the sale of goods for resale.

alternatives Choices; other methods.

Reading and Writing Practice

603

co·op·er·a·tive

and o

Transcribe: 1,000

co·or·di·nate

intro

par

well-run hyphenated before noun

if

555-6611

1900

Transcribe: 1900 First Avenue

[138]

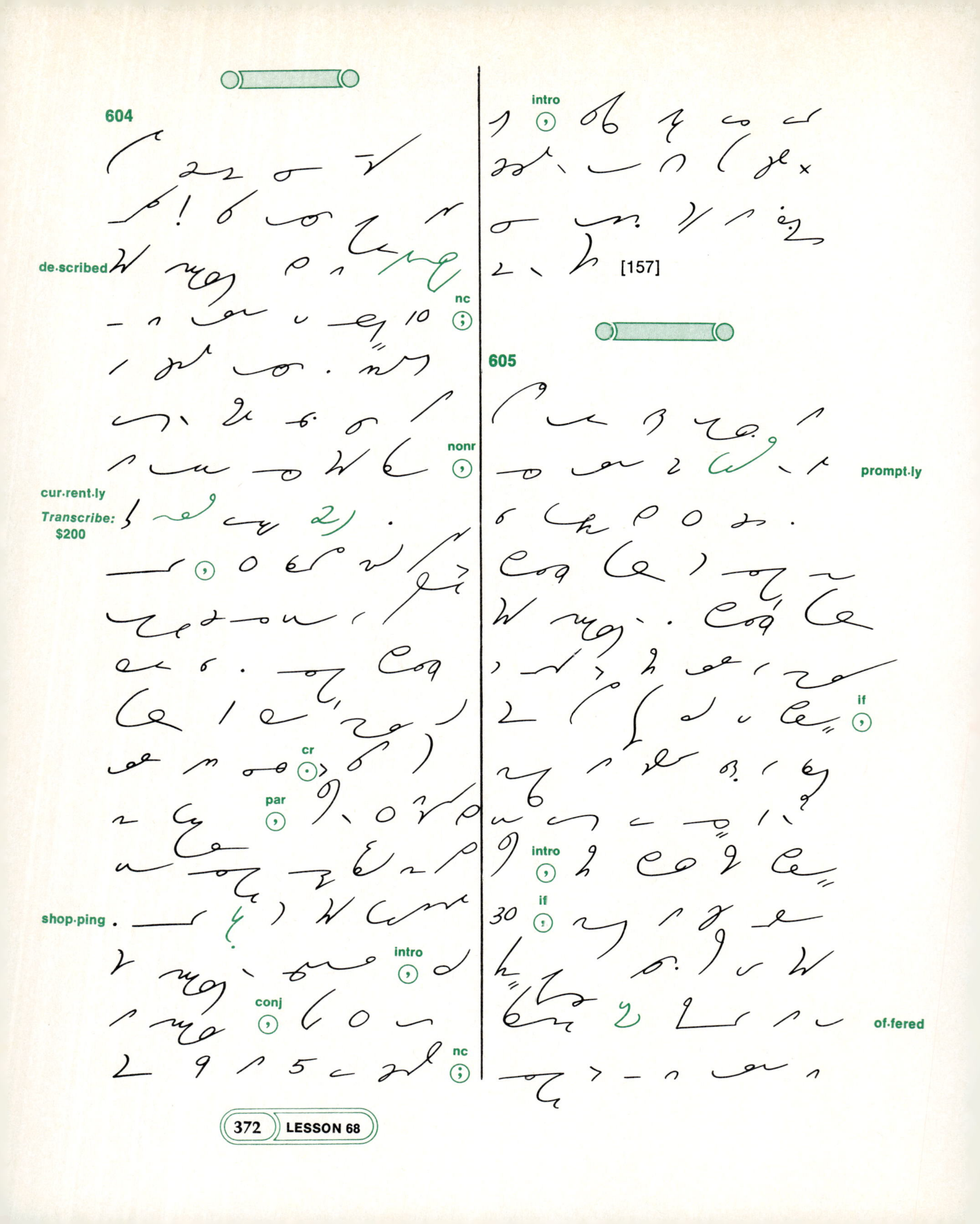

604

de·scribed

nc

nonr

cur·rent·ly

Transcribe: $200

cr

par

shop·ping

intro

conj

nc

intro

[157]

605

prompt·ly

if

intro

if

30

of·fered

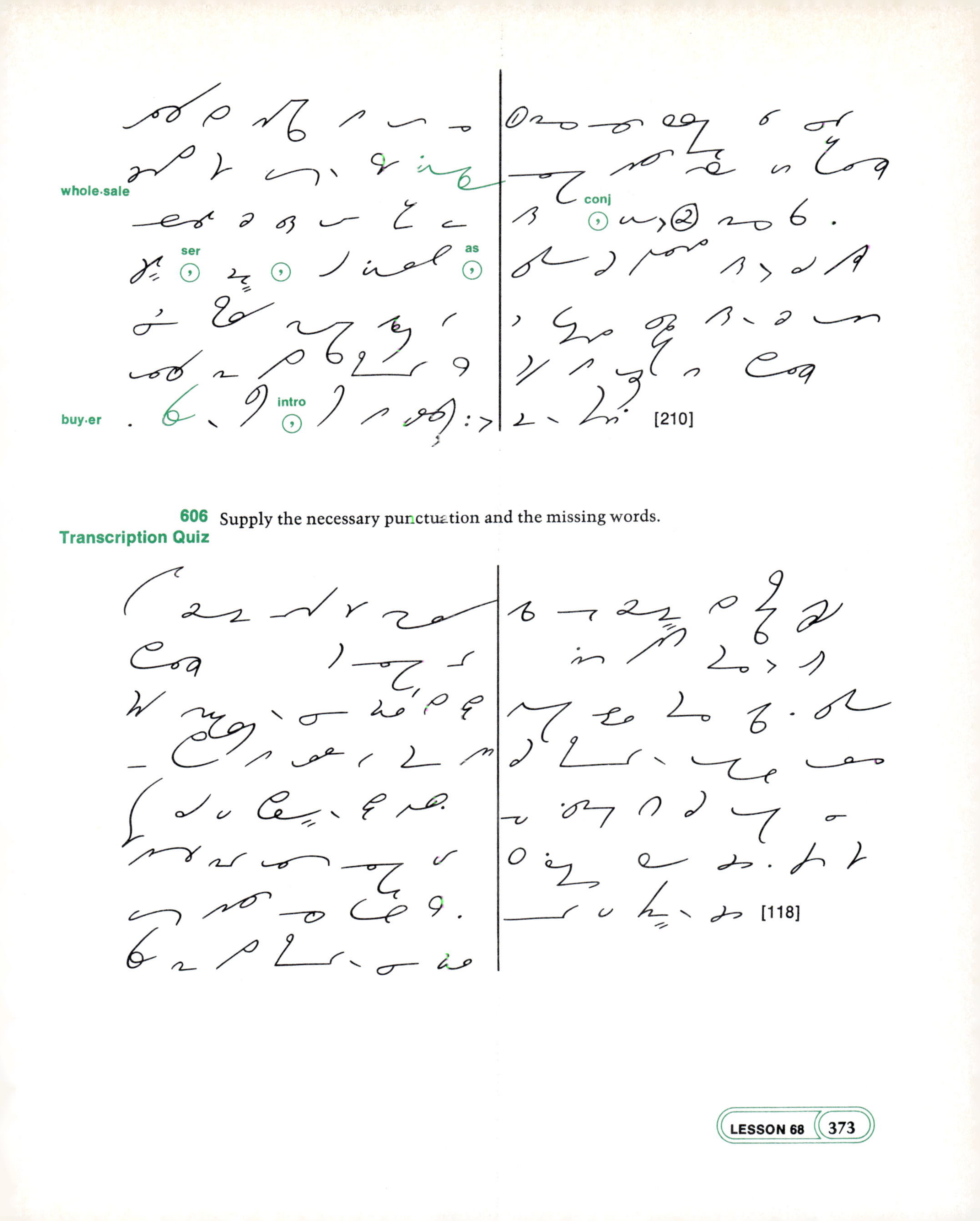

whole·sale

ser

as

conj

buy·er

intro

[210]

606 Supply the necessary punctuation and the missing words.

Transcription Quiz

[118]

Warmup Write the third paragraph of the phrase letter on page 360 as rapidly as you can and as often as time permits.

Developing Word-Building Power

607 Word Endings

-cal

1

-ble

2

-ual

3

-ther

4

1. *Practical, economical, critical, radical, logical, medical.*
2. *Sizable, sensible, payable, vegetable, available, reliable, possible, acceptable, impossible.*
3. *Individual, actual, factual, eventually, natural, naturally.*
4. *Rather, whether, brother, bother, mother, father, neither, either, gather.*

Building Transcription Skills

608 SIMILAR-WORDS DRILL forward, foreword

forward To or toward what is ahead.

I look forward *to seeing you.*

foreword Preface.

I read the foreword *of the book.*

---

609 Business Vocabulary Builder

inaugurate To dedicate ceremoniously; observe formally the beginning of.

hindrance Obstacle; something which delays.

productive Effective in yielding results.

Reading and Writing Practice

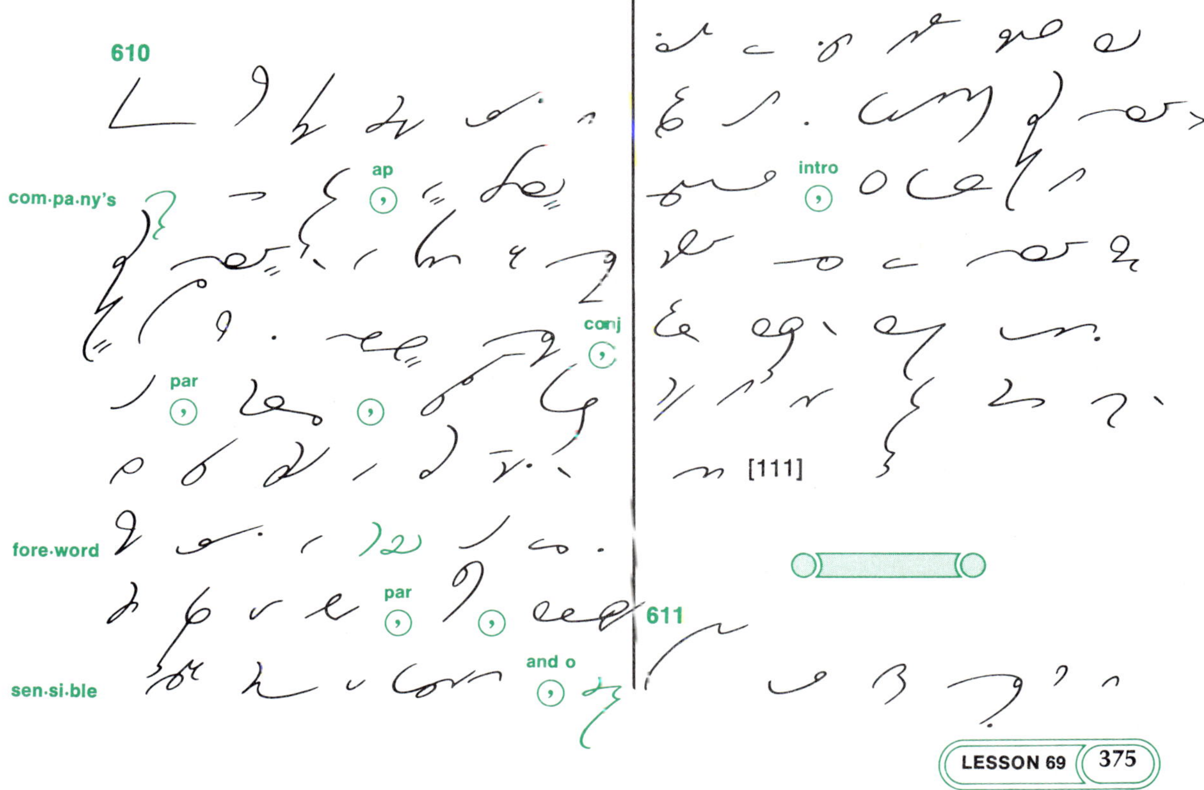

ap

enjoyed

believe

as

ap

[109]

612

eventually

and o

ap

inaugurate

intro

and o

well-trained = *hyphenated before noun*

nc

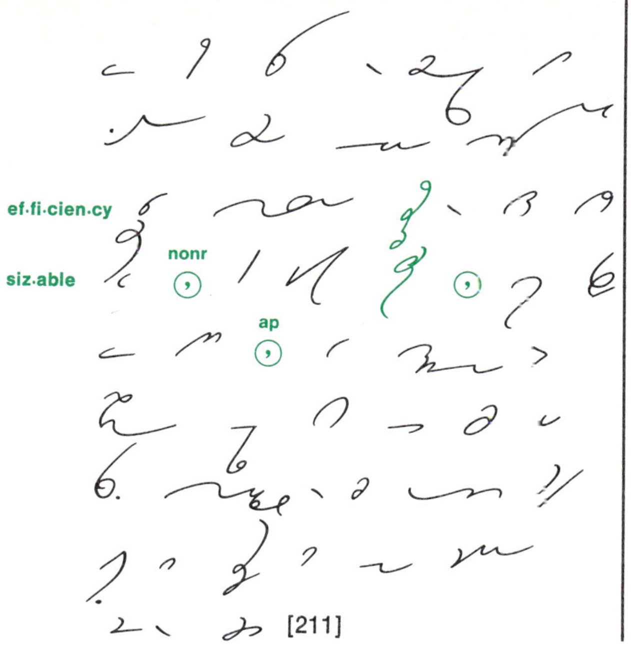

ef·fi·cien·cy

siz·able

nonr ,

,

ap ,

[211]

613

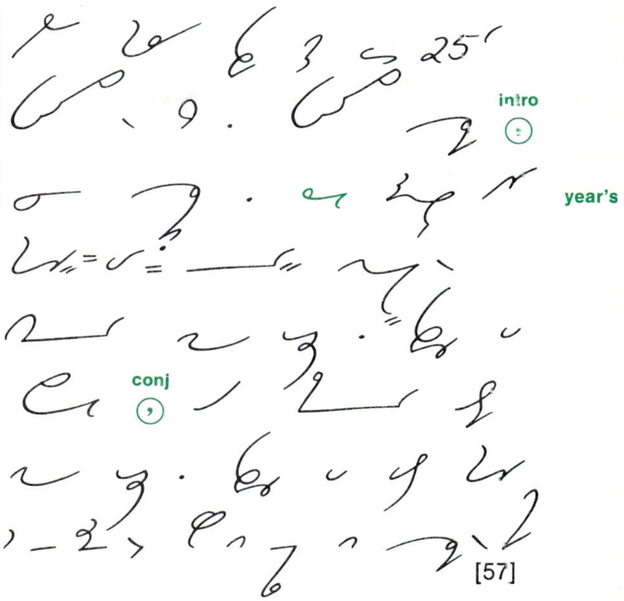

intro :

year's

conj ,

[57]

614 Transcription Quiz Supply the necessary punctuation and the missing words.

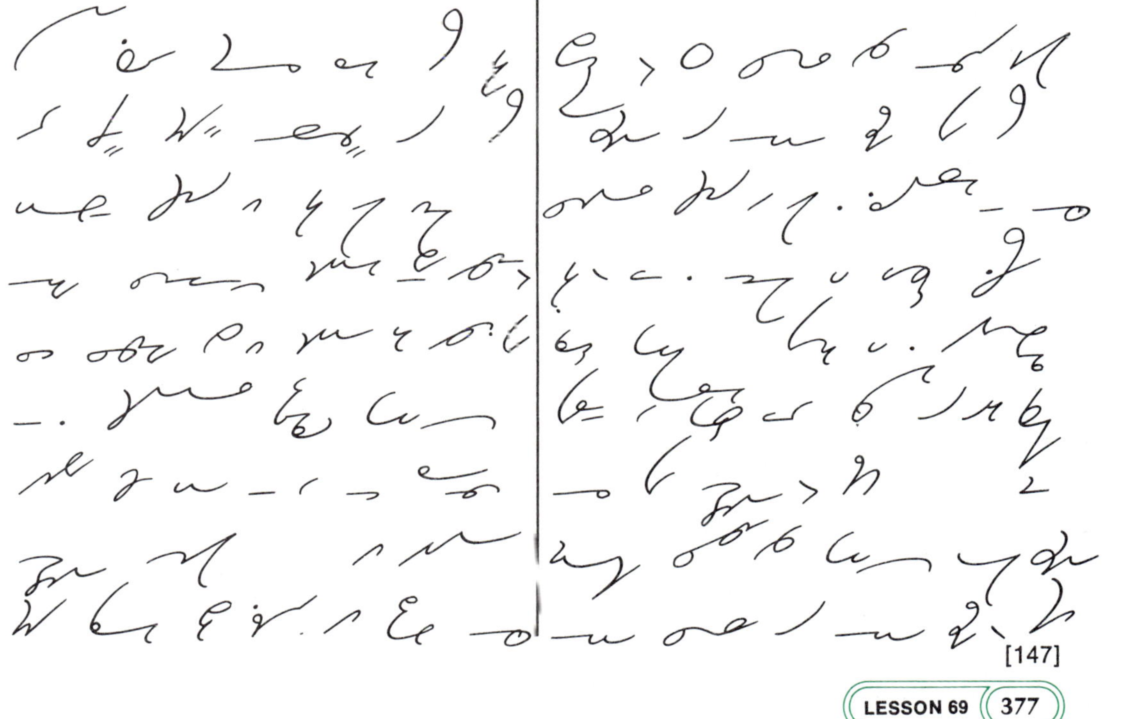

[147]

Warmup For the final time, the phrase letter on page 360 is your warmup. In your best shorthand, write as much of the letter as time permits.

Developing Word-Building Power

615 Shorthand Vocabulary Builder

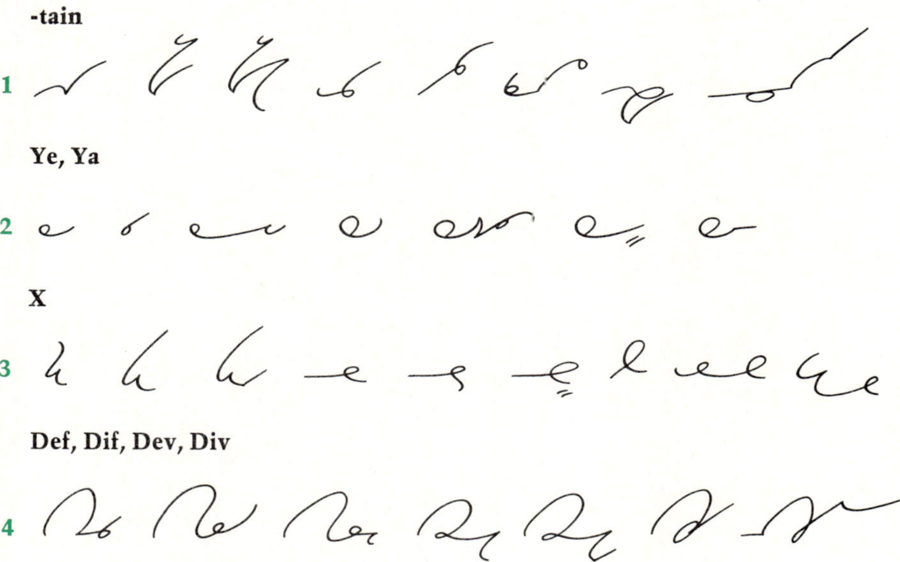

1. *Contain, obtain, obtainable, retain, detain, certainly, captain, maintained.*
2. *Year, yet, yellow, yard, yardstick, Yale, yarn.*
3. *Fox, box, boxed, mix, mixes, Max, tax, relax, perplex.*
4. *Definite, different, difference, develop, developed, divide, individual.*

Building Transcription Skills

616 Business Vocabulary Builder

excessive More than is usual; extreme.

eliminated Removed; excluded.

abide To accept without objection.

Reading and Writing Practice

617

intro

dyes

par

nonr

su·per·mar·kets

ser

wheth·er

par

when

[112]

618

as

and o

sweep·ing

af·fect

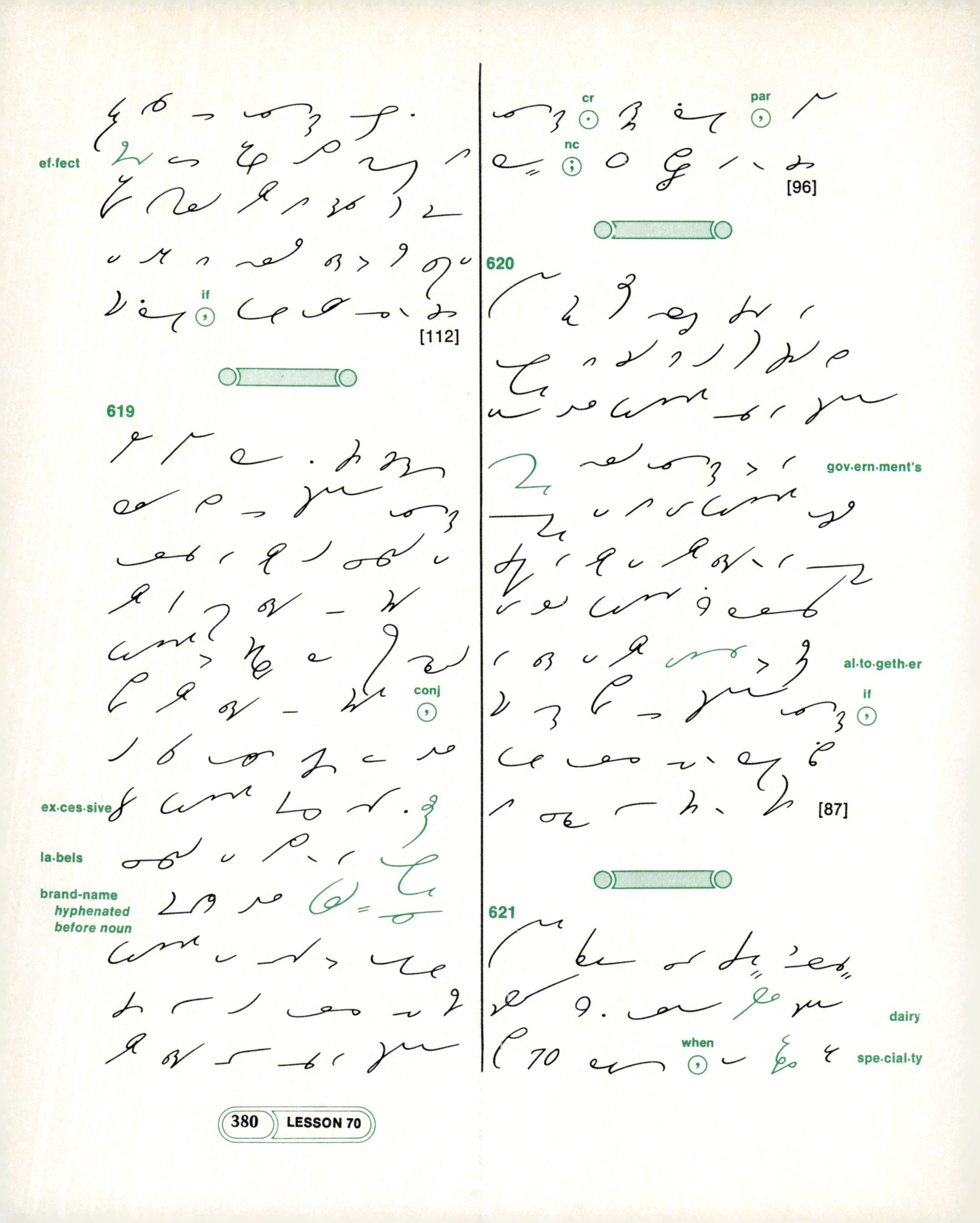

ef·fect

cr

par

nc

[96]

if

[112]

620

gov·ern·ment's

619

al·to·geth·er

if

conj

[87]

ex·ces·sive

la·bels

brand-name
hyphenated before noun

621

dairy

when

spe·cial·ty

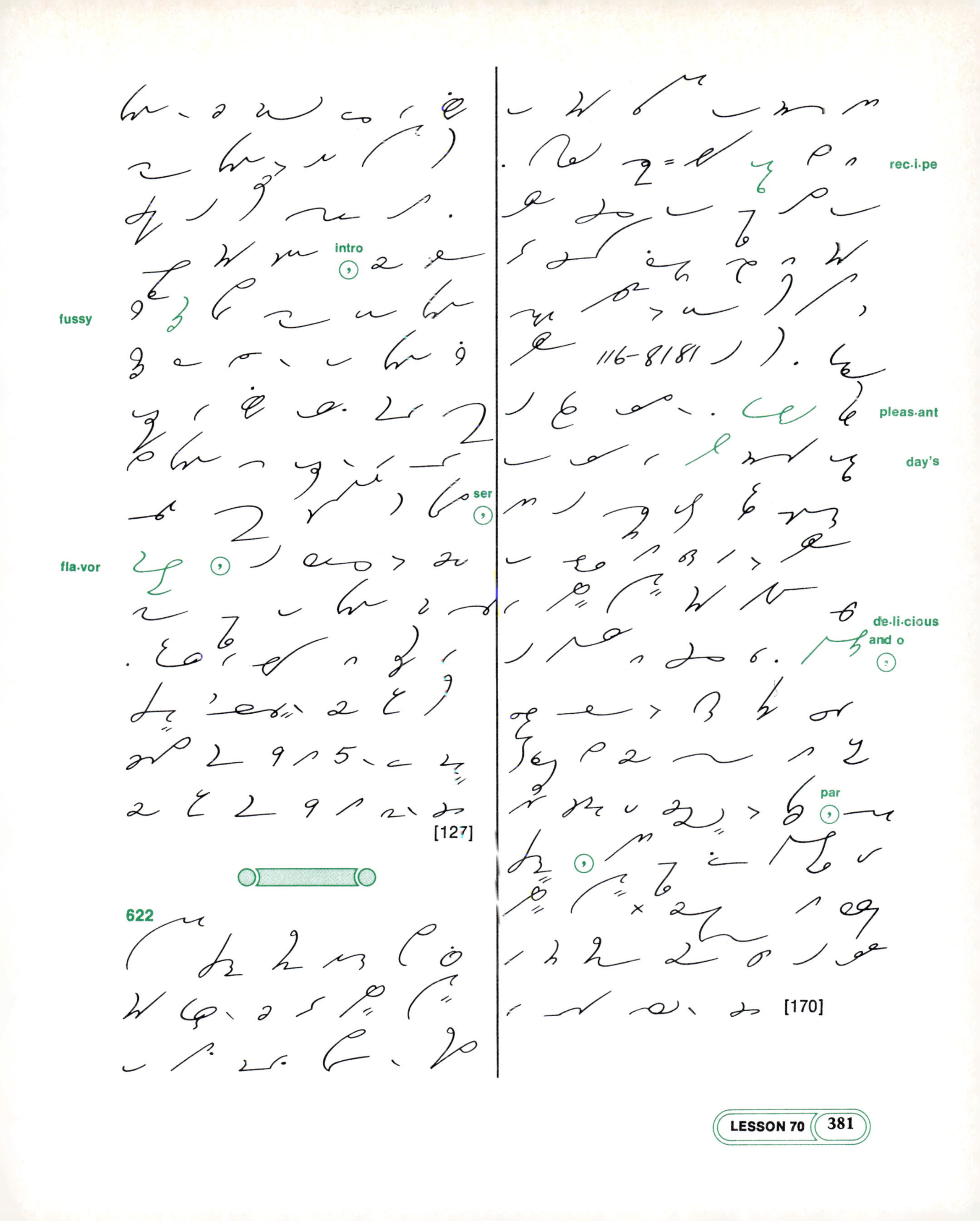

fussy

intro

ser

flavor

[127]

622

recipe

116-8181

pleasant

day's

delicious

and o

par

[170]

The Secretary on the Job

623 DON'T WASTE THE PAUSES

Ms. Davis

Don was

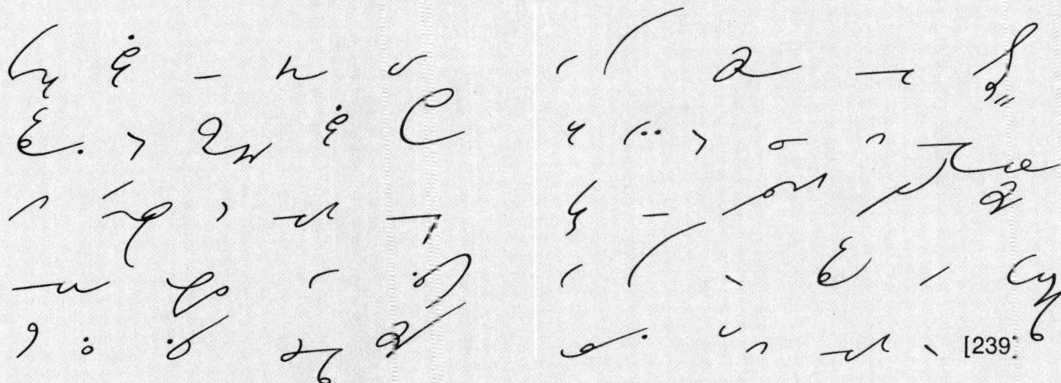

A good secretary is a valuable part of a business organization. A good secretary represents the office, the company, and the employer at all times. A good secretary maintains confidences, does not gossip, and does not even listen to gossip.

CHAPTER

Transportation

How did you get to school, and how did your relatives get to work this morning? How did the food you ate for breakfast and the clothes you are wearing get from the farm and factory to you? Unless you live within walking distance of school or work, you used some form of transportation to get to your destinations.

You might have traveled in a car, bus, or subway. Or, perhaps you even had to cross a stretch of water on a ferry boat. It is also possible that one of your relatives had to travel in a plane to get to work. Unless you grow wheat in your own backyard to make bread or you raise sheep for wool, the food you eat and the clothes you wear probably have had to travel to the stores by some form of transportation.

Transportation is the vital industry that moves people and goods from place to place. Without it, almost all activity in this country would come to a virtual standstill. The United States has been called a "nation on wheels." There is not a minute of the day or night when cars, trucks, buses, trains, or planes are not crossing and crisscrossing the nation's highways, railways, or airways.

And, of course, transportation is not confined within the country's boundaries. International ship lines and airlines are constantly carrying people and goods from one part of the world to another. Technology has even enabled us to send vehicles to other planets and to land people on the moon.

It has often been said that transportation and civilization go hand in hand. Certainly the advancement of civilization has been made possible by the constantly improving means of movement.

The business of moving people and goods from one place to another is one of the largest industries in the United States and employs millions of people. The majority of people employed in the transportation industry are involved in moving goods rather than people. Trucks, trains, and boats primarily carry goods, while automobiles, buses, and planes mainly transport people.

The necessity for transportation in our daily lives makes this industry one of the most important in the country today. Jobs in the transportation industry provide the excitement and the challenge of helping to keep the nation moving smoothly. The letters in this chapter deal with the transportation industry.

Building Phrasing Skill

624 Phrase Builder

Reading goal: 50 seconds.

The

1

For

2

Be

3

Omission of Words

4

1. *To the, in the, for the, at the, by the, that the, when the, on the, of the, if the, from the.*
2. *For this, for that, for them, for our, for which, for which you, for me, for us, for my, for these.*
3. *To be, he could be, I would be, who would not be, they will be, I will not be, they can be, he cannot be, this would be, we might be able, you should be, you can be, if it will be, there will be, you will not be.*
4. *Two or three, three or four, one or two, men and women, many of them, one of the.*

625 Warmup Phrase Letter

This is your warmup phrase letter for Chapter 15. How fast can you read it? How fast can you copy it?

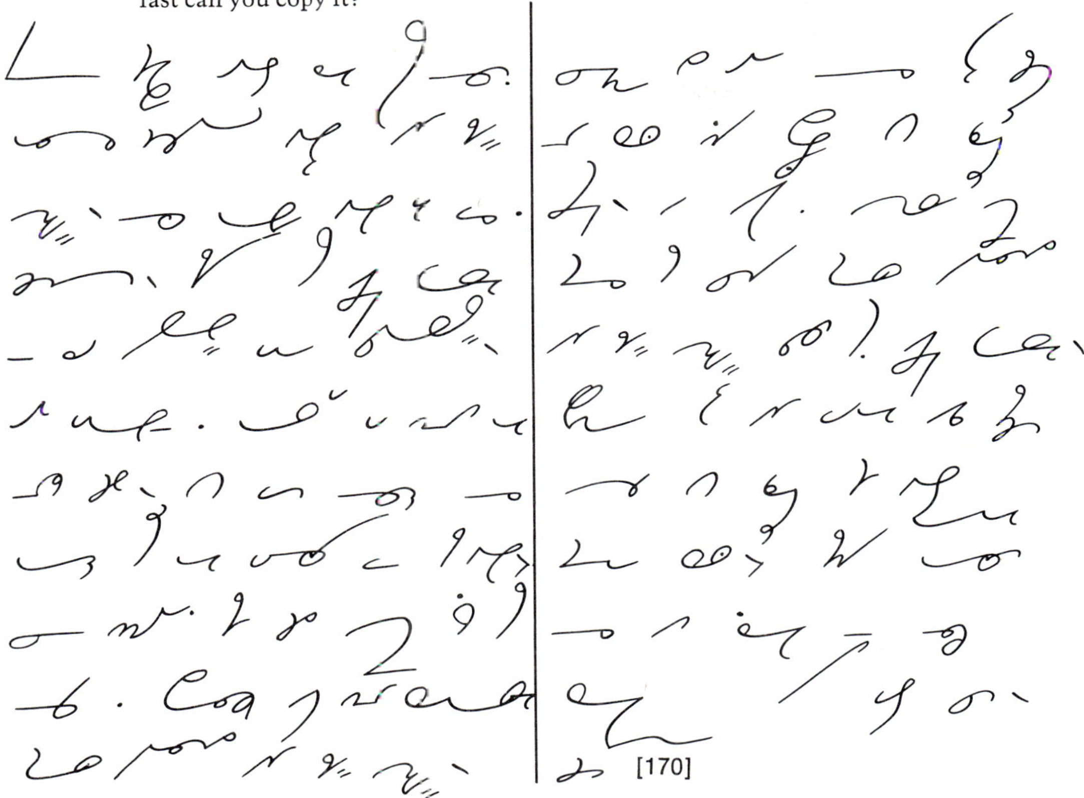

Building Transcription Skills

626 OFFICE-STYLE DICTATION restorations

Occasionally an executive will dictate a word or phrase and then change it. Upon reflection, however, the dictator may decide that the original word or phrase was better.

The reports are excellent—no, **good***; oh, perhaps* **excellent** *is better.*

The best way to handle this situation is to write the restored word or phrase as though it were a completely new form. You write the word *excellent*; then strike it out and substitute *good*; finally, you strike out *good* and rewrite *excellent*. The shorthand notes would look like this:

Do not try to indicate that the original outline for *excellent* is to be restored. This effort may make your notes difficult to read, with the result that you might not be able to transcribe them correctly.

Illustration of Office-Style Dictation

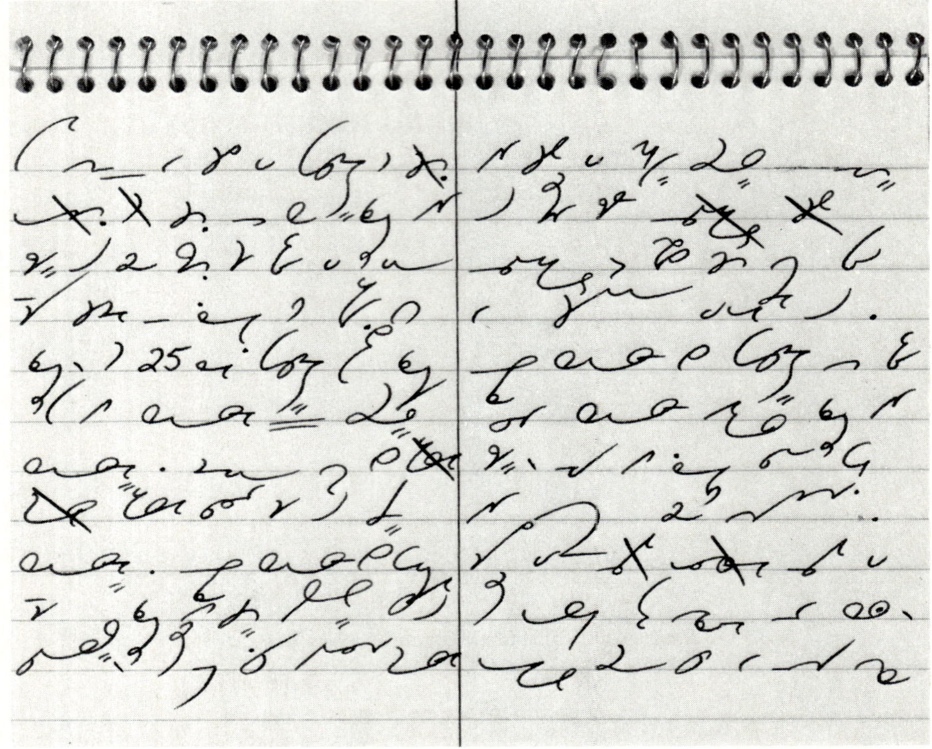

627 Business Vocabulary Builder

layover Scheduled stop between parts of a trip.

interstate Between states.

testify To make a statement based on personal knowledge or belief.

metropolises Chief cities in regions.

Reading and Writing Practice

628

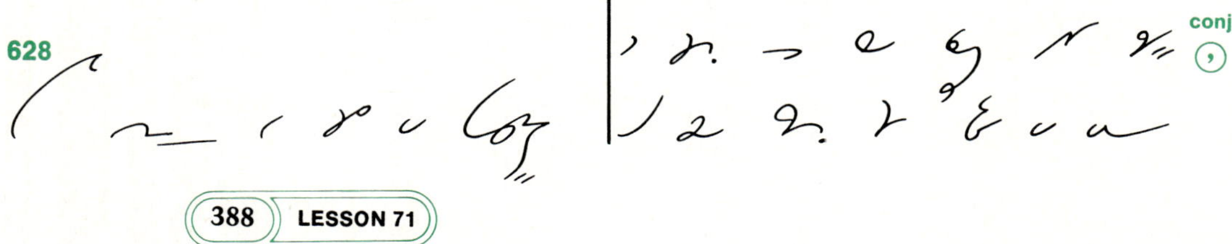

cit·i·zens

ap

ap

ser

ser

flights

intro

two-page *hyphenated before noun*

cr

par

[207]

629

heart·en·ing

as

ser

nec·es·sary

two-hour *hyphenated before noun*

hours'

if

when

[162]

630

as

ap

routes

ser

intro

per·mis·sion

oc·curred

nonr

par

com·mer·cial

intro

[151]

631

if

de·luxe

and o

known

intro

intro

freight

102,

5

whether

intro

and o

[154]

632 Transcription Quiz Supply the necessary punctuation and the missing words.

23

Co.

[160]

Warmup Your warmup letter is on page 387. Practice the first paragraph, writing it as rapidly as you can and as many times as you can in the time available.

Developing Word-Building Power

633 Brief-Form Chart

Your reading goal: 20 seconds.

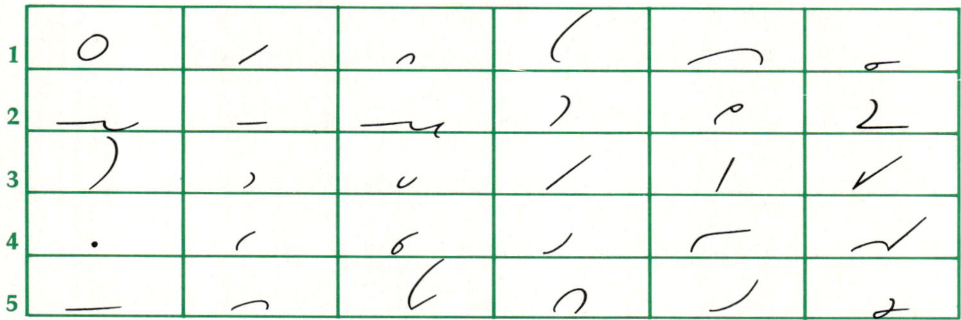

1. *I, it-at, you-your, be-by, good, when.*
2. *Mr., in-not, Mrs., for, they, from.*
3. *Have, is-his, of, would, which, should.*
4. *A-an, the, with, there (their), them, could.*
5. *Am, can, but, this, and, send.*

634 Geographical Expressions

1
2

1. *Harrisburg, Vicksburg, Pittsburgh, Fitchburg, Greensburg, Plattsburgh, Lynchburg, Newburgh.*
2. *Louisiana, Tennessee, Georgia, Kansas, Nevada, Virginia, West Virginia, Wyoming.*

Building Transcription Skills

635 SPELLING FAMILIES -el, -al, -le Always be careful when you must transcribe a word that ends with the sound of *l*; the word may be spelled *-el*, *-al*, or *le*. When in doubt, look it up!

Words Ending in -el

trav·el	**la·bel**	**nick·el**
pan·el	**can·cel**	**tun·nel**

Words Ending in -al

per·son·al	**ter·mi·nal**	**vi·tal**
ru·ral	**fi·nal**	**cen·tral**

Words Ending in -le

am·ple	**sam·ple**	**an·nu·al**
cir·cle	**sim·ple**	**en·able**

636 Business Vocabulary Builder

rural Of or relating to the country or countryside.

routes Traveled ways; highways.

board *(verb)* To get on a ship, train, plane, or bus.

crucial Essential.

Reading and Writing Practice

637 Brief-Form Letter

Trav·el·er

intro

ru·ral

if

cheat·ed

if

am·ple

sights

intro

one-time first-class *hyphenated before noun*

at·ten·dants

conj

[150]

638

ex·traor·di·nary

conj

par

na·tion's

when

when

conj

intro

when

intro

[137]

639

ap

con·ser·va·tion

geo

Transcribe:
9 a.m.
4 p.m.

pan·el

cr

and o

[126]

640

yes·ter·day's

geo

geo

or·di·nar·i·ly

conj

en route

when

al·ready

conj

at·ten·dants

conj

cru·cial

intro

vi·tal

par

in·debt·ed

ser

[209]

641 Transcription Quiz Supply the necessary punctuation and the missing words.

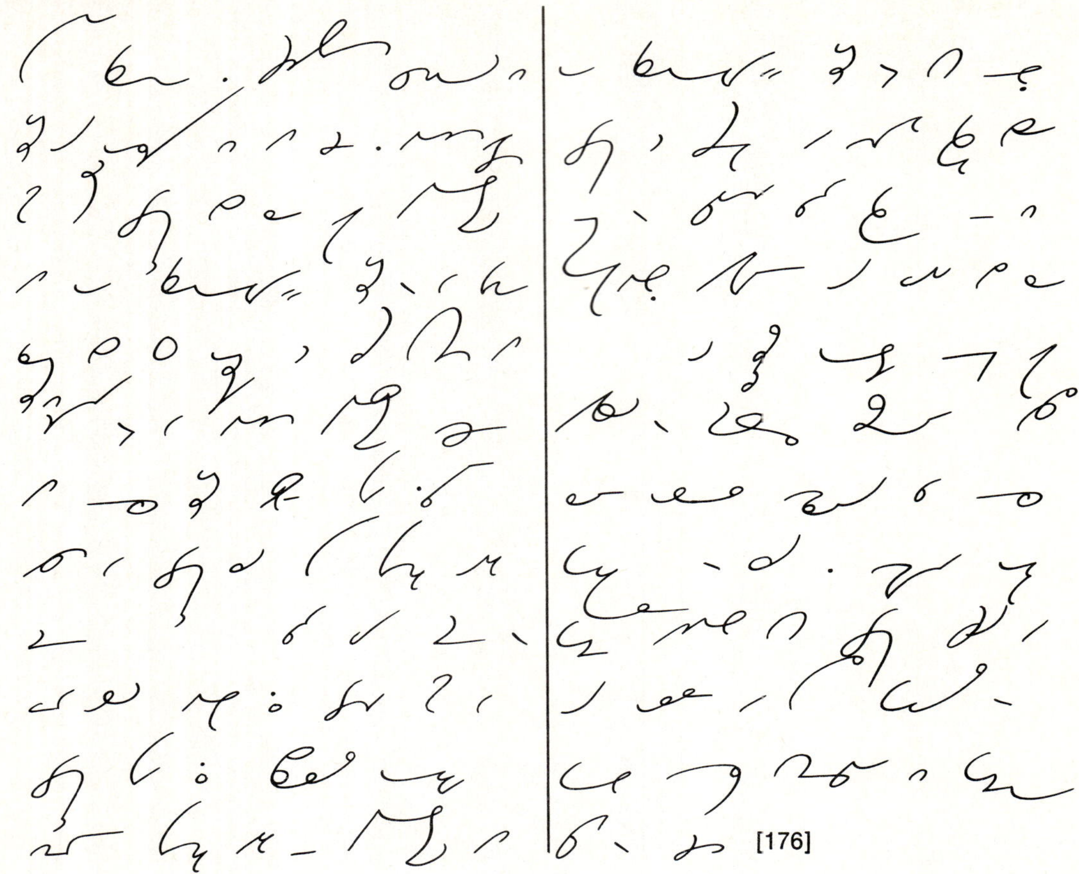

The secretary never speaks about confidential company business to friends out of the office. Even casual remarks can lead to trouble.

Warmup Your warmup letter is on page 387. Copy the second paragraph as rapidly as you can and as often as you can in the time available.

Developing Word-Building Power

642 Word Families

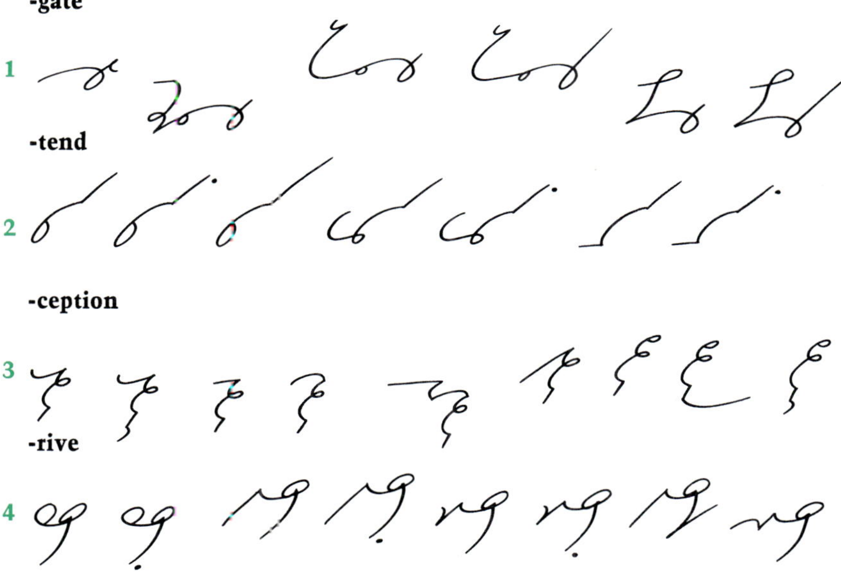

1. *Gates, investigate, obligate, obligated, navigate, navigated.*
2. *Attend, attending, attended, pretend, pretending, intend, intending.*
3. *Reception, receptions, inception, conception, misconception, deception, exception, exceptional, exceptions.*
4. *Arrive, arriving, drive, driving, strive, striving, derived, contrive.*

Building Transcription Skills

643 GRAMMAR CHECKUP all right

This expression should always be written as two words. Some transcribers mistakenly spell it *alright*. They are perhaps influenced by the spelling of such words as *altogether*, *always*, and *already*.

A good way to remember that *all right* is spelled as two words is that its opposite, *all wrong*, is spelled as two words.

It will be all right *with me.*

---

644 Business Vocabulary Builder

memorable Worthy of remembering.

authentic Genuine; actual.

inception Beginning.

Reading and Writing Practice

645

mu·se·um

intro

in·cep·tion

au·then·tic

ser

worth·while

city-owned hyphenated before noun

so·lic·it·ing

if

Transcribe: $1 $1,000

[187]

646

as

intro

Transcribe: 50 percent

50,

conj

rais·ing

cr

fund-rais·ing hyphenated before noun

647

ap

13

Transcribe: Flight 1616

1616

com·pa·ny's

cr

13

ser

14

15

nonr

all right

par

Transcribe: 2 a.m.

intro

[147]

648

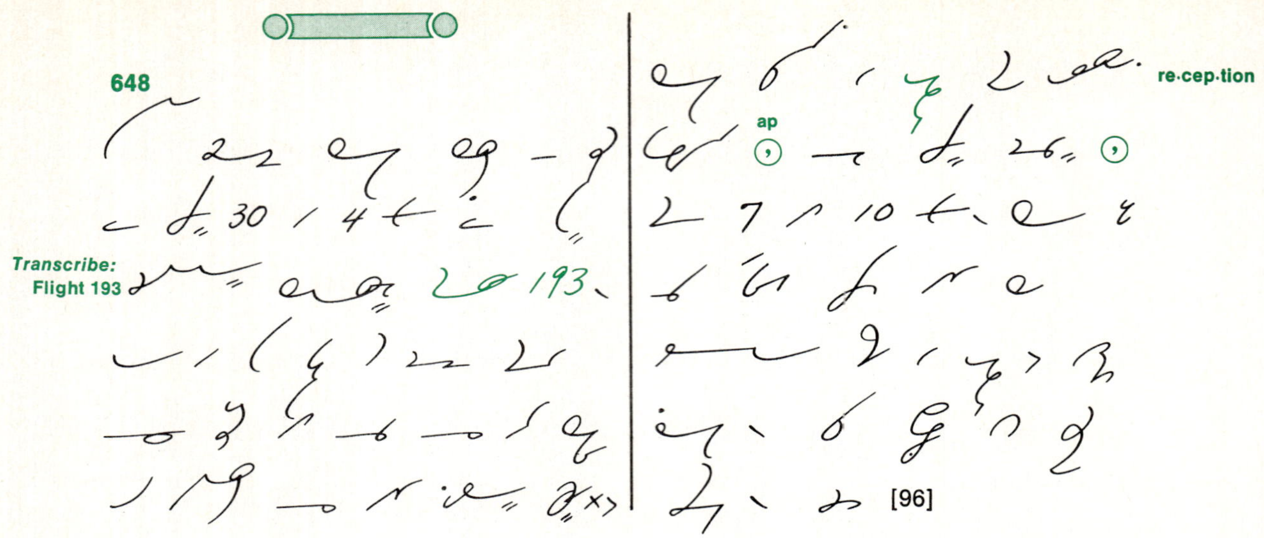

649 Supply the necessary punctuation and the missing words.

Transcription Quiz

[167]

Warmup Your warmup letter is on page 387. Copy the third paragraph of this letter as rapidly as you can and as many times as you can in the time available.

Developing Word-Building Power

650 Word Beginnings and Endings

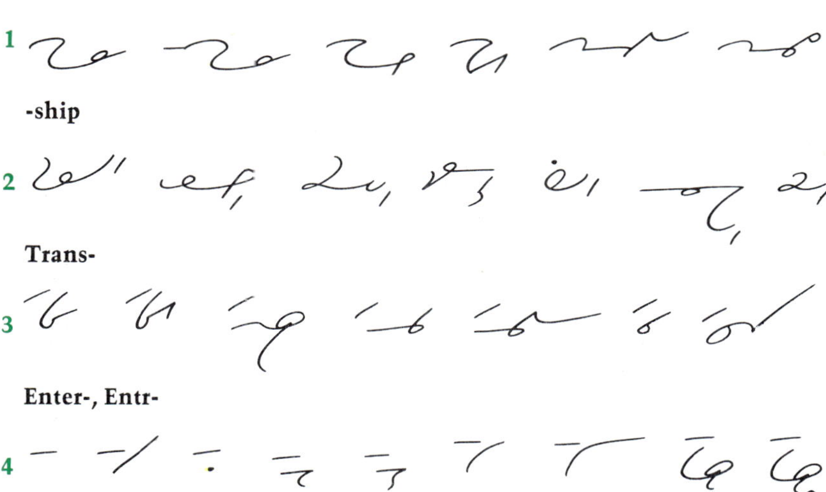

1. *Complete, incomplete, completion, competition, commuter, committee.*
2. *Friendship, relationship, fellowship, steamships, hardship, membership, worship.*
3. *Transport, transportation, transcribe, transmit, transmittal, transit, transacted.*
4. *Enter, entered, entering, entrance, entrances, entertain, entertainment, enterprising, enterprisingly.*

Building Transcription Skills

651 SIMILAR-WORDS DRILL loose, lose, loss

loose *(adjective)* Not tight; unattached; not fastened.

The fan belt is loose.

lose *(verb)* To be deprived of.

Did you lose *your keys?*

loss *(noun)* That which one is deprived of.

The loss *was $500.*

---

652 Business Vocabulary Builder

commuter One who travels from one place to another, usually to work.

portals Doors; openings.

feasibility Possibility; reasonable expectance.

initiate To begin; to start.

Reading and Writing Practice

653

as

fa·cil·i·ty

dai·ly

re·mod·el·ing

when

lat·er

al·most

por·tals

when

ar·ea

busi·est

[170]

654

par

nc

of·fi·cial·ly

par

conj

conj

intro

if

[167]

655

main·te·nance

when

nonr

re·luc·tant·ly

when

conj

when

brake

ser

intro

conj

[154]

656

dis·tress·ing

to·day's

and o

conj

loss

se·vere

ap

intro

loose

intro

brake
in·ci·den·tal·ly

intro

los·ing

par

36-month
hyphenated before noun

36 =

conj

cr

[224]

657
Transcription Quiz

Supply the necessary punctuation and the missing words.

12

[137]

Warmup Your warmup letter is on page 387. Copy the entire letter as rapidly as you can. If time permits, write it a second time in your best shorthand.

Developing Word-Building Power

658 Shorthand Vocabulary Builder

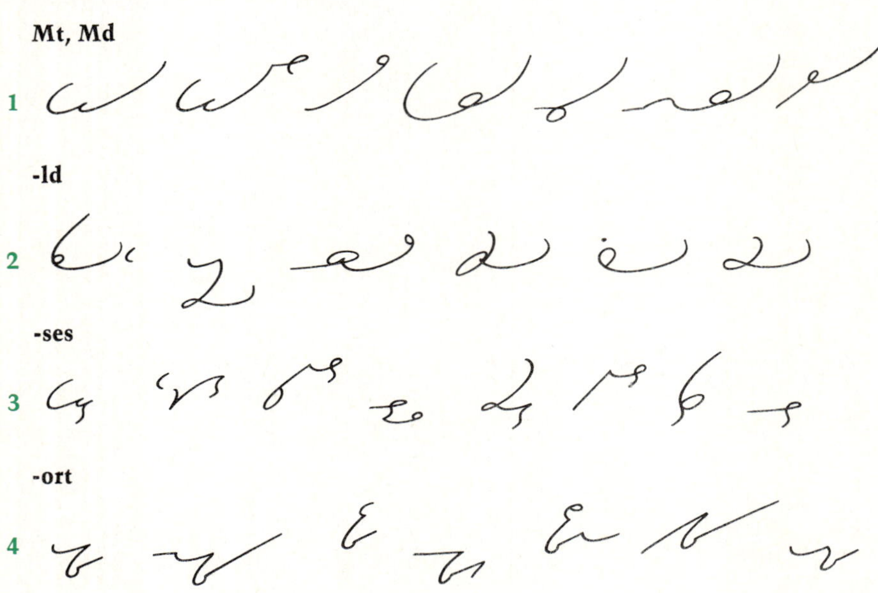

1. *Prompt, promptness, empty, blamed, named, unclaimed, deemed.*
2. *Buildings, revealed, mildly, filed, hailed, failed.*
3. *Process, circumstances, addresses, necessary, versus, dresses, basis, misses.*
4. *Report, unreported, support, importation, exporter, deported, resort.*

Building Transcription Skills

659 Business Vocabulary Builder

perimeter Boundary or outer limits of an area.

adversely Acting against or in a contrary direction.

tolerate Endure.

mobility Ability to move.

Reading and Writing Practice

660

out·skirts

conj

traf·fic

ser

pol·lu·tion

intro

sub·urbs

cross-coun·try hyphenated before noun

as

intro

[148]

661

nonr

re·lieve

ad·verse·ly

par

pre·lim·i·nary

when

nc

[113]

662

re·spon·si·ble

cit·ies

ser

intro

com·pa·ny's

two-week *hyphenated before noun*

if

and o

when

per·son·nel

ap

[230]

663

Transcribe: 10 million

Transcribe: $50 million

com·pa·nies

mo·bil·i·ty

ser

dis·sat·is·fied

conj

when

per·son·al

cli·ents

and o

par

if

cus·tom·er

par

[253]

The Secretary on the Job

664 WHAT WOULD YOU DO?

C.

2. What would

1. Suppose

A.

B.

C.

3. A conference

A.

B.

4. While

A.

B.

C.

ANSWERS

1. C.

2. B.

3.

4. C.

[490]

CHAPTER

Office Equipment

The planning of a modern office layout—which involves allowing sufficient space for present and future employees, arranging for the efficient flow of work from one work station or department to another, and selecting appropriate equipment and furnishings—has become a profession in itself. If you took a tour of a modern office, you would realize why this is true.

Historically, the office started its humble beginning in nothing more than a row of rooms organized almost haphazardly, which housed the employees necessary to handle the company's business. But as technology provided the know-how to speed up production and communications processes and as competition grew fiercer, the pace of business accelerated and the number of employees needed to keep the wheels turning also increased. Sophisticated equipment, much of it based on computers, added to the confusion. It soon became apparent that some attention had to be given to the corporate environment, not only to facilitate smooth operation among departments but also to make the working place more comfortable for employees. Studies found that employee efficiency and productivity increased in an environment that was conducive to thinking, stimulating enough to provide group interaction, and flexible enough to accommodate change.

The modern office looks considerably different from its earlier counterpart. Floors are carpeted and ceilings are soundproofed to cut down noise from typewriters, telephones, and human voices. Colors replaced institutional gray or green and are used extensively to accentuate and brighten hallways, ceilings, walls, and furniture. Colors may also serve as a traffic coding system to distinguish different areas for such functions as sales, accounting, data processing, and so on.

Furniture is designed for efficiency and comfort. Desks have plenty of work space and easy-to-reach spacious drawers for papers, stationery supplies, and reference books. Even chairs are specially designed for particular types of work and can be adjusted to the height of the individual to eliminate fatigue and discomfort.

Office machines have changed too. Most are electric and many are computerized. Typewriters, photocopiers, and calculators, no longer finished in traditional black, are color coordinated to complement the surroundings.

Other sources of color—plants, paintings, and sculpture—put finishing touches on the scheme. And, of course, lighting is designed to provide comfortable illumination.

The bare light bulb and the rolltop desk of the office of fifty years ago are gone forever.

The letters in this chapter will give you an idea of the type of correspondence sent and received by companies that deal in office equipment.

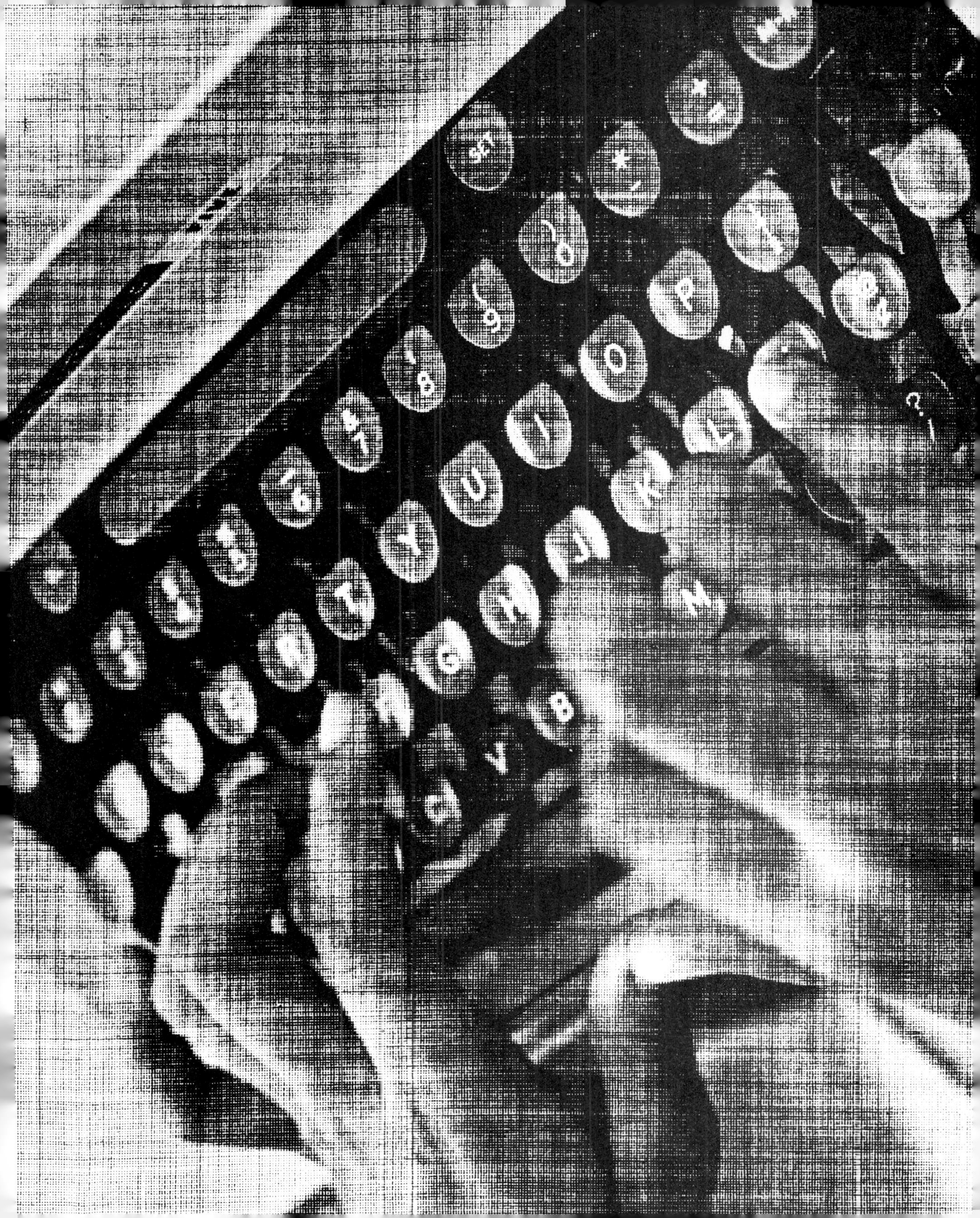

LESSON 76

Building Phrasing Skill

665 Phrase Builder

Reading goal: 50 seconds.

Some

1 

Special

2 

Each

3 

Ago

4 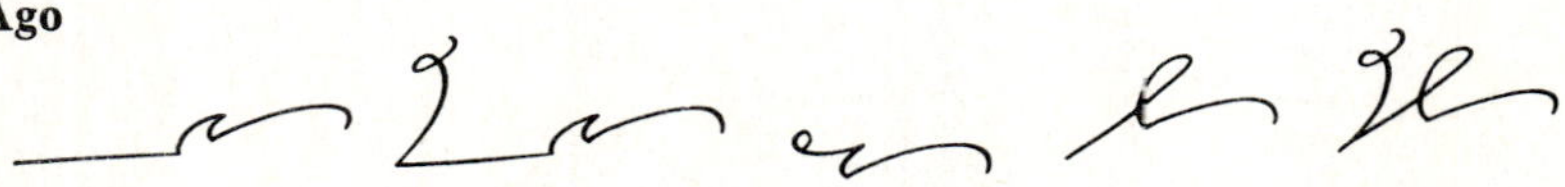

1. *Some of the, some of these, some of that, some of our, some of them, some time ago.*
2. *Your order, your orders, you ordered, as soon as, as soon as possible, of course, of course it is, of course it will.*
3. *Each time, each one, each one of the, each one of them, each day, each morning, each case, each other.*
4. *Months ago, several months ago, years ago, days ago, several days ago.*

666 Warmup Phrase Letter

How fast can you read this letter? How fast can you copy it?

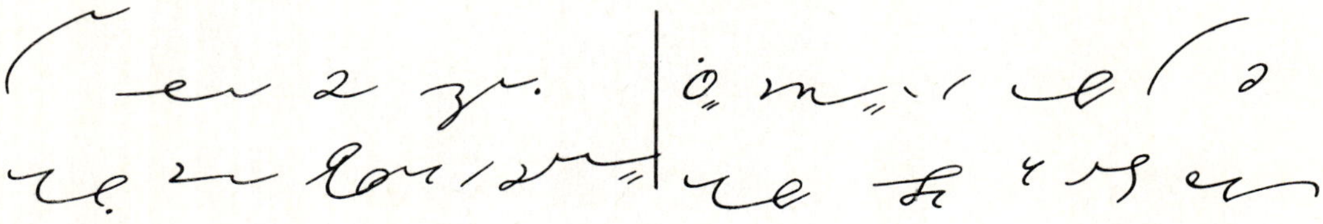

[112]

Building Transcription Skills

667 OFFICE-STYLE DICTATION transpositions A business executive may occasionally decide to transpose words or phrases. The simplest way to indicate the transposition of a word or phrase is to use the printer's sign for transposition.

The dictator might say:

The offset duplicator is the least expensive and most effective machine for our needs —make that **most effective and least expensive**.

In your shorthand, you would make the change in this way:

You would then be careful, when you transcribe, to type the word *and* after the word *effective*.

Illustration of Office-Style Dictation

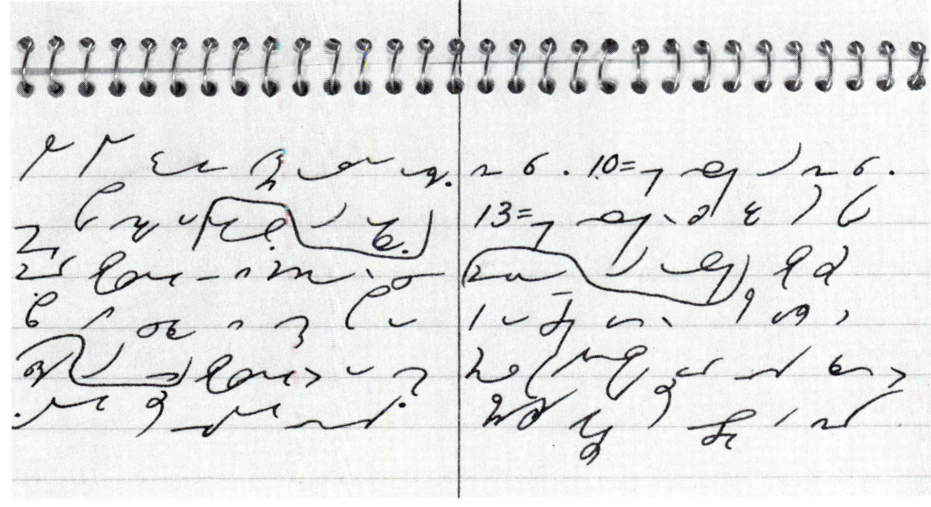

668 Business Vocabulary Builder

interchangeable Permitting mutual substitution.

distinctive Having unusual style.

malfunction Failure to operate in the normal or usual manner.

Reading and Writing Practice

669

re·plac·ing

10-inch

13-inch

hyphenated before noun

in·ter·change·able

par

if

[118]

670

as

ser

be·lieve

intro

pur·chas·ing

conj

[97]

671

Transcribe: Model 121

121

high-qual·i·ty hyphenated before noun

and o

121

121

com·pa·ra·ble

nc

121

ser

dis·tinc·tive

121

when

[153]

672

121

ef·fi·cient·ly

conj

ap

conj

oc·ca·sions

par

conj

Smith's

cr

[132]

673

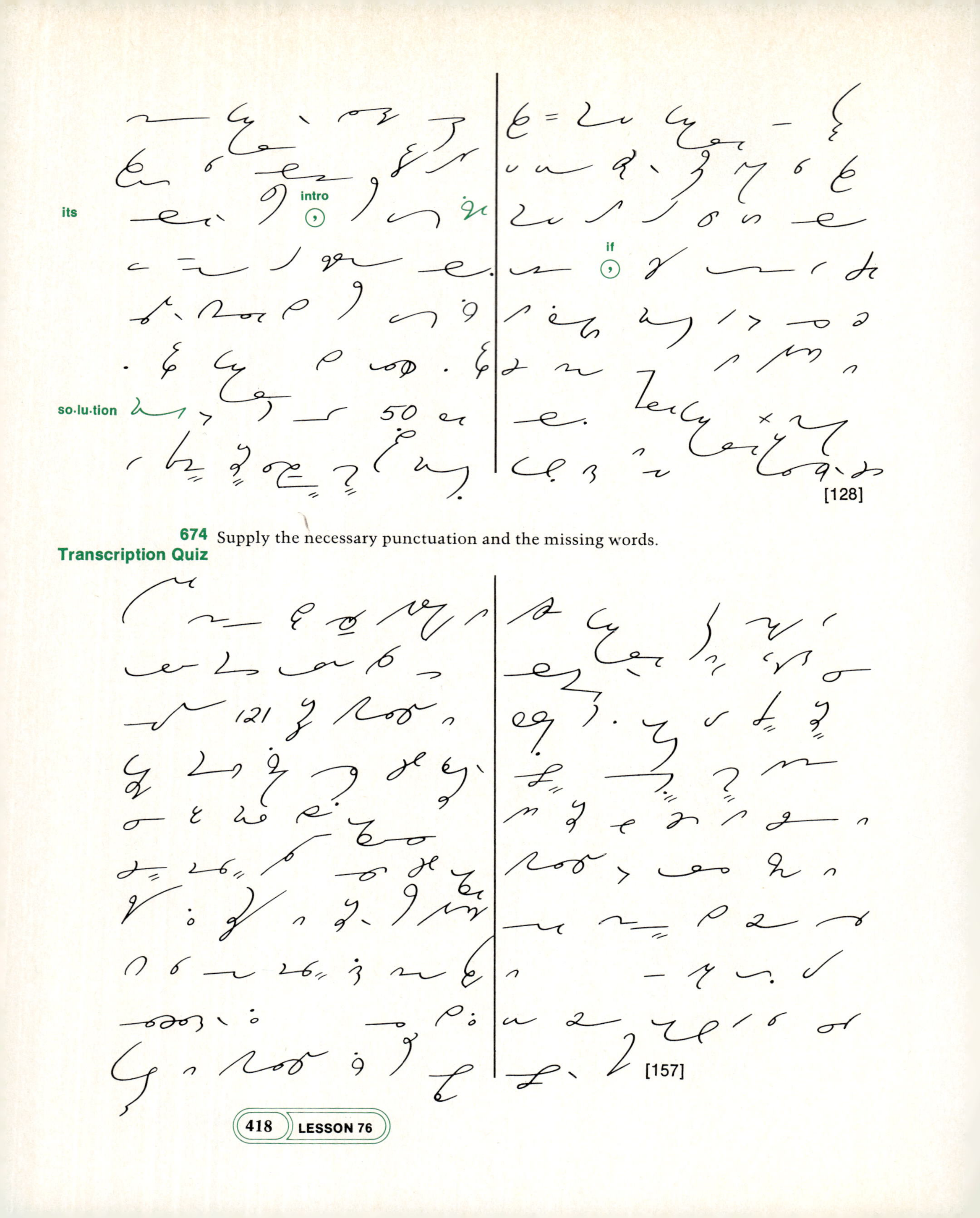

its

intro

so·lu·tion

if

[128]

674 Supply the necessary punctuation and the missing words.

Transcription Quiz

[157]

LESSON 77

Warmup Your warmup letter is on page 414. Write the first paragraph as rapidly and as often as you can in the time you have available.

Developing Word-Building Power

675 Brief-Form Chart

Your reading goal: 20 seconds.

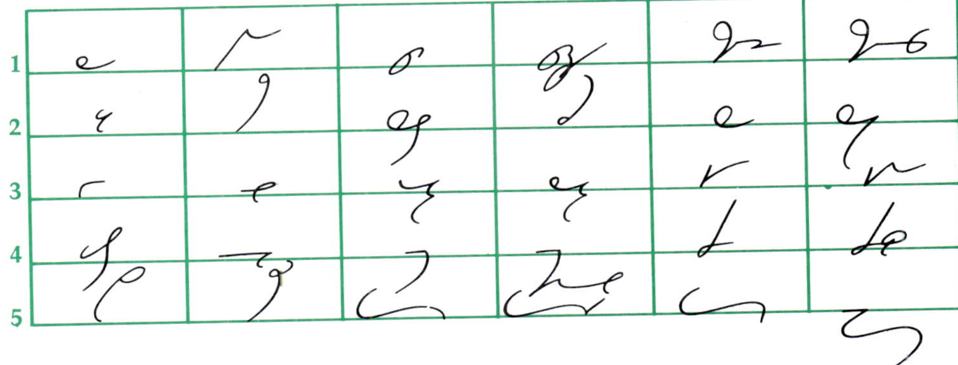

1. *Were, Dr., out, outside, afternoon, aftermath.*
2. *Was, ever-every, wherever, very, where, whereby.*
3. *Than, next, responsible, irresponsible, shorten, shorter.*
4. *Whatever, Ms., never, nevertheless, general, generalize.*
5. *About, several, progress, progressed, progression, unprogressive.*

676 Geographical Expressions

1

2

1. *Framingham, Birmingham, Nottingham, Cunningham, Buckingham, Billingham.*
2. *Iowa, Idaho, Missouri, South Carolina, Wisconsin, South Dakota, Oklahoma, Rhode Island.*

Building Transcription Skills

677 SIMILAR-WORDS DRILL correspondence, correspondents

correspondence Communication by letters.

When you need correspondence *materials, write us.*

correspondents Those who communicate by letter.

One of their correspondents *is sending me a copy of the material.*

678 Business Vocabulary Builder

foresee To see beforehand; to anticipate.

likelihood Probability.

erroneous Containing errors; mistaken.

mutually Directed by each toward the other.

Reading and Writing Practice

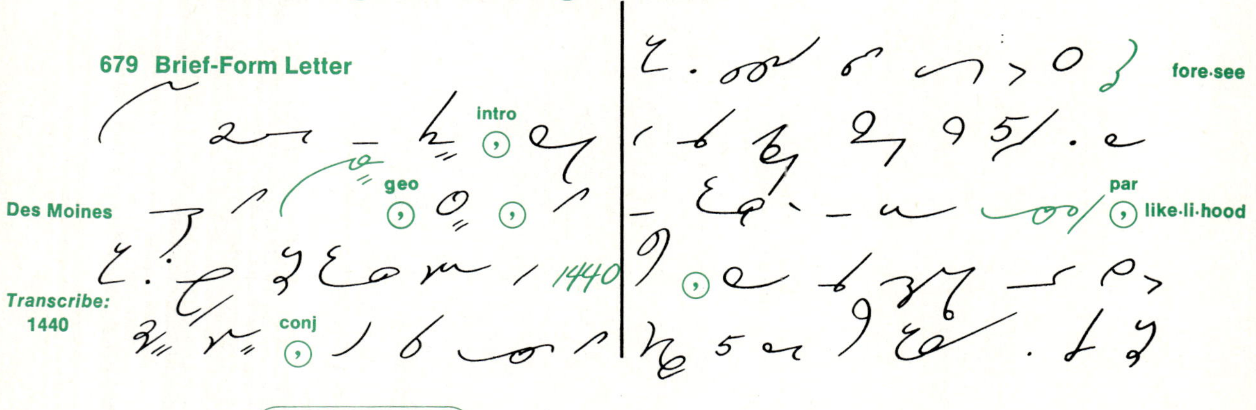

when

nonr

if

par

[153]

680

nc

par

Des Moines'

wel·comes

ar·ea

if

oc·ca·sion

ap

[110]

tem·po·rary

681

ac·knowl·edge

cop·ies

ap

un·for·tu·nate·ly

intro

ap

geo

cor·re·spon·dence

if

[107]

682

par

conj

cor·re·spon·dents

suf·fi·cient

and o

up-to-date *hyphenated before noun*

[111]

683

par

billed

ser

ten-day *hyphenated before noun*

as

ap

er·ro·ne·ous

[116]

684

intro

too

if

[83]

685 Supply the necessary punctuation and the missing words.
Transcription Quiz

[159]

Many young people who have special talent or interest in drama, music, art, journalism, politics, and so on, have found that secretarial training works almost like magic in gaining entrance to these areas of work.
John Robert Gregg

Warmup Your warmup letter is on page 414. Write the second paragraph of the letter as rapidly as you can and as often as you can in the time available.

Developing Word-Building Power

686 Shorthand Word Families

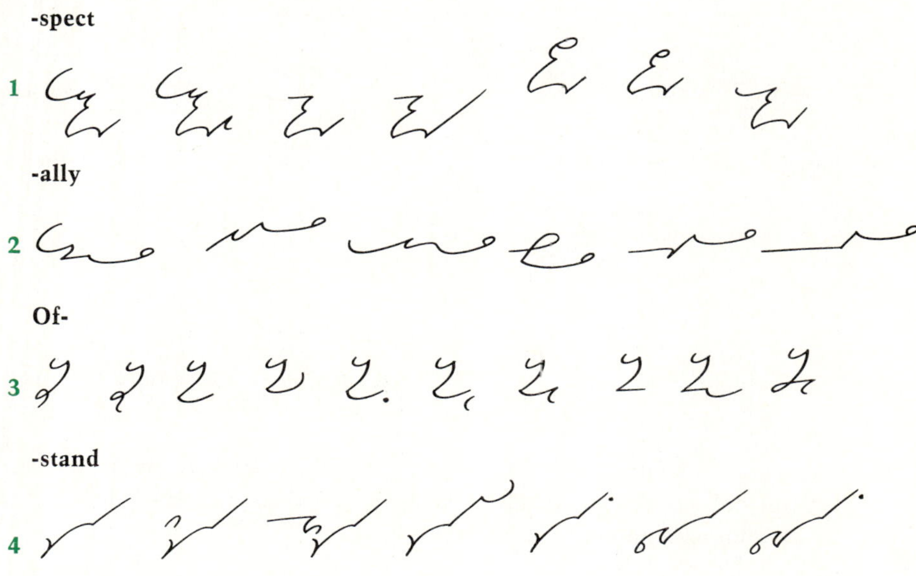

1. *Prospect, prospects, inspect, inspected, aspect, expect, respect.*
2. *Personally, totally, locally, nationally, mutually, mentally.*
3. *Office, offices, offer, offered, offering, offerings, offers, often, oftener, offense.*
4. *Stand, understand, misunderstand, standard, standing, withstand, withstanding.*

Building Transcription Skills

687 SPELLING FAMILIES r in past tenses

Past Tenses in Which R Is Doubled

oc·curred	de·ferred	trans·ferred
pre·ferred	in·ferred	con·ferred
con·curred	re·ferred	blurred

Past Tenses in Which R Is Not Doubled

of·fered	cov·ered	hon·ored
dif·fered	ma·jored	suf·fered

---

688 Business Vocabulary Builder

par Equal level.

tier One of two or more rows arranged one above the other.

vertical Upright; upward.

deferred Put off; postponed.

● Reading and Writing Practice

689

out of date no noun, no hyphen

and o

if

los·ing

as

par

ser

per·son·nel

intro

com·pa·ny's

priv·i·lege

and o

[164]

690

ef·fi·cient·ly run
no hyphen after ly

par

ap

con·ve·nient

[117]

691

de·ferred

oc·cu·pan·cy

trans·ferred

Transcribe:
9 a.m.

[97]

692

conj

ref·er·ence

lo·cal·ly

of·fered

intro

oc·curred

par

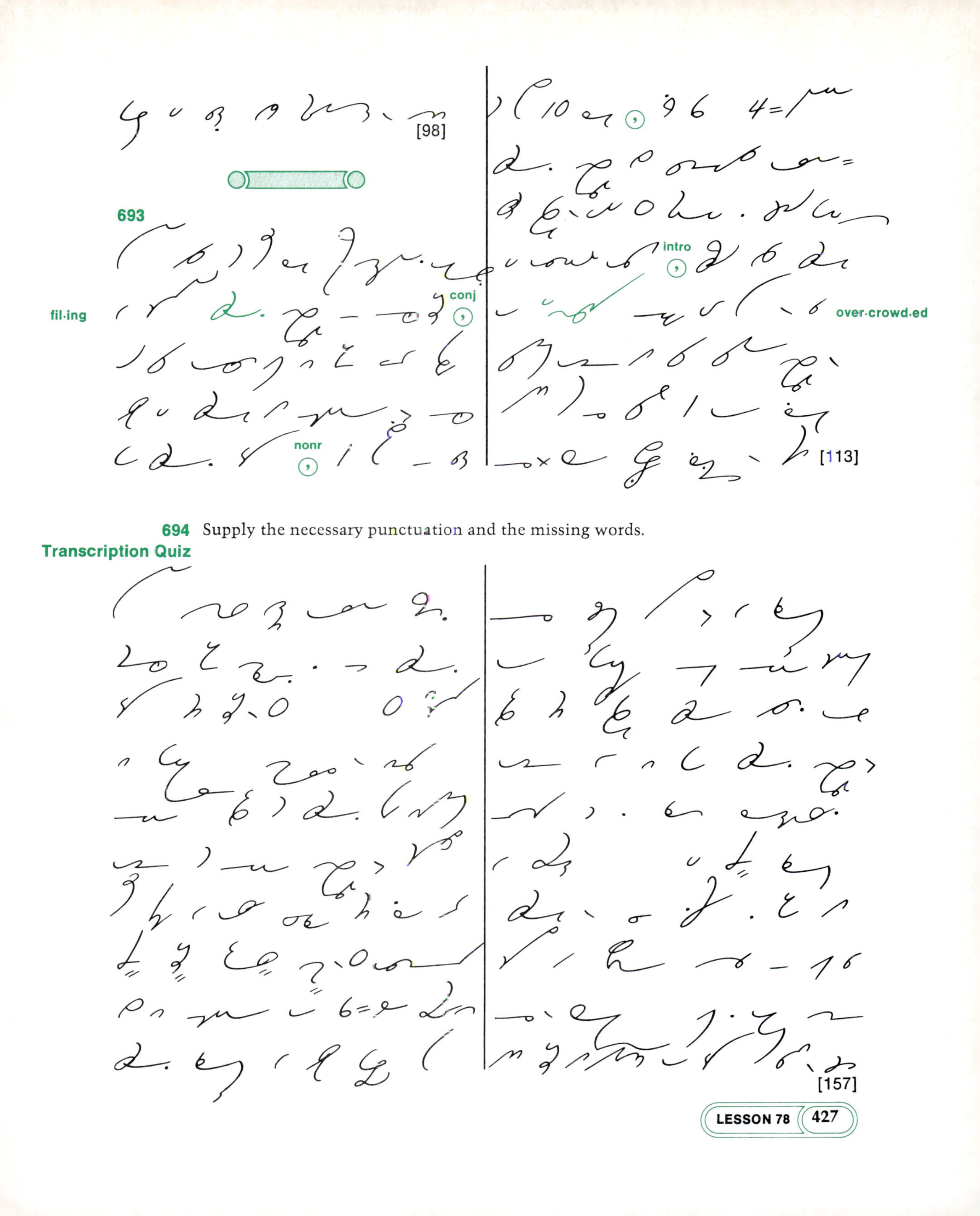

[98]

693

fil·ing

conj

nonr

intro

over·crowd·ed

[113]

694 Supply the necessary punctuation and the missing words.

Transcription Quiz

[157]

Warmup Your warmup letter is on page 414. Write the third paragraph of the letter as rapidly as you can and as many times as you can in the time available.

Developing Word-Building Power

695 Word Endings

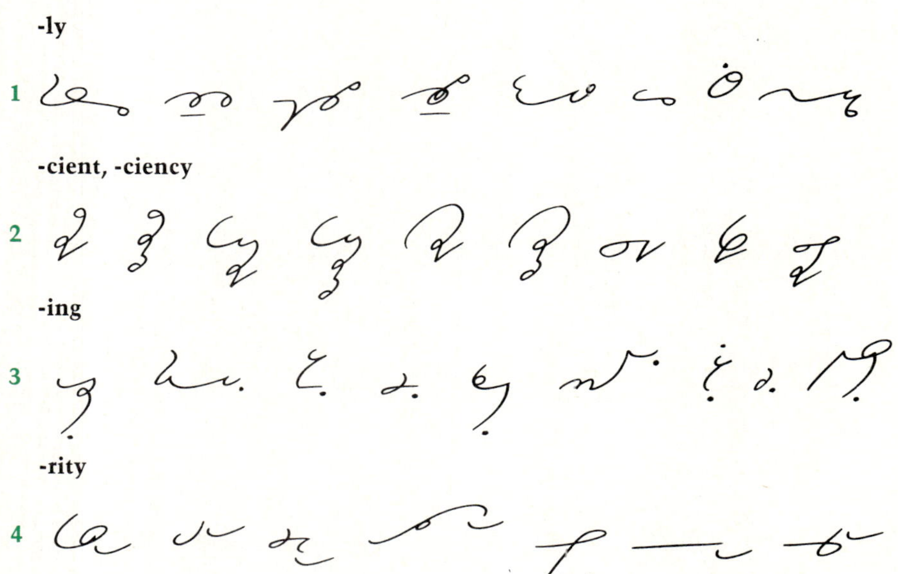

1. *Frankly, quickly, unfortunately, quietly, slowly, only, highly, closely.*
2. *Efficient, efficiency, proficient, proficiency, deficient, deficiency, ancient, patient, inefficient.*
3. *Receiving, following, opening, sending, serving, wondering, hoping, seeing, driving.*
4. *Priority, authority, sincerity, integrity, majority, minority, maturity.*

Building Transcription Skills

696 GRAMMAR CHECKUP let, leave

Let and *leave* are two words that people often misuse. You will have no difficulty using these words correctly if you will remember the following definitions.

leave To move or go away from; to depart.

I will leave *home at 6 o'clock.*

let To permit; to allow.

Let *(not* leave*) me help you.*

Hint: If you are in doubt as to whether *let* or *leave* is correct, substitute *permit* and *depart*. If *permit* makes sense, use *let*; if *depart* makes sense, use *leave*.

---

697 Business Vocabulary Builder

bond paper A strong, durable paper.

embossed Raised in relief from a surface.

expedite Accelerate the progress of; facilitate.

Reading and Writing Practice

698

sup·plies

ream

Transcribe: No. 24

geo

nc

conj

im·me·di·ate·ly

your

[115]

699

as

mer·chan·dise

nc

intro

and o

com·pa·ny's

cr

when

re·ceive

conj

ex·pe·di·tious·ly

par

[129]

700

fi·nan·cial

ref·er·ences

much-need·ed
hyphenated before noun

par

[96]

701

wel·come

nonr

conj

in·qui·ries

ser

leave

ap

15 nc

sep·a·rate·ly

[153]

702

ir tro

and o

lu·cid

[79]

703 Transcription Quiz Supply the necessary punctuation and the missing words.

[113]

Warmup This will be your final warmup on the phrase letter on page 414. Make one copy of the letter in your best shorthand.

Developing Word-Building Power

704 Shorthand Vocabulary Builder

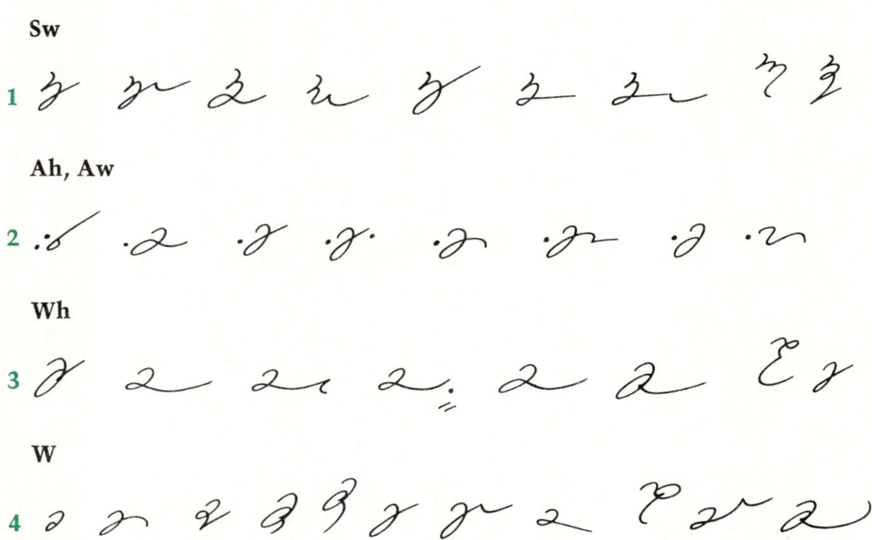

1. *Suite, sweater, swear, swore, suede, swim, swimmer, swoop, swift.*
2. *Ahead, aware, await, awaiting, awake, awaken, away, awoke.*
3. *White, wheel, wheels, Wheeling, whale, while, whisper, wheat.*
4. *We, week, west, wise, wife, wait, waiter, wink, wipe, winter, wild.*

Building Transcription Skills

705 Business Vocabulary Builder

functional Designed from the point of view of use.

modular Constructed with standardized units for flexibility and variety in use.

remodeling Altering the structure of; reconstructing.

Reading and Writing Practice

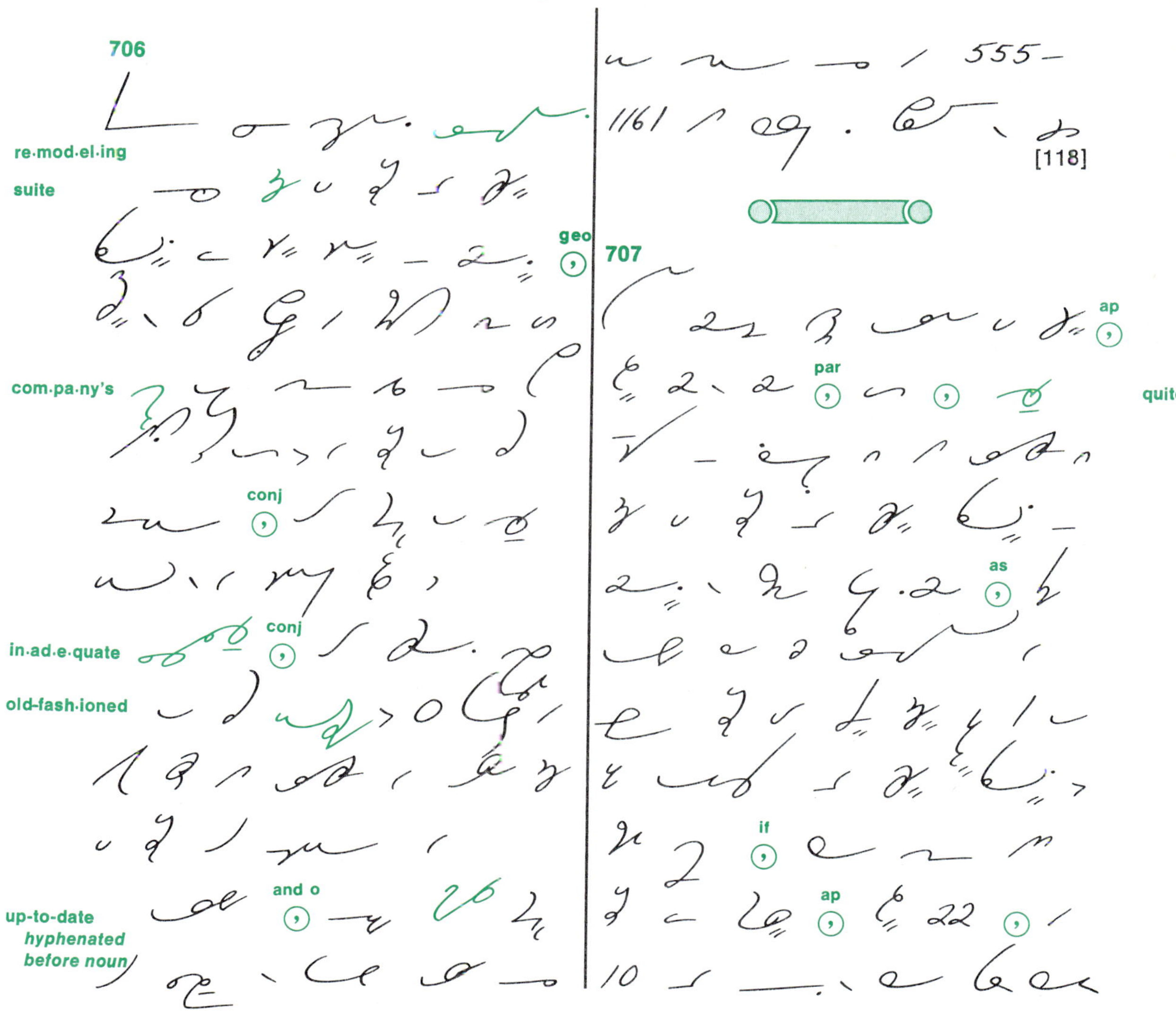

sam·ple

[117]

708

dis·cuss

cho·sen

conj

when

for·ward

[77]

709

nonr

ser

mod·u·lar

drap·er·ies

par

intro

wheth·er

pro·ceed

[98]

710

cop·ies

intro

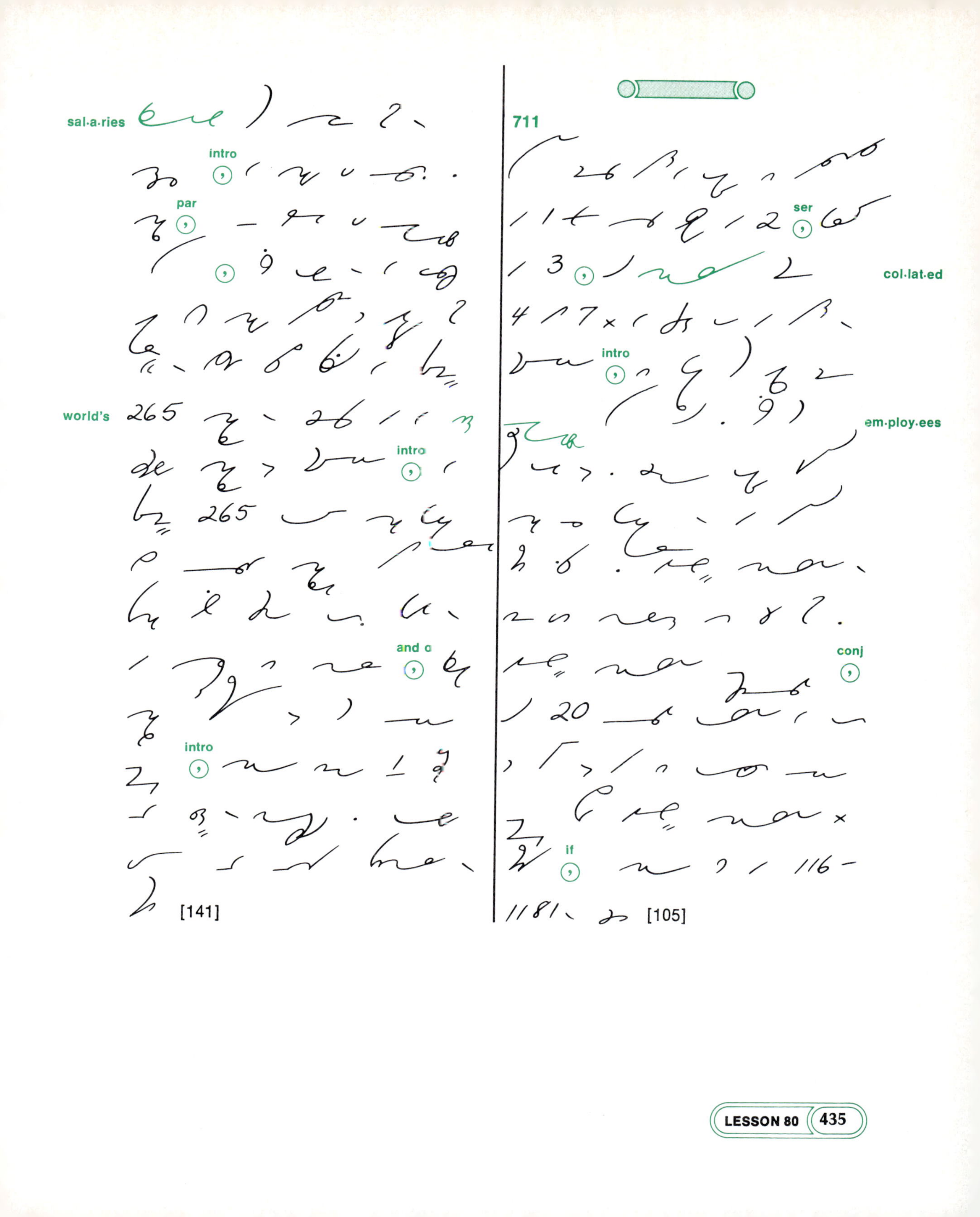

sal·a·ries

intro

par

world's

intro

and o

intro

[141]

711

ser

col·lat·ed

intro

em·ploy·ees

conj

if

[105]

The Secretary on the Job

712 YOU AND YOUR FUTURE

What have you

One high school

If you can

[413]

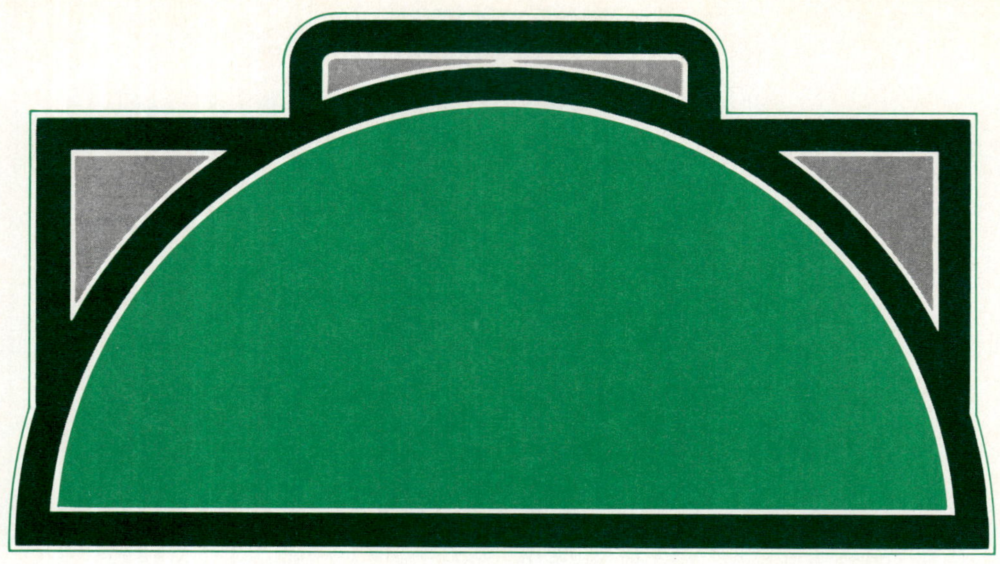

Appendix

Recall Drills

JOINED WORD ENDINGS

1 -ment

2 -tion

3 -tial

4 -ly

5 -ily

6 -ful

7 -ble

8 -ther

9 -ual

10 -ure

11 -self, -selves

12 -ort

13 -tain

14 -cient, -ciency

DISJOINED WORD ENDINGS

15 -hood

16 -ward

17 -ship

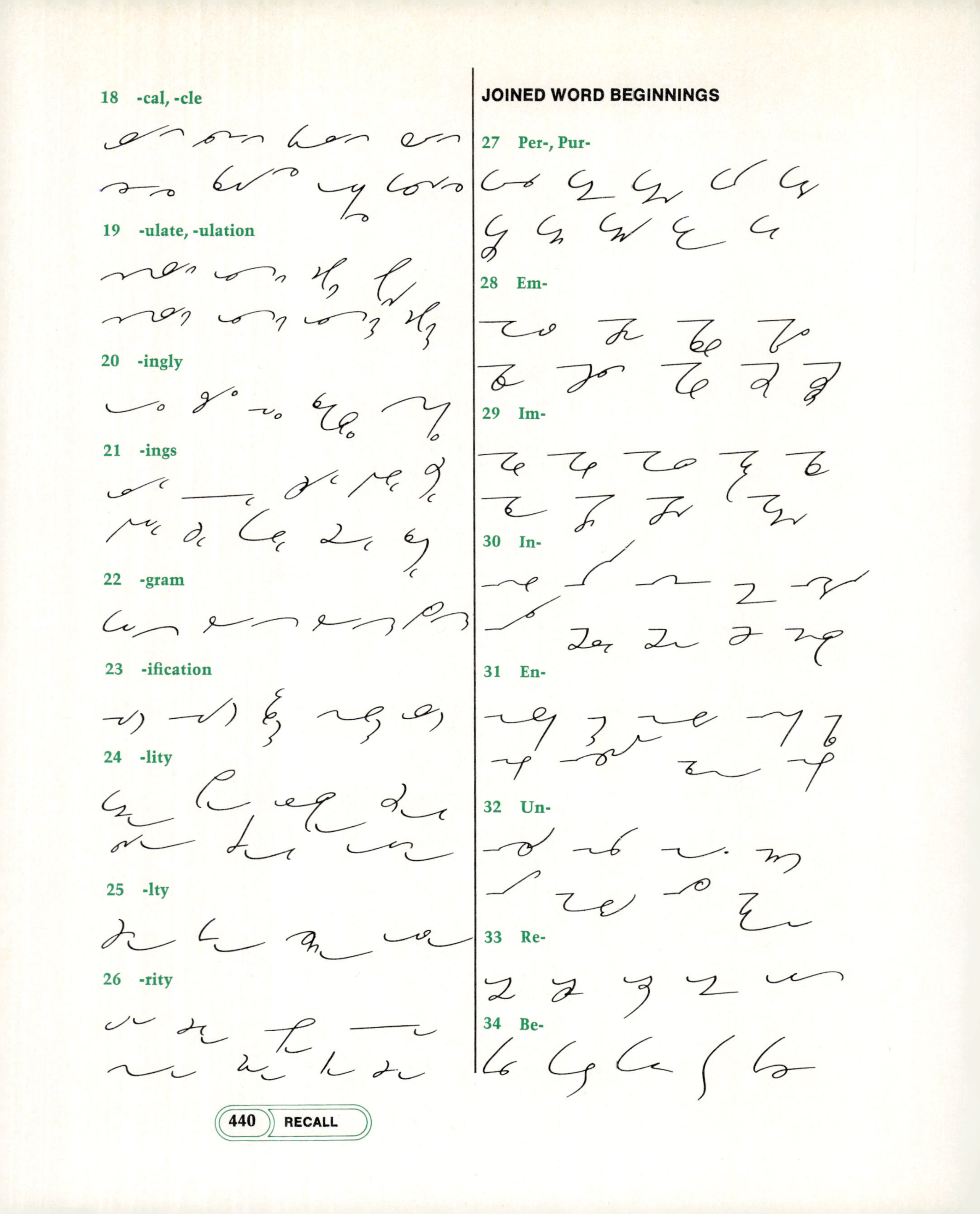

18 **-cal, -cle**

19 **-ulate, -ulation**

20 **-ingly**

21 **-ings**

22 **-gram**

23 **-ification**

24 **-lity**

25 **-lty**

26 **-rity**

JOINED WORD BEGINNINGS

27 **Per-, Pur-**

28 **Em-**

29 **Im-**

30 **In-**

31 **En-**

32 **Un-**

33 **Re-**

34 **Be-**

35 De-, Di-

36 Dis-, Des-

37 Mis-

38 Ex-

39 Com-

40 Con-

41 Sub-

42 Al-

43 For-, Fore-

44 Fur-

45 Tern-, Etc.

46 Ul-

DISJOINED WORD BEGINNINGS

47 Inter-, Etc.

48 Electr-, Electric

49 Super-

50 Circum-

51 Self-

52 Trans-

53 Under-

54 Over-

Addresses for Transcription

The numbers of the following names and addresses correspond to the numbers of the supplementary letters in the Instructor's Handbook for *Gregg Dictation and Introductory Transcription, Series 90.*

CHAPTER 1

1 Ms. Jane O'Brien, 1200 Avenue C, Elkhart, IN 46514

2 Memorandum to Mr. Jones from L. C. Short

3 Mr. William Lee, Eastern Printing Company, 500 Wilson Road, Harrison, NY 10528

4 Mrs. Martha Thompson, General Manager, Texas Insurance Company, 527 Lakeshore Drive, Dallas, TX 75214

5 Mr. James Blake, 1600 Broadway, Westport, WA 98411

CHAPTER 2

6 Memorandum to Miss Kelley from C. R. Baker

7 Mr. Carl Smith, East Coast Sales Company, 215 Beacon Street, Philadelphia, PA 17815

8 Mr. Anthony Adams, Adams Furniture Company, 1080 Lakeside Avenue, New Haven, CT 06519

9 Nelson Manufacturing Company, 300 Third Avenue, Springfield, OH 45512

10 Miss Betty Green, Personnel Director, International Manufacturing Company, 41 South Street, Concord, NH 03303

CHAPTER 3

11 Memorandum to Mr. White from Bill Lopez

12 Memorandum to Mr. Best from Carl Murphy

13 Mrs. Marvin Lee, Manager, National Manufacturing Company, 160 Franklin Avenue, St. Louis, MO 66111

14 Mr. Richard Burns, Sales Manager, Burns Printing Company, 14 Garden Lane, St. Paul, MN 55114

15 Memorandum to Mrs. Strong from James Reed

CHAPTER 4

16 Mr. William R. Jennings, President, General Publishing Company, 801 Lexington Avenue, Seattle, WA 98112

CHAPTER 4 (Continued)

17 Mr. Harold Sullivan, 1311 Central Avenue, Baltimore, MD 21233

18 Mr. Charles Best, 37 LaSalle Street, Chicago, IL 60644

19 Mrs. Janice Smith, Virginia Advertising Company, Richmond, VA 22301

20 Miss Lois Baker, General Products, 151 Harbor Avenue, Detroit, MI 48207

CHAPTER 5

21 Mr. Edward Fisher, Credit Manager, Eastern Supply Company, 18 East Main Street, Newark, NJ 07118

22 Memorandum to Mrs. Powell from B. B. Billings

23 Mr. Alexander Ball, Credit Manager, Southern Wholesale Company, 115 Day Street, Little Rock, AR 72203

24 Mrs. Janet Simmons, Credit Manager, Southern Furniture Company, 2150 Pine Street, Newton, AL 36352

25 Mr. Edward Carter, West Coast Manufacturing Company, 18 Central Parkway, Portland, OR 97250

CHAPTER 6

26 Mr. J. R. Mild, Customer Service Representative, Miami Leather Shop, 14 Dade Boulevard, Miami, FL 33125

27 Mr. Charles A. Alexander, National Products Company, 15 Baker Street, Atlanta, GA 34615

28 Mr. Nathan Taylor, Taylor Clothing Store, 34 Baylor Street, Lincoln, NE 68119

29 Mr. J. L. Garcia, Smith Publishing Company, 424 Davis Drive, Eastport, ME 04631

30 Mr. Jerome Case, Credit Manager, Mason's Department Store, 220 Central Avenue, Bloomington, IN 46217

CHAPTER 7

31 Mr. E. J. Morris, North Carolina Carpet Company, 1300 Butler Road, Charlotte, NC 27701

32 Mrs. Sarah Smith, Office Manager, New Jersey Manufacturing Company, 300 State Street, Montvale, NJ 07080

33 Miss Glenda Washington, 17 Cullen Drive, Houston, TX 77004

34 Mrs. L. V. Mason, 640 Clark Street, Helena, MT 59601

35 Mrs. Jane Rice, Customer Service Manager, Eastern Department Store, 416 Central Avenue, Wilmington, DE 19968

CHAPTER 8

36 Mr. John C. Lee, 166 Glenview Drive, Missoula, MT 59801

37 Mr. Alvin Smith, United Insurance Company of America, 415 Bryan Avenue, Denver, CO 81009

38 Mrs. Mary Kelley, 127 Oak Drive, Madison, WI 53925

39 Mr. Henry Jennings, 18 Lake Street, Spokane, WA 98112

40 Miss Clara Case, 48 Mill Road, Hartford, CT 06531

CHAPTER 9

41 Mr. Gordon Underwood, Box 129, Springfield, OH 45387

42 Miss Sylvia Smith, Editorial Director, Eastern Publishing Company, 15 Stevens Road, Rockville, ME 04732

43 Mrs. Marilyn Jones, 211 Dover Road, Baltimore, MD 21202

44 Miss Dorothy Brown, Sales Manager, General Publishing Company, 480 Park Avenue, New York, NY 10022

45 Miss Patricia Keith, 108 First Avenue, New York, NY 10010

CHAPTER 10

46 Ms. Catherine Green, 180 Oak Street, Springfield, NJ 07093

47 Mr. Marvin R. Baker, 315 Valley Street, Burlington, IA 52601

48 Mr. Rolando Garcia, 361 Main Street, Cincinnati, OH 45227

49 Mrs. Alfred Temple, 1141 Park Street, Los Angeles, CA 90022

50 Miss Helen Lang, 1315 Woodward Drive, Detroit, MI 48207

CHAPTER 11

51 Mr. H. L. Cunningham, 3104 Beacon Street, Boston, MA 02215

52 Miss Martha Green, 210 York Avenue, Atlanta, GA 30312

53 Mr. Carl Chase, 141 Third Avenue, Wilmington, DE 19804

54 Miss Lena Bennington, 106 East Broughton Street, Marquette, WI 53947

55 Mrs. Glenn James, 1611 Westerly Road, Providence, RI 02891

CHAPTER 12

56 Mr. Jack Moss, 156 Eagan Street, Spokane, WA 99362

57 Mr. Harold B. Carter, 96 East Park Avenue, Jackson, MS 38949

58 Dr. A. B. Stein, 1611 Hancock Avenue, Milton, DE 19968

CHAPTER 12 (Continued)

59 Mr. R. C. Smith, 130 State Street, Jackson, AK 99762

60 Ms. Sally Brown, 713 South Pine Street, Denver, CO 80202

CHAPTER 13

61a Mrs. R. A. Mason, 271 Glenview Drive, LaMarque, TX 77104

61b Mr. Sam Bradley, 1400 South Main Street, Houston, TX 77032

62a Ms. Joyce Cunningham, 1400 South 12 Street, Omaha, NE 65118

62b Ms. Joyce Cunningham, 1400 South 12 Street, Omaha, NE 65118

63a Ms. Clara Harrington, 1471 Parkridge Drive, Washington, MO 66111

63b Washington Business Club, 732 Main Street, Washington, MO 66101

64a Mr. James Worth, 21 West 121 Street, Milwaukee, WI 53925

64b Alabama Drama Association, 92 West 21 Street, Birmingham, AL 36350

65a Mr. Joseph Winston, 321 Main Avenue, Austin, TX 76034

65b Miss Hazel Lee, President, Texas Fine Arts Club, 4200 South First Avenue, San Antonio, TX 75010

CHAPTER 14

66a Mr. Jason M. Jones, 1300 State Street, Chicago, IL 62900

66b Miss Wanda White, Red Barn Restaurant, 1490 Wabash Avenue, Chicago, IL 62904

67a Ms. Anita Green, 351 Ash Street, Scranton, PA 18509

67b Mr. Elton Gates, 14 East 12 Street, Bay City, NC 27834

68a Miss Juanita Long, 315 River Road, Alexandria, NE 68119

68b Mr. A. B. Harper, 400 South Trent Street, Alexandria, NE 68110

69a Mr. Alvin Hersh, 1407 Central Boulevard, Miami, FL 33125

69b General Electronics, 4400 East 12 Street, New York, NY 10001

70a Mr. A. C. Jones, 341 First Street, Trenton, NJ 07080

70b Ms. Carol Smith, 1407 East Riverside Drive, Trenton, NJ 07081

CHAPTER 15

71a Mrs. Alice Smith, President, Central Airlines, 400 Broadway, Peoria, IL 61604

71b Mr. L. C. Taylor, President, General Manufacturing Company, 321 First Avenue, Brownsville, TX 73701

72a Miss Clara White, Madison Wholesale Company, 140 Main Street, Reading, PA 19607

72b Mr. Alvin James, 141 Commerce Street, Memphis, TN 38128

CHAPTER 15 (Continued)

73a Miss Aletha Jackson, Head, Department of Accounting, Jones and Company, 1800 State Street, Chicago, IL 60670

73b Miss Aletha Jackson, Head, Department of Accounting, Jones and Company, 1800 State Street, Chicago, IL 60670

74a Mr. Carl D. Madison, President, Greenburg Chamber of Commerce, 402 Oak Drive, Greenburg, MO 66110

74b Miss Grace Stern, Driver Education Instructor, Greenburg High School, Greenburg, MO 66112

75a Mr. Calvin C. Smith, Manager, National Moving Company, 1400 Beacon Street, Boston, MA 02143

75b Mr. J. C. Duffy, 402 South Brentwood Avenue, Troy, NY 10721

CHAPTER 16

76a Mrs. Joan Rogers, The Lexington Company, 1241 Grayson Street, Birmingham, AL 35055

76b Mr. Marvin Wood, Service Manager, General Office Machine Manufacturing Company, 200 Main Drive, Little Rock, AR 72203

77a Ms. Mildred Brice, National Office Furniture Company, 14207 South Main Street, Atlanta, GA 34615

77b Miss Jan Morris, The Wilson Company, 314 East Sutton Drive, N.W., Atlanta, GA 34600

78a Mr. Abraham Tate, Ajax Office Furniture Company, Los Angeles, CA 90056

78b National Communications Systems Incorporated, Main at Elm, Flint, MI 48706

79a Montana Office Supply Company, 230 Skyline Drive, Missoula, MT 59801

79b Mrs. Harvy Wilson, Manager, General House Moving Company, Bozeman, MT 58702

80a Miss J. V. Williams, Central Construction Company, 200 Oak Street, Wheeling, WV 26003

80b Mr. L. R. Wilson, President, The Wilson Company, 400 State Street, Wheeling, WV 26003

Index of Building Transcription Skills

The number next to each entry refers to the page in the text in which the entry appears.

Brief Forms of Gregg Shorthand

IN ALPHABETICAL ORDER

	A	B	C	D	E	F	G
1							
2							
3							
4							
5							
6							
7							
8							
9							
10							
11							
12							
13							
14							
15							
16							
17